Presented to Purchase College
by
Gary Waller, PhD Cambridge

State University of New York
Distinguished Professor

Professor
of Literature & Cultural
Studies, and Theatre &
Performance, 1995-2019
Provost 1995-2004

Modern Language Association of America

Research and Scholarship in Composition

Lil Brannon, Anne Ruggles Gere, Dixie Goswami, Susan Hilligoss,
C. H. Knoblauch, Geneva Smitherman-Donaldson, Art Young,
Series Editors

1. Anne Herrington and Charles Moran, eds. *Writing, Teaching, and Learning in the Disciplines.* 1992.
2. Cynthia L. Selfe and Susan Hilligoss, eds. *Literacy and Computers: The Complications of Teaching and Learning with Technology.* 1993.
3. John Clifford and John Schilb, eds. *Writing Theory and Critical Theory.* 1994.

Writing Theory and Critical Theory

Edited by
John Clifford and John Schilb

The Modern Language Association of America
New York   1994

For James Berlin and Kenneth Burke,
whose democratic vision inspired us all

The following publishers have generously granted permission for the use of extended quotations from copyrighted works: "Democracy," from *The Wild Flag* (Houghton Mifflin). © 1943, 1971 by E. B. White. Originally in the *New Yorker*. Guidelines accompanying E. B. White's essay "Democracy" in *The Norton Reader*, edited by Arthur M. Eastman. Seventh edition (Norton, 1988). "Tribute," from the *New Yorker*. © 1943, 1971 by The New Yorker Magazine, Inc.

Library of Congress Cataloging-in-Publication Data

Writing theory and critical theory / edited by John Clifford and John
  Schilb.
      p.   cm. — (Research and scholarship in composition ; 3)
    Includes bibliographical references and index.
    ISBN 0-87352-575-2 ISBN 0-87352-576-0 (pbk.)
    1. English language—Rhetoric—Study and teaching—Theory. etc.
  2. Literature—History and criticism—Theory, etc.   3. Criticism.
  I. Clifford, John.   II. Schilb, John, 1952–   III. Series.
  PE1404.W744   1994
  808'.042—dc20   93-50595

Published by The Modern Language Association of America
10 Astor Place, New York, New York 10003-6981

Set in New Aster

Printed on recycled paper

Contents

Preface to the Series

The Research and Scholarship in Composition series, developed with the support of the Modern Language Association's Publications Committee, responds to the recent growth of interest in composition and to the remarkable number of publications now devoted to it. We intend the series to provide a carefully coordinated overview of the varied theoretical schools, educational philosophies, institutional groupings, classroom situations, and pedagogical practices that collectively constitute the major areas of inquiry in the field of composition studies.

Each volume combines theory, research, and practice in order to clarify theoretical issues, synthesize research and scholarship, and improve the quality of writing instruction. Further, each volume reviews the most significant issues in a particular area of composition research and instruction; reflects on ways research and teaching inform each other; views composition studies in the larger context of literary, literacy, and cultural studies; and draws conclusions from various scholarly perspectives about what has been done and what yet needs to be done in the field.

We hope this series will serve a wide audience of teachers, scholars, and students who are interested in the teaching of writing, research in composition, and the connections among composition, literature, and other areas of study. These volumes should act as a lively orientation to the field for students and nonspecialists and provide experienced teachers and scholars with useful overviews of research on important questions, with insightful reflections about teaching, and with thoughtful analyses about future developments in composition studies. Each book is a spirited conversation in which you are cordially invited to join.

Series Editors

Introduction

This volume of original essays is the third in a series designed to meet the need for "a carefully coordinated overview" of the "major areas of inquiry in the field of composition studies." When we started to plan *Writing Theory and Critical Theory*, we indeed felt able to define "the most significant issues" that connected the words of our title. When we made an open call for submissions, however, we encountered a formidable range of perspectives on our topic. Even when we solicited essays from scholars familiar to us, we often failed to anticipate what they would eventually write. Of course, this collection does not simply parade idiosyncratic views; rather, it features several recurring themes that our own dispositions have helped shape. Nevertheless, the book can lead authors, editors, and, yes, readers down unexpected paths. As with research on other topics in this series, the body of work linking writing theory and critical theory continues to grow in many ways. In introducing the following essays, we inevitably propose a certain framework; at the same time, we acknowledge that it is inevitably provisional.

Even the book's title reflects decisions we have made. The term *writing theory* can denote trends related to writing, rhetoric, and composition. To be frank, we feel less secure with our other key term, *critical theory*. We mean it to indicate various strands of contemporary thinking that have influenced literary studies, including deconstruction, hermeneutics, postmodernism, feminism, neo-Marxism, neopragmatism, psychoanalysis, reader response, and cultural studies. The series editors originally proposed the term *literary theory*, but we ultimately decided against this term, for two reasons. First, the schools of thought we have cited transcend literary studies; they infuse other fields like philosophy, history, and the social sciences. Second, literary scholars themselves have drawn on these schools to question the very idea of "literature" as a unique (and uniquely valuable) mode of discourse.

We follow many advocates of these approaches when we turn to *critical theory* as an alternative rubric. It has the virtue of signaling a preoccupation of all these schools: critique of current discursive practices and social structures. As a term, *critical theory* is somewhat problematic because of its original association with the Frankfurt school, a circle of German cultural critics who fled to the United States during World War II. Members of this group—including Theodor Adorno, Max Horkheimer, and Herbert Marcuse—did hold some ideas peculiar to them. In one form or another, though, several of their concerns have reemerged for the contemporary theories that we have in mind. Even if these theories do not use the Frankfurt school's vocabulary or adopt its orientation, they pursue some of its characteristic themes: the illusions of Enlightenment rationality, the nature of political authority, the construction of human subjects, the role of language in mental representations, the power of mass culture, the need for self-reflection, and the need to adapt previous social theories to modern (or postmodern) circumstances.

We became acutely conscious of recent developments linking writing theory and critical theory when we looked back at an earlier essay that we wrote on this topic. Entitled "Composition Theory and Literary Theory," it appeared in the 1985 MLA volume *Perspectives on Research and Scholarship in Composition*. In the essay, we attended most to reader-response theorists, because they joined many composition scholars in depicting students as active shapers of meaning. We noted that a few specialists in composition were turning to deconstruction or to other forms of poststructuralism, and we pointed out that various scholars were proposing *rhetoric* as a rubric for unifying English studies. We concluded by highlighting two opposing curricular visions: Terry Eagleton's notion of rhetoric as the study of mass culture and E. D. Hirsch's "cultural literacy," which we equated with support of the canon. (Subsequently Hirsch dissociated himself from the great-books curriculum while continuing to advocate the teaching of mainstream knowledge.)

A good deal has changed since we wrote that essay. At that time, we focused on composition and literature as unified entities that needed to overcome the differences *between* them. Recent history indicates growing differences *within* these fields. Scholars now argue regularly about what the mission, methodology, and content of each field should be. For example, as David Shumway notes in this volume, empirical research has become a subject of intense debate in composition after dominating the field for almost two decades. Both composition and literature have spawned theory and antitheory camps; in her essay, Beth Daniell analyzes composition's version of this trend. Since 1985 certain visions of a unified English curriculum have also emerged or grown stronger. Nowadays many English faculty members wish not simply to amalgamate composition and literature but, rather, to elaborate a third term that would displace or subsume them. As Susan Miller and Kathleen McCormick indicate in their essays, one new candidate is *cultural studies*. An increasing number of scholars in literature as well as composition have turned to *rhetoric* as a possible disciplinary framework; see, for example, the proceedings of the 1987 MLA conference on doctoral programs in English (Lunsford, Moglen, and Slevin).

There is as yet no consensus on how to define these two terms. Scholars in literature and composition still need to decide which methodologies and topics constitute the purview of cultural studies (Schilb, "Cultural Studies"), and a tension still exists between classical and deconstructive understandings of rhetoric. The classical view associates rhetoric with persuasion, while the deconstructive view focuses on the destabilizing interplay of tropes. Many composition specialists insist on the continued viability of the classical tradition (see Murphy; Connors, Ede, and Lunsford). The contributors to this volume do not oppose classical rhetoric; some, including Suzanne Clark and Susan Wells, explicitly value elements of it. But, in keeping with the book's title, most primarily investigate the resources that deconstruction and other forms of critical theory can bring to the study of discourse. Rather than see deconstruction as an end in itself, these authors, like many current theorists, enlist its strategies for the larger purpose of cultural critique. When they focus on linguistic instability, they ultimately relate it to particular social actions at particular moments in history. Several of the contributors—for example, Susan Miller, Kathleen McCormick, Kurt Spellmeyer, James Slevin, Linda Brodkey, and Victor Villanueva—attempt to fuse rhetoric with cultural studies and to give clear new dimensions to each.

The school of thought that we emphasized years ago, reader-response theory, still thrives in composition and literary studies. Yet, under the surging influence of feminism, neo-Marxism, minority perspectives, postcolonial thought, and the work of Michel Foucault, reader-response theorists in both fields have increasingly turned to ideological critique. They see readers and writers not as free, individual agents but, rather, as the products of discourses that frequently serve the state. Reader-response theory continues to examine individual reading and writing performances. Now, however, it often analyzes them as modes of subjection or resistance to dominant institutions. This approach, too, appears throughout the essays that follow. Most notably, Slevin analyzes the ways in which composition students are themselves constructed as *Norton* readers.

In effect, several of the essays in this volume critique a movement that we did not forecast in 1985: social constructionism. It was introduced to composition by theorists like Kenneth Bruffee, Patricia Bizzell, and Elaine Maimon. They in turn drew on neopragmatists like Richard Rorty and Stanley Fish, who emphasized the incorrigibly social foundations of human thought. This movement usefully disputed composition's previous emphasis on the isolated writer and acontextual skills. As a result, a flood of scholarship emerged that identified ways in which writing demands vary with context, a prime example being the differing standards of the academic disciplines. Many composition specialists, however, now question aspects of this trend. Clark, in her essay here, worries that it may once again purge emotion from academic reason. As Spellmeyer indicates, many suspect that conventions do not regulate discourse as much as social constructionism has claimed they do. He also makes the increasingly familiar charge that social constructionism emphasizes conformity. Several contributors, whether or not they fault this movement explicitly, call for a more radical criticism of existing institutions. They believe that composition should not just invoke "the social" and proceed to affirm particular discourses; for them, the various components of "the social" must be anatomized, evaluated, and quite possibly transformed.

Such analysis must include English departments themselves. As institutions, they shape whatever relations can be posited between writing theory and critical theory in the first place. When we discussed the possible relations between the two in 1985, we chose not to dwell on the historically low status of composition in the English curriculum. In part, we wanted to emphasize developments in theory; in part, we hoped that the situation of writing instructors would improve. Since then, composition has indeed gained respect as a field, as the very existence of this MLA series attests. The number of graduate programs in composition and rhetoric has increased and so has the number of tenure-track positions. Nevertheless, many English departments have yet to give composition a status equal to that of literature. They continue to regard the interpretation of poetry, fiction, and drama as inherently more valuable and to relegate composition to overworked, underpaid graduate students or part-timers. They identify composition with teaching, and teaching with mere service to the rest of the college or university. Various contributors allude explicitly to these circumstances, including Susan Miller, Kurt Spellmeyer, Sharon Crowley, and Ross Winterowd. We suspect, however, that all the contributors want English departments to grant composition genuine parity. After all, relations between writing theory and critical theory are not just theoretical; they emerge from, and impinge on, people's working lives. While the specific curricular visions proposed here vary, they reflect a common imperative: to challenge systems that disenfranchise people by narrowing the available discourse. English departments, because they continue to marginalize the field most responsible for identifying possibilities of discourse, cannot be exempt from this critique.

We have organized the volume into four sections, although we are aware that their concerns overlap. The essays in "Refiguring Traditions" propose ways of using critical theory to historicize and assess orthodoxies of writing instruction. First, Susan Miller submits that British cultural studies and related schools of thought can help composition rethink its long-standing penchant for mechanical correctness. Drawing on such figures as Stuart Hall, Terry Eagleton, Louis Althusser, and Michel Foucault, she explains how composition itself emerged from a dubious institutional agenda. In the late nineteenth century, Miller points out, the American academy sought to incorporate a broader range of students while maintaining old social hierarchies. Composition emerged as the ideal sorting mechanism: certain students would have to undergo its "low" rituals of purification, while others could proceed to the "high" study of literature. Composition, Miller argues, broke from the rhetorical tradition when it constructed the student writer as a particular human subject, one who concentrates on private, individual experience. To reverse this drift, Miller suggests, present-day composition specialists must emphasize the social functions of writing and cultivate the historiography that she has demonstrated.

Kathleen McCormick also refers to theorists associated with British cultural studies as she examines a typical composition assignment, the research paper. McCormick points out that when textbooks discuss this assignment, they often give a conflicting message: even though they indicate that sources are subjective, they press students to be objective in researching and writing papers. McCormick emphasizes that an ideal research paper would not embrace relativism. Rather, she would have students place their perspectives, as well as those of their sources, in a historical context. Students doing this kind of research would probe contradictions among sources, acknowledge marginalized voices, note the effects of various ideological positions, and envision better discursive practices.

A similar concern with society, history, and culture leads James Slevin to challenge the way in which writing courses usually teach classic essays. Centering his discussion on the composition favorite

"Democracy," by E. B. White, he observes that anthologies like *The Norton Reader* (Eastman) and theorists like Frederic Bogel encourage a formalist appreciation of the piece. Slevin would have students use critical theory to examine the essay as a debatable response to exigencies of its time, an approach he demonstrates by looking to the *New Yorker* issue where it first appeared. In addition to reviewing the strategies of White's text, Slevin analyzes other texts in the same issue, showing how they all seek to negotiate relations of gender, race, and class.

Alluding to a wide range of theorists, Kurt Spellmeyer critiques a more recent development in composition: its focus on the conventions of various discourse communities. Above all, he questions Kenneth Bruffee's influential view of how knowledge is socially constructed. In brief, Spellmeyer claims that Bruffee ignores power relations and the ways that people can challenge discursive constraints. While he admits that Bruffee's emphasis on social context is a significant advance over the empiricism of Locke, he believes that Bruffee slights the institutional and political circumstances in which knowledge is produced and circulated. The idea, suggested by the sociologist Max Weber, that modern society is an "iron cage" can help counterbalance Bruffee's idealism. Spellmeyer argues, however, that Weber resembles Bruffee in underestimating people's ability to resist conventions. Elaborating a more optimistic view of human agency, Spellmeyer cites studies of convicts who alter prison policies. He also finds support in the anthropology of Victor Turner and Sally Falk Moore, who depict culture as a dynamic process rather than as a fixed set of rules.

Suzanne Clark expresses another concern about writing theory's turn to social constructionism. Even though she admires much about the development, she fears that it will perpetuate the modern intellectual tradition of denigrating the sentimental. Clark argues that feminists should be especially concerned, because sentimental discourse has usually been linked to women. She finds Julia Kristeva's work helpful in its envisioning of a more central place in academic reason for this discourse and for women themselves. Academic reason's contempt for sentimentality has entailed contempt for rhetoric as well, in particular for the appeals of ethos and pathos. By neglecting these elements of classical rhetoric, Clark asserts, academic reason limits its own public influence. She believes that social-constructionist writing theory will meet the same fate if it insists on excluding the sentimental.

Like Clark, Susan Wells relates contemporary theory to classical thinking, but her essay focuses on what writing teachers might learn from student writing and from three texts: Plato's *Phaedrus*, Jasper

Neel's *Plato, Derrida, and Writing,* and Mikhail Bakhtin's "Discourse in the Novel." For Wells, all these works signal the "doubleness" of writing. They show how the written text manipulates time, fictionalizes the author, and moves through shifting circumstances. Wells thinks that Neel seeks to manage such doubleness, whereas Plato and Bakhtin join her in affirming it. Ultimately she advocates writing courses that examine "questions of evidence, documentation, and verifiable support" but that do so by giving students "permission to lie"—that is, to play roles, imagine situations, and engage in counterfactual inquiry. Like Bakhtin, Wells calls for writing instruction that emphasizes the multiple voices within a text.

The essays in our next section analyze the "language and authority of theory." Although theory has become a central topic of composition and literary studies, recent developments have thrown into question its motives, meanings, and claims. While composition has grown more self-consciously theoretical, several scholars in the field have begun to argue that theory conflicts with practice. Believing that theory promotes jargon and aristocratic disdain for pedagogy, they fear that critical theory will team with writing theory to keep writing teachers institutionally powerless. Advocates of theory in composition also clash with empirical researchers who have enhanced the field's prestige over the last two decades. The first group accuses the second of lacking political awareness; the second accuses the first of dismissing reasonable quests for evidence. Meanwhile, some literary scholars who previously were dedicated to theory have grown less sanguine about its potential to transform behavior. The prime doubter is Stanley Fish, who takes great pleasure nowadays in proclaiming that theory has no consequences. Other figures—including Jacques Lacan, Hélène Cixous, Jacques Derrida, and Paul de Man—have warned against treating theory as a mechanism of policy. Whatever one thinks of all these developments, efforts to merge writing theory and critical theory must take account of them.

Beth Daniell begins her essay by noting the widening rift between theory and practice. Like Fish, she sees theory as a rhetorical and political practice that lacks the cognitive authority to dictate new perspectives and habits. Daniell takes up Fish's idea that consequences may follow not from theory but from theory *talk,* which can help composition build communities or perpetuate hierarchies. She uses Louise Wetherbee Phelps's *Composition as a Human Science* to identify potential strengths and weaknesses in the theory talk of the field. When composition specialists expound a theory, Daniell argues, they should consider its premises, limitations, and beneficiaries. Furthermore, they should relate it to the exigencies of the classroom and make it accessible to a wide audience.

Joseph Harris's title, "The Rhetoric of Theory," indicates a framework similar to Daniell's. Also citing Fish, Harris suggests that theories of writing be judged according to their performative effects: "The final test of a theory . . . is what we can do with it, what kinds of talk and writing it makes possible for ourselves and our students." He applies this criterion to various examples of composition scholarship, emphasizing not their cognitive authority but, rather, their implications for practice.

David Shumway also argues that knowledge claims are rhetorical as he analyzes the debate in composition between empirical researchers and advocates of critical theory. Citing Linda Flower and James Berlin as exemplars of these groups, he reviews two charges that Berlin makes against Flower's work in cognitive psychology: that it vainly pretends to mirror reality and that it supports the capitalist system. While Shumway disagrees with Berlin to an extent, asserting "that empirical research is not inherently instrumentalist and that it entails no particular epistemology at all," he acknowledges the naïveté of Flower's claim that her work captures raw experience. Ultimately he urges composition scholars to consider empirical research "a particular form of argumentation." In this respect, he believes, it can serve critical theorists like Berlin who may find ethnographic work especially suitable for their purposes. Nevertheless, he also recommends that critical theorists keep identifying particular uses of empirical research that do reinforce capitalism.

Robert Brooke, Judith Levin, and Joy Ritchie conclude this section by forging other links between theory and practice. They relate Lacan's concepts of transference and countertransference to their writing pedagogies, but these authors note that they cannot straightforwardly apply such concepts because their own situations differ from Lacan's. Instead, they resort to "wild analysis," reshaping Lacan's insights in the light of their classroom experiences. With this aim, they address matters that Lacan slighted, including feminism and the knowledging-building activities of groups. The structure of the essay also reflects the authors' methodological emphasis. In alternating parts, Brooke, Levin, and Ritchie each discuss particular forms of transference and countertransference in their academic careers.

The essays in the penultimate section of this volume address issues of narrative and narrative theory. As Joan Didion claims in the evocative opening of *The White Album*, "[W]e tell ourselves stories in order to live." Set in 1968, Didion's text asserts that "we live entirely, especially if we are writers, by the imposition of a narrative line upon disparate images" (11). Some twenty-five years later, critical theorists echo Didion's prescient insight through reference to the fictiveness of all discourse, the arbitrariness of professional conventions, and the situatedness of disciplinary epistemology. Writing theorists have also of late been drawn to the important role narratives and narrative theories play in structuring the complex disparateness of composition and rhetoric.

Judith Summerfield's essay, the first in this section, introduces readers to some salient aspects of narrative that apply to composition theory and practice. In postmodern composition studies the significance of narrative goes beyond genre; it is seen, instead, as a defining feature of human nature. Symbolic actions and the telling of stories, Summerfield notes, are thought to be ways of coming to know; they are strategies for particular representations of reality. From that perspective, what writers select out of the "shifting phantasmagoria" of reality becomes a provisional stand-in for the truth (Didion 11), within disciplines as well as in the back alleys of our minds. Each of these circumstances encourages a pluralistic and multiple epistemology. Turning to the pedagogical relevance of narrative, Summerfield points out that student writers have always had difficulty with authenticity when writing in the first person. She liberates the narrator from stability and unity, problematizing the "I" who writes as a specific role the writer may assume, as a choice that may expand the possibilities for who that writer might become.

Douglas Hesse theorizes about narrative but focuses more specifically on its connection to the complexity of time. For Hesse the essay is a situational, constructed experience combining what happened— as constructed in the author's mind—with the actual writing about the event. Hesse claims that a writer's observations become more compelling within the familiar conventions of story, that propositions carry more force embedded in a plot. He also suggests that students gain authority through a belief that narrative can give order and significance to disparate experience.

Lester Faigley avoids unintentional irony in his piece, describing his course on postmodernism and politics by announcing little hope for resolution or full political applicability in the debates raging within poststructuralism, postmodernism, critical theory, and feminism. In the course, a quest for possible interconnections provides intellectual stimulation for the students whose cogent voices are intertwined in Faigley's narrative. The central problem arises in the debate between Jean-François Lyotard and Jürgen Habermas, between an assertion that there are no grand narratives or universal truths and a belief in the rational use of language, in a defense of modernism and Enlightenment humanism. Faigley's students actively debate this conflict in response to texts by Chris Weedon, Victor Vitanza, and Patricia Bizzell. Bizzell, Faigley notes, tries to bridge postmodernism and politics by suggesting that teachers should "aver provocatively" political stances that might require a foundation, for example, developing "civic virtue." When Linda Brodkey, Faigley's colleague at the University of Texas, tried to do just that in a freshman course called Writing about Differences, she was attacked and finally defeated. The irony, Faigley points out, is that politics and writing are obviously melded at the university even though they remain problematic in his course. Only if professors lived outside history, he concludes, could they simply transmit knowledge to students. In actual classrooms, "the experience of reading theory collaboratively and dialogically does not rise above contingent existence but plunges everyone more deeply into the historical particularities shaping the scene of instruction."

Linda Brodkey's essay tells three stories about her struggle to create a writing course based on difference: one on pedagogy, another on publicity, and a final one on institutional postponement. Brodkey begins with a theoretical justification for the course, which would have focused on exploratory discourse, argumentation, and warrants. Her postmodern inclinations were clear: she planned to give reason a modest place in argumentation and to balance "the need for a measure of certainty against the provisional 'truths' and 'realities' of poststructural language theories." That is, Brodkey hoped to teach rhetoric as "a set of contingent principles for examining issues in situ." The people who objected to the course did not, however, concern themselves with this approach to rhetoric; they apparently did not want a writing course to focus on difference. For her most critical opponents, the very notion of writing about difference meant political indoctrination. Brodkey provides a compelling analysis of their tactics in distorting her explicitly stated goals for the course, whose eventual postponement, she claims, was based more on negative publicity in the popular press than on any careful study of the course's merits. Brodkey's narrative, of course, offers her own perception of what happened, and, as she implies, it remains to be seen whose version of the brouhaha will prevail. We asked Ben McClelland, Mark Clark, and Patricia Harkin to comment on this important conflict and respond freely to Brodkey's narrative.

Ben McClelland develops a thoughtful navigation analogy to suggest that Brodkey might have been more successful had she been less inno-

cent about the inevitable "eddies and hidden undercurrents" that be-
devil the journey of academic reformers. McClelland believes that his
ability to alter the direction of the writing program at the University
of Mississippi was based on his understanding of the university as a
"confluence of ideologies," that is, his wary realization that multiple
and agonistic forces impinge on curriculum reform, however routine
it may seem to those inside writing programs. In retrospect, the heated
departmental debates at the University of Texas before Brodkey arrived
seem to have created such a volatile climate that her concern with
difference—a widely accepted interest in composition studies—ignited
a firestorm of hostility. Regardless, McClelland is clear that we can and
should learn to navigate the unique political contexts of our institutional homes without shrinking from our professional mission. Like
many in the profession, he wants to believe that the Texas case was an
anomaly and a cautionary tale but not cause to alter our progressive
course.

Mark Clark's essay concerns the nature of Brodkey's opposition.
Clark believes that Brodkey wanted to make explicit how difference
works in texts, and he wonders why her opposition was afraid of such
exposure. Distinguishing a pedagogy of difference from difference as
a topic, he thinks that the topic might, as opponents of the course
claimed, be problematic. Brodkey's focus on a pedagogy of inquiry,
however, seems "much more critical, democratic, and liberating," and
Clark does not understand why Brodkey's opponents assumed that the
course would be biased. Couldn't any course content be political? Are
students so dim-witted, he wonders, that they can easily be indoctri-
nated against their will? Clark suggests that the way students and
teachers use texts ultimately makes the difference between political
indoctrination and methods of reading and writing that put difference
at the center. In keeping with most contributors to this volume, Clark
explicitly situates himself as an instructor who values difference in
pedagogy; consequently, he laments the Texas failure to institute such
a desideratum.

Patricia Harkin wants to know whether theory can teach us how to
act in the painful circumstances Brodkey describes. Appropriately, she
examines Brodkey's story within the context of contemporary narrative
theory, noting that the Texas tale is told by its hero; hence, Harkin
thinks, Brodkey constitutes the events as tragic romance or irony. For
example, while Brodkey's theoretical acumen fails against the powerful
but egregious Right, it also constructs a sympathetic audience of readers who understand that only the intellectually inferior could misun-
derstand her sophisticated theoretical motivation. Any inconsistency

in Brodkey's account, Harkin claims, is a "salient mark of a politically active postmodern feminism that is as close as we are likely to come to the heroic." Perhaps Harkin's most compelling point is the crucial moral for composition studies that she sees in Brodkey's narrative: "No longer content merely to copyedit the sons and daughters of Texas taxpayers, Brodkey and her helpers took language itself as their province," which Harkin sees as a "strident *non serviam.*"

The final section of *Writing Theory and Critical Theory* consists of a seminar in which the contributing authors examine past and future developments in composition. These days, the professional, philosophical, and cultural contexts of the field are so saturated with new theories and competing narratives of knowledge that, as writing theorists, we must inevitably allow our ideas to become fluid, tentative, alert. A generation ago we entered Kenneth Burke's cocktail party just to listen, and soon we were engaged. We began reading linguistics, psychology, education, and, recently, literary theory; now, among many other things, we read critical theory. We look within ourselves to understand why certain traditions seem unsatisfactory; we struggle at our own institutions, in our own departments, for informed practice. In our various subject positions as scholars, workers, and citizens, we try to profess values of equality and justice. As individuals with unique histories, we move in certain directions, and yet somehow we move together, forming the kind of intellectual and political alliances that sustain us, that enable us to sit alone for hours writing for an audience that we believe in and that we hope in turn can believe in us. Collaboratively, we have created a diverse and committed unity, a vibrant discipline.

As editors of this volume, we asked some of the participants in this professional dialogue to contribute to our symposium. These authors chart some of the changes, some of the intellectual forces that made a difference in their thinking about reading and writing. Their intellectual autobiographies serve as representative anecdotes of the diverse ways that literary theory, critical theory, and composition studies commingle in the thinking of professionals who are trying to understand the connections they have made, the changes they have undergone, and the emotional and intellectual dynamics of their choices. This text concludes, then, with their stories.

Louise Rosenblatt is an articulate link to the humanistic thinking of Franz Boas, Ruth Benedict, and John Dewey. This interdisciplinary perspective has always been a source of strength in her work, although it also probably contributed to her marginalization by the powerful and parochial New Critics. Her understanding of the reading process was inspirational to theorists looking for more sophisticated models of composing. In her earliest work, *Literature as Exploration* (1938), she championed democratic values that affirmed the creative and intellectual potential of active readers. Her transactional approach suggested ways to explain how meaning gets made, and her democratic vision revealed a social purpose for writing. Insisting on a wider social context for reading, Rosenblatt helped compositionists understand that writing is already situated in the world, always doing cultural work, inevitably affirming ways of forming and seeing that have significant sociopolitical implications. Her current wariness of writing theory's social turn comes from her concern that postmodernism's decentered, written subject will denigrate the active social agent. For Rosenblatt, the Foucauldian subject imprisoned in language is anathema; she wants to look beyond the pessimism of some postmodern ideas to see a solution in her pragmatic roots. Many compositionists agree with her assessment that it is futile to theorize a thoroughly constructed subject, and many of us hope that we can help students develop and use a critical consciousness. We admit that we are written, but in that metaphor we see the possibilities for reinscription.

Robert Scholes takes a look back at such canonical literary theorists as Erich Auerbach and Northrop Frye to explain how composition came to be synonymous with style. During the sixties, however, Scholes moved away from such isolated views of writing. His work with hypertext, for example, led to *The Practice of Writing* (coauthored with Nancy Comley), an imaginative textbook that combined an informed perspective on reading and writing with a practical understanding of pedagogy. Scholes notes that critical theory enriched his views on the ways thinking can take place. Certainly that asset is evident in *Textual Power*, in which he shows how deconstruction can lay bare the false oppositions that English departments have constructed to privilege male critics and diminish female compositionists. His critique also demonstrates that a commitment to equality can be the ethical bridge from one discipline to another, enabling us to use critical tools to build more democratic structures.

Ross Winterowd has long been seen as the lonely voice of rhetoric crying in the literary vastness of the MLA. As an intellectual compositionist with broad interests, Winterowd has felt the injustice of being on the wrong end of the MLA's hierarchy. Upholding broader, more demanding criteria for the life of the mind than does the specialized Victorian or Shakespearean, Winterowd has become, for the generation of writing teachers who have followed him, a symbol for how arbitrary the standards of scholarly communities can be. Consequently, Winterowd's meditation here is not filled with equipoise; instead, he is angry. But he offers us an understandable context: a profession in which teachers who pursue the close reading of canonical texts are hegemonically secure while composition teachers flounder in the basement with workbooks and endless student essays. Fortunately, most composition theorists, including the editors of this collection, have not had the same vexed professional experiences as Winterowd has. We are certainly familiar with myopic traditionalists, but today composition studies is too important to be excluded. We are grateful for Winterowd's perseverance, but we think that Burke was right to encourage us to work for change within organizations. And since this text is, in fact, being published by the MLA, we read that change as an epiphany, a sanguine harbinger.

Elizabeth Flynn focuses less on the outcast fate of compositionists and more on the professional consequences of a specific essay she wrote, "Gender and Reading." Although the essay was nominally response-oriented, Flynn hoped for a cognitive approach to reading. Today, a decade later, her position is more social. Flynn is a compositionist, but she has strong commitments to theory and feminism and, like a growing number of contemporary theorists, can productively work in all three fields. Indeed, her work suggests that our received notions of specialization are no longer very useful. Through postmodern lenses, Flynn now sees in her early essay traces of women's ways of knowing, social construction, and nonstable identities.

Sharon Crowley notes her early commitment to composition studies in the seventies when the field was still dominated by linguistics and psychology. Like Winterowd, Crowley was also made painfully aware that literature and composition are unequal and that students' writing can never live up to the idealist standards of a universal, timeless canon. But Derrida has come to her rescue, enabling her to see the rhetorical tradition afresh, especially Plato's desire to control writing and his caricatures of the Sophists. Both strategies are perhaps not unlike the traditionalist's view of postmodern composition. Interested more in what theory can do for the profession than in the purity of theory, Crowley worries about agency in critical theory. Like many others, she hopes that her work can contribute to noncoercive change through a heightened consciousness.

Victor Villanueva entered the profession after Winterowd, Crowley, and others had created an environment in which an emphasis on difference would be possible. Like many theorists today, Villanueva refuses to separate sociopolitical values from intellectual work, striving instead for an ethical and professional coherence. The conservative ploy to reify tradition demands a repression of social experience that no longer serves. Villaneuva's essay, which describes his experiences with racism and class bias, is an indication that compositionists new to the profession are confidently refusing demarcations of the social and the scholarly. His movement against hegemony flows directly from the Bakhtinian voices that his life has created within him. The resulting acknowledgment of his contradictory consciousness leads him to texts sympathetic to his lived experiences. For Villanueva, then, social-epistemic rhetoric is not just a current trend in the profession but an ethical imperative central to his sense of self. His assertion that rhetoric is politics characterizes a new generation of compositionists.

We have asked two members of this new generation, Susan Carlton and Beverly Moss, to comment on these personal narratives. Not surprisingly, both are impressed by recent attempts to examine individual professional positions through what Carlton calls a "guiding model of intelligibility." Carlton and Moss use their own experiences to reinforce the necessity of eliminating restrictive dualisms and of grounding reading and writing both in theory and in the world. As editors, theorists, and practitioners we are encouraged that, true to Burke's dialetical fable of history, a new group of theorists has caught the "tenor of the argument" with bright prospects for keeping "the discussion . . . vigorously in progress" (*Philosophy* 110–11).

John Clifford, *University of North Carolina, Wilmington*
John Schilb, *University of Maryland, College Park*

PART I

Refiguring Traditions

Composition as a Cultural Artifact: Rethinking History as Theory

Susan Miller

Composition studies is by now well enough established as a field to have its own historical subfield, a specialization in the history of academic discourse and instruction in it. This specialization is most heavily indebted for its formation to Edward P. J. Corbett's 1965 *Classical Rhetoric for the Modern Student*, which set a precedent for the scholarship of James Murphy, Winifred Horner, Robert Connors, Sharon Crowley ("Evolution"), and James Berlin (*Writing*). These and many other historians of rhetoric and composition generally take one of two nonadversarial stances. The first, which might be called neoclassical because it relies on ancient rhetorical traditions, follows the methods of traditional "big" histories by describing a rhetorical canon, a list of prominent names from Aristotle to Linda Flower and John Hayes and beyond. The second, more naturalistic and new-historicist, details curricula, textbooks, organized practices, and trendsetting models for teaching composition since its late-nineteenth-century beginnings as a distinct university-level curriculum.

Each of these historical methods is connected in contemporary composition studies to a joint project, a proselytizing intellectual agenda for the field as a whole. The active intellectual politics that has elsewhere opposed two brands of "big" and "new" history has been cooperatively merged in composition studies so that the historians named here, and many others who have been less vocal about their motives, can pursue what Stephen North cites as an "avowedly propagandistic agenda" (97). They want, with greater and lesser commitment to actual applications from the past and greater and lesser commitments to highlighting the political implications of such applications, to urge teachers of composition to theorize their diverse practices. This wish—to describe an intellectual foundation for teaching that still suffers in quality and in professional status from its ad hoc reputation—firmly unites composition history with composition theories in efforts that encourage change in actual, not just in prominently published, ways of conceiving of writing instruction. But as a cultural approach to history might teach us, we have not yet accounted for the origins and subsequent conduct of composition courses in ways that explain the need for this agenda. We have not as yet placed composition in the originating cultural context whose current inadequacy might lead to the changes in practice that this agenda desires.

The target of both these historical schools, and the issue I want to readdress from a cultural historian's perspective, is the inevitably marginal and tedious emphasis on correctness and propriety, in the form of instruction in mechanics, spelling, and grammar, in early composition courses. This limited early and continuing model ("theory") of instruction might be summarized as teaching that has used many "reformist" and "progressive" methods to persuade students to enthusiastically write texts that are finally, stringently, *corrected*. This model has little to do with the comprehensive rhetorical instruction that guided advanced discourse studies before composition was instituted as a discrete required course. It may have even less to do with controlling the actual writing situations that today's students face. But mechanistic and rote models for teaching, what our historians cum propagandists cum theorists want to replace, still unfortunately endow composition with its particularly bourgeois yet marginalized, conventional but palpably unpleasant, flavor.

In fact, explaining to practicing composition teachers that a broadly conceived intellectual history of their practices suggests a range of desirable theoretical and practical alternatives to this model has not done a great deal to change entrenched images of what composition courses are for. Historicism has done less to influence the conduct of composition than its scholarly excellence warrants. As Richard Larson's survey of contemporary practice for the Ford Foundation indicates, new theories of composing and of interventionist, process-oriented teaching methods have done little to change the actual curriculum in college writing. And as publishers readily verify, grammar handbooks and workbooks are still the most easily sold versions of discourse instruction we have. Composition courses, first taught in universities as required freshman-level work in the 1890s, did and still do emphasize conventionally universal ideas, paradoxically standardized "personal" voices, and "correctness" over analyses and productions of discourse in the light of particular purposes and audiences.

These courses consequently did and still do require students to expose their writing to what Peter Stallybrass and Allon White identify, in *The Politics and Poetics of Transgression*, as a "bourgeois gaze" of disapprobation, clinical scrutiny by an *idea* of convention. In many settings, these courses are not much intellectual fun to take or to teach. But equally important, their long-term results for students are rarely measured in concrete terms or even recognized as important, except when we acknowledge the completion, successful or not, of a freshman initiation rite that is frequently designated "socialization." Most composition curricula and teaching practices have been organized neither with regard to the effects that students think these courses have nor with reference to the writing situations that students encounter after they leave these courses. Graduates of composition courses are not imagined as actual writers, people who have (or have not) been given the knowledge and practice they might use to negotiate among the many privileging mechanisms that define consequential writing in the shifting range of discourse communities that they do and will inhabit.

This lack of responsiveness to a newly highlighted intellectual tradition, as well as the somewhat self-justifying definitions of what composition courses are for, suggests that we have not yet found a persuasive history or a convincing way of telling it. We have not, that is, explained the difference between the two traditions: the rich rhetorical one that appears to have created a highly literate elite and the corrective tradition that abruptly displaced it without having empowered its students as virtuosi in the act and the goals of writing. If we are to explain why the field's new histories, theories, and research have so little purchase on its continuing practice, its past requires retheorization. Specifically, we must look at composition as a cultural practice rather than as an intellectual development, a way of viewing it that arose in specific nineteenth-century social and material worlds. In other words, we need once again to problematize the kind of identities we accept for, and deny to, composition students and their teachers, and we need to question the cultural purposes that composition has, in its universal expectation, "served." Doing so at least reveals the social contexts that created (and now result from) the "standard" approaches to learning to write.

The model supporting this rereading comes primarily from British cultural studies, which draws on a number of theoretical sources to explain particular social phenomena without creating a dichotomy between systems and the individuals whose experience appears to occur apart from, or even in opposition to, those systems. This school has usefully addressed the way institutions—impersonal structures of procedure, common sense, and received values—regularly turn out individuals whose thinking and writing "freely" duplicate and perpetuate the structure of that institution and its hegemonic results. Stuart Hall especially has attempted to undertake the kind of interpretation that would repair the split—maintained by Marxist, Foucauldian, poststructuralist, and feminist theories since Louis Althusser's 1970 essay "Ideology and Ideological State Apparatuses"—between structuralist analyses of institutions and accounts that privilege the experience of individuals. As Hall puts it, "The question of [ideological] reproduction has been assigned to the marxist, (male) pole, and the question of subjectivity has been assigned to the psychoanalytic, (feminist) pole. Since then, never have the twain met" (102). That is, this perspective typically theorizes states, classes, and universities as self-perpetuating abstract structures and analyzes the interiority of personal experience as though it were exempt from total systems. But Hall's new reading of these split Althusserian interpretive fields emphasizes Antonio Gramsci's insights about the consensual, cross-class, -race, and -gender ways in which ideological structures enacted through institutions call for specifically constructed human identities. In Gramsci, these identities, by virtue of their relative positions, cooperate with institutions, and with one another, to maintain the basic structures of a society. Consequently, Hall and others informed by this perspective do not comfortably separate and oppose ways of analyzing "high" and "low" classes, discourses, or "mentalities," for their manifestations operate in shifting and blurred local patterns that implicate both sides of the traditional methodological dichotomy between them.

This theoretical mutuality between what we perceive as impersonal, even deterministic, structures and personal, even creative, identities is particularly relevant for us as we reread the history of composition. Usually we maintain the vivid discrepancy between this field's institutional situation and its theoretical and pedagogical emphases on individual teachers and student writers. Often, the perspective of individuals, seemingly isolated teachers and students, counters cultural theory's address to the institutional workings of ideology. Objections to what appear to be only deterministic theories—But *I* teach well. *My* students learn to write. Do you think *I* participate in this supposed conspiracy?—assert a priority for independent thought, the avowed content of much composition instruction. But in the cultural theory pursued by Hall and Gramsci, such reactions, like all ideas, are clearly social, not individual, phenomena. Thinking never escapes the media of language, rituals, and behaviors in which individuals are repeatedly positioned, long after their Lacanian, early-childhood falling into language. Consequently, while the experience that stimulates such questions is certainly real, it has never been innocent—or capable of explanation only by reference to psychological limits on its experiencing. Our seemingly private experience is inserted in "chains of connotation and social practices" that articulate it (Hall 112).

If we accept this perspective and look for the mutuality between institutional practices and personal instances that it insists on, we can quite specifically examine the distinct American practice of instructing postsecondary students in a generic form of writing as a primary site for enacting and for inculcating an identifiable set of culturally reproduced ideologies. To explain the workings of the cultural site that composition is and has been, we would not isolate and describe the educational institution, course content, students, or teachers of writing as independent "subjects" who act autonomously or are acted on as individual entities. In writing this history, we would look for neither a closed intellectual tradition of rhetoric nor the insights of individual teacher-theorists in various movements in teaching. Instead, we would read early composition courses and their enduring habits as ways of speaking and learning that cooperate with—and simultaneously help to establish—dominant social, political, and economic ideas.

We need to reestablish the scene of the nineteenth-century composition course and its newly "subjected"—identified and cooperative— student before we consent to this new take on it. Imagine that you are a new scholarship student at Harvard in 1893, the first member of your merchant family to attend an institution of higher learning. Among your first classes is a requirement to take English A, because you are not among the few who have aced the Harvard entrance examination. In this class, which you and two hundred fellow students attend daily, your teacher assigns a book called *Principles of Rhetoric* that stresses capitalization and punctuation rules. He (the precise pronoun here) requires that you write a theme every day. Some of the topics assigned are A Snowy Ride with the Doctor, The Condition of the Roads in My Neighborhood, and Our Newsboy. Every day, with no instruction in rhetorical invention, you compose a brief essay on these topics and others like them; every day, your teacher returns papers to you with marks identifying (in unflattering terms) your errors, misstatements, incomplete thoughts, infelicitous language, and illegible handwriting. Your grades in this course are tied to those errors, so you strive to correct yourself and are corrected, by a teacher who is one of twenty staff members teaching two thousand students in English A (see Kitzhaber, *Rhetoric*).

Historians of composition often point to the disruption in classical rhetorical education that this admittedly conflated narrative represents, and they commonly acknowledge that this classroom was a product of new university curricula designed to accommodate a greatly expanded student body in a newly commercial and newly managed society. The student in this class will not hear Edward T. Channing's *Lectures on Rhetoric*, intended for seniors at Harvard College, nor can he assume that his instruction is, as it was in the days of Channing's Boylston professorship, required of every Harvard graduate. Some students are excluded from routines in these classes of two hundred; some are not producing daily themes in sections of a course that is now "directed" by a composition "supervisor," the journalist A. S. Hill, who has been recruited from a nonacademic profession.

These and other elements of this narrative have been treated as its "unspeakable" details (in Althusser's terms, its forbidden vision), as subtexts that we should footnote, ignore, or explain without reference to their obvious implications for the social functions of our hypothetical student's instruction. For example, composition historians usually overlook how this student's class fits a new and explicitly unified curriculum, offered in a new cultural site, the English department. Accounts of these departmental beginnings almost always include a list of concurrent political and social situations. Western expansion, post–Civil War dislocations and unease, industrialization, the "impact of science," and the 1862 Morrill Act, which established land-grant universities, are often mentioned as the cultural context in which English departments were born (see Berlin, *Rhetoric* 20; Parker 347).

Historians also regularly privilege one of the two elements of the English curriculum to explain how English departments appropriated the central position in the new university curricula. Composition, many historians have stressed, was the social underpinning that permitted new English departments to overcome the classics and science in a struggle for curricular power. This argument emphasizes the material circumstances that designated composition a useful contribution in a newly "managed" economy. Yet highly theorized histories of English studies, like Terry Eagleton's "The Rise of English" and Jane Tompkins's "The Reader in History," attend only to literature. It was an ideological substance that could replace organized religion and its spiritualized submissiveness with a different, but not culturally new, emphasis on the inspired origins and flawless language of idealized, now nationalistic, texts.

Nonetheless, both reading and writing, composition and literature, composed this new discipline devoted to vernacular written language. Not long before, English education featured women teaching a "pink sunsets" brand of belles lettres in colonial and redbrick British academies and the teaching of primary-level grammar to prepare students for classical language instruction; the founding of English as a central discipline thus required that *letters* be defined as both textual generation and textual analysis. These new departments placed all aspects of vernacular language in a whole system, a cooperative unit that could respond to a threat to the social status of the elite.

This threat was a significant rupture in the "normal" conditions for education. Before the nineteenth century, this normalcy had positioned higher education as a moral center from which an elite could maintain its cultural control. As Gerald Graff emphasizes in *Professing Literature*, the classical college was unembarrassed by its focus on "well-bred men," who needed literary, not vocational, preparation for their professions. It ensured social cohesiveness through its graduates' memories of shared study in the uniform curricula, and it ensured their moral connection to the Hegelian human spirit by conveying the exemplary messages of "great" Greek and Latin literature. Through Latin and Greek language, colleges also transmitted what Hegel called "the alphabet of the Spirit itself," perfect grammatical correctness (qtd. in Graff, *Professing Literature* 29). But in the antebellum and later nineteenth century, these missions were in danger. College graduates were increasingly becoming the patrons, not the producers, of the culture we mean when we think of Matthew Arnold and of a selective, idealized, quasi-religious textual tradition (Graff, *Professing Literature* 19–36).

Consequently, the new university in the nineteenth century had a symbolic mission that was at least as important as its commercial responses to changing economic and demographic patterns were. The university was still under pressure to maintain the stratification systems that had been coded as morality in the old colleges, but it was also organized to meet the perceived needs of new students who expected training and participation in privileged culture. Events in what Arthur Applebee calls the "extra-curriculum" also pressured universities to reorient their agendas to maintain the status of both institution and graduate (12). Outside the university, troublesome imitations of its social leadership were appearing in widely read periodicals that offered reading lists and advice on composition and linguistic propriety. Gender- and occupation-based clubs, as well as educational institutes and societies, offered settings where literature might be read and where homegrown but serious essays and research reports might be critiqued and discussed.

Equally important, the bourgeois culture in which these new threats to the education of the elite resided was forming new categories of "high" and "low" whose dominance, in the nineteenth and much of the twentieth century, would be increasingly absolute. New published sources of popular education promoted these categories in a wide-spread domestic discourse, organizing a sexually coded bourgeois cultural hysteria that opposed cleanliness to license and impropriety. Best-selling treatises like Edwin Chadwick's *Report . . . on an Enquiry into the Sanitary Conditions of the Labouring Population of Great Britain* (1842) and Henry Mayhew's *London Labour and the London Poor* (1861–62) established absolute rejection of (and fascination with) sewer, slum, and other unregulated, "dirty" locales. This emphasis on the domestic propriety of well-scrubbed appearances—reflected, in soap advertisements of the 1890s, in equations between policing and washing the home—suggested that one might conquer sin by proper housekeeping as well as by institutionally prescribed religious and educational fervor (Stallybrass and White 125–35). All these nonacademic organizations of a new social "common sense" were signs of increasingly blurred American systems of privilege. Entitlements to social standing were diffused beyond the moral centers of religion and comparatively straightforward programs for higher education in early colleges.

This symbolic context, as much as a catalog of political and economic events, explains how the discipline of English quickly defined the center of new university curricula. As Richard Ohmann points out, the selection of literature and writing as the "important" content of English studies fitted these circumstances perfectly, "as though established by a national authority." But Ohmann dichotomizes the two sides of the English curriculum as the labor of composition and the bourgeois leisure of reading literature. He claims that "composition spread like kudzu, mainly because its utility was incontestable" ("Reading" 16, 17).

On the contrary, if we stay with questions about the cultural functions of English as a whole (and with what we know of the limited utility of its classic freshman composition), it is clear that the principle at issue here was not composition's practical, industrial uses, which a traditional Marxist would naturally highlight. Primarily, composition contributed to establishing English as a unified *symbolic* system—a nationalizing authority that produces particular sensibilities that respond to an Althusserian "call" to identity, the structurally reproductive cultural "hailing" that, for instance, makes a woman with children a socially recognizable and evaluated "Mother." The university, ambivalent about its formerly unentitled, newly admitted students, needed to establish an internal boundary, a way to stratify diverse participants in what had been perceived as one dominant American group. As the symbolic domain of a national vernacular literature was suddenly produced to control an actual public realm, an equally new but easily identifiable, low, and now alien "writing" could simultaneously represent a murky, improper realm of language. That is, nonliterary writing by the unentitled became an organized discourse on composition, the unentitled domain that would perfectly complete the formation of a newly conceived, privileged, and discrete literary canon. This discourse offered connotations of mythic improprieties that earlier colonial countertexts of nonliterary vernacular writing had not suggested. It became the unscrubbed, unsanctified "other" beside quasi-religious literary texts.

In this interpretation of early practices and their continuing symbolic and actual hold on composition, English, by virtue of establishing composition, placed literary authorship above popular writing, the inadequacies of which had not been at issue in a "universal" colonial literacy. More important for our purposes, English pointedly compared literary authorship with inadequate student composition. In the era's disturbing social, economic, and political blurrings, English represented not "work" versus "leisure" but, as Charles Eliot, the president of Harvard, explicitly said in his 1869 inaugural address, both "principles" and a "test" (qtd. in W. Douglas 129). Composition was to be the mechanism by which Harvard and other "new" universities might initiate, while closely judging and categorizing, its students. Earlier assumptions that college students were automatically entitled to participate in discursive controls on the public and private patriarchal realms were now translated, through composition, into a plausible fiction that new university students were "not good at English."

It is, consequently, more telling than we might recognize at first that our exemplary student is, at the urging of Harvard's A. S. Hill after only a few years of supervising this curriculum, taking English A as a freshman (Kitzhaber, *Rhetoric*). This course is not symbolically, and soon will not be actually, part of a continuous and universal requirement to learn rhetoric throughout four years of instruction (see Russell on Harvard's early, multilevel cross-curricular rhetoric requirement). The student's performance in this course will determine how much more "writing" he must take and, specifically, how soon he will be admitted to the "principles" taught by vernacular literature—what one nineteenth-century English teacher identified as "our national ideals . . . , our race ideals . . . and our universal ideals" (qtd. in Applebee 68).

The course in composition thereby became a primary site of cultural reproduction, a local instance of the newly reproduced national ideology that would attempt to maintain the licensing systems of an older hierarchy in a new formation. This ideological repetition required that, for the first time in the history of education, institutions of higher learning would make an issue of the specific *graphic* correctness of a student's vernacular written language. Earlier registrants at Harvard and other colleges did not often submit (to) vernacular compositions; when they did, they were not thereby designated as members of a particular category—they were not "placed." As recently as 1859, parents of a Vermont student sued their school district to excuse their child from writing compositions, arguing that learning to speak, not to write, was the child's proper task (Heath, "Ethnohistory" 35).

But our new student has taken Harvard's entrance exam; his infelicitous handwriting, spelling, and syntax have become a matter of public record. The reports of the Harvard Board of Overseers, widely circulated in the late nineteenth century, gleefully detailed his failings with the sympathy and understanding we might expect of young boys looking at a circus sideshow. Only two percent of his peers have actually been exempted from this course, but its new symbolic force asserts to our student that he could have escaped it. Imaginatively, at least, he might be among the already entitled, a group that constitutes the "better" class he may (or may not) eventually join.

Our student is now subject to the disapproving "gaze" of composition. Its obsession with mechanical correctness, usually explained as an instance of the era's "linguistic insecurity," is also usually referred to as the wrong end of rhetoric, perhaps an illegitimate graphic version of that ancient discipline's final but important domain of "delivery." But because the institution now needed to convey ambivalence about this student's entitlements to retain its stratification systems, this mindless practice had a logic beyond the new, historically appropriate emphasis on the written document over the oral speech. Taken from elementary instruction in classical languages that had already served the transmission of the Hegelian and the puritanical spirit, a new institution of writing, in the form of "composition," lifted out of these indigenous classical contexts a variety of disparate parts that we have mistakenly identified as demeaned elements of the rhetorical instruction that formerly empowered public discourse. Composition instruction instead comprised grammar based on lessons in classical languages, a new emphasis on graphic conventions largely standardized by printers, pedagogical practices designed to teach translation, "model" texts, the aura of gentility around privileged oral usage, and practice in composing that had once been a small part of continuing oral rhetorical curricula. These excavations and their collective relocation in one curricular entity formed a discrete institutional appropriation of vernacular written language. In combination, they placed newly required vernacular student documents, and the new university students who wrote them, in a problematically hazy but always demeaned relation to each of these distinct cultural texts.

This particular way of emphasizing mechanical correctness additionally translated the student's written language into a potentially diseased student "body." This body was examined, categorized as "diseased" or "well" in specific anatomical places, and made available for new "treatments." It could be "cleaned up," "polished," and even "pruned," in all the invasive ways that the correction of language implies. Our student was now exposed to the institution as his predecessors never were and as no "author" collaborating with editors and publishers ever is. He was exposed in a most vulnerable spot—his written vernacular language.

This exposure involved more than a topological mapping of surfaces, for vernacular language also now publicly constructed topics that had, for thousands of years, been private. By asking students specifically to write about "what they knew" instead of to compose addresses on traditionally assigned matters of public policy and debate, the course in composition made not only graphic conventions but once-personal opinions visible to the institution. An isolated "individual," imagined even now, after Althusser, as independently experiencing "life" outside the language, rituals, and behaviors that construct it, became the imagined "real" subject of this course. This new individual was expected not to create significant public addresses as his predecessors who received a rhetorical education had been but to be initiated into sensitivity, responsiveness, and the separation from consequential action that Romantic teaching methods promoted by emphasizing interiority over public engagement. As Eagleton has argued, following Althusser, this student thereby acquired the covert "subjectivity" also required of students of literature ("Subject" 98). By suggesting that the only topic of interest to students is private, isolated experience, the student's assignments construed a prepolitical, presexual, preeconomic student identity. Within these limits, this newly hailed subject might be "creative"—about nothing consequential to his surroundings. And if that spark did not appear, he might be individually blamed, as today's students often are, for exclusion from a socially constructed discourse that defines *creativity* and *originality* as access to literary insight.

These practices undertook progressive educational "reforms" that were also re-formations. They focused on—while new handbooks were simultaneously codifying—a correct written vernacular language, as a matter of fostering and gauging politeness and good breeding. But they also followed what Pierre Bourdieu calls "the whole trick of pedagogic reason" (qtd. in Stallybrass and White 95), appearing to require only insignificant personal concessions in the form of a polished surface of language but actually extorting from students their practical needs and desires to participate in the traditional privileges of higher education, a consequential substantive textuality comprising many forms of public discourse. Unlike earlier students whose vernacular clubs and fraternities had directly (sometimes violently) critiqued individual faculty members, college rules, and town-gown relations, these students would compose no significant criticisms of the new university and its official discriminations among students or of the entire society's new organizations and stratifications. They would write about their newsboys in this repressive new container for what Hill explicitly referred to as the "mother tongue" (qtd. in Kitzhaber, *Rhetoric*). The surface of writing, what the institution insisted on seeing, would constantly say "aah." Composition would be, if ambivalently, a national course in well-bred silence.

One cannot, of course, teach or direct such a course without being implicated in its mission. Those assigned to place, treat, and correct this student's verbal body were also new identities extrapolated from images of classical schoolmasters, but they were newly endowed with a cultural call to discriminate "high" and "low" discourses in the duality quickly organized by the entire English curriculum. As such, composition teachers of whatever gender entered and constructed an institutional space for the same nineteenth-century sexual hysteria that fostered scrubbed domestic and linguistic surfaces. Like their counterparts in bourgeois homes, these teachers became blurred figures of both authority and service who would initiate, discipline, instruct, comfort, and regulate students in their movement from linguistic privacy to institutional exposure. Just as the nurses Freud described oversaw the child's painful renunciation of home language for classical study, these teachers guided the student's transition to academic maturity. But as supervised staff members without the curricular freedom or space for reflection that they and their peers might assume when teaching literature, they also relayed the new discriminatory mechanism of the "test" of composition. Much like women in soap advertisements that featured rear views of a woman scrubbing a gentleman's front stoop, they symbolized a formerly hidden domestic labor, now organized and regulated in a moral public mission. In images we can easily connect to Freud's historically concurrent description of the blurred feminine figure of mother and maid (see S. Miller 136–38), these teachers both conveyed institutional concessions to the new students who were producing "other" language and simultaneously rehearsed students in linguistic ideals.

Composition was clearly a site for the "low," in all its senses, cooperating with the discursive "high" now located in vernacular literature rather than in religion and the classics. As an instrument of a new kind of higher American education, required composition organized formerly "undiscoursed" domestic and private social practices, even those once obtained in private literacy education, in new, rigid definitions of those practices as an established public system. Like the asylums, hospitals, schools, barracks, and prisons—and examinations— that Michel Foucault describes, the quickly prominent new course helped ensure the maintenance of bourgeois reason (see *Discipline* 184–94). A new logic of stratification and licensing contained and enabled both literature and composition.

Consequently, the scene our exemplary student inhabited represents an instance in cultural history when ordinary language was taken into an organized vision and defined as the language of "outsiders" whose teachers were ambivalently perceived priests mediating between high and low. Without jettisoning the intellectual history we have retrieved from traditional and new historiographies for rhetoric, we must explicitly understand and elaborate on this *cultural* context and its ideological workings if we are to explain why so few root metaphors for composition studies have changed in the light of recent theories and research. The discrepancy between new intellectual history, theory, and research in composition and the continuing corrective practices of generations of its professionals has much to do with our failure to work through the symbolic social and political functions of composition courses that these practices still serve. The field is still hailed by, and still answers, a call to persuade students of their insufficiency as against "important," if now not necessarily canonical, writers.

This resistance to cultural work accounts for other resistances in our collective will to renovate our field. We still rely on separations of high and low, private and public discourses, despite new theoretical discussions of literary canon formation, literary history, and the social construction of class and gender differences in which private and public participate. We still divorce student writing from consequential textuality and thereby simply and powerfully convey ambivalence about students and their discursive positions in the academy, their private reasons for writing, and the professions they will eventually enter. In addition, our institutional structures simultaneously elevate and devalue a particularly moral yet distasteful Calvinistic "work" of composition while they practically devalue yet spiritually privilege a self-contained experience of literature. We still regulate, supervise, place, and exempt composition courses and their students, largely without acknowledging the political connotations of this language or noticing its massive contradiction to equally problematic expectations of thought, originality, insight, and critical awareness. And we export these contradictions within our larger institutions, still seeking to colonize the linguistic practices of other departments to maintain a universal standard while claiming, in writing-across-the-curriculum efforts, that we best understand their discrete discourse communities, the situational origins of their evaluative standards, and even the difference that establishes their ideas of meaning.

Each of these oppositions contains a contradiction that helped establish English studies as a whole, a pointedly social-symbolic logic that nineteenth-century academia accepted—as we cannot—as its sustaining common sense. As literary studies critiques the origins and social results of privileging a closed canon of literary texts that perpetuates embarrassingly monolithic values, we might also reevaluate the history of composition and our own experiences of it in the light of its parallel cultural origins and parallel social results. Until we do, we will not have a genuinely new paradigm for composition that replaces its original division of good and bad writing with our new expertise in historicizing, theorizing, and teaching students to enjoy the variable relations of writers to their texts.

University of Utah

"On a topic of your own choosing and with a clear position of your own, use at least seven unbiased, accurate, and authoritative sources to write a balanced and objective paper that gives a complete picture of the subject you are investigating"

Kathleen McCormick

1

The title of this essay is not entirely fanciful: it is not far removed from the kind of instructions students receive in most college textbooks on writing the research paper. Let us look, for example, at two representative passages from textbooks currently in use:

> Remember that research should take you beyond mere reporting, beyond just finding information. Be prepared to demonstrate your ability to evaluate the information and ideas that you discover, to arrive at a clear, well-thought-through conclusion, which gives the reader something to think about. . . . Some excellent topics do not concern issues as such; they pose the general question, "What is being done in this area?" Your research in such a case does not move toward a judgment as to who is right. Instead, the research consists of assembling information from various sources in order to present your readers with a composite picture.
>
> (Weidenborner and Caruso 8, 9)

Does the source seem biased? Writers have opinions that they support in their writing, but some writers are more open-minded than others. Is the author's purpose in writing to explain or to persuade? Does the author provide a balanced presentation of evidence, or are there other perspectives and evidence that the author ignores? Be aware of the point of view of the author and of the publication you are examining. An article in a magazine of political opinion such as *The National Review* can be expected to take a conservative stance on an issue, just as a *New Republic* article will express a more liberal opinion. Your own paper, even when you are making an argument for a particular viewpoint, should present evidence for all sides. If you use opinionated sources, you can balance them with sources expressing opposing points of view.   (Veit, Gould, and Clifford 297)

Both these passages offer students contradictory advice. The first example tells students that they should, on the one hand, develop conclusions of their own, that research is more than "mere reporting"; on the other hand, the passage indicates that some of the best topics require students simply to "assemble" information from various sources. What exactly is the difference between reporting and assembling? Students learn that their papers should "evaluate" information and arrive at interesting conclusions but that excellent topics require no "judgment" by the writer.

The second passage acknowledges that all sources speak from a particular perspective—all writers and publications have "opinions" and "points of view"—and yet it also suggests that "balanced" sources are able to rise above the merely perspectival. Indeed, sources with particular points of view become increasingly denigrated as the paragraph develops. They are said to "ignore" evidence for alternative positions, to be "opinionated," and to need to be "balanced" by alternative positions. The two passages establish a series of oppositions—between the production of knowledge and the mere telling of it, between balance and bias, between fact and opinion—and yet they also unwittingly demonstrate the impossibility of maintaining these distinctions.

In *Lenin and Philosophy*, Louis Althusser points out that while the school is the most dominant ideological state apparatus, "hardly anyone lends an ear to its music: it is so silent!" (155). Within the American academy over the last two decades, an increasing number of teachers and theorists have become attuned to this "music." The schools, and the detailed structures within them, carry subtle and not so subtle ideological messages that, in Althusser's famous metaphor, "interpellate" or hail students to take up the position of a subject in and of the dominant ideology. Scholars now frequently comment on the ways in which educational structures construct subjects, and broad-ranging educational critiques often accompany these commentaries. One thinks of Paulo Freire's "problem-posing" pedagogy (66–74), Gerald Graff's "conflict model" of education (*Culture Wars*), and Henry Giroux's "critical literacy" (*Schooling* 155–72), all of which call for teaching students to perceive the interconnectedness of social conditions and the culture's reading and writing practices, to analyze those conditions and practices, and to take action within and against them. Further, over the last decade, teachers have increasingly used literary and rhetorical theory to develop new curricular and pedagogical practices that can empower students to read and write from more critically literate perspectives.[1]

This essay deploys some of the insights of contemporary cultural theory, not to theorize the curriculum in general or to theorize about pedagogy, but to analyze in detail one particular educational practice—the research paper—as some characteristic college textbooks describe it to students. While I realize that all teachers do not use these textbooks, they are particularly popular in freshman-level writing classes because of what Althusser would call the "educational means of production" (*Lenin* 154–57). Such courses are largely staffed by inexperienced graduate students who receive little if any teacher training and who therefore rely on textbooks that map procedures out simply and easily for them and their students.

In and of itself, the research paper may at first seem harmless enough, perhaps even trivial as a topic for cultural critique, but it functions in the United States in much the same way as the written examination does in Britain: it is a major form of testing that allows students to accumulate discrete credits toward a degree. Alan Sinfield's 1985 essay on Shakespeare and education, whose title I invoke in my title, is the most extensive cultural-materialist critique to date of the equivalently detailed British testing system, which enables students to pass from one educational level to another. Here I perform a similar analysis of the predominantly and characteristically American institution of the research paper.

I read textbook instructions less for what they overtly tell the student (like the two already quoted, they may, in fact, function quite helpfully) than for symptoms of the tensions or contradictions in our culture that these instructions often unconsciously reproduce (for a discussion of symptomatic reading, see Macherey 94). In particular, I look for points of contradiction within these texts to force them to reveal the ways in

which—despite their explicit injunctions to students to think independently and evaluatively—the modes of reading and writing they advocate actually prevent students from developing critically literate
reading and writing practices. My analysis is a self-conscious application of some methods of Marxist criticism, which, as Tony Bennett
defines it, "so 'works' upon the texts concerned as to *make them* 'reveal'
or 'distance' the dominant ideological forms to which they are *made* to
allude" (*Formalism* 141). Thus, I do not claim that my reading of these
textbooks is valid because it possesses ontological priority (Bennett,
"Texts" 5); rather, I see it as valid because of its *effects*. It takes these
textbooks out of the contexts in which they are generally used, and in
which their methods of instruction seem natural, and reads them
against the grain, working them to make them reveal ideological interests to which the analysis makes them allude. While symptomatic analysis of literary and other cultural texts has become commonplace in
cultural studies circles in the last decade, it is rarely applied to such a
humble and apparently innocent apparatus as the textbook. Yet because textbooks hold a contradictory position within the social formation as both educational instruments and profit-making commodities,[2]
they can be particularly useful in revealing some of the tensions within
our culture and within our own profession.

The bulk of current textbook instruction on writing a research paper
consists of painstakingly detailed mechanical directions on using the
card catalog, taking notes on sources, accessing online catalogs, revising sentences and paragraphs, making an outline, and quoting and
documenting sources. These almost obsessively detailed instructions
police what is at once, contradictorily, the private or personal activity
of reading or writing and a shared scholarly activity. However useful,
such detail covers over a glaring absence: the lack of serious discussion
about interrogating sources and placing them in larger cultural and
historical contexts. For example, the texts fail to explore the ways in
which sources may be complicit with, or may work to challenge, the
existing social order or the ways sources relate to issues of power and
privilege. In short, these texts contain little instruction in what Giroux
calls "citizenship education," the development of "forms of knowledge
and social practices" that make students "critical thinkers" and that
empower them "to address social problems in order to transform existing political and economic inequalities" (*Schooling* 9).

Such absences are rich material for cultural analysis. Like the acad-
emy itself, the textbook is linked, perhaps inherently, to the residual.
Major publishers—Norton; Heath; Macmillan; Harcourt; St. Martin's;
Holt, Rinehart, and Winston; Little, Brown—who control much of the

enormously lucrative textbook market are tied primarily to profit and therefore to adoptions; they thus view with suspicion, and often censor, material that could offend potential customers, regardless of its apparent educational content. As a representative of Holt, Rinehart, and Winston, for example, has said, "When you're publishing a book, if there's something that is controversial, it's better to take it out" (qtd. in Starr 103).

In the mid-1980s, I and a group of colleagues from the Carnegie Mellon literary and cultural studies program managed to persuade D. C. Heath to publish two theoretically innovative textbooks, *Reading Texts* (McCormick, Waller, and Flower) and *The Lexington Introduction to Literature* (Waller, McCormick, and Fowler). We were able to do so at least in part because we could guarantee that we would use the books at our own university, because we were willing to go on the road to persuade other departments to adopt the textbooks, and because Heath, nervously but not ungenerously, was convinced that our approach—a mixture of reader-centered pedagogy and cultural materialism—was an emerging trend. Nonetheless, at all stages of production, we were cautioned about not getting too far ahead of the dominant understanding of literary studies; about, for example, balancing innovative teaching approaches with selections of traditional literary texts; about emphasizing reader-response criticism rather than cultural materialism as the "new" aspect of our approach. As I look now at my and my collaborators' attempts in these textbooks, particularly in *Reading Texts*, I can see how developments in our outlooks and broader trends in the academy make constant revision necessary. I would today seek to make a number of different editorial compromises from the ones we made at the time. Our editors also instructed us to think always of the practical implications of our approach for the classroom teacher. This was, in fact, good advice—even if the way we profited from it differed somewhat from the way it was meant. It directed me, for instance, to consider how other textbooks dealt with what I came to see as the necessary microlevels of pedagogy, such as the research paper.

2

[Your research paper topic] should be a topic that you can consider objectively. A controversial question may motivate your research, but if you have strong preconceptions concerning it, they may distort your judgment. . . . A weakness of many students' papers is that they record material from their reading but do not venture opinions of their own.   (Coyle 11)

[T]he fundamental activity of research is to establish what *is*. How you feel about the situation, or how you should feel, is a proposition of value; what should be done about the situation is a proposition of policy. But the explanation of the situation itself remains a matter of fact.   (Metcalf 33)

Lasting persuasion usually depends on a convincing presentation of evidence based on what seems to be undeniable fact. . . . Think of your paper as being mainly written in your own voice.
                                (M. Walker 100, 113)

Conventional research papers have two significant, unstated goals: first, to teach a way of *reading* that will accord culturally dominant points of view the status of transcendent knowledge, thereby discrediting counterdominant positions; second, to teach a way of *writing* in which individuals can authenticate their subjectivity only by their "discovery" of, and subsequent alignment with, the "objectivity" of the dominant. These two goals are in line with Sinfield's analysis of British examination papers in "Shakespeare and Education." Sinfield contends that the examinations embody "the two fundamental mystifications of bourgeois ideology": they require "the projection of local conditions on to the eternal," and they construct "individual subjectivity as a given which is undetermined and unconstituted and hence a ground of meaning and coherence" (138, 140). By equating objective truth with what is dominant at a particular conjuncture—"project[ing] local conditions on to the eternal"—research paper instructions encourage in students an intolerance of, disdain for, and distrust of all that is not part of mainstream culture. Further, by assuming that the objective rightness of the dominant will be relatively self-evident to student-researchers who presumably know little about their topics, textbook instructions in effect tell students that they must somehow intuit transcendent truths. In other words, they must discover a "ground of meaning and coherence" and then write about these truths in a way that is at once original and objective. This process of interpellation into the dominant is indeed efficient; such instructions not only indoctrinate students into a particular way of reading the world—as ordered and explicable—but further require that students employ a rhetoric of order and objectivity in their own writing in order to validate themselves as individuals.

Traditionally, most textbooks describe authoritative sources through the language of objectivism: the best sources are "accurate" (Veit, Gould, and Clifford 296; Winkler and McCuen 39) and "unbiased" (J. Johnson 70), and their goal is "to inquire about the truth" (Metcalf 82). At times objectivity seems to take on moral and political as well as epistemological significance. Objective sources are described as "reliable" (Coyle 74; Watkins and Dillingham 262; J. Johnson 70), "safe" (Metcalf 83), "authentic" (J. Johnson 70), and "trustworthy" (J. Johnson 72). In contrast, sources that are outside the mainstream are "worthless, silly, and misleading" (Winkler and McCuen 39), and as nearly every textbook points out, "controversial" and overwhelmingly "biased." Textbooks often indirectly link the dominant with objectivity by directly linking bias either with easy targets, such as eyewitness accounts of UFOs, or with journals that overtly express particular political opinions or special interests.

Such instructions hark back to a phase in the history of the discipline in which it was thought that objectivity might accord literary studies some of the respectability of the hard sciences. While research paper instructions in some textbooks have recently begun to change in response to reader-centered criticism or the process approach to writing, the changes have largely (though not entirely) been cosmetic. In trying to accommodate the insights of student-centered approaches without rethinking basic definitions of knowledge and subjectivity, textbook instructions have often become more conflicted, silently reinforcing the dominant from a "reformed" perspective.

Indeed, some textbooks—especially those that seem to have added insights from reader-centered theory—are often explicitly contradictory about the distinction between biased and unbiased sources. On the one hand, they argue that sources are always perspectival or biased, since different groups (or at least different "individuals") in a society may have conflicting viewpoints on complex topics; on the other hand, they retain the residual assumption that the best sources are unbiased. Brenda Spatt, for example, contends that sources should be "trustworthy," yet she recognizes that "few knowledgeable people are entirely detached or objective." She goes on to argue, usefully, that " 'bias' is not a bad word, nor is it quite the same thing as 'prejudice,' " but then asserts, contradictorily, that "awareness of bias may weaken your belief in the author's credibility; it is the person who is both knowledgeable and without bias whose opinions tend to carry the most weight" (303). While "bias" might not be a "bad" word at the start of the passage, it becomes increasingly pejorative as the passage develops. Similarly, Jean Johnson writes on one page, "It is impossible to find completely unbiased sources" (78), and yet on another, she notes, "If your subject is controversial, you will want to make sure that you use unbiased sources" (70).

Contradictory statements such as these enable us to glimpse something erupting through the surface not only of the textbooks but of the wider ideological conflicts that have produced them, something the textbooks and the ideology itself are trying to repress—that objectivity is a constructed category and that things appear "entirely objective" only from a particular perspective. Dave Morley argues that dominant texts "privilege a certain reading in part by inscribing certain preferred discursive positions from which its discourse appears 'natural,' transparently aligned to 'the real' and credible" (167). Thus, a given discourse seems to be objective to readers only if they read the text from the position it privileges. Therefore, textbooks that encourage readers to regard certain texts as objective unwittingly prevent students from adopting a critical stance toward those texts, from analyzing the ways in which the texts' arguments are necessarily positioned within larger cultural beliefs and struggles.

Some textbooks appear to be afraid to face the possibility that knowledge is not absolute. This fear may arise because, in the absence of a historicized theory of culture, discourse, and subjectivity, a lack of objectivity seems to threaten to turn into either the relativism most recently embraced by deconstructivist theories (de Man; J. H. Miller, *Fiction*) or the subjectivism of reader-response criticism (N. Holland; Bleich, *Criticism*) and some process approaches to writing (Elbow, *Power* and *Teachers*; Macrorie). Since both relativism and subjectivism preclude the possibility of determining any intersubjectively verifiable criteria whereby one could develop a "valid" position, it is understandable that textbooks would want to avoid these positions, and they do so by lapsing into the belief that "good" sources are objective.[3] It is quite possible, however, to argue that no position is objectively true without aligning oneself with relativism or subjectivism. The way to avoid these positions is not to reassert the existence of transcendent truths but, rather, to recognize that all discourses, including one's own, are situated and to evaluate their effects rather than their claims to objectivity. The rhetorical devices, symbol systems, and metaphors that any discourse employs have significant effects—they structure the thoughts, values, actions, and alliances of those who use it. And while no discourse can claim to have unmediated access to knowledge or to be truly objective, the effects of one discourse can be seen as more desirable than those of another—once one establishes a specific set of criteria by which to judge them.

In discussing the relation of Marxism to poststructuralism, Tony Bennett (following Ernesto Laclau) contends that Marxism should "conceive of itself as a set of discursive interventions . . . which must prove their validity through their effects rather than by claiming any kind of prior ontological privilege" ("Texts" 5). The effects Bennett seeks are similar to those sought by Giroux and Graff and to those that I advocate in this essay: "to disrupt the prevailing array of discourses through which subject identities are formed . . . so as to produce new discursive articulations that will produce new subjects and new forms of political alliance" ("Texts" 5). Students become able to analyze, intervene in, and possibly change the systems of social relations in which they find themselves only when they learn discursive practices that enable them to interrogate the larger cultural, historical, and political effects of the texts they encounter daily, from the newspaper to MTV to the sources they use for their research papers.

Most current textbooks try to keep readers within the dominant not only by sustaining in them a belief that objectivity exists but also by convincing them that they too—almost intuitively—will be able to write "objective" papers. To accomplish these goals, textbooks must teach students to marginalize or discredit any source that threatens to reveal objectivity as a culturally produced category rather than a transcendent one: students, therefore, learn to treat with suspicion controversial and contemporary issues that lack clear-cut answers. They are repeatedly warned to question whether controversial sources are "balanced or one-sided" (M. Walker 56) or whether the sources are "aware of their biases" (J. Johnson 70). Further, the textbooks tell students that a controversial subject may be difficult to "consider objectively" because "preconceptions" may "distort" the reader's judgment (Coyle 11). Noncontroversial subjects and sources, therefore, are by implication more likely to be balanced and unbiased and are thus "safer" for students to choose, despite injunctions by almost all the books that students should find an interesting topic.

The textbooks also often warn students against choosing topics involving complex current political and ideological debates, not because these topics cannot be dealt with objectively (there is, after all, always a dominant or commonsense view to fall back on), but because such a view may not yet have been articulated in public: "reliable information may be unobtainable" (Coyle 11). Stephen Weidenborner and Domenick Caruso tell students to avoid topics, such as abortion and public prayer, in which "the controversy derives solely from opinion" because "such questions can only be resolved by each individual in light of his/her personal values." While the authors baldly admit that such topics may be "more important to more people than any topic you will write about," they nonetheless see those subjects as inappropriate to the task of student research (8). The clear message is that certain topics—those that would require students to interrogate explicit points of contradiction in the culture, to examine and possibly critique the cultural means by which forms of knowledge and belief are produced, or to analyze the effects of certain belief systems—are taboo. Instead, the textbooks often encourage students to use biographical or historical subjects because these topics are easily defined and limited (Spatt 272)—that is, one can be more "objective" about them. But as Louise Smith argues, "Every issue, even every topic, is charged *somehow* for *someone*."

Because distinguishing biased from unbiased sources is important to the success of the student's paper, one would expect the textbooks to provide fairly detailed information on how to read and analyze sources. The instructions, however, are quite brief; the textbooks uniformly attribute to students an intrinsic ability to distinguish—without training or even explicit instruction—biased from objective sources. This absence in virtually all the textbooks is crucial for a symptomatic reading because it lays bare both the kinds of reading strategies they encourage students to adopt and their underlying complicity with the dominant.

How is the student, presumably one just beginning to learn about the topic, to tell a biased from an unbiased source? Instructions on detecting bias often amount to not much more than whether an argument sounds good. Sylvan Barnet and Marcia Stubbs tell students that a reliable argument should "strike you as fair" (351). On what is the student to base such intuitive judgments? How can one decide if an argument is "fair" in the absence of a large amount of information on it? Brenda Spatt tells the student, "Jot down . . . any rough impressions about the author's reliability as a source" (291–92). But if students are researching subjects like the ones that Spatt suggests, such as the Berlin Olympics of 1936 or the Battle of Gettysburg, about which they probably know very little, how could they possibly have rough impressions about the author's reliability? And even if they did, how could they assume that their impressions were at all accurate?

Some remarks of Richard Veit, Christopher Gould, and John Clifford may suggest an answer. Discussing an essay by Manuela Hoelterhoff in which she criticizes Disney World, the authors point out that Hoelterhoff has "alerted" readers to her "bias" by conceding that Disney World "is almost universally admired" and by clearly taking a different position (170, 171). Is one to conclude that positions in line with the dominant view of Disney World are unbiased? While this conclusion may not be the one that the authors intend, it is likely to be the one that students will draw if their instructions are simply to detect bias by using their intuition. Perhaps Anthony Winkler and Jo Ray McCuen are the most revealing when they tell their readers to "use common sense" (39). Common sense is surely the most unreflective means of passive acquiescence to the dominant that exists—and something that research should help to problematize rather than justify. As Catherine Belsey argues, while common sense might appear to be "obvious and natural," it is in fact "ideologically and discursively constructed, rooted in a specific historical situation and operating in conjunction with a particular social formation." The "obvious" and the "natural," Belsey contends, "are not *given* but *produced* in a specific society by the ways in which that society talks and thinks about itself and its experience" (*Critical Practice* 3). Textbooks credit the student's common sense with the ability to intuit objectivity only because they have mystified the notion of individual subjectivity, assuming that, as Jonathan Dollimore puts it, "the individual [is] the origin and focus of meaning" (qtd. in Sinfield 140), and because they have universalized the particulars of their own historical moment.

Students are often instructed not only to use their intuition to determine if a text is biased but also to check the credentials of authors and the respectability of the publication in which the article occurs. When a textbook tells students to use various directories to determine the objectivity of sources, it encourages in students an uncritical acceptance of allegedly objective sources. There is no discussion of how an author or publication gets into—or, perhaps more important, gets excluded from—one of these indexes. Objectivity is invariably linked with the common sense of the dominant.

Finally, the procedure for evaluating bias is not only unclearly specified in the textbooks, it is also supposed to remain unvoiced in students' papers. Most evaluations—in which students separate "reliable" from "unreliable" sources—are to be done well before students begin writing their papers. That the teacher does not see the student's process of evaluating sources indicates the extent to which it is meant to remain a product of commonsensical intuition rather than critical thinking. If it became explicit, the student—or the teacher—would have to clarify the premises underlying it, and if those premises came under scrutiny, the whole procedure could fall apart, for the premises themselves would be shown to be constructed, not transcendent, and situated within a particular ideological context.

A premise or an assumption that is seen as contingent rather than objectively true must be explained and analyzed; it cannot simply be accepted as fact. Under what circumstances did it become dominant? Who benefits from it? Do different premises operate in other social formations? Counterdominant positions also need to be evaluated rather than silently dismissed as false. Who holds the counterdominant positions? What might change if they became dominant? Who would benefit? Who might be hurt? In what ways is the tension of the immediate problem embedded in larger cultural contexts? If one wanted to try to change the dominant position(s), what problems would likely occur? What larger systems of social relations work for or against changing the dominant position? Questions such as these have no place in students' research processes as currently defined. But in the absence of these questions, it seems unlikely that students can ever critically evaluate either their particular research topic or the social problems and issues they confront daily and on which they are expected, as citizens of a democracy, to take a stand.

3

My discussion has focused thus far on the reading instructions that students are given for doing research. I turn now to the writing instructions. By and large, all the textbooks offer students the same basic formula for writing their research papers. Students are to find an issue that has a clearly delineated mainstream position but that is just controversial enough to make their papers seem to constitute a decisive and personal choice for a particular position. The paper is to be a "discovery" of the objective truth of the dominant, and to qualify as such, it must have three primary characteristics: it must be without contradictions, it must be objective, and it must align the students' subjectivity with the alleged objectivity of the dominant and, therefore, authenticate both.

Textbooks, predictably enough, recommend that students' final drafts resemble the sources the students have judged to be unbiased. The papers must be "coherent" (J. Johnson 177; Spatt 368; M. Walker 110; Winkler and McCuen 89), "balanced" (Veit, Gould, and Clifford 361; Weidenborner and Caruso 119), "unified" (J. Johnson 177; Spatt 368; Winkler and McCuen 89), and "complete" (J. Johnson 178; Spatt 371). A seemingly innocent directive about the paper's organization also suggests a particular way of conceiving of knowledge in the world: by the time students write their papers, they should be able to neutralize contradictions among sources and use those differences to create a "complete picture" (McCormick, "Cultural Imperatives" 202–06).

Let us look at an example, from Melissa Walker's *Writing Research Papers*, that unwittingly demonstrates how a student's early observations on contradictions among sources are effectively eliminated by the end of the paper. The student, doing research on Eleanor Roosevelt, observes on a note card that different sources offer different explanations of Roosevelt's motivation to enter public life. While certain standard sources, such as the *Encyclopedia Americana* and the *Encyclopaedia Britannica*, argue that Roosevelt wanted to keep her husband's name before the public, other sources suggest that "as a public person E[leanor] R[oosevelt] pursued her own interests and not necessarily those of her husband" (M. Walker 89). (I should point out that this example is included in the textbook to show students how to date and initial a note card that contains their own opinions, not to instruct them in how they might develop those opinions. Nonetheless, it is fascinating for a symptomatic analysis.) The student's comment about the contradictions among sources could begin to pose serious questions not only about Roosevelt's relation to her work but also about the relation of those contradictory representations of her to larger ideological tensions about the status of women and their work. Who, for example, benefits from representing Roosevelt's work as that of a faithful wife? Who benefits from representing her as a more independent political leader? Have interpretations of her always been conflicted in this way, or are representations of her as an independent woman the contemporary result of feminist revisionist history? What does the history of interpretations of Roosevelt tell us about the relation between the dominant groups in a culture and the stories that get told about the past? In what ways do supposedly factual historical accounts help to perpetuate or challenge the dominant ideology?

Needless to say, the student does not ask questions like this. The final paper does present Roosevelt as a woman whose political activity was independent of her involvement with her husband, and it does give a number of sources to "support" this position. It does not, however, ask why contradictory accounts of Roosevelt exist in the first place or why encyclopedias represent her as a mere supporter of her husband. Further, it does not explore the student's investment in seeing Roosevelt as an independent woman. All these questions are crucial to a critically literate view of Roosevelt, and they all require cultural analysis. Only briefly, in the final paragraph, does the student allude to the tensions among the representations of Roosevelt:

> Eleanor Roosevelt is widely recognized for her aggressive and creative approach to her responsibilities as the wife of the presi-

> dent of the United States. A little investigation reveals, however,
> that she was an independent thinker and a leader in her own
> right.   (M. Walker 128)

The student presents this position as objective and relatively obvious,
requiring only "a little investigation," but we are left, having seen the
earlier note card, with a nagging question. Why, if "a little investigation" is all it took, do the major encyclopedias seem less inclined than
this student and some other sources to recognize Roosevelt's independence from her husband?

Why does this paper fail to problematize a contradiction in the representation of Eleanor Roosevelt? It is because the goal, like that of most
research papers, is to simplify and homogenize, not to interrogate the
tensions within a given field of inquiry. Spatt, for example, tells students that they "may decide to exclude those [sources] that do not
mesh easily with the others" (291). Even when students are told that
they may acknowledge sources that disagree, they are given no instruction on how to analyze why the disagreements might exist in the first
place:

> You may simply report the disagreement, especially if you have
> no basis for trusting one source more than the others. Or you
> may choose one source if it seems more trustworthy than the
> others. . . . Or you might try to verify the fact by further research.
>   (Weidenborner and Caruso 130–31)[4]

None of these options assumes that the controversy itself might be
worth investigating, nor is it clear by what criteria the students would
determine the validity of an argument.

Such directions teach students to believe that, if they know enough
(though one never discovers how to learn "enough"), they can resolve
any contradiction; contradictions are a kind of fall from objectivity
that, paradoxically, one must get rid of before one can discover the
"complete picture" about an issue. An alternative view for which I am
arguing, however, sees contradiction as a fundamental aspect of human history that ideology works to conceal, simply to make existence
more bearable: "In the name of comprehensibility the collective mind
invents systems (religions, philosophies, mythologies) that allow it to
attain to some notion of coherence" (Dowling 53–54). From this perspective, the research paper—far from smoothing over contradictions
in the name of a false coherence as it now does—should interrogate

contradictions to reveal the ways in which the dominant represses history, to analyze the effects of that repression, and, potentially, to reconstruct history from alternative perspectives for different ends.

Textbooks instruct students not only that they must resolve contradictions in their papers but also that the persuasiveness, indeed the very integrity, of those papers depends on a stance of objectivity: "Lasting persuasion usually depends on a convincing presentation of evidence based on what seems to be undeniable fact" (M. Walker 100; see also Spatt 303, 306; J. Johnson 70; Winkler and McCuen 102).[5] The student's finished paper is, therefore, supposed to be "like" the preferred sources. A symptomatic reading of such instructions would suggest that, despite some claims to the contrary, the ultimate goal of the research paper is to report knowledge: "Write as if you were passing the information [from your sources] on to your readers" (J. Johnson 142). Knowledge is, therefore, something that is "transferred" from one source to another; it is certainly not produced by the student.

Finally, the so-called student's point of view is often the perspective of one or more of the sources (generally those that most represent the dominant position) that the student "chooses" to adopt. Weidenborner and Caruso directly tell students that they should "make whatever modifications are needed" in their own position "to bring it into conformity with the sources" (76). If students speak "in their own voices," it is generally only to repeat the stories they have learned from others: "The paper becomes your message to your readers about the discoveries you have made during your search" (J. Johnson 141). Spatt, for example, tells her readers, "In writing about history, you may also have to consider your point of view," but that "point of view" turns out to be someone else's:

> If, for example, you set out to recount an episode from the Civil War, you first need to establish your perspective: Are you writing from the Union's point of view? the Confederacy's? the point of view of the politicians of either side? the generals? the civilians? industrialists? hospital workers? slaves in the South? black freedmen in the North? (274)

While this list of potential perspectives may look exhaustive, it omits the student's—that of a culturally situated eighteen- or nineteen-year-old who is living in the 1990s, who may be Hispanic or black or white, who resides in the North or South, and so on.

As I have noted, some textbooks influenced by reader-response criticism and the process approach to writing do not tell students to flatten out differences among sources or to take up the positions of their sources. Andrea Lunsford and Robert Connors, for example, state that "disagreements among sources can provide particularly fruitful areas to consider and may provoke you to new insights all your own" (559). Richard Veit, Christopher Gould, and John Clifford, despite other statements to the contrary, repeatedly tell students, "You do not want to be merely a passive consumer of ideas"; "you must be an active, analytical reader and writer"; and "you are fully entitled to think of yourself as a scholar engaged in a scholarly enterprise" (169, 205). Their textbook, in a separate chapter on writing an argumentative research essay, encourages students to "write an argument of [their] own" (410). But in the absence of a rationale for critiquing sources, in the absence of a theory of the student as a subject in history, and in the absence of explicit instruction on developing, historically situating, and evaluating one's own positions, it is difficult to conceive of how students are to go about constructing new insights or an original argument.[6] Veit, Gould, and Clifford state that the purpose of an argumentative essay is to "test ideas in a sincere search for truth" (410), implying once again that truths are universal. Only by recognizing that truths are situated within larger systems of production, however, can students begin to contextualize their own and others' positions and to develop an argument for the value (not the truth) of one perspective over another.

Imagine students caught within this web of conflicting instructions. They should choose an interesting topic but not a controversial one. They must be objective but not too objective. They should use their own ideas but change those ideas if their sources do not confirm them. They must give a complete picture, but they must not use biased sources. If we ever needed evidence for the poststructuralist emphasis on the decentered subject, we find empirical confirmation of it in these textbooks.

4

To change the function of the research paper—that is, to stop quietly defending the existing social order and start actively examining, critiquing, and possibly altering it—we must wrench the research paper from the universal-individual paradigm that it currently occupies and draw it into the social and historical. We must address three areas in particular. First, teachers and textbooks should give students new criteria for evaluating arguments. Students must learn that a simple suggestion of truthfulness does not determine the validity of a position, for the idea that language can transparently and transcendently depict the real is an illusion. All discourses, from advertising to history to the tenets of common sense, are inscribed in ideology. They are all perspectival, and none is value-free. But criteria do exist for evaluating diverse arguments. One can judge positions by their social and historical effects rather than by their claim to absolute truth. Students performing those evaluations must situate the arguments they encounter in larger historical and ideological contexts and ask such questions as Who holds this position? Who benefits from it? and How has it evolved over time? This approach requires students to address topics that are contestable (indeed, the very kind of topic that textbooks currently warn students against), to pay serious attention to marginalized as well as dominant positions, and to determine for themselves the criteria by which they will judge the effects of these diverse positions. Students will obviously have to engage in some historical research both to explore how their subject became contested and to determine criteria for judging the various arguments they encounter. While this may sound like a tall order, teachers willing to limit the number of potential research topics can assign group projects in which students perform much of this historical research well before they write their individual research papers (see McCormick, "Reading").

In requiring students to learn to evaluate their sources ideologically, I am by no means suggesting that they be taught a facile knee-jerk response to political correctness. Political correctness—when it is more than just a trumped-up accusation by a paranoid right wing—is a variation on an old objectivist paradigm: it sees some positions, because they meet certain predetermined ahistorical criteria, as transcendently superior to others. What I am advocating, in contrast, is much closer to Giroux's "citizenship" education or Freire's "dialogic" education. In these systems, students learn to analyze and critique the social and political consequences of all discursive practices, to recognize social injustice even if it does not directly apply to them, and to develop, historically situate, and defend positions that they believe in and that could potentially lead to alternative practices (see McCormick, "Always").

The culturally situated research paper also requires students to revise their ideas of themselves as subjects or agents in the world. Students' points of view must be conceived of not as either objective or subjective but as what Morley (following Marcel Pêcheux) calls "interdiscursive"—"the product of the effects of discursive practices traversing the subject throughout its history." When readers read a text, they experience it neither from an unmediated or objective perspective nor from a personal or subjective perspective. Rather, they approach a text as products of other discourses they have experienced in other social or institutional settings (Morley 164, 163). These discourses impinge on the students' particular readings of a text—even if those students try to feign an attitude of objectivity as they are instructed to do in traditional research papers. While one can never fully see one's own ideological situatedness, conceiving of the self as an interdiscursive subject rather than a free individual can (paradoxically) enable students to develop greater agency than they might otherwise have had; such a radical reconception of the self may lead students to examine the various discursive practices that have produced them and that both enable and delimit their possible actions. We must encourage students to interrogate—within the research paper itself—the contradictory ways in which both they and their sources are situated in relation to the issues they are exploring.

Finally, students' papers should go beyond analysis and critique of the effects that result from various positions and, as Giroux argues, should seek to develop alternative practices—contingent on the contexts in which students find themselves—that might eventually work to transform those aspects of the social order they have critiqued. I am thus arguing not only that students should take up their own positions on issues but that they should explore the kind of action that might be necessary to effect the change they want. To meet this goal, students must have at least an incipient sense of the embeddedness of their particular topic in larger systems of social relations.

If, as teachers of reading and writing, we want our students to be able to recognize and question some of the mystifications of the dominant ideology, we must seriously interrogate the ways in which our own pedagogical practices are often—even if unwittingly—complicit with the dominant. We need sustained analyses of even the most seemingly insignificant or natural material details of our profession, including our writing textbooks and our research paper assignments. By wresting research paper instructions from the contexts in which they are usually read, we can call into question their status as "natural" or "transparent" and thereby expose their ideological interests. Only after our current teaching methods have been disrupted can we begin to envisage practices that could produce alternative ways of learning and thinking.

University of Hartford

NOTES

[1] See, for example, Scholes, *Textual Power*; Cain; Berlin and Vivion; Sadoff and Cain; Kecht; Donahue and Quandahl; Atkins and Johnson; Graff and Gibbons; Nelson; Davis; Meese; and *The Politics of Teaching Literature* and *Literary Theory in the Classroom* (special issues of *College Literature*). Finally, in the area of textbooks, see Waller, McCormick, and Fowler; McCormick, Waller, and Flower.

[2] Starr reports that over a billion dollars is spent annually on college textbooks, and he notes that the combined sales of elementary, high school, and college textbooks "surpass the sales of all hardcover and paperback books sold in the United States" each year (101).

[3] One current textbook, Lunsford and Connors's *The St. Martin's Handbook*, is something of an exception, even though it shies away from any culturally based orientation. More consistently than most textbook writers, Lunsford and Connors maintain the stance that "even the most seemingly factual report, like an encyclopedia article, is necessarily filled with implicit, often unstated, judgments." They go on to argue that "there are no neutral facts in the world of meanings," suggesting that students must always query their sources (551, 552). This approach seems a decided advance on other books that repeatedly lapse into a residual objectivism. But Lunsford and Connor's argument finally is individualist rather than cultural: the reason "facts" are not neutral is not that they are constructed by discourses in broad ideological contexts but that they are constructed by unique individuals. "The point is," they conclude, "that all knowledge must be interpreted subjectively, by people. As a result, a writer may well tell the truth and nothing but the truth; but he or she can never tell the *whole* truth because people are not all-knowing" (552). Lunsford and Connors thus retain the opposition between objectivity and subjectivity; they simply come down on the side of a reasoned subjectivity.

[4] Similarly, Marius and Wiener offer students three choices in considering differing opinions, all of which suggest that students should be able to decide, with relative ease, which position is "correct": "In dealing with contrary evidence, you have three options: 1. You can argue that the contrary evidence is invalid because it has been misinterpreted by your opponents and that it therefore does not damage your position. . . . 2. You can concede the contrary evidence but argue that your point of view is still superior. . . . 3. You can change your mind" (528–29).

[5] Yet students are also warned against choosing a topic that is too objective. As Weidenborner and Caruso tell their readers, topics with a "single, accepted answer" such as "Why is the sky blue?" are inappropriate because "they have been answered to everyone's satisfaction" (7–8).

[6] In an unusual move, Kaufer, Geisler, and Neuwirth devote most of their textbook to teaching students how to analyze and evaluate diverse sources on a given issue and how to make an original—or "new"—contribution to the issue (230). This book, unlike most others, encourages students not to be

afraid to explore tensions and differences among competing arguments, and it suggests that there is no single, objective solution to any problem. Nonetheless it does not teach students to interrogate the larger cultural and historical factors that produced those tensions or to question the political (or even moral) implications of their own new solutions. Thus, its ahistoricism not only reasserts a faith in the power of the individual to come up with new arguments but, by making newness the sole criterion for the student's position, appeals to—and encourages—the student's self-interested individualism. The criterion of the new, thus, paradoxically guarantees that the student will stay within the confines of the old, the dominant, which privileges the individual over the social.

Reading and Writing in the Classroom and the Profession

James F. Slevin

This essay explores the relation between ways of reading and their implications for writing and teaching students to write. It is grounded in a close analysis of several texts, especially a short canonical text by E. B. White, but it is essentially about the relations between texts and contexts, about competing ways of analyzing texts, about (as a consequence) competing ways of understanding rhetoric and rhetorical theory, and so, finally, about the politics of reading and writing.

I begin with an anecdote from Mary Louise Pratt, who tells this story about the dedication, in 1876, of the Statue of Liberty:

> On that occasion, a sizeable number of male dignitaries and two or three of their wives gathered round the base of the statue to perform the official dedication, while members of the New York City Women's Suffrage Association circled the island in a rented boat protesting the event. In a statement issued separately, the suffragists declared themselves amused that the statue of a woman should be raised to symbolise liberty in a country where women lacked even the most minimal political rights.
>
> ("Utopias" 49)

Please keep that image in mind. I return to it, and to the conceptual framework that Pratt uses it to establish, shortly. For the moment, however, I want to turn to an essay by White that first appeared in the 3 July 1943 issue of the *New Yorker*. Now known by the title "Democracy," the piece is so widely anthologized and so regularly taught that it has become a permanent part of the canon:

> We received a letter from the Writers' War Board the other day asking for a statement on "The Meaning of Democracy." It

53

presumably is our duty to comply with such a request, and it is certainly our pleasure.

Surely the Board knows what democracy is. It is the line that forms on the right. It is the don't in don't shove. It is the hole in the stuffed shirt through which the sawdust slowly trickles; it is the dent in the high hat. Democracy is the recurrent suspicion that more than half of the people are right more than half of the time. It is the feeling of privacy in the voting booths, the feeling of communion in the libraries, the feeling of vitality everywhere. Democracy is a letter to the editor. Democracy is the score at the beginning of the ninth. It is an idea which hasn't been disproved yet, a song the words of which have not gone bad. It's the mustard on the hot dog and the cream in the rationed coffee. Democracy is a request from a War Board, in the middle of a morning in the middle of a war, wanting to know what democracy is.

I begin my analysis of this text by addressing the apparatus that accompanies it in the *Norton Reader* and by suggesting that these questions constitute what it means for students to become "Norton" readers:

The Reader

1. Look up democracy in a standard desk dictionary. Of the several meanings given, which one best applies to White's definition? Does more than one apply?
2. If White were writing this piece today, which of his examples might he change and which would he probably retain?
3. Compare White's definition of democracy with Becker's (p. 832).

The Writer

1. White's piece is dated July 3, 1943, the middle of World War II. How did the occasion shape what White says about democracy?
2. Translate White's definition into nonmetaphorical language. (For example, "It is the line that forms on the right" might be translated as "It has no special privileges.") Determine what is lost in the translation or, in other words, what White has gained by using figurative language.
3. If you didn't know that White was the author of "Some Re-

marks on Humor" (p. 1076), what specific features of his use
of metaphor in that piece might enable you to guess that he
was?
4. Using White's technique for definition, write a definition of an
abstraction such as love, justice, or beauty.

(Eastman 833–34)

The aim of reading in the *Norton* textual apparatus seems to be a
thoroughly ahistorical understanding of the text as an object of analysis
and, in a related matter, as White's property. When the piece first
appeared in the *New Yorker*, it was untitled and unattributed. Essentially, the notion of reading displayed here is passive and obedient:
the reader's role is simply to understand—by acts of consulting (a
dictionary), translating (updating examples), and comparing (with the
definition of another writer).

The conception of "the writer" is pretty much the same—ahistorical
and passive. History (like a world war) is an occasion for a point but
not an essential element of the point. History shapes the text but is not
in turn shaped by it. Questions of historical difference are repressed.
White himself seems situated only in the most casual way in this moment in history, and it is assumed that one can understand this complex
historical situation by a simple appropriation of certain stereotyped
notions of the Fourth of July and World War II; no serious research or
historical inquiry is invited. The students' posture is appreciative and
uncritical—they are to consider what White gains by metaphor but not
what he might lose or conceal. And the text's relevance to other writers
is also, in the sense used here, only occasional: White's essay is to be
used as a model for composing a similar text on a different abstraction.
Writing is thus seen as a form of uncritical imitation.

Reading, then, means understanding the point and appreciating the
technique. Writing involves the reproduction of the qualities that get
exhibited in White's style. Reading and writing are acts of attentive
acquiescence.

The import of these questions becomes apparent when one examines
a serious reading of the essay that seems to me a useful response to
such questions as these. In my examination, I do not so much challenge
this particular reading (a reading that, in its own terms, I find perfectly
fine) as bring into the foreground the assumptions that make such a
reading possible; I then question some of those assumptions.

Frederic Bogel's close analysis of this text is concerned with the
relation between the essay's ideas about democracy and the style that
conveys these ideas. That is, what democracy means for White is em-

bodied in, and so inseparable from, the essay's metaphoric style. Bogel argues that

> White's metaphoric strategy is an integral part of his conception of democracy. Each of those metaphors is not just an equation but an alchemical process that transforms a single, sterile abstraction ("democracy") into the fruitful concreteness and specificity of everyday reality. (171)

Democracy is not an idea but "a series of lived, concrete experiences" assembled to dramatize and reinforce one important meaning for White: that the abstraction "democracy" has meaning only in and through everyday life. Moreover, White's decision to embody this meaning through metaphor—through what Bogel considers the "luxury" of metaphor at a time of national constraint and self-denial—dramatizes another of the text's meanings: that democracy makes possible the freedom of "innocent luxuries" (171), like the cream in one's coffee or the pleasures of metaphor in a time of more sobering prose. Writing and reading this style are themselves among the meanings of democracy.

In a characteristic formalist move, Bogel argues that the style itself communicates a meaning in two ways. That is, Bogel draws two semantic implications from the essay's style: first, democracy is a matter of how people live their lives, day in and day out; and, second, human beings do not live by strict necessity alone. The metaphoric style dramatizes or embodies a vision of democracy that transcends what Bogel calls "the impoverishments of a siege mentality" (172).

Bogel can draw these conclusions—he can read this way—because he wants to conceive of prose as a thoroughly fictionalized rhetorical situation. He establishes a defense of this particular model, distinguishing between implied and real writers and readers. He argues:

> Once we make this elementary distinction between a person speaking and the person created by speech or writing, we can begin to analyze the rhetorical—rather than the historical or "real-life"—situation of virtually any piece of written discourse. We will be careful not to confuse author and speaker, or actual audience (ourselves) and dramatic audience, or referent and referential effect of language. . . . (178)

> To extend this recognition, in a mildly systematic way, to as many aspects of a prose utterance as possible is to begin to see it as just

that: a piece of prose rather than a slice of life, a rhetorical situation rather than an historical event. Terms such as "speaker,"
"dramatic audience," and so on simply help us to make this enabling abstraction from all that is, an abstraction that disengages
an object of analysis from an endless context and allows a discipline to come into being.   (179)

Why does Bogel (or, more generally, the critical approach he represents) want to separate prose from life? Why prose "rather than" slice
of life; why rhetorical situation "rather than" historical event? Why not
both verbal construct and historical action? He speaks of this brack-
eting off of history as an "enabling abstraction from all that is," but
what, precisely, does it enable? And what kind of understanding does
it disable? What might we as critics and teachers want to say, or feel,
about the discipline that thereby comes into being? My primary question is, what does Bogel mean by "an endless context"? What exactly
is he objecting to? Or, in other words, is it possible that the relevant
context is not endless or at least that some more limited context might
be helpful to us in our efforts to understand writing—and to get students interested in doing it themselves?

Bogel's analysis illustrates the extent to which contemporary writing
theory evokes a rhetorical tradition through the frames of formalist
literary theory—a theoretical contradiction that I now wish to examine
in some detail. I want to clarify, though, the exact nature of my disagreement with Bogel. I genuinely admire the care and insight with
which he reads White's text; Bogel's analysis of the ways the text functions is highly enlightening. My own argument explores what I take to
be absent from his approach, an absence typical of the reductive ways
in which we currently teach "reading" in "composition" classes. It
seems ironic, and yet typical, that Bogel's practice here departs from
the kind of analysis he undertakes when dealing with literary texts in
other contexts. In the context of literary study, his work reflects, responds to, and is helping to shape new theoretical approaches to eighteenth-century literature, approaches not unlike the one I propose. I
take these contradictions as further evidence of an important issue in
the teaching of writing; even critics who are alert to many of the issues
I raise here tend, when concerned with "composition," to use methods
of analysis at odds with their understanding of textuality and textual
practices. It is this tendency, and not Bogel's accomplishments as a
scholar and critic, that I wish to call into question.

To do so, I present a fairly straightforward reading of White's essay
in the context of its original appearance in the "Talk of the Town"

section of the 3 July 1943 issue of the *New Yorker*. I would like to reconstruct this context by looking carefully at several of the essays, stories, and advertisements that surround the essay, beginning with a piece called "Tribute," which appeared near the end of the "Talk" section:

Tribute

For all we know, this may *really* be the story to end stories about notes that pass between maids and mistresses, and vice versa. A lady who is away from her apartment a good deal these war days has a habit of leaving little notes for the maid, containing instructions about the various things to be done while she's away. "When the order comes from the grocer's," she is likely to write, "please put the milk in the icebox right away, so it won't spoil." Or "Be sure to remind the laundry man about those pillowslips that were missing last week. I can't find them anywhere, and I'm sure he lost them." Things like that. The lady realized that they may have been a bit fussy in tone, but she never suspected that there was anything wrong about them until the other day, when she came home earlier than usual and found the maid folding one of the notes and putting it in her purse as she was making ready to leave. "Why, Edna!" the lady said, "Are you taking that home with you?" "Yes'm," said the maid. "I always takes your notes home with me." The lady was touched, but she was also puzzled. "You do?" she said. "But what do you do with them?" "Oh, I shows them around to my friends." "Really, Edna!" the lady said, still more or less touched. "Why do you do that?" "Well, Ma'am," said Edna, "it amuses them."   (15)

Let's look first at the title. The *Oxford English Dictionary* defines *tribute* as "something paid or contributed as by a subordinate to a superior; an offering or gift rendered as a duty, or as an acknowledgement of affection or esteem." Clearly, the title evokes the latter, currently more common meaning, though it does so ironically, referring to the maid's final "tribute" to her mistress. But this title contains a whole reservoir of meanings having to do with subordination and duty, and the title, like the effect of the piece as a whole, is made possible by the continuing relevance of this system of subordination. The story takes for granted other power relationships as well—the grocer who delivers the goods, the laundry man who picks up and returns the laundry. In a world of tribute in this other, older sense, the social hierarchy is well intact, and the squelch occurring at the lady's expense will not affect the order of things.

I want to speculate a bit about the ways in which different classes are related in "Tribute." I see three strata: The "we" who speaks the text, the lady, and the maid and her friends. The strata are set up hierarchically on the basis of writing and reading, on the extent to which one is empowered to produce written discourse. The notes that the lady writes tie the strata together; they are the texts that the strata share. This is a story about the power relationships embedded in the activities of reading and writing.

The story—which clearly belongs to the lady, in spite of her final status in the discourse—is curiously disembodied and unspecified. No details are given, except for the conversation between the lady and Edna, which occurred "the other day."[1] The story turns on a moment of discovery, when the lady returns home early to find her maid making off with a note. It is a moment of appropriation: the maid appropriates the note, and the lady appropriates the maid's action by conducting a kind of surveillance—a series of questions that emerge from her naïveté but that enact her wholly unchallenged right to interrogate her maid. The social hierarchy guarantees that the appropriation of the note will elicit an appropriation of Edna's privacy.

The central emotion of the piece is amusement. The textual power of the black women, which is not insignificant, derives from their capacity to alter the genre of the notes—from a discourse of utility (exposition) to a discourse of amusement (literature). Because the mode of reception is literary, the piece makes it into the *New Yorker* and simultaneously establishes the alignment between the "we" that speaks the story and "them."

But this literary event—this amusement—takes place not in the notes but in the use to which the notes can be put. Edna does not say, interestingly enough, that "they [the notes] amuse" her friends, even though the plural has been used before. She says, rather, that some ambiguous "it" amuses them. The referent for "it" cannot with any certainty be determined, but it seems to mean that the act of showing, and not the notes themselves, is what amuses her friends. A literary performance of these texts of power becomes a way to survive the indignities of servitude. Edna, like the *New Yorker*, understands these performances: to *show* the note is what matters. The act amuses herself and her friends and, now, the *New Yorker* readers.

This momentary alignment has no other basis in the social world of the magazine. Edna and her friends are not *New Yorker* people; they are not going to read this piece, and that is certainly part of its appeal.

In this regard, the use of dialect is essential to the continuing amusement that makes for the literariness of the piece for the *New Yorker* audience. Edna speaks three sentences: the first two are conspicuously incorrect; the third (the squelch) is, as it must be to be a squelch, correct. The way the story unfolds depends for its effect on this social placement, the powerful representation of Edna's subordination to the dominant discourse. Were the maid to speak standard English, the anecdote would hardly seem as amusing, for its effect depends on the reproducing—at the moment of the alignment between "we" and "Edna" to poke fun at the lady—of Edna's class and racial difference.

The story establishes an agonistic struggle for control of what the notes mean or can mean, and the exercise of authority is crucial. Since the lady's notes are the central texts around which the brief anecdote unfolds, it is significant that readers never actually see any of them. The texts themselves are hypothetical, invented instances. Readers are told about the kinds of notes the lady is "likely to write": "Things like that." The male speaker presumes a knowledge of the lady that allows him to concoct representative notes rather than produce the real ones. The phrase "she is likely to write" has about it a certain detached and distant authoritativeness; the woman is the sort of person one knows so well that one can simply present the sorts of things she is "likely" to do. The words "she never suspected" suggest authorial superiority—in intelligence and moral (or at least social) values. The woman operates at the level of the "fussy"; the male voice operates as a more perceptive social observer. This presumption is the basis for much of the humor in *New Yorker* cartoons at this time, and it suggests that the piece might be a written version of that genre.

Indeed, just before the "Talk of the Town" section in this issue of the *New Yorker* is a cartoon advertisement for Hollander Furs with significant parallels to this short anecdote. An affluent woman not unlike the "lady" in "Tribute" is speaking to a white maid in a "Domestic Employment Agency." While the lady's husband stands in the background holding open, invitingly, a fur coat, the lady says, "and you can wear my Hollander Mink-Blended Muskrat on your day off." The advertising copy adds, "There's no guarantee that a fur coat will solve your servant problem, but there's always hope—especially when it's a Hollander fur" (5).

This cartoon ad, and the "servant problem" it alludes to, has a fascinating textual history in itself. The wartime lack of domestic help—that is, *white* domestic help (as white women found jobs elsewhere)—became a source of humor at the expense of "maids and mistresses."

For example, the 8 May 1943 issue of the *New Yorker* features a piece entitled "Miracle":

> A dignified elderly lady sailed into one of Bloomingdale's elevators the other day, and boomed, "Maids' uniforms, please." Another lady, a distressed-looking young matron with a small daughter, impulsively grabbed the old lady's arm and squeaked, "For God's sake, tell me where you got her." (15)

The 22 May issue, in the lead piece in "Talk of the Town," comments on news reports that a "desperate New Jersey housewife, advertising for a maid, offered, in addition to the usual wages and prerogatives, the use of her mink coat on days off" (11). Six issues later, this bit of news becomes an advertisement, another instance of the interchangeability of content and marketing. During this period, a number of "Talk of the Town" pieces base their social satire on blatantly racist stereotypes; in "Trouble," in the 6 March 1943 issue, another black servant (a "colored cook") is "borrowed" by an artist from her employer and is represented as unable to cope (" 'Po-ah me, Po-ah me' " [15]). This blending of racist and sexist views comes together in the story of Edna: the wartime employment of white women in business and industry led to the "servant problem" that the Hollander Furs ad depicts and that underlies the power relations established in "Tribute."

The positioning of these fairly complex power relations in "Tribute" is achieved textually; everything—including the documents on which this discourse centers—is controlled by the speaker, who utters four sentences entirely in his own voice. Three of the four sentences average forty words apiece (24, 36, and 57); they possess a complex, intricate style—with much subordination and a tone of assurance. The fourth is an effective sentence fragment of three words ("Things like that"). The other fourteen sentences—mostly dialogue—average nine words apiece. Indeed, the discourses of the women represented within the piece are less than one-quarter the length of the sentences of the authorial voice. In this dramatization of authority and power, the dominant figure establishes, and finds amusing, a scene of struggle between two conspicuously less dominant groups, a struggle amusing only to those who can enter without difficulty into the "we" that delivers the words to readers. This story is finally a male vision of two women, who are depicted with the kind of bemusement that enacts—as a frame for the story's racial and class hierarchies—a gendered hierarchy.

What is going on here, moreover, is not just this one incident but a tradition, a genre, of discourse. It is the genre of "stories about notes that pass between maids and mistresses." As "the story to end [such] stories," it might seem to be about the end of a genre. The announcement catches the reader's attention, but it seems, as the story unfolds, to be in favor of putting an end to these stories, as if this kind of discourse has run its course. This story cannot be topped; the squelch is too perfect.

Lingering behind the boast is, of course, the sinister warning that the genre has reached a point of endangerment. When black people can appropriate "our" discourse and read against its intentions, when they can gather to resist mainstream meaning and ways of meaning, when they can in effect gain some interpretive and discursive power of their own by reading and talking in opposition to "our" rhetoric— when this happens, then things may have gone too far. I think the text retains this implication while allowing for another way of reading— and thus another way of imagining the reader's response.

The italicized *really* ("For all we know, this may *really* be the story") suggests another genre—"the story to end stories" genre—that implies an agon of storytelling, an outdoing of previous stories. It is a form of the challenge or the dare. As it announces the end, it actually invites further competition, just as it brags that it will now outdo what has preceded. The beginning, "For all we know," has about it an openness to sequel. As a form of action in the world, the story invites more "ladies" to offer up stories that will somehow embarrass themselves, their help, or both. This invitation to participate is a perverse form of democracy; it is a way of opening up this most selective of media to the readership, of allowing everyone to have a place there, or at least a moment of exposure. In the community that the "we" embraces, this offer passes for democracy in action.

The questions that I have been asking about this text—and the way of reading that these questions elicit—suggest an alternative to the methods of critics like Bogel and textbooks like the *Norton Reader*. Mary Louise Pratt, in her important article "Linguistic Utopias," offers a way of conceptualizing these different interpretive models. She sets up a distinction between what she calls a "linguistics of community" and a "linguistics of contact":

> Many commentators have pointed out how our modern linguistics of language, code, and competence posits a unified and homogeneous social world in which language exists as a shared patrimony—as a device, precisely, for imagining community. The

prototype or unmarked case of language is . . . the speech of adult native speakers face to face . . . in monolingual, even monodialectical situations—in short, the maximally homogeneous case linguistically and socially. This is the situation where the data are felt to be "purest," where you can most clearly see the fundamentals of how language works, with minimal distortion, infelicity or "noise." Now one could certainly imagine a linguistic theory that assumed different things—that argued, for instance, that the best speech situation for linguistic research was one involving, for instance, a room full of people each of whom spoke two languages and understood a third, and held only one language in common with any of the others. A UN cocktail party, perhaps, or a trial in contemporary South Africa. Here, one might argue, is where you can most readily see how language works—it depends on what workings you *want* to see, or want to see first.   (50)

The linguistics of community posits a unified social world, a utopia of harmony and fraternity; it is a world imagined as essentially horizontal, leveled. Like most utopias, it is imagined as an island, free of internal difference and external intrusion. As Pratt suggests, it can explain some things: two persons of the same class talking in the same language face to face. But it has little to say about some other things: about a trial in South Africa, where defendants speak a language that differs from the court's; about how a male doctor talks to and understands a woman patient; about how poor children, black and white, enter into the discourse of mainstream American education.[2]

Pratt is interested in these things, and so she is interested in a linguistics that explores the relation between different languages and groups. She terms this a "linguistics of contact," and she asks her readers to imagine

a linguistics that . . . placed at its centre the operation of language *across* lines of social differentiation, a linguistics that focused on modes and zones of contact between dominant and dominated groups, between persons of different and multiple identities, speakers of different languages, that focused on how such speakers constitute each other relationally and in difference, how they enact differences in language.   (60)

For example, what she calls "community" or "utopian" linguistics analyzes apartheid in terms of the separateness of whites and blacks, seeing each as insular, as an isolated island where members of each group talk only among themselves, relating only to themselves. A linguistics of contact looks at "particular forms of relatedness of whites and blacks. . . . It sees apartheid as activity, something people are doing, something enacted through practices in which difference and domination are ongoingly produced in conflict" (60).

Pratt recognizes the profound disruption such a linguistic model occasions. Returning to the image of the Statue of Liberty, she points out:

> To include both the island full of dignitaries and the boatload of suffragists in the same picture is to introduce a deep cleavage indeed into the imagined community. It is to bring even the dominant class into a zone of profound internal incoherence and conflict that is almost unbearable to confront.   (55)

But that conflict is precisely what must be confronted, and she calls for "a linguistics that [places] at its centre the workings of language across rather than within lines of social differentiation, of class, race, gender, age." This project has a critical and interventionist aim. It is meant to encourage understanding of "the workings of domination and dehumanisation on the one hand, and of egalitarian and life-enhancing practices on the other" (61).

In discussing the two short pieces from the *New Yorker*, I have been trying to sketch the operation of these two competing linguistic models. One I associate with White and formalist critical practice; the alternative I associate with Edna, her friends, and Pratt. White in his writing, and formalists in their critical methodology, offer a linguistics of community, a linguistic utopia whose aim is to unite difference and harmonize conflict. Edna and her friends suggest a linguistics of contact, a way of understanding the meeting of dominant and resistant forms.

This latter perspective leads to questions about the power relations between authors and readers; about reading as a way of resisting as well as understanding texts; about gender, race, and class generally; and, specifically, about how poor people, black people, and women might locate themselves in the pages of the *New Yorker*. It leads to questions quite different from those the *Norton Reader* teaches students to ask. In the *Norton Reader*, White's piece escapes its historical moment by an act of literary transcendence. The possibility of such an escape is the burden of formalist argument; the methodology that formalist argument proposes is aimed at securing this removal of the text from history and the questions that a historical investigation would raise.

How might one read White's short essay to enable just such a historical investigation? In other words, what kinds of questions might "Tribute" and the surrounding advertisements encourage readers to raise
about White's piece? In Pratt's phrase, I want to see "Democracy" in
terms of "the workings of language across rather than within lines of
social differentiation, of class, race, [and] gender. . . ."

Some social differences at work here are clear enough; for example,
who is the "we" in "Democracy"? If you read the *New Yorker*, you know
that it is simply a convention of the "Talk of the Town" section that
begins each issue. But what kind of persona does it establish? What
attitude toward the subject and toward the reader is implied in that
persona? A corporate personality seems to be speaking here, speaking
for more than one person (but not for everyone); it is the voice of
documents constructed by kings and popes—in addition to *New Yorker*
writers—and the voice of power and authority that permeates the advertisements surrounding the text. Even if *we* (you and I) are used to
it, being "used to it" raises important questions: Does the use of "we"
establish a kind of "us" against some undefined "them"—them folks
that don't read the *New Yorker*? Are readers being summoned to implicate themselves in this "we" and, in so doing, to rally against "them"?
What sort of seduction is this? How does it differ, if at all, from the
ads? How far are readers willing to go? Where is White in all this,
coming back to the *New Yorker* for an attractive salary in part because
sales and advertisement revenue were slipping and the publisher hoped
that White could reverse the trend? What does it mean, for a writer, to
have become something of a commodity, a revenue-gaining device—
as successful as his or her salary would warrant? And how does such
a writer's "situation" compare with the questions about "the writer"
that the *Norton Reader* offers for students' consideration?

The *New Yorker*'s construction of class distinctions, in its very bril-
liance, might blind readers to subtler forms of social differentiation,
particularly gender. The advertisements portray women who, as do-
mestics and consumers—in either case domesticated—are clearly contributing to the war effort. One ad for La Cross "Nail Refreshments"
nail polish, for example, invokes the wartime work opportunities
("Wear one shade while you swirl for the USO, another while you
twirl a red rivet for Victory") but ultimately does so to locate civic
responsibility in sexual surrender, as the woman portrayed in the foreground awaits the leering soldier in the background (3 July 1943: 6).
A similar ad is for a nail polish called, significantly, "Shore Leave"—
"Launched by Peggy Sage." It comes in "as gay and sparkling a bottle
as ever launched a ship! A shining new red with a 'Navy blue' dash." A

Central Park setting finds a sailor wooing a young woman in a row boat, as the ad copy advises her to "Get Shore Leave . . . and stand by for action!" (3 July 1943: 1). These images are powerful, and their import, if not their explicitness, seems reproduced in the iconography of the definition of democracy, which does not exploit but, rather, erases gender. The references there, when gender-specific, are male— the stuffed shirt, the high hat, the ball game. This definition moves easily between, and so identifies, the male and the universal.

The identifications presupposed in White's essay go beyond issues of class and gender, touching as well on questions about national culture and its appropriation of historically rooted ideals. The text takes for granted the reader's familiarity with the standard iconography of American culture; what is occurring here is the Americanization of the concept of democracy. Is democracy universally identified with baseball games or mustard on hot dogs or the imagery of popular bemusement at the affectations of dandies? For all the appeal of these metaphors to one nation of readers, the text dramatizes a recurrent problem in "America's" notion of itself and of democracy: democracy is "ours." It is not a question of politics as a branch of philosophy but, rather, a question of nationalism as a motive of public policy, and so alternative versions of it—say, today, in Latin America or Africa or Asia—must always be measured by this standard. Only those who accept this nationalistic standard seem invited to apply themselves to this text. What if you are troubled by such a standard? How, then, do you read it? Does it open up a space for you?

I wonder whether we can accept even the modest hypothesis that at least most Americans are embraced by this text. For example, what are the implications of White's serial arrangement—the unsubordinated, undifferentiated accumulation—of fifteen different metaphors for democracy? No one, especially no one who has read his *Elements of Style*, would otherwise accuse White of lacking a sense of priorities. But he accords statements about important principles of government and the rights of individuals (one person, one vote; voting itself; a free press) the same status as statements about the casual accessories and familiarities of a certain class of readers, readers who can take both these rights and these accessories for granted. The text's syntax and organization, then, take quite a lot for granted, embracing only those who *can* take quite a lot for granted. Indeed, far too much is taken for granted there—and then, in July of 1943. The notion of "the feeling of privacy in the voting booths, the feeling of communion in the libraries, the feeling of vitality everywhere" implies, by an unwitting exclusion, a certain class; it aligns the text unavoidably with the class that is excluding others. In 1943, in large sections of this country, especially the South, few black people were allowed to vote, and no black people were allowed to use the local public library. They were Ednas. They felt no privacy in voting because they couldn't vote, and they surely felt no communion in the library, because they could enter it only to pick up a book for a white person. For these people, and for many white people in many parts of the country, in 1943, there was not quite that "feeling of vitality everywhere" to which this text presumes its readers will agree. The cover of this Fourth of July issue of the *New Yorker* portrays three rows of people: five military men in the front, five military women behind them, and, in the back, seven "supporting" citizens (civil defense officers, workers, mothers, children). Not one of these seventeen figures is a person of color.

I would like to turn now to Bogel's summary of his reading of White's essay:

> But of course these two "arguments"—that figurative language is necessary to define democracy, and that democracy permits such luxuries as figurative language—are really two faces of a single argument, an argument defining democracy, in part, as that form of government which recognizes the necessity of certain luxuries. For how can we call mere luxury what is essential to the definition of democracy? (172)

Democracy is a form of government in which luxury is a necessity, and hence—implicitly—a right. Why am I not surprised to find a definition of democracy like this in the pages of the *New Yorker*? Bogel—despite himself—has arrived not at the semantic implications of a decontextualized form but, rather, ironically, at the ideological implications of a document inseparable from a particular moment and medium. He helps to explain, again despite himself, the utter appropriateness of its original context. White's essay belongs not in his collected works, or in the *Norton Reader*, but here where it began, amid ads for Cadillacs and fur coats and nail polish, alongside a story about a lady and her maid who can't speak proper English.

In a statement about democracy spoken by an imagined collectivity, a "we," formalist critical practice finds a harmony of form and content, style and meaning. From an alternative theoretical model, recuperated from the community of readers buried in "Tribute," one finds instead acts of exclusion, neglect, and domination. White's piece wasn't just "there"; it was *doing* something in 1943, in the pages of the *New Yorker*, just as it is *doing* something today, in the pages of the *Norton Reader*.

But what it was and is doing must be seen across boundaries of class and race and gender and national culture, seen in relation to those for whom democracy's promise remained, and remains, unfulfilled.

I want to make clear my own critical analysis, for it might all too easily be misconstrued. I am not offering this reading of White's essay as an exposé, a fidgety dramatization of his failure to be politically correct. No one who has read his *Harper's* and *New Yorker* pieces on world government (the latter collected in *The Wild Flag*) could consider him a nationalist, much less a chauvinist; no one who has read his moving "On a Florida Key" could think him, with any fair appraisal of his own cultural context, a racist. I choose to discuss White, and this essay in particular, in part because he is anything but an easy target for simplistic ideological tuition. The concerns and questions I raise— that arise, I believe, out of his essay understood as a written action occurring in a particular historical and textual context—are meant to make a larger point, not about White's personal failure, but about the misshapen ways of reading that delimit our understanding of what texts do.

Seen in this way, White's text, in at least one dimension, stands in resistance to the time's dominant political formation. Indeed, I would like to return to what seems most admirable in White's short piece, apparent in context. The most conspicuous and powerful alignments of the time were those that appropriated a devastating human event, the war, for the purposes of marketing—to make a buck. The war itself became the major rhetorical device, the surefire basis for making an appeal. In the same issue in which White's essay appears, for example, is an ad that celebrates how "Westinghouse helps in every zero hour [and] fights with millions of man-power hours." The ad visually links a scene of battle with a scene from a Westinghouse factory and then juxtaposes both to a pastoral scene (father, mother, and daughter on a picnic) and the promise that "even finer Westinghouse products . . . will bring a new measure of freedom and enjoyment to the men and women of a world at peace" (3). A generation of affluent consumers soon to flee the cities for the "pastoral" suburbs took with them loyalties constructed by rhetoric such as this. The issue also contains an advertisement for Cadillac, its name and crest superimposed on the representation of an attack led by one of its tanks, indeed the "Commando of the Tanks." The ad translates wartime profiteering into a discourse of technical skill and civic duty: "Thus Cadillac's forty years of 'know how' is being most effectively used in the service of the nation." The ad goes on to detail "other projects entrusted to us" that appropriate for patriotic purposes the "outstanding skill and craftsmanship of the type upon which the Cadillac reputation and tradition are founded" (31).

White removes his definition from the military alignments that mark the rest of the discourses in the issue; indeed, his version of democracy is moving in its silence on war. And, in his elegant condescension toward the "Writers' War Board" and its arch-formalist chairman, Archibald MacLeish, White resists the government's unrelenting effort at this time to control the work of writers.[3] This resistance makes the piece, finally, not a timeless truth but a moment of powerful eloquence.

White's condescension toward the Writers' War Board arises from his distaste at being manipulated into playing along with the deceptive effort to "boost morale." The two pieces that immediately follow White's in "Talk of the Town" are intended to do just that. The first evokes the terror of Soviet and Nazi imperialism (in a dark image of mutual destruction). The second, pointing to the terrifying consequences of Italian fascism, fantasizes a "volcanic eruption" that fixes the figure of a "six-year-old goose-stepping through the streets with a tiny rifle on his shoulder"—the child suffocated and sculpted by the hardened lava to become "a delight to archeologists and perhaps a warning to laymen . . ." (13). These pieces display the sadism that characterized mid-war mobilization of public attitudes. White, to his credit, refuses to participate. He is not prepared to endorse the rhetoric of World War II or to suppress his conception of democracy to satisfy the immediate needs of the military.

And yet White's very "American" definition of democracy idealizes American traits, further developing the notion of a perfectly good society confronting a perfectly evil one. Whatever else he might resist, White cooperates in constructing a purified version of the American polity—that is, he suspends his critical judgment and implicitly encourages his readers to suspend theirs. He thus participates in the general wartime tendency to numb critical attention to American social problems, to see the war as wageable only to the extent that it is an uncomplicated crusade. Complexities are ignored; the future that might arise from this uncritical acquiescence to a manufactured national image (the future of the Cold War, of Vietnam, of Ronald Reagan) is not considered. This is Norman Rockwell gone to college, addressing an audience that takes pride in its superiority to Rockwell's sentimentality but that fails to acknowledge its own, albeit more sophisticated, sentimentality.

Any decontextualized approach to prose analysis, especially one that appropriates a formalist version of the rhetorical situation, neglects all these dimensions of White's text. This method of reading brackets real writers and real readers, as well as the social, political, and cultural circumstances of their existence. It separates the text from the circumstances of its existence—the material conditions of publication. And it brackets the text's operations across lines of social and racial differentiation. In contrast, the view of reading and writing I am suggesting expands, indeed radically alters, the rhetorical schema. It introduces not implied but actual authors and readers, as figures constituted by period, class, gender, race, and age. It sets discourse within the economy of textual production, within the institutions that enable and constrain it, that shape it and misshape it. And it examines the way the text's language—by both what it says and what it does not bother to say—produces and reproduces unjust social hierarchies.

This framework, by including these considerations, includes our students as well, includes what and how they write in a discipline enabled by this different version of rhetoric. At the same time, the notion of what we mean by reading is also reconceived as more than a passive reception of the text and more, even, than an active encounter with a text; it is an encounter with the social contexts of both the text itself and the reader. Such a framework, with its primary focus on the production and consequences of discourse, can foster a different understanding of critical education. This extended and contextual view of critical analysis is, if nothing else, more relevant to students; it provides them with occasions for *wanting* to read texts closely. Critical reading becomes more than just a casual intellectual exercise. Moreover, for me, it would be easier to devise writing assignments on White's essay— assignments that promote careful textual analysis—if I could use the other discourses from the *New Yorker*. Students who have a rigorous understanding of what it means to look critically at a piece of writing may look at their own writing in this way—in the context of institutional requirements and expectations, power relations in and out of the classroom, and their own aims as writers and even as citizens who want to write.

Critical literacy, literacy that is historical and contextual, encourages and enables writing of a like kind. Such reading, I think, prompts interesting writing that serves to develop critical reflection, especially when students choose areas of their own to investigate in this manner. Such literacy helps students develop a clearer sense of writing not just as a process but as a form of production, a way of entering and shaping the world. It can make all of us as writers aware that our voice is not necessarily our own, that it is not simply one possibility among a repertoire of private, personal voices; rather, it is, or can be, an imposed voice, constructed not by us but for us. It makes us aware that the organizational and stylistic choices we make are not just aesthetic but ideological; they have profound implications for the ways in which we invite others into, or exclude others from, our texts, and so they have implications for the kinds of social relations that our texts produce. Writing—even school writing, maybe *especially* school writing—can thus be seen in historical terms, as related to larger cultural and social issues that can intrude on the texts we teachers and our students construct without our bidding and occasionally even without our knowledge.

From the perspective of formalist literary theory, teachers of writing have been consigned to a lower status because we are concerned with history, with social practice, with a wide range of texts, not just the canon, and with the uses, not just the forms, of writing. We are subjugated (the word is not too strong) for profoundly political reasons, no matter what our personal politics happen to be.[4] The sort of reading I would recommend, and the kind of writing and the teaching of writing to which it leads, can enable us to situate our projects within powerful conceptual models—like Pratt's, for example—that can produce social change. I would locate the study and teaching of writing within post-structuralist cultural theory's historicizing and problematizing of texts and textual studies. On the level of both theory and academic politics, writing teachers have much to gain by forming connections with scholars and teachers operating from within these new theoretical perspectives. But to do so, rhetoric and composition must be understood as a branch of the theory of culture and the history of cultural production.

Rhetoric and composition as an academic field has much to contribute to this work, to the development of these theories and particularly to the elaboration of curricula and pedagogies that transform theory into practice. Our concern with the *production* of texts, production occurring within institutional constraints and engaging in the construction of social relations, constitutes an important supplement to the analysis of textual reception and signifying practices that current literary and cultural theory undertakes. Those of us who work closely with students and their writing are in a position to envision, create, and sustain curricula and pedagogies that transform this theory into practices consistent with its stated, but as yet unrealized, goals.[5]

Georgetown University

NOTES

[1] There is no source for this story, though one must presume that "the lady" mentioned it to someone at the *New Yorker*. She is unquestionably a *New Yorker* lady, and the perspective is entirely hers: We do not read, at the beginning, something like "A black maid of our intimate acquaintance reports from the Upper East Side a story to end stories about notes that pass between maids and mistresses. This black servant is quite busy these war days. . . ." In fact, we cannot even imagine reading that.

[2] Many sociolinguists have studied the discourses of doctors and patients; for a study of the linguistics of contact in the schools, see Heath, *Ways with Words*.

[3] The "Goings On about Town" section in this issue shows that most of the sixteen new motion pictures are patriotic propaganda (e.g., *Action in the North Atlantic, Desert Victory, Immortal Sergeant, Mission to Moscow*). The "intriguing" summary of the recently released *Casablanca* is itself perhaps even more revealing: "Intrigue in the North African metropolis when the Germans were still running loose there" (6).

[4] For a more complete development of this issue, see Slevin, "Depoliticizing" and "Politics."

[5] For their helpful comments on an earlier version of this essay, I wish to thank Kathryn Temple, Joseph Sitterson, Gerald Graff, Sabrina Barton, Geoff Waite, and Locksley Edmondson.

On Conventions and Collaboration: The Open Road and the Iron Cage

Kurt Spellmeyer

Nothing changes more rapidly than the basics. In 1923, when Charles Harvey Raymond published his *Essentials of English Composition*, the basics had to do with "thought," especially, as he observes in chapter 1, its "Completeness" and its "Clarity." "*Thought*," Raymond wrote, starting with what he must have judged to be the last word on the subject,

> is the process by which the mind discovers the relation between two or more ideas. The relation itself, when clearly perceived in the mind, is called *a thought*. An example will make this point clear. The words *tramps, dusty road, hot sun*, convey to us three separate and distinct ideas. The word *tramps* gives us an idea (that is, "calls up in our mind a picture") of ragged and unkempt individuals. The words *dusty road* give us an idea of a somewhat neglected highway. . . .
>
> It is not apparent what relation any one of these three ideas bears to either of the other two; therefore we say that the ideas do not as yet convey a thought. Let us add enough words to convey a thought: *The tramps were plodding along the dusty road under the hot sun.* (5–6)

For readers today, in our post-Wittgensteinian, post-Saussurian era, this description of the writing process might seem strange, even bizarre. When we talk about writing now, we begin with forms of life or systems of signs, speech acts or language games, rather than with "ideas" in their relation to one another. Starting with words, we tend to let ideas take care of themselves, and we can do so in good conscience because we assume that ideas are a product of language and that language determines what we see and what we say before we see or

73

say it. Precisely because we start with words instead of minds or the phenomenal world, most people are likely to assume that deciding which ideas belong with which is less a matter of thinking clearly than of knowing well a certain set of codes or the rules of specific "games."

But Raymond had never read Saussure and Wittgenstein. Like other scholars of his generation in the United States, he remained more or less a neo-Lockean, as I believe his remarks on thought demonstrate. "Let us then suppose," Locke had written in his *Essay concerning Human Understanding*, "the Mind to be, as we say, white Paper, void of all Characters, without any *Ideas*; how comes it to be furnished?" (104). Behind every word, the *Essay* argues, we can find some corresponding idea, whether simple, complex, or abstract; behind every idea, we find the memory of some sensation left on the mind's receptive surface like chalk marks on a slate or the shapes left in warm wax by a seal. And because ideas mediate between words and things, no one should accept on faith an automatic correspondence between the two of the kind that Locke's opponents presupposed (Aarsleff 57–63). Since our words may be at odds with reality, Locke advises us to test them against experience through the exercise of critical reason—and it is here, with thinking properly, that Raymond starts his textbook on the art of composition. Tramps *plod*, and the sun *shines*—not the other way around—since our ideas, stored in memory, tell us to expect just this state of affairs. If bad writing comes from bad thinking, then bad thinking comes from the careless recollection of such ideas. And as a safeguard against our carelessness, Raymond not only advises beginners to review their memories with the greatest circumspection but also warns against the yoking together of what nature has kept wisely apart, as when writers combine in a single sentence thoughts unconnected by experience or when they lodge a subordinate "thought" within the precincts of a main clause (19, 36).

"The tramps were plodding along the dusty road under the hot sun." Although I cannot believe that Raymond had aspirations to symbolic metacommentary, few images could better represent the activity of thinking as Locke conceived it. Locke, we might say, awakened one morning to find himself shut up in the prison-house of language, but unlike people now, he was determined to break out and set off along the broad, open road of certainty. The philosopher John Yolton explains it this way: "What Locke was asking was, 'How can we escape the appeals to authority, the confusion of words for things?' " And Locke's answer, Yolton tells us, was, " '[M]ake careful observations . . . study things not words' " (70). No matter what Raymond's aspirations might have been, the image of the tramps invites us to see ourselves as observers of the same kind, more or less free agents in our relations with the world. For readers today, of course, his invitation has lost much of its power to persuade: we know that he bears witness to the way things *were* rather than the way things *are*, and our awareness of this difference— an awareness that the basics always necessarily change and that even the evidence of our senses is the product of language and culture— makes his textbook read like a compendium of beliefs once held by some idyllic, prelapsarian tribe. Between "things are" and "things were," conventions now interpose themselves—as the patterns, structures, and relations implicit in our signifying systems—and our discovery of conventions has made the open road seem like an impossible dream (cf. Locke 162–63; Saussure 65–78).

What has replaced the open road as our guiding metaphor is *community*, a term we use to indicate the conventional, prestructured character of everything seen and said. Yet the metaphor of community has limitations of its own that we cannot afford simply to ignore. Renouncing the illusion of a "real world" knowable through experience and reflection, we have enclosed ourselves (and our students, we should not forget) in the prison-house of a culture irreparably sealed off from the world since the codes themselves, in the last remove, are all we can be sure of. If there is a way out, as I want to argue here, it leads away from both Locke and the idea of community toward a less reductive image of social life, one large enough, and loose enough, to make room for words and things and minds together. In no portrayal of that life will we ever see ourselves figured honestly unless we look past the instability of knowledge. We will never understand either words or things—and we will never understand ourselves—until we recognize that basics always change because we need and want them to.

Getting off the Road

> After we came out of the church, we stood talking for some time together of Bishop Berkeley's ingenious sophistry to prove the non-existence of matter, and that every thing in the universe is merely ideal. . . . I shall never forget the alacrity with which Johnson answered, striking his foot with mighty force against a large stone, till he rebounded from it, "I refute it *thus*."
>
> (Boswell 333)

Almost no one can doubt with much sincerity that the Lockean road has reached its dead end. Though Dr. Johnson's famous kick may have refuted Locke's opponent Bishop Berkeley, at least in the minds of admirers like James Boswell, we know too much about Java, the Brazilians, and the ancient Celts to believe that any number of well-kicked stones can guarantee that kicking signifies the same thing to every observer. As we have learned, it is signifying—the specific position occupied by an act like kicking in the larger, cultural framework of symbols, codes, attitudes, and behaviors—that makes all the difference between Johnson's London and Kuala Lumpur. Disparate languages, disparate histories, disparate economic systems might credibly be said to have fashioned disparate worlds, behind which we cannot peer to find extracultural certainties. And if these worlds are indeed the products of different cultures, then education must be related in some essential sense to learning the various ways of producing worlds—of seeing what the culture allows one to see and acting as the culture permits one to act.

But this lesson was not the one learned by the students of Raymond's day. Instead, they were told that knowledge is discovered through acts of disciplined attention and that the mind operates, when it operates correctly, like a camera obscura whose contents must be carefully reviewed (Locke 562–73). Absurd as we may find this idea now, it enabled neo-Lockeans to assure themselves that every person had at his or her disposal the resources to contest the wisdom of the ancients, the dictates of common sense, and the authority of the state. "Study things not words" sounded like good advice to those convinced, as Locke was, that institutions have a tendency to get things wrong in ways conducing to their own advantage and that education should be less a process of enculturation than a training in resistance and humane skepticism. Innocuous as Raymond's textbook may have seemed at the time it went to press, his bland assumptions about ideas had cleared the way two centuries earlier for revolutions that shattered Europe's ancien régime. Yet this same advice, or so the story goes nowadays, helped to precipitate the social disaster recalled by Kenneth Bruffee in his seminal essay "Collaborative Learning":

> For American college teachers the roots of collaborative learning lie neither in radical politics nor in research. They lie in the nearly desperate response of harried colleges during the early 1970s to a pressing educational need. A decade ago, faculty and administrators in institutions throughout the country became aware that, increasingly, students entering college had difficulty doing as well in academic studies as their native ability suggested they should be able to do.... The common denominator ... was that, for

> cultural reasons we may not yet fully understand, all these stu-
> dents seemed to have difficulty adapting to the traditional or
> "normal" conventions of the college classroom.   (637)

While Bruffee indicates at the start of his essay that he will leave
unexamined the "cultural reasons" for the crisis, his subsequent discussion of language and social life nevertheless closes in on the cause—
which I take to be the legacy of Locke.[1] With its idealized image of the
solitary, skeptical observer, the pedagogy of the open road eventually
produced, in Bruffee's view, something like an entire generation of
students who had never understood writing, learning, and knowledge
as social or "collaborative." Confronting this massive forgetfulness,
Bruffee tries to shift the center of heuristic gravity away from discrete
individuals in their relations to ideas and back to social systems; away
from private significance and toward the common, "normal" structures
of signification that enable us to know tramps as tramps, and roads as
roads, however differently we each may perceive them firsthand. He
reminds his readers, in other words, that although a plain and simple
world may exist, our capacity to know it as a "world" indeed, and
not as a meaningless flow of impressions, ultimately depends on the
shaping power of culture itself: we may survey the roadside fields and
farms with more or less acuity, but what we see and what constitutes
seeing are always already socially constructed. On these terms, we are
never free agents, nor is what we say an account of things as they really
are. Knowledge, Bruffee reasons, is made rather than found—and
made by communities, among which he numbers departments of English as well as the more mundane associations of neighborhoods and
families. And just as he argues that communities make the world or
some portion of it through acts of "collaboration," so he suggests that
the various modes of collaboration are themselves constructed. If the
world is made, then people make it in predetermined, rulelike ways:
not just anyone gets to collaborate, and not just in any fashion, but
according to established routines or "conventions" ("Learning"
640–41).

For the better part of a decade, Bruffee's analysis of knowledge as a
collaborative construction has so thoroughly carried the day in composition circles against the vestigial Lockean strain that even undecided
bystanders, troubled by the broader implications of his argument, find
themselves persuaded that there is no going back. Still, the implications
remain no less troubling if we consider Bruffee's work not simply as
epistemology but also as an account of social life. Surveyed from this
perspective, the world he evokes bears more than a passing resem-

blance to the one described eighty-eight years ago by the sociologist Max Weber in his pioneering study of industrialization, *The Protestant Ethic and the Spirit of Capitalism*. Somewhat anachronistically, I would like to point out that Weber concurs with Bruffee in regarding knowledge as a construction from top to bottom, and he agrees as well that the activity of constructing knowledge unfolds in specific institutional settings, according to specific norms, which are themselves constructed. As Weber tells it, cultural values—such as the Puritan idea of work as a sacred calling—produce transformations of the social structure, such as the shift from mercantilism to large-scale, industrial capitalism. Although Bruffee never reaches quite this broadly, he and Weber appear to agree about just how wrong Locke was and about how completely we live our lives within frameworks of assumptions collectively built and maintained.

Yet it seems to me that an enormous distance separates Bruffee's modest reaffirmation of "the social" from Weber's agonized study. Instead of simply noting that social life is constructed, Weber writes about how and why the Western world was constructed in one particular fashion: we might say (anachronistically again) that he rehistoricizes Bruffee's dehistoricized account and that the history he uncovers is tragic in the strictest sense of the word:

> The Puritan wanted to work in a calling; we are forced to do so. For when asceticism was carried out of monastic cells into everyday life, and began to dominate worldly morality, it did its part in building the tremendous cosmos of the modern economic order. This order is now bound to the technical and economic conditions of machine production which to-day determine the lives of all the individuals who are born into this mechanism, not only those directly concerned with economic acquisition, with irresistible force. Perhaps it will so determine them until the last ton of fossilized coal is burnt. In [the Puritan Richard] Baxter's view the care for external goods should only lie on the shoulders of the "saint like a light cloak, which can be thrown aside at any moment." But fate decreed that the cloak should become an iron cage.   (*Protestant* 181)

Weber shows us, one could say, the dark side of collaboration. The protagonists of his tragedy are seventeenth-century religious innovators whose theology of work as a sacred calling promised to transform the factory and the home into pews within the spacious nave of a universalized sacred space. But this transformation, in fact, did not happen, and church and home together were annexed by the factory. If the Puritans worked hard because they wanted to serve God, their grandchildren worked even harder because hard work was what common sense told them to do, long after "the sacred" had ceased to command their respect or even their momentary interest. And the logic of the factory—the logic of production as the alpha and the omega—continues to dominate our society, and it will do so, Weber prophesies, "until the last ton of fossilized coal is burnt." What matters to us in composition is not simply that Weber may be right but that Bruffee never asks some version of the questions Weber asks. If everything is a "social construction," then how do our constructions operate? When students join our "communities," when they accommodate themselves to our demands, whose interests, exactly, do they wind up serving?

The matter of interests, however, is the one Bruffee least wants to explore. Despite the elaborate rationale he has refined over the years to support his heuristic of social learning, he admittedly intends nothing more ambitious than a short-term therapy for students disabled by their misplaced belief in individual experience. While granting that the movement for increased collaboration started with a call to eliminate "from education what were perceived" as "destructive authoritarian social forms," he takes pains, nevertheless, to distinguish the "radical" (and British) wing of the collaboration movement from its more pragmatic, less politicized American counterpart ("Learning" 636). Whereas British educators meant to challenge the status quo, American proponents of collaboration were desperately struggling to shore it up by helping their students "adapt." On the one hand, Bruffee recognizes that "traditional classroom learning . . . left these students unprepared"; on the other hand, he continues to endorse the current disposition of knowledge as though this disposition had no complicity in preserving the classroom practices he dismisses as a crashing failure ("Learning" 637). With his concern for the social origins of knowledge, Bruffee should have given some attention to the cultural and historical reasons for the apathy he remembers. Other theorists in other disciplines, more willing to look past the classroom, might seek out the sources for this apathy in contradictions of the kind that Weber posits: the contradictions, say, implicit in a social order that long ago ceased to provide any rationale for its continued operation except conventionality itself, coupled with the crushing power of the "technical and economic conditions" (Weber, *Protestant* 181). Bruffee appears never to have entertained the possibility that academic "communities" might be less than truly communal or that, once new initiates have earned their admission, they are likely to be given a smaller measure of respect and latitude than genuine coworkers are. By accepting the academy's fields and departments as bona fide "communities" and by representing their practices as embodied in rulelike conventions, he unintentionally underwrites a status quo that may be at odds with collaboration itself— if we take the term to imply a form of life arising from truly shared concerns. In Weber's world, such concerns have disappeared, and we are left with a meaningless and irresistible instrumentality; it is perhaps to this unhappy state that Bruffee's apathetic students were responding. Bruffee hopes that the next generation of student-writers will feel like active agents in spite of their marginality and powerlessness, which he leaves unexamined—and unmodified.

Turning his back on the open road, but also on the kinds of problems that Weber explores obsessively, Bruffee tries to lure students into the classroom by "proving" that the construction of knowledge is a shared, egalitarian project. And for this proof, he calls at first on Michael Oakeshott, Richard Rorty, Clifford Geertz, and Stanley Fish, each of whom uses conversation as a master trope for the whole of cultural life. In the highly liberal form of conversation envisaged by most defenders of collaborative learning, the participants refine their interpretations of the world through an open exchange of ideas and the practice of mutual critique. While no single participant can claim definitive knowledge at the outset, all the participants, in their search for consensus, may draw steadily closer to a shared perception, a collective truth. Even if we set aside the obvious question—What if they fail to reach a consensus?—I would like to point out that the model of conversation, generous as it seems, can scarcely do justice to the actual constraints on discourse in many classrooms, constraints of a uniquely institutional sort. Although the model of culture as conversation expresses an ideal that may be implicit in the act of speech itself—the utopian desire for an all-inclusive, unconstrained community—the production of knowledge in most disciplines today seldom approaches this ideal.

If Bruffee seems not to have noticed the discrepancy, neither does he seem to have noticed the enormous difference between Oakeshott's capacious "conversation" and Thomas Kuhn's account of "normal," or everyday, scientific practice, to which Bruffee repairs after his brief invocations of Geertz and Fish. Whereas Oakeshott claims for his grand theme the "conversation which, *in the end*, gives place and character to every human activity and utterance" (199; emphasis added), Kuhn is concerned with the more immediate processes that shape the knowledge of particular practitioners. Oakeshott's subject is culture writ large, while Kuhn's is the practice of a discipline in all its specificity, and this practice, at least as Kuhn represents it, looks distinctly unlike a conversation. Predictable and highly formalized, Kuhnian normal science empowers its specialists to pose only the smallest range of questions and to seek answers using methods no less predictable and constraining. Taken together, the questions, methods, and permissible answers constitute what Kuhn refers to as a paradigm. And because he believes that paradigms exert a virtually nonnegotiable force on research, he adopts "puzzle solving," rather than conversation, as the closest analogy to the work of normal science:

> We have already seen . . . that one of the things a scientific com-
> munity acquires with a paradigm is a criterion for choosing prob-
> lems that, while the paradigm is taken for granted, can be
> assumed to have solutions. To a great extent these are the only
> problems the community will admit as scientific or encourage its
> members to undertake. Other problems, including many that had
> previously been standard, are rejected as metaphysical, as the
> concern of another discipline, or sometimes as just too problem-
> atic to be worth the time. (37)

The binding force of a Kuhnian paradigm is not merely the cultural continuity of knowledge built up from past achievements but also the more rigid and coercive social or systemic pressure brought to bear by scientific institutions. Whereas scientific knowledge derives its cultural continuity from examples, attitudes, and commitments—from a framework that, once learned, can be taken for granted from then on—a coercive social pressure is exerted by the departments, funding agencies, and professional journals that authorize and encourage, sanctioning some research projects while actively suppressing many others. But if Bruffee fails to distinguish clearly enough between cultural horizons and social structures, he follows Kuhn's lead in this regard, since Kuhn himself uses the term *paradigm* to cover both aspects of science at once: the dimension we mean when we speak of tacit knowledge or shared assumptions and the dimension we mean when we speak about research grants or junior colleagues who get the ax when tenure time comes around. Because Kuhn himself ignores the distinction, in spite of his avowed concern with the particular relation between scientific knowledge and the communities of practice, his study of revolutions is conspicuous for its omission of royal patrons, universities, munitions programs, and industrial applications—its omission, in short, of the social actors and social sites that have shaped the "conversation" we call science. And yet without some attention to these institutional particulars, Kuhn has shown us less than half the historical picture.

For theorists of conversation like Oakeshott and Rorty, conventions become conventional by virtue of their common use-value, their hermeneutical openness to multiple purposes: one person uses a word; another hears it, likes it, and then passes it on. Words and ideas gain currency, albeit often only in transit, because they help us to cope—to keep, as Rorty says, the "conversation going." Once they stop performing this function, we should be free to dispose of them (269, 373, 378). Kuhn's paradigms, however, have a different status, determining in an essentially lawlike fashion the course of future activity. Rather than offer provisional sites for multiple purposes, Kuhnian paradigms seem to be little more than tacit *rules*—a word Kuhn employs fairly often—and he reduces normal practice along similar lines to a more or less unbending routine.[2] Professional science invariably leads, he tells us, "to an immense restriction of the scientist's vision and to a considerable resistance to paradigm change" as practice becomes "increasingly rigid" (64). But I would argue that if Kuhn is prepared to describe those who labor under such conditions as a genuine community, then we might with no greater violence apply the term to inmates of the nearest prison, who will wear the same clothes, awaken and sleep at the same time, and devote their daylight hours to the "normal" practice of, say, manufacturing license plates. Even those of us who are not inmates can appreciate that compliance with existing social structures does not a community make, although Kuhn suggests that it should, since paradigms shape not only the rulelike practices of scientists en masse but also the assumptions and motives—the culture—underlying the activities of individual researchers (191). That such a uniformity of attitudes persists in the sciences seems improbable at best when it continues to be elusive in every other area of institutionalized human achievement. For this reason a number of historians and philosophers—among them Stephen Toulmin (*Human Understanding* 98–130), Paul Feyerabend (*Realism* 269–70), Stanley Aronowitz (262–65), and Sandra Harding (*Science* 197–202)—have challenged Kuhn by maintaining that diversity is (or might be, in the absence of domination) the norm rather than the "abnormal" exception. Feyerabend especially has drawn a sharp contrast between science as a potentially pragmatic, egalitarian cultural project and "science" in its current social forms: between, that is, science as a true conversation, open and uncoercive, and "science" as a repressive, monological grind (*Against Method* 18–19). While Feyerabend, from Bruffee's point of view, might appear to have set off down the Lockean road once again, a theory of knowledge that cannot come to grips with the existence of the iron cage is simply too "good" to be true.

Prisons, Conventions, and Conspiracy

Such a theory is too good—or too bad—to be true because the Kuhnian account does not allow us to imagine social life as anything other than a cage; it does not allow us to see why a prison is *not* a community and never can be. By Kuhn's definition, and Bruffee's, a prison might even offer the best example of community, for there are few other social spaces in which conventions at their most explicit and rigid, their most rulelike, bind saying and doing so completely. Consider this passage from Piri Thomas's autobiography, *Down These Mean Streets*:

> Every day at Great Meadows Correctional Institution was the same. Our lives were regulated by the sound of a trumpet. It blared at 7:30 A.M. every morning to get us up for breakfast and work. It blared again at 12:00 noon for lunch, and at 3:30 P.M. it signalled the end of the workday and time for supper. There was also yard recreation, and then around 5:00 P.M. it sounded for lock-in time. We remained in our cells from fourteen to sixteen hours to await another day of the trumpet.
>
> Saturdays and Sundays we were off and had yard privileges most of the day, until 5:00 P.M.. In summertime, we had movies on Sunday; in wintertime, we had them on Saturday and Sunday. You could either go to the movies, stay in the yard, or keep to your cell. You couldn't go home. (qtd. in Orland 65)

If shared conventions alone make a community, then a prison ought to be one. Ordinarily, people experience their daily routine as an invisible second nature, so familiar and so loosely followed that it requires scrutiny only in response to disasters or flagrant anomalies, but many of the narratives told by former inmates suggest that the conventions of prison life command ceaseless attention as *conventional*, that is, as always already in place (Orland 64–77). Like Thomas, the boxer Rubin "Hurricane" Carter recalls, "Each morning, at six o'clock sharp, a nerve-shattering bell would blow me out of my bed, demanding I wash, shave, and clean up my cell. Two more bells would dispatch me off to eat." Then, after thirty-five minutes, "another bell would order me to work" (Orland 66). In the prison, everything is conventional in the strict, rulelike sense of the term, and yet Carter soon came to understand what theorists often forget: that conventions and rules are binding only because someone or something can make them binding. As one Connecticut inmate told a researcher, "The main beef of the prisoners is not the lack of rules" but "the stupidly capricious and arbitrary misapplication of the rules. . . . Every guard who is so inclined passes his own set of private rules" (Orland 69). What differentiates a prison from other social settings, in degree if not in kind, is neither the rigidity of its conventions nor the capriciousness with which these conventions are maintained or modified—neither stability nor change by itself—but the inmates' lack of control over both stability and change. The difference between a prison and true community is, in other words, largely a matter of power.

It is always possible to argue, of course, that all societies operate as prisons do. On the outside as on the inside, each of us is obliged to act out roles we never chose, in a drama we never authored. Even our most sublimely "original" moments cannot escape the grid of constructed meanings and uses: deviant or rebel, we never cease to play some role in some drama. If prisons are communities, then the difference between life in the Rahway penitentiary, where Carter spent the best years of his adulthood, and life here in New Brunswick, twenty-odd miles away, is simply that the former makes brutally explicit the constructed nature of social life everywhere. People outside the Rahway prison, or so this reasoning goes, can retain the illusion of their freedom only because they have forgotten, or perhaps have never noticed, the existence of constraints that ceaselessly obtain. For those on the inside, the illusion is repeatedly shattered—by convention, needless to say—with bugles and bells, but the Rahway prison a community remains.

To see the prison in this light, however, is to miss a great deal about the prisoner's lived experience: it is to miss altogether the community itself. While prisoners lead the most conventional of lives, often to the point of outrage and sometimes to the point of madness, their behavior cannot be explained through recourse to conventionality alone. In reality, as the sociologist Philip Priestley tells us, "things are not so simple. Practically every published account of prison life suggests that prisoners organize themselves to oppose" enforced institutional arrangements. Among other things, they create inmate subcultures, "*sub rosa* societies which exist in the interstices of the official regime and which serve to meet some of the otherwise unmet human and economic needs of their prisoner members" (6). Within the structures of the institution, within the system of regulations designed to normalize behavior down to the level of the most basic bodily functions, inmates develop ad hoc networks of intersubjective agreement and cooperative action to improve their relative advantage within the prevailing relations of power.

The dynamics of prison life escape our understanding until we begin to recognize the existence of this hidden, ad hoc dimension that sustains the real communities. Though the institutional structure of prisons in the United States has remained more or less unchanged since the 1960s, the sub-rosa societies have transformed themselves more rapidly and more radically. A decade of liberal prison reforms allowed small numbers of inmates to get training in law, and these inmates went on, despite the odds against them, to win cases that crucially shifted the balance of power within many prisons, especially as this balance affected the conditions of inmate labor and the opportunities for future collective action (Berkman 39–50). "Jailhouse lawyers" used the courts to bring unions into prison shops and books into prison libraries, and they helped the inmates themselves to gain a measure of control over the management of the prisons. Assisted by some of these same advocates, Black Muslim prisoners across the country were able to win the right of open worship, and Islam subsequently became a powerful force for their resistance to both white guards and white inmates (Berkman 50–56). Still other groups pursued changes of a different kind, changes not simply in the inmates' material circumstances but also in their self-understanding. Evidence gathered in 1958 reveals that prisoners typically considered wardens and guards to be "legitimate agents of state power." More recently, inmates at many prisons have come to see their confinement within the context of a worldwide proletarian struggle. Efforts by inmates to develop a program for their political education have, in the words of Ronald Berkman, "radically altered" the prisoner's "conception of himself, the prison, and the society that incarcerated him." According to Berkman, the "growing class consciousness" of many inmates has helped them "to overcome the feeling that incarceration signals a pathological disorder." Prisoners have started to recognize "that only a certain stratum of society is incarcerated, despite people of all classes being involved in criminal activity" (160). Once we look beyond the level of Kuhnian conventions, we see in the prisons not one community at all but many different communities, contingent and strategic—each moving through various stages of evolution or dissolution, each struggling to define itself and advance the interests of its constituency.

Prisons are not communities, nor are communities prisons, because the prisoners want to get out but cannot. As Thomas puts it, "You couldn't go home" (qtd. in Orland 65). The difference between a prison and a "home," which I take to be something like a real "community," has to do with the latitude allowed social actors who are struggling to achieve the closest possible correspondence between the world as experience tells them it should be and the world given to them by their circumstances. Within the confines of the prison, inmates create a kind of home on the basis of their shared sense of the world as it should be, and because they share this sense, their relations with one another are never governed by mere conventions. Conventions like the ones that Kuhn and Bruffee describe appear on the scene only after the members of a particular group, having lost their past accord, try to restore it by appeal to precedent or authority or, worse yet, by force, though none of these—force least of all—can do anything to appease those for whom the community has already begun to resemble the prison itself. Far from preserving consensus, strict rules and conventions indicate how far consensus has already eroded. There may be no "private rules," as the Connecticut inmate supposed, but everyone can interpret institutional policies to suit his or her private advantage—the guards in their effort to exert control and the prisoners in their desire to throw it off. Consensus, by contrast, has other sources.

Beyond Community

If the example of prison houses shows us anything, it is that we need to reconceive social life in ways that make room for change and difference as well as like-mindedness, that allow us to acknowledge intersubjectivity but also the reality of dissent. As we search for such a model, however, we join colleagues from other disciplines who have arrived there long before us. Writing in 1974, when English departments were just starting to unravel, the art historian T. J. Clark bitterly complained about the "cheerful diversification" of new perspectives on his subject, each "taking its place alongside of other varieties—formalist, modernist, sub-Freudian, filmic, feminist, radical." "For diversification," he told his audience, "read disintegration" (qtd. in Preziosi 166). Fourteen years later, and in a very different field—feminist philosophy—Elizabeth Spelman made the following observation about the diversity emerging there:

> Most philosophical accounts of "man's nature" are not about women at all. But neither are most feminist accounts of "woman's nature" . . . about all women. There are startling parallels between

what feminists find disappointing and insulting in Western philosophical thought and what many women have found troubling in
much of Western feminism.   (6)

Their differences aside, Clark and Spelman both describe a disarray
that Kuhnians might see as evidence of crisis, a time when the paradigms have visibly failed and normal practice has broken down. Yet
the "crisis" has continued for the better part of two decades, and it
appears unlikely to resolve itself soon. As another art historian, Donald
Preziosi, has documented, the current disarray in his field did not begin
in 1974, or 1964, or at any moment of deviation before then; rather,
this disarray reflects long-standing, fundamental disagreements about
art, its uses, and its meanings—disagreements that precede the formation of the discipline (19). In this same spirit, Spelman offers a tight
case for concluding that what we think of as "woman," far from being
a transhistorical, transcultural universal, is everywhere different and
everywhere contested, just as it should be in women's studies.

   Those who find these arguments congenial may be tempted to write
Clark off as a reactionary, but when he speaks ruefully of disintegration, he expresses attitudes we all share to some extent—about knowledge and language and, most of all, about culture. Early students of
culture—Emile Durkheim, Max Weber, Bronislaw Malinowski, A. R.
Radcliffe-Brown, and Ruth Benedict—writing at the very moment
when the modern nation-state had reached its full flower, ascribed to
each society something like a distinctive worldview, a total way of life.
Weber wrote, for example, about the "ideal types" of political authority
established by each civilization (the Chinese, the Indic, and so forth;
see *Theory*); Durkheim described a *conscience collective* (415–47); and
Benedict, building on the work of Franz Boas and Malinowski, affirmed
in 1934 that the "significance of cultural behavior is not exhausted
when we have clearly understood that it is local and man-made and
hugely variable. It tends also to be integrated. A culture, like an individual, is a more or less consistent pattern of thought and action" (46).
The presuppositions of total coherence led Benedict and her successors
to view each isolated aspect of social life (curing illness, preparing
food, cleansing the body, burning the dead) as a small mirror image of
the encompassing pattern. And her contemporary B. L. Whorf, whose
influence Kuhn acknowledges in *The Structure of Scientific Revolutions*,
went one step farther by trying to demonstrate that the thought and
behavior of a society—the Hopi, for example—were largely predetermined by its language (134–59).

   Because the idea of culture as a single pattern or system leaves little room for change or difference, or for the kind of struggles *within* constraint that sociologists like Berkman have identified, more recent theorists of social life have had to look beyond traditional holistic accounts like Benedict's. The most influential of these theorists is almost certainly Michel Foucault, whose *Archaeology of Knowledge* proposes a rethinking of discourse in order to uncover the pervasiveness of "discontinuity" (9, 203). Toward this end, he rejects both the Lockean account of knowledge as the outcome of critical reflection applied to sensible experience and the image of culture as an internally coherent structure or ensemble of structures. One way to see his project in the *Archaeology* is to regard it as a handbook for those who want to retrace the historical development of knowledge without presupposing the existence of enduring "patterns" on any level. If we wish to understand medical science, in other words, Foucault warns us that we will not learn much by looking at societies en masse (comparing Chinese medicine, say, to Western medicine) or even at the defining characteristics of a particular era or age (comparing Renaissance medicine to modern medicine). Nor will it be possible to understand the development of medical knowledge by studying medicine "in itself"—its current practices and literature. Instead, Foucault argues that we need to consider not simply the emergence of institutions for medical practice within a field of related, sometimes competing institutions but also the emergence of a medical discourse within a field of related, sometimes competing discourses. Only then can we make sense of the appearance, inside the discipline proper, of standards for assessing the validity of research. Yet even as Foucault describes the production of knowledge in this highly methodical fashion, he underscores the persistence of discontinuity at every level. While he acknowledges the existence of rules governing practices and discursive formations, he insists that the rules keep changing. The history of individual disciplines and discourses is a history of unforeseeable breaks, redirections, and innovations. For this reason, as Hubert Dreyfus and Paul Rabinow conclude, "There is no complete system," "no way" for the historian of discourse "to determine in advance the conditions of possibility" for the future. "One can only describe specific systems and determine which kinds of . . . statements actually did occur" (55–56). But Dreyfus and Rabinow also recognize that Foucault's undertaking in the *Archaeology* still makes it difficult for us to see how these breaks and restorations take place. Characterizing his efforts as a "methodological failure" (79–85), they point out that, after completing the *Archaeology*, Foucault turned his attention to nondiscursive practices and to relations of power, which promised a more useful understanding of how knowledge changes.

In the last years of his life Foucault abandoned the search for the structures behind social change and focused instead on the conscious strategies used by human agents in the act of remaking structures; he turned, we might say, from the cage to the process of dismantling the cage and then transforming it, perhaps, into something else (Dreyfus and Rabinow 250). He did not live long enough, however, to pursue the implications of this move from structures to strategies, from a world in which institutions form and deform people at will to one where people reform their institutions through struggle. In Foucault's last works, a decentered subject returns to a once-subjectless scene, but the relation between the subjects and the scene remains far from clear. If people are always oppressed by their institutions and perpetually engaged in resistance, then why do institutions exist at all? Foucault may be no better than Kuhn at helping us to see why some places are prisons and some are not.

For a clearer sense of the difference, we might look at research done in 1975 by Victor Turner and Sally Falk Moore. Speaking from the "point of view of social dynamics," Turner maintains that

> a social system is not a harmonious configuration governed by mutually . . . interrelated principles. It is rather a set of loosely integrated processes, with some patterned aspects, some persistencies of form, but controlled by discrepant principles of action expressed in rules of custom that are often situationally incompatible with one another.　　　　　(qtd. in Moore 216)

There is, in other words, always a degree of slippage between custom (or culture) and social structures, between evolving human purposes and more stable institutions—and neither the structures nor their cultural underpinnings are consistent in themselves. Although social systems provide a "loosely integrated" framework for future action, they cannot predetermine the shape, pace, or direction of this action on any scale, if only because no system is free from inconsistencies, and no society—no community, as we might put it—has yet managed to escape all the vestiges of difference and dissent. But to escape them at some future time would be, Turner argues, an absolute disaster, since inconsistencies permit the fabrication of new knowledge in response to changing circumstances or the re-formation of established knowledge on behalf of those hitherto excluded from the inner circles of social power. At the risk of losing Turner's precision, we could say that within every institution different communities form and re-form as each member tries to play a role in reshaping ostensibly stable conventions. Instead of arising from any prior like-mindedness, these communities are *produced* by the arguments over what counts as truly common and over how the commonalities ought to be respected. All the while, of course, the commonalities themselves keep getting recast (Turner 272–99).

Unnerving as Turner's position may be for people trained to value only what appears unchanging (rules, patterns, principles of organization), his colleague Moore presses these insights to their logical culmination when she describes social life as fundamentally ad hoc,

> a continuous struggle between the pressure toward establishing and/or maintaining order and regularity, and the underlying [fact] that counteractivities, discontinuities, variety, and complexity make social life inherently unsuited to total ordering. The strategies of individuals are seldom (if ever) consistently committed to reliance on rules and regularities. For every occasion that a person thinks or says, "That cannot be done, it is against the rules, or violates the categories," there is another occasion when the same individual says, "Those rules or categories do not (or should not) apply to this situation. This is a special case." (219–20)

As an anthropologist who has studied legal practice, Moore never loses track of institutional decorums, founding texts, and the power of precedent. Yet her insight is precisely that none of these can stabilize normal practice as Kuhn understands it. Even if explicit rules are firmly in place, their application remains indeterminate—subject to interpretation, disagreement, and struggle. From a post-Turnerian perspective, normal practice may look much more like a conversation after all, much less like puzzle solving. And collaboration undergoes a similar metamorphosis: no longer just a working-with, it is also to some extent always a working-against.

Modest almost to the point of self-evidence, Moore's analysis nevertheless deftly overturns almost everything that Bruffee and his supporters have told us about conventions, communities, and collaboration. But if Moore leaves Bruffee far behind, she very nearly does the same with Weber and the iron cage. Rather than suppose that our society has come to be driven irresistibly by a single, all-pervading rationale, she sees in social life, modern and "primitive" alike, two distinct but complementary processes: first, the process through which "people try to control their situations by struggling against indeterminancy, by trying to fix social reality, to harden it, to give it form and order and predictability"; and second, the process "by means of which people arrange their immediate situations (and/or express their feelings and conceptions) by exploiting . . . indeterminacies" (234). While society appears to assume enduring forms, day-to-day cultural life requires their continuous revision or replacement. Societies change, and never stop changing, because no system can accommodate everybody's situation equally and because a culture, as something shared by everyone, can continue only if its members remake society, over and over, for their own ends. The social constructionists in our own field seem to have overlooked both this process of remaking and at least one of its implications: that although culture is indeed a construct, there are no rules for constructing society itself because the act of construction always begins where it is needed, at the points of discontinuity, tension, exclusion, and rupture. Nor, strictly speaking, do conventions exist, if we mean by this term lawlike rules or invariant procedures—there is only a perpetual series of infractions and disputes, jerry-riggings and makeshifts. Through conventions in the root sense of the word, as strategic places for "coming together," different groups or factions within a community can meet and renegotiate the terms of their future involvements. One need not go to Turner's Africa or Moore's legal archives for confirmation. Speaking from the discipline of art history, Preziosi has reached similar conclusions. "In constru(ct)ing the visual environment," he writes, "we work with a mass of elements that have been codified in the course of individual and collective history." Such "codifications," however, "are invariably ironic and transitory, perpetually subject to transformation and deformation" (154). If Turner, Moore, and Preziosi are correct, then we might think of our disciplines less as places defined by agreement and more as sites of problem posing and negotiation—places where the "transformation and deformation" of codes can occur.

Toward a Pedagogy of Negotiation

Perhaps the most persuasive evidence I might offer to support the Turnerian view—and certainly the most readily accessible—is the collection that includes this text: a collection of essays on composition and pedagogy, sponsored by an organization, the Modern Language Association, that has resolutely avoided any contact with either subject for the better part of a century. If we assume that the moral sensibilities of English professors in the 1990s are not notably advanced over those of their predecessors, why this concession, and why now? Surely part of the reason is the shifting balance of power inside the university as a whole. While the number of English majors, never great, has declined at many universities in proportion to the total undergraduate enrollment, the teaching of composition goes on as inevitably as ever, and the courses once viewed as a kind of family scandal by Chaucer scholars and hero-worshiping Carlylians have become, if not quite a source of pride, at least a way of paying the bills. Other reasons might be offered, certainly, but indeterminacies in "the profession" have given us the opportunity to assert ourselves where we were once unwelcome. By doing so, and in the prestige dialect of theory talk, we demonstrate to one and all the fairness of the English apparatus, whose defenders now can claim that they have had no hand in prolonging the invidious distinction between literary studies and composition. And we, for our part, gain something not so very different from this painless exoneration—a small measure of the visibility that our forerunners never achieved.

Still, our belated membership in the MLA's expansionist community demands that we preserve some regard for its distinctive conventions. Better to sound like Frank Lentricchia or Barbara Herrnstein Smith than Donald Murray. But writing about composition requires a manner, and not just a matter, that marks us as Murray's successors to some degree, successors whose audible presence in the discourse of English language and literature is probably about to change it. In our concern with the making of texts as opposed to their consumption through scholarship and criticism, we are going to remain inescapably allied to the old nuts-and-bolts discourse of composition. Or we might, alternatively, achieve a new understanding of production itself as a deeply problematic undertaking—and by doing so draw closer to literary studies after all, where the problematic seems increasingly to have found a permanent home. If everything goes well, if composition assumes the status of a "field," on a par with Restoration drama or critical theory, then we may eventually choose to "forget" about the current transitional period, which could look, in retrospect, like an undignified, unedifying struggle. And one way to forget that this struggle ever occurred will be to maintain that our discourse has always followed certain rules and abided by certain precepts, when in fact we have had to reinvent the discipline and the language and the institutional role, just as our successors will, if they stay in business at all.

The kind of dissimulation that would deny the reality of this reinventing—and the need for it—occupies a prominent place, as I have argued here, in the discourse on society generally, but it also occupies a special place in the discourse on writing, a discourse whose origins Gérard Genette describes as follows:

> One can grasp easily enough . . . the way in which rhetoric produces [conventions]: it ascertains a *quality* in the text that might or might not have been there—the poet describes (instead of designating with a word), the dialogue is abrupt (instead of connected); then [rhetoric] substantializes this quality by naming it—the text is no longer descriptive or abrupt, it *contains* a description or an abruption. It is an old scholastic habit: opium does not put one to sleep, it possesses a soporific power. There is in rhetoric a *passion to name* which is a mode of self-expansion and self-justification: it operates by increasing the number of objects in one's purview. . . . Rhetorical promotions are arbitrary; the important thing is to promote and thus to found an Order of literary dignity.   (*Figures* 53)

We make texts, Genette tells us, through hermeneutical struggle—through appropriations, resistances, alliances, subversions, outright mutinies, each of them chancy and undignified undertakings, begun in blindness to the outcome. But after the fact, in keeping with what may prove to be the oldest convention of them all, we dignify our uncertainty with the name of order and our resistance with the name of collaboration. And by naming the stages of our struggle in this manner, by giving free play to the "passion" for an ideal consistency, we slyly induce those who follow us to say nothing new: we induce them, no matter what they write and no matter how much, to be satisfied with a repetition of our words, a repetition tantamount to silence. Far from ignoring the constraints that every writer must acknowledge—the nature of the subject, the expectations of a readership, the authority of prior achievements—the rhetoricians of Genette's critique typically operate by obscuring these very constraints, which arise from the changing world beyond the text rather than from some secret place within it.

But Aristotle made this point as well, that we should look not to language for an explanation of language but to the shifting terrain of public life. Instead of prescribing definitive limits to public discourse, the *Rhetoric* explores the means of employing the various discourses already current: his treatise sets out to establish what the discourse of his time had actually become, not what it must be forever after. Aristotle's method there is fundamentally inductive and historical, as it is in his researches on plant and animal life and in his writings on politics, for which he prepared by collecting the constitutions of more than a hundred city-states. And yet Aristotle keenly understood the uncertainty of "the good and bad" for humankind, caught up as our pursuit of the good must be with decisions about means and ends that depend on our wisdom as much as on our knowledge (*Ethica*, bks. 1 and 2; *Rhetorica*, bk. 1). Freed from the search for rules, a "Turnerian" rhetoric might in the same spirit stop trying to decide what discourse has to be and take as its focus the problems, questions, and uncertainties that remain to be addressed in and across the disciplines, problems usually withheld from students until they have mastered the basics. But no basics of this kind exist; nothing is *intrinsic* to literary criticism or history or political science. All we have are questions, texts, and contexts for discussion, and these are where we should begin when we teach and study writing.

If Locke mistakenly sought in "Ideas" a permanence and reliability that language could not offer, then perhaps now, well after the "linguistic turn" has overtaken us, the time has come to stop pursuing permanence anywhere else. Every writer presumes, of course, that a text should be relatively clear and coherent, that it ought to exhibit, at the barest minimum, a beginning, a middle, an end. Yet the most appropriate form a beginning should concretely assume in an essay like this one—an essay posing Bruffee against Locke, Turner against Bruffee, and Moore against a whole tradition—is anyone's guess. I suspect that readers who have followed my somewhat tortuous argument to its end will be less inclined to ask whether I have observed the conventions than whether I have written something that will help to answer questions of importance to them—and it is precisely my venturing beyond the customary that makes possible a real convention, a genuine "coming together." In composition, as in most other fields, we have placed far too great an emphasis on what stays the same in knowledge, at the expense of the capacity to use knowledge as a means of dealing pragmatically with change. While we are not exactly on the open road, we are never altogether trapped within the iron cage, which becomes most fully a prison only after we have consented to the illusion of its solidity.

Rutgers University, New Brunswick

NOTES

[1] Although Bruffee blames Descartes for theories of knowledge that privilege the individual observer, Locke might have been a more appropriate choice because of his influence over the English-speaking world. For Bruffee's critique of "Cartesianism," see "Social Construction" 776.

[2] In *The Structure of Scientific Revolutions* Kuhn provides a fairly loose definition of *paradigm*, one that is not always consistent. First he associates paradigms with "rules and standards" (11), then he describes paradigm changes as changes in the "rules of the game" (40), and later he says that researchers typically follow "the paradigm rules quite closely" (83; see also 38–39). At other places, however, he de-emphasizes the rule-rule character of normal scientific practice, referring instead to a "network of commitments." Rules, he suggests, "derive from paradigms, but paradigms can guide research even in the absence of rules" (42). Still, the paradigms are binding in ways that seem, by Kuhn's account, quite inflexible.

Rhetoric, Social Construction, and Gender: Is It Bad to Be Sentimental?

Suzanne Clark

> *It is probably necessary to be a woman (ultimate guarantee of sociality beyond the wreckage of the paternal symbolic function, as well as the inexhaustible generator of its renewal, of its expansion) not to renounce theoretical reason but to compel it to increase its power by giving it an object beyond its limits.*
> —Julia Kristeva, "From One Identity to Another"

> *All truths arise out of dialectic, out of the interaction of individuals within discourse communities. Truth is never simply "out there" in the material world or the social realm, or simply "in here" in a private and personal world. It emerges only as the three—the material, the social, and the personal—interact, and the agent of mediation is language.*
> —James Berlin, *Rhetoric and Reality*

Academic arguments are marked by the conviction that reason ought to take priority over emotion. I do not argue against reason here. As Julia Kristeva has pointed out, the discourse of reason cannot be simply overturned. Instead I argue that the well-known and gendered opposition of reason and emotion is misleading. If we take a social-constructionist view of meaning, the liminal operation known as the sentimental shows how emotion too falls under the domination of cultural conventions but also how both reason and emotion participate in the irrational. By "sentimental" I mean a gendered and despised discourse, now often defined by the act of revulsion against its excess and by denial that leads us to claim that our preferences are "not sentimental." The label helps us construct intellectual discourse in the academic community—sentimentalists are not allowed. This restric-

96

tion has serious consequences for the relations not of reason and emotion but of academics and society, consequences that are evident in the problems women face as writing subjects. Modernist literary criticism in particular has attacked the tradition of women's writing as sentimental (for a critical examination of this history, see S. Clark, *Sentimental Modernism*). Sentimentality is regularly associated with women's discourse and its history, rhetorical emotion, conventional sympathy and the banality of mass culture, and a certain domestic order governed by middle-class maternalism, which the middle-class paternalism of intellectual institutions would like to condemn or keep in its place.

What the pseudostruggle of critical reason and sentimental emotion obscures is something other than the idea of emotion.[1] It obscures the performance of exclusion, the defining and reproducing of an intellectual class as gendered. This pseudopposition also covers up the vulnerabilities of reason, the ways in which even academic texts are traversed by unknown, unintended, and disruptive elements. The opposition to emotion, and especially to the pleasures of mass culture, conceals the extent to which the ascetic and critical academy is a product of that very culture. Social-construction theorists in particular ought to take account of the social construction of intellectual work. And feminists need to insist that social construction acknowledge the operations of gender.

To say, as James Berlin puts it, that "all truths arise out of dialectic" is to wreck the paternal authority of reason, which is vested in the identity of a conscious subject (*Rhetoric* 17). Critical theory produces a crisis in the subject's relation to discourse, opening up to the unsettling other the process of reproducing subjectivity. If this crisis about the subject of argument is not to become a permanent alienation that coalesces around the skeptical identity of a rational subject, we need to account for the rhetorical production of the crisis—its embodiment. Our cultural unconscious in this process, I suggest, comes into view with the operations of the sentimental.

Feminists have been all too conscious of the problem of sentimentality: from its beginnings in the eighteenth century, the word has seemed to promote a stereotyped and normalizing emotional responsiveness that both defined the value of feminine discourse and trapped women within it. For two hundred years, strong women writers (think of Harriet Beecher Stowe; think of Alice Walker) have made sentimental rhetoric, with its appeals to personal feelings of love and sympathy for the oppressed, an instrument of cultural and political power. And in the name of reason other strong women writers have tried, for two hundred years, to distance themselves from this very sentimentality (think of Jane Austen's bias toward "sense" in *Sense and Sensibility*; think of Mary Wollstonecraft's warnings that women's sentimental childishness kept them from developing into rational maturity and independence).

The fate of sentimentality is deeply entangled with the fate of rhetoric itself, its disconnection from the literary and the aesthetic, and its decline with respect to the discourses of science. The sentimental arose in the eighteenth century in conjunction with the establishment of the middle class and its division of discourse into the gendered realms of public and private, political and domestic, male and female, with the accompanying promotion of the Enlightenment project to purify reason of its emotional, material heterogeneity. Women began to write, and at first the sentimental marked the new sensibility in a positive way, emphasizing the importance of sympathy and of moral responsiveness to others. Men like Samuel Richardson (with *Clarissa*) and Laurence Sterne (with *A Sentimental Journey*) were important to the development of the sentimental; so were the moral sense philosophers and David Hume and, in France, Jean-Jacques Rousseau. The sentimental was everywhere connected to appeals for moral progress and a democratic equality, entering even into the documents of the American and French Revolutions.

Before Romanticism tried to make a decisive separation between the (feminine) sentimental and the masculinity of the sublime imagination, philosophers (Hume and Kant) were beginning to think of sentimentality as both gendered and perverse. As John Mullan traces the developing history, the sentimental first accompanied a sense that the pathos of emotional appeals contributes to sociability. Before the end of the eighteenth century, however, this perception had already begun to change—for example, in the work of Adam Smith—so that a representation of emotional display began to seem antisocial, subversive of rational control, or even diseased. By the end of the eighteenth century, sentimental women were already beginning to appear, to male thinkers, not sympathetic or social but hysterical.

The conception of the rhetorical situation, with its appeals to ethos, logos, and pathos, was translated into a faculty psychology. Nevertheless, the importance of the rhetorical situation, and of the sentimental to rhetoric, was still intact in George Campbell's *Philosophy of Rhetoric*. And sentimental rhetoric was still taught, through Campbell, to American students for more than half the nineteenth century, when it gradually gave way to a more linear and utilitarian or, at best, pragmatic notion of the act of communication, a notion that stripped away the sentiment.

By the time John Genung systematized it in 1886, rhetoric, having fallen prey to the utilitarian, seemed to be no more than a program of practical methods, "the art of adapting discourse, in harmony with its subject and occasion, to the requirements of a reader or hearer" (1), an art clearly separate from the logic or truth on which it ought to be based. Genung, in other words, makes no claims for rhetoric as a discursive practice working to produce (or socially construct) either knowledge or ideology. Furthermore, he asserts (as a man of his times would) that "insincerity" is the most frequent fault in the writer, visible in "unconsidered use of conventionalisms, stock expressions, outworn figures, and the like" (5). But of course in its eighteenth-century origins, sentimentality was precisely a set of communally agreed-on conventionalisms and stock expressions that would appeal to communally held emotions and values: the virtuous would be held in high "esteem" for their "benevolence," but their "delicacy" might make them vulnerable to the "cruel" and the "unkind." Genung denies the social construction of ethos, or the speaker's credibility, and pathos, or emotional appeals, and that conventionality is what the melodrama of sentimental abstraction relentlessly exposes.

Feminism reveals its difficulties with social construction in the issue of the sentimental. In 1977 Ann Douglas published her influential *The Feminization of American Culture*, in which she argues that nineteenth-century sentimental rhetoric was responsible for the degradation of public argumentation and for the advent of a manipulative mass culture in the twentieth century. Recently Madeleine Grumet suggested that women teachers and indeed the whole (feminized) profession of teaching are caught within the process of denial that Douglas associated with sentimentalism, a kind of dishonesty or "rhetoric of false praise" that appeals to values it does not really promote—nostalgia for motherhood and maternal care without support for the hard realities of women's work (41).

The problem here is a confusion between the advocacy of values (sentimental appeals) and the way power works in the social construction of knowledge. The word *sentimental* often marks the point at which women's interests are denied by the more powerful (those who wield the epithets). Feminists sometimes write as if, by claiming to be "not sentimental," they will keep women's interests from seeming illegitimate. For example, in "Healing the Wounds," Ynestra King argues that ecofeminism can heal the nature-culture split. "The western male bourgeois subject," King writes, "disempowers and sentimentalizes his mother, sacrificing her to nature." That is, he says he cares about her, just as he says he cares about the old-growth forest—at the same time that he is getting out the chain saw in the name of culture and reason. King says that "the embodied woman as social historical agent, rather than product of natural law, is the subject of ecofeminism" (130). This is a socially constructed subject. King calls for an ecofeminist politics based on "reconciliation." She needs to recognize, however, how that reconciliation depends on our telling the male bourgeois subject that he should stop cutting down the trees, not that he is wrong to sentimentalize his mother *or* nature—it is precisely the sentimental appeals to an ecological reconciliation that work to advance ecofeminism. Describing the Indian "Chipko Andolan," or "hugging movement," King tells of women influenced by Gandhi who hugged trees to save them from loggers: "Yet this is not a sentimental movement; lives depend on the survival of the forest. For most women of the world, interest in the preservation of the land, water, air, and energy is no abstraction but a clear part of the effort to simply survive" (132, 133). She seems to equate sentimentality with abstraction, but isn't that abstraction just a mark of shared understanding? I think I know what she means—that these women, unlike others who might write passionately about the forests, are making the connection between their feelings and survival. But by this rather pragmatic criterion, all poetry may come to seem mere sentimentality; everything aesthetic could seem sentimental. If there were no survival value in trees, would those who appreciate them have no argument? But here, too, the word *sentimental* is being used to shortcut an argument that wants to hierarchize values according to some kind of logic. *Sentimental* puts that argument on the basis of us and them instead.

Because King's project is to rejoin rationality and feeling, the merely aesthetic or any disjoined feeling seems unacceptable to her. But let us remember how these distinctions repeat the moment of the Enlightenment subject. King writes:

> We thoughtful human beings must use the fullness of our sensibility and intelligence to push ourselves intentionally to another stage of evolution—one where we will fuse a new way of being human on this planet with a sense of the sacred, informed by all ways of knowing, intuitive *and* scientific, mystical *and* rational . . . a *rational* reenchantment. (134)

Thus while she agrees with my argument here—she argues for a return of sensibility in particular, as I do—she is also caught in the fabric of necessary categories that our language and our culture maintain.

Against her will (I imagine), she repeats the prejudice against sensibility in argument.

Current usage represses the history of the sentimental and treats the term as a form of invective. A review that calls a work "sentimental" is understood as a damaging judgment. The author's rationality is in question, and so is the credibility of the argument. If you are the victim of a "sentimental" epithet, you have been excluded from a magic circle. It is as if your readers are too tough for you, and you are too much of a sissy for them, as if you have let your own emotions run away with you and, furthermore, mistakenly counted on winning your reader by pathetic appeals rather than by a less indulgent, more ascetic rhetoric. You have, in sum, violated the post-Enlightenment standards of serious discourse, and you are in danger of becoming an outcast as far as the community of straight-thinking intellectuals is concerned. Frequently, if you are reviewed in, say, the *New York Times Book Review* and your book edges dangerously close to tenderness, the reviewer will reassure the reader, as Pat Barker did in a positive essay on Dan McCall's *Triphammer*, that the work has "no sentimentality." One answer to the question asked in the title of my essay is that, indeed, it is bad to be sentimental, unless you enjoy excommunication from the community of intellectuals. My position is that a strong barrier against acknowledging pathos, a barrier marked by these anxieties about sentimentality, works to keep academic argument from being powerful or effective in the public arena. However newly acceptable rhetoric may seem, it is still not at one with reason.

Excessive emotion suggests that a discourse is influenced by something else, perhaps personal experience, a desire to appeal to the personal experience of others, or the violence and desire of the body's fluctuating life. But why do we want to exclude these experiences from the academic conversation? From the critical point of view, the inhabitants of our everyday world seem mostly too ignorant to recognize their own sentimentality: you may be one of them, submerged in banality. Surely you could not be intellectually honest and be sentimental on purpose—even Roland Barthes became suspect in his later years for admiring his mother. Emotional appeals may sell automobiles or social reform, but (don't we believe?) they are propaganda devices, logical fallacies having nothing to do with truth, reality, or knowledge. It is the claim that we can connect emotionality and knowledge—in fact, the desire to persuade—that reveals the sentimental as rhetoric instead of transparent truth or reasoned argument.

Even though sentimentality is a despised rhetoric, there is always the supposition that another audience does not despise it nearly enough: those others who are overly emotional, or sensitive, or perhaps ignorant—who (unlike us?) buy greeting cards, write love letters, and watch television. But perhaps most of you, men and women alike, would admit that those sentimentalists are other sides of yourselves. From the perspective of critical academic discourse, those others (and other selves kept private) are marked as feminine, though they are not necessarily women. Indeed, the apparently ahistorical pejorative—sentimental!—has an uncanny connection with the history of writing by women.

The mode of address I have been using, invoking you as a presence in my discourse, is itself sometimes identified with the feminine and the sentimental. Is the familiar stricture against this rhetorical "you" an innocent one? The sympathetic evocation of a person—the personification—in these constructs has marked such poetic relations as Keats's apostrophe to the urn or the nightingale in his odes and HD's address to the sea, which signaled the advent of imagism: "Whirl up, sea—/ Whirl your pointed pines" ("Oread"). It also characterizes the relation of the female novelist to her "dear reader." These connective modes of address challenge the isolation of private purposes and throw a metaphorical bridge across the distance between discrete texts, speaker and other. Making a place for the familiar stranger, such invocations introduce a wobble into the structure of a rhetorical agreement that is based on an identification of subject and reader and on the threat of a decentering, a teasing out of thought.

The intersubjectivity figured forth by sentimentality reveals how the relation of self and other in discourse is metaphorical. The sympathetic personification gives a face to the audience we address, marking the juncture of rhetoric as figure and rhetoric as persuasion. But the poststructuralist turn to rhetoric shares the awkwardness that feminists encounter with sentimentality. Rhetoric has occupied a complex series of positions during the long history of reason's antagonism to emotion. The period since the Renaissance has been marked by the rise not only of Ramist logic and the positivism of science but also of the middle class and its gendered distinctions between public reason and the rhetoricity of private, feminine sensibility.

A decline in the authority and range of rhetoric as a resource for argument, which, since Ramus, has accompanied the notorious exclusion of invention from rhetoric, may be connected to the gendering of emotional and personal life by domestic discourse. Roland Barthes, in his early history "The Old Rhetoric," reveals not only his distrust of rhetoric's normalizing force but also his fascination with the genealogy of its figurativity and invention. Is not rhetoric itself sentimental, with its codes and conventions certainly, but also with its location of meaning in the situation, in the connectedness between an ethos represented by the subject and the pathos of the audience, arising in dialectical response?

Since Plato's critique of the Sophists, rhetoric has periodically been blamed for separating persuasion from a foundation of truth. Rhetoric has also suffered from the hugely elaborated economy of modern reason, with its quest to substitute technology for rhetoric, to purify itself of the contingent human body. As Stephen Toulmin writes of rhetoric's history, in *Cosmopolis: The Hidden Agenda of Modernity*, this unyielding desire for certainty and control has worked to separate science, logic, and even philosophy from the discourses of civil society and from the kinds of knowledge represented by Renaissance humanism, to which he recommends a return. Alas, though Toulmin advocates a return to the practical, the oral, the particular, the local, and the timely, he does not acknowledge how all these have been stored away in domestic discourse (as sentimental) while modernity has pursued its agenda or how his restoration might depend on the work of feminism to reclaim the status of the gendered other. These uses of the past require that we confront the political unconscious of modern reason in its normalizing operations.

Feminism can provide a model for rhetoric that addresses its doubly flawed relation to the history of modern reason. If rhetoric has been suspect because persuasion seems separable from truth, it has also been allied with strategies of domination, with hierarchies of male-female, master-slave. Susan Jarratt has argued, in "The Role of the Sophists," that feminine writing has much in common with the sophistic tradition and that it offers us a way to escape the metaphysics of truth inherited from Plato. Dale Bauer describes how a feminist pedagogy, because of (not in spite of) its necessary contentiousness, introduces the dialogic into classroom hierarchies of knowledge and ignorance. As feminism unsettles certainties, it also speaks from a position of commitment.

Social-constructivist arguments, however, have not made good use of feminism's ability to help characterize rhetorical knowledge. The governing narrative of antisentimentality is the illusory trajectory away from middle-class emotion and middle-class subjectivity. In *Rhetoric and Reality*, James Berlin portrays the development of writing instruction in this century as a conflict of epistemologies: objective or positivitistic theories, subjective or expressionistic theories, and transactional or rhetorical theories. Berlin seems to give us a way out: after all, as he points out, "The truths of rhetoric . . . are by their very nature uncertain, open to debate, contingent, probable. They deal not just with the empirical or rational analysis of experience, but with the emotional, aesthetic, and ethical—in other words, with the total range of human behavior" (15). A powerful critical consensus has developed around the antifoundationalist idea that knowledge is socially con-structed and therefore rhetorical. While social construction includes emotion and ethics in rhetoric, however, it has difficulty accounting for gendered subjectivity. Berlin outlines a critique of "expressivist" rhetoric: appeals to personal or emotional experience imply a notion of subjectivity that is humanistic and idealistic (and elitist) rather than rhetorical. But this connection between emotional appeals and the humanist subject only occurs because emotion itself has been rele-gated, by post-Enlightenment social and ideological configurations, to the domestic space of women, the opposite of male rationality. As Nancy Armstrong has argued in *Desire and Domestic Fiction*, the figure of the domestic woman has served as part of the construction of mid-dle-class individuals.

Academic writing in American institutions of higher education has been developed within the ambitions of the middle class, which higher education has both defined and supported. Academic reason, eschew-ing emotional appeal, evokes the gendered ideology of that middle class as firmly as popular sentimentality might. In Berlin's social-con-structivist approach, discrimination about sensibility or emotions rests on appeals to hierarchies that are intertwined with discriminations of class. Attacks on the sentimental can apparently be translated simply as attacks on the middle class and thus on an ideology that ought to be questioned. From such a point of view, sentimentality is bad because it is a symptom of class ideology. Students who turn to personal experi-ence as the basis of their arguments ought to be awakened to their unconscious politics.

In the rush to a rhetorical pluralism that embraces social construc-tion and the dialogic, however, there is an unconscious appeal to a logic that ought to make us—feminists and rhetoricians alike—pause. Gregory Clark has written, in *Dialogue, Dialectic, and Conversation*, a brief version of the case for the social perspective. He takes us from Kenneth Burke, Mikhail Bakhtin, and Kenneth Bruffee through John Gage to Patricia Bizzell, arguing for a democratic view of how meaning is negotiated. It is not easy to disagree. But somehow (like Toulmin) Clark fails to include feminists in the conversation. And that omission at the least should make us wary. Even though, citing Greg Myers, he seems to acknowledge that ideology functions as a kind of social

unconscious, what he really imagines is a pluralism of conscious individuals: "The problem is that the rhetorical statements we use to construct our communities are inevitably propelled by private purposes
that demand . . . consensus by attempting to establish publicly the
correctness of our beliefs in order to deny the validity of beliefs that
differ" (56). But surely—from a social-constructionist point of view—
"private purposes" cannot be the problem. Ideology works not as the
private agendas of individuals but as a kind of unconscious within the
very forms of communication, and to ignore the unconsciousness of
that operation is to leave us at its mercy. Thus feminists need to keep
looking at the way gendering marks the unconscious separation of right
reason from excess and defeats the hopes for relatedness suggested by
the dialogic, the dialectic, and conversation.

Academic argument—especially the debate invoking critical theory
and advocating a social perspective—is itself still distorted by its censorship of emotion and subjectivity. This fear of the sentimental, I
suggest, is itself a form of sentimentality, a mark of how academic
discourse at its most critical is still grounded in a kind of foundationalism—a nostalgia for objectivity. Even though poststructuralist theory
has made the case for a positioned, rhetorical understanding of knowledge, arguments are carried out as if the full triangulation of the rhetorical situation could be ignored—as if only the formal logic, or logos,
mattered, as if logos functioned in opposition to the audience-speaker
relations figured in ethos and pathos, as if recourse to sympathy and
to shared commitment were an irrational move rather than an aspect
of ethical reasoning. The intellectual conversation, however, is not
simply a multiplicity of positions but a process open to the irrational,
and it is perhaps most dangerously open not to emotional irrationality
but to the political unconscious inscribed in the discourse. The historical gendering of the logic-rhetoric opposition has much to do with the
peculiar unloveliness of academic discourse as well as its recurrent
setting of reason against emotion. The effects of this gendering continue to prevent academic argument from understanding the consequences of rhetorical situatedness. An important marker of this
unconscious disability is the recurring critical use of the epithet *sentimental* as a shorthand for critique. The distancing of academic discourse from rhetoric will remain a problem, rather than a sign of
rationality, so long as being sentimental remains bad.

This limit to the warrants that critical discourse seems willing to
grant rhetorical inquiry is troubling because the normalization of academic and intellectual discourses works against all of us as intellectuals
writing seriously. Though feminism may be most familiar with the

double bind, I do not mean to restrict the problem to women. What is at stake, I argue, is no less than the effective power of our lives as academic theorists, critics, and rhetoricians. The critical stricture against the sentimental points to an ascetic discipline that cuts us off from what others plaintively invoke as the real world, from sensibility, from community, as well as from using or acknowledging the functions of voice and personal experience. Most painfully, it cuts us off from effective pedagogy and from seeing what interests those in higher education might share with public school teachers. Even though contemporary critical theory longs to position itself and to insist on a tough resistance to liberal ideology, the dismissal of sentimentality denies its own rhetorical situation within a discourse of invective and scapegoating that belongs to the liberal history of gender. Therefore contemporary critical theory also eliminates any possibility of a critical interrogation of these very categories, which are always already dismissed, or of the place of academic discourse within the ideologies of humanism, which are strongly dependent on the gendered differentiations evoked by sentimentality.

Intellectuals are offended by the coerciveness of sentimentality: our culture seems to demand that arguments be sentimental if they are to be heard. Refusing to be sentimental seems like an intellectual critical freedom. In fact, however, refusing to be sentimental is falling prey to the illusion of an independent rationality. Is objectivity really a resistance to middle-class culture and its ideology—or is that objectivity a confirmation? By scorning the appeals to emotion that appear in civic debate as well as in advertising, academic intellectuals reinforce the separation of the academy not from the influence of the banal but from power. By eschewing sentimental appeals, we are indulging ourselves in an illusion of academic freedom, autonomy, and authority that has visible countereffects. While politicians wave the flag, higher education loses its status and authority.

In the classroom, university professors may scorn the "touchy-feely" sensitivity of elementary teachers or the hysteria of feminists, but they may also be out of step with the very relationships that make learning effective. Janet Emig wants the profession to address teaching and learning theories: "In most departments of English, there is a terrifying naïveté, a proud and boastful absence of any such theory. In my own department, for example, theories of learning and of teaching are regularly dismissed as matters of 'mere affect' " (88). Much psychological learning theory is based on a positivistic notion of reason rather than on a rhetorical epistemology like psychoanalysis, but the dismissal of pedagogy is not likely to be on those grounds. Perhaps the multiple decentering of the teacher's presence represents our attempt to sidestep the impossible contradiction: the professor bases his (yes, maybe still sic) authority on the command of reason and the denial of emotion, while the class—that multiplicity of discourses—experiences this stance as disembodied and abstract. The professorial ethos is authoritative in an empowering way—that is, as a stance students might identify with—only to the extent that they can (and wish to) take up a position defined not only as "objective" but also as white, middle-class, and male.

The professor does not need to become hysterical to remedy this situation; rather, "he" might, like "women," practice the wise and perverse hysteria that Julia Kristeva recommends. Most professors would need to add no more than a small admission of their other selves into the classroom to deconstruct the absolute (or tragic) irony that threatens us. A resonance in the voice while reading Shakespeare—or Kathy Acker—has often been enough. Marking the precariousness of reason, bliss introduces undecidability into reasoned discourse. Marking the emotional context of reason, pleasure introduces not only the sentimental but also social construction into reasoned discourse. Kristeva says, "It is the critic's task, and there is hardly a more comical one, to coagulate an island of meaning upon a sea of negativity" ("How Does One" 109). Irony then appears in its comic guise. These relationships allow the reproduction of subjects within discourses, the taking up and performing of an ethos that is neither natural nor insincere.

Academic discourses have tended to reproduce a certain reasoning subject rooted in the gendered, middle-class formations that have constructed the institutions of American higher education during the past century. But professors who adopt committed positions—as feminists, as advocates of the oppressed—risk a recuperation, by the gendering of mass culture, in which these positioned stances soon appear (the moment they have lost their novelty and begin to work effectively to organize coalitions, as with feminism and also all the "politically correct") as themselves sentimental. As the feminist philosopher Alison Jaggar says, "The 'myth of the dispassionate investigator' functions . . . to bolster the epistemic authority of the currently dominant groups, composed largely of white men, and to discredit the observations and claims of the currently subordinate groups including, of course, the observations and claims of many people of color and women" (158).

We are not, we hope, the despised and inadequate subject of sentimentality, even if we are women. But if we join with the post-Ramist and Enlightenment project to define the critical and the progressive against banal and regressive sentimentality, we are repeating the gesture that would aspire to replace the messy tangle of ideology and convention with a scientific distance, the gesture that would despise rhetorical knowledge as well.

University of Oregon

NOTE

[1] As Crosswhite has argued, following Heidegger's notion of *mood*, "It is an essential virtue (and compromise) of rhetoric to conceive of argumentation as essentially connected to an audience, specifically one in a particular mood. And it is one of the chief aims of rhetoric to instill in its practitioners the ability to create the necessary mood in which work can go on—in rhetoric proper, the work of persuasive argumentation" (36). Crosswhite wishes to reinstate an essentialism not of the subject or of mood but of relation, of the rhetorical situation.

The Doubleness of Writing and Permission to Lie

Susan Wells

> *In order to attack writing and sophistry, Plato becomes a writer
> and a sophist. This is disingenuous.*
> —Jasper Neel, *Plato, Derrida, and Writing*

Disingenuous: The word comes from *ingenuous*, which is derived from
the Roman term for someone born within the territories, a free man
marked by a noble and open demeanor. Another derivative of this term
is *ingenuity* (*ingenious* has a distinct parentage), which meant, until
the seventeenth century, aristocratic bearing. A cognate, *ingenio*, surfaces in the backwaters of the history of rhetoric. The Spanish baroque
rhetorician Baltasar Gracián writes, *"Todo gran ingenio es ambidextro"*
(170), declaring that every great power of invention is double (see
Grady). Jasper Neel's critique of Plato, then, is staged on a ground
littered with contradictory terms, doubled words.

I begin at this place of doubling, borrowing some of Gracián's *gran
ingenio* and investigating our discomfort when, as writing teachers, we
confront something double. We come upon the double both in our
students' writing and in classroom practices; we also find it in the texts
that are reshaping literary theory, particularly the work of Jacques
Derrida. I use Jasper Neel's book *Plato, Derrida, and Writing* as a representation of that discomfort, which can be found in our teaching practice and, on a given day, in the work of any composition scholar.

Debate on this doubling of rhetoric and writing has been organized
in an archaic form, as a discussion of the *Phaedrus*, an early Platonic
dialogue in which Socrates disputes the efficacy of both writing and
rhetoric. Derrida takes the *Phaedrus* as the central text for analysis in
his chapter "Plato's Pharmacy" in *Dissemination*; Neel devotes *Plato,
Derrida, and Writing* to successive analyses of Plato and Derrida, culmi-
nating in a defense of process theories of writing as they are understood

within composition theory. I move from Neel to Derrida, returning often to the *Phaedrus*; my search is for a conception of the doubleness of student writing that supports our understanding of the complexity of students' work; that search eventually takes me to Mikhail Bakhtin.

Neel's book, like many of the other important texts in composition theory, is self-consciously programmatic: its project is to establish the study of writing as a serious discipline, by confronting the Platonic distrust of writing, and to show that writing instructors who focus on process instruction are already deconstructionists. This project is remarkable, especially as a description of an emergent discipline: writing, for Neel, must be "saved from philosophy" before it can "receive attention as a legitimate field of study" (xi). What does Neel mean here? Is philosophy staking serious disciplinary claims to the study of student writing? Certainly, disciplines have been formed through attacks on current methods of study. But when Marx undertook a critique of political economy, he began with the most advanced economic theorists of his time, not with Hesiod's *Works and Days*; Freud elaborated a theory of the unconscious in controversy with Josef Breuer, not with Aristotle on the emotions. Ours is not a society in which Plato's critique of writing has had much purchase; the *Phaedrus* is a canonized text, and Derrida has worked through many of the implications of the logocentrism it instantiates, but the practices and social supports for writing continue to operate, hegemonically, on quite a different social level. And Neel is no novice: he has seen people hired and paid and tenured to give serious attention to writing; no one has to argue with Plato to establish a discipline that is already institutionally entrenched.

Neel's language in his introduction to *Plato, Derrida, and Writing* suggests a different kind of project. Writing has been "stolen" (6), a theft that can be redeemed only by silencing the voice of Plato. Only such a rescued and vindicated writing can (should) be worthy of serious study. Writing begins to exfoliate itself as double: writing, the action that produces the text we read, does not yet exist, because its power has been taken up and engrossed by the disingenuous Plato, who, doubling himself ingeniously behind the figure of Socrates, steals from all future voices their potential power. Writing has been violated and must be restored.

The locus of the restoration is to be the writing subject, a subject whose ambidexterity, particularly in its relation to time, scandalizes Neel. The rhetoric of *Plato, Derrida, and Writing* is firmly located in temporality: it addresses questions that have been postponed "too long" or that "it's time" to open (x, xi). But Neel faces in Plato an antagonist who did not make good on his temporal debts. The speaker of the

Phaedrus locates himself freely in time: Plato, writing in 367 BC, imagines the Socrates of 410 BC hoping that Isocrates will turn to philosophy. This doubled location troubles Neel, since it requires Plato to use the very powers of writing that he has spent the dialogue criticizing: "The only way he can speak in his own absence, speak in someone else's voice, and speak out of his own time is in writing" (*Plato* 23). And it is this doubled and contradictory position that Neel finds disingenuous.

So it is: disingenuous, not the frank rejoinder of the free man but a sneak attack, a discourse from outside the gates. And therefore possibly useful to us, and to our students, who are also, from time to time, defined by exclusion. Let us consider in this light a student text, a selection from an untitled essay that I refer to as "Autobiography":

> My alarm clock went off at 6:00 am. It was light out already. I didn't sleep very well the night before. As I walked down to the kitchen to get a cup of coffee, my eyes barely open and still coated from Mr. sandman, I ran into my father leaving for work. He kissed me on the cheek and wished me luck at my first day of high school then fled out the door.
>
> I pressed my shirt and uniform skirt the night before which made getting ready easer. I was ready before my sister as usual. She was always late for everything. Beth had been attending Bishop O'Hara for two years. This was an old scene for her so she couldn't care less if she was on time or not. However it mattered to me. I wanted to be right on time. I kept screaming to her from the bottom of our steps to hurry up.
>
> My mother flew down our dirt road all the while screaming at my sister for being late. I sat silently in the front seat with my tablet gripped tightly in my hand. I was so nervous I didn't even turn on the radio. I just gazed out the window at sights I've seen a thousand time. Looking at them as though I had never seen them before.
>
> We arrived at the school at 8:02 only two minutes late thanks to my moms driving and the absence of traffic. Their was a few other people getting dropped off also. She waited till the others pulled away and moved up to the back door. She gave us both kisses and shoved us out of the car. Or at least that's what it felt like.[1]

The student who describes her first day of high school with such breathtaking vulnerability can never be called disingenuous. But we might ask what distinguishes her story from that other account of a young person hurrying toward instruction, the one that begins with Socrates's "My dear Phaedrus, whence came you, and whither are you going?" (263).

Both narratives are marked by a doubling of the speaking subject. But, obviously, the *Phaedrus* organizes this doubling through the conventions of the third person narrative, while "Autobiography" splits the narrator into a present speaker and a past object of representation. Both narratives work to control and manipulate the passage of time—the *Phaedrus* by doubling its temporal location, the student essay by slowing the tempo of described events. Both texts exploit self-contradictions. The *Phaedrus* is, as Neel points out, a piece of writing against writing; it dramatizes contradiction in Socrates's interpolated speeches. The student writer's controlled and dispassionate narration contradicts her past tension and insecurity. Both narratives, finally, are impelled and organized by desire: Socrates's desire for Phaedrus and his more peremptory desire for philosophical discourse; Plato's desire for a society that would have turned Isocrates from rhetoric to philosophy; the student's desire that her passage into adolescence would have been marked and savored, the desire to have been "right on time."

Neither text, then, is marked by any singleness or purity of subjectivity, intention, or temporal location. The *Phaedrus* is distinguished from the student essay, in this regard, only by its conscious objectification of the speaking subject, its dramatization of contradictory discursive relations, and its overt performance of the manipulation of time. The *Phaedrus*, in a word, is self-conscious, a text that understands itself to be double and that insists on duplicity while replicating and complicating it. The student essay sutures the doubled protagonist, the rectified time, and the attentive narrator into a reparative account; "Autobiography" needs no redemption because the text is itself a restoration, a repair of the past effected without the inconvenient aid of philosophy. It would seem, then, that what prompts Neel's objection is not the doubleness of Plato's text—the most naive texts share this doubleness—but the text's knowledge of its doubleness, a knowledge Neel assigns to Plato and repeatedly laments in the catchphrase "I wish I didn't think that Plato knew that" (*Plato* 38, 44, 50, 55).

Self-consciousness, for Neel, prompts bad pedagogy and the end of thought: students who reflect on the self-division that writing inevitably performs on them are necessarily paralyzed or destroyed, like the Catholic girl Neel describes, who cannot examine her position on abortion, or the fundamentalist boy buffaloed by a first reading of the Book of

Job (*Plato* 92–96). For Neel, to allow the double consciousness of the *Phaedrus* to enter the writing class is to administer a drug so toxic that students will either withdraw from writing altogether or forget how to achieve even temporary and provisional closure.

Surely we have heard these charges before. Philosophy corrupts the young, casts so much doubt on received ideas that its practitioners cannot perform their duties as citizens, tempts us to impiety, and leads us outside the walls, into the territory of the disingenuous. Perhaps it even makes the worse case appear to be the better one. If our enterprise, the study of writing, is to prosper, if we are not to be ensnared by the deceptive teleologies of truth that lead us ineluctably from the writing classroom to the study of literary texts, then philosophy, in the person of the author of the *Phaedrus*, must be silenced. It is the argument of the scapegoat, the argument deconstructed in the *Phaedrus*. And it is not Neel's argument alone: composition studies has repeatedly defined itself by excluding some dangerous kind of knowledge, some destructive kind of writing. What is excluded shifts, but the position of exclusion remains. The 1966 Dartmouth Conference, on the teaching of English, urged the exclusion of literary analysis; early basic writing teachers avoided the long essay and focused on smaller units of writing; contemporary basic writing teachers forgo small units in isolation in order to focus on whole texts. Writing teachers can find, in the current literature, injunctions against self-expressive writing, personal narratives, and assignments like those that students have done in other classes. All these excluded elements stand for something else that we would like to exclude from the study of writing—its doubleness, which is demonstrated most forcibly in the *gran ingenio* of philosophy.

I turn now to an alternative way of reading the doubleness of writing, moving from the *Phaedrus* to Derrida and back again, with a long detour through Bakhtin. Let me begin with the *Phaedrus*'s own cautionary tale about doubleness, the allegory of the chariot drawn by two horses, the well-behaved and honorable white horse and the ill-conditioned and insolent dark horse. Although there is a long Christian tradition of reading the allegory as a representation of the immortal soul linked to the corrupt body, we might productively read the text in a different way. All three elements—the two horses and the charioteer—are parts of the soul. And the soul, in Plato's story, needs the dark horse as much as it does the white. Face-to-face with the beloved, the white horse draws back in shame; it is the dark horse that forces the soul "to approach the beloved and to remember the joys of love" (296). The dark horse is the agent of memory, repeatedly drawing the soul toward the beloved, peremptorily demanding union with the beloved. Socrates tells us that the charioteer tames and humbles the dark horse, but his story shows us that the dark horse also subdues its partners and persuades them to at least come close to the beloved instead of simply falling back in awe. And as Socrates concludes the allegory, it is the dark horse that has the last word:

> When they [lover and beloved] meet, the wanton steed of the lover has a word to say to the charioteer; he would like to have a little pleasure for his pains, but the wanton steed of the beloved says not a word, for he is bursting with passion which he understands not.   (298)

If we read the allegory in terms of our concerns here, the doubleness of writing expresses the written text's location in time, the duplication of the writing subject, the contingency of the text's propositional content. This doubleness shadows everything candid, open, and noble in the text—it is disingenuous—and so it threatens to bring the text to grief. But without this doubleness, and without the dynamic of desire and memory in which it entangles the text, writing remains inert, disabled by the shame of its becoming (or, as we call it, "the process"). The work of writing—and of teaching writing—is an elaborate performance of pretending to tame the dark steed, all the while making sure that it has the last word.

If we expand our reading to the concerns of the discipline, we could see the chariot as a figure of the relations between writing theory and literary theory, the two often housed together uncomfortably in English departments. Each discipline reproaches the other: composition, as in Neel's book, reproaches literary criticism for its divorce from the actual, from the work of students; literary theory denounces writing instruction, or rhetoric, for its brutal self-interest, its complicity with the social. It is a quarrel between the ingenious and the disingenuous, each side finding in the other its dark horse, each battling for the right to name the beloved—the fullness of language? the fullness of the real?—each side falling back in terror as soon as it approaches its own object of desire, and each rudely reminding the other of what it has forgotten.

The repertoire of academic liberalism contains an established trope for handling this kind of division: value both sides, for different reasons, and enjoin them to be mutually respectful and cooperative. Thus, empiricists and theorists, new historicists and deconstructionists, cognitivists and social constructionists are counseled to avoid reductive dichotomies and to get along. This is exactly the path I do not want to take: the energy and force of this oddly harnessed pair is derived from contestation and from the persistent bad manners of the dark horse.

What happens, then, if we assume that literary theory and rhetoric are contestatory, if we use that contest to reflect on the doubleness of writing? Nothing good: rhetoric itself divides into hostile parts, and the doubling of writing threatens to become uncontrolled. We can find a representation of just this problem in the *Phaedrus*, where writing and rhetoric slide into and out of each other:

> SOCRATES. Do you know how you can speak or act about rhetoric in a manner which will be acceptable to God?
> PHAEDRUS. No, indeed. Do you?
> SOCRATES. I have heard a tradition of the ancients, whether true or not they only know; although if we had found the truth ourselves, do you think that we should care much about the opinions of men?
> PHAEDRUS. Your question needs no answer; but I wish that you would tell me what you say that you have heard.
> SOCRATES. At the Egyptian city of Naucratis, there is a famous old god, whose name is Theuth.   (322)

And Socrates goes on to tell the story of the origin of writing. After a series of earlier interchanges that distinguished writing as a mere technique from the disciplinary practice of rhetoric, the dialogue now collapses rhetoric into writing; if rhetoric deals with the contingent, the probable, the less than certain, then writing provides a false defense against that uncertainty, a false stability and clarity. Derrida, reflecting on these oppositions in "Plato's Pharmacy," allows rhetoric to remain buried in the house of writing; his arts of memory do not distinguish this corpse from those of the other guests at Socrates's feast of discourse. Rhetoric, however, had already arrived in the dialogue through Lysias's text and Socrates's imitation of it, the two interpolated speeches on why the nonlover should be preferred to the lover. In those speeches, we can discern the ways in which rhetoric is already a kind of writing.

The speeches resemble the sophistic school exercise called the *progymnasmaton*, in which students made speeches on fanciful topics (Kennedy 103). The fanciful topic in this exercise—that the nonlover is to be preferred to the lover—conveniently demonstrates the central Platonic case against rhetoric, that it makes the worse case appear to be the better one. Socrates's amorous, deceptive speech—doubly deceptive, since he says that he is only pretending to be a nonlover to conceal his passion for the young man—is in fact already a kind of writing. The hidden speaker takes up multiple positions in relation to the discourse. The addressed is ostensibly a generic and undifferentiated "young man" but also the material listener, Phaedrus. The speech is therefore displaced, operating at the intersection of the public and private, the space of writing. In silence, Derrida passes over this radical swerve from rhetoric to writing, this placement of writing within the intersubjective project of persuasion. He accepts the substituted topic of writing for the provocation that introduced it into the dialogue: a rhetorical performance; a play with opposites, presented as a seduction; an erotic speech that already includes the elements of writing within its structures. Rhetoric becomes writing, but a kind of writing that is already rhetorical, just as the rhetoric from which it was generated was already writing.

The conceptual structure of the *Phaedrus*—and, for that matter, of *Dissemination*—figures the doubleness of writing as a substitution of rhetoric for writing, positioning over the displaced performance and the doubled subjectivity that characterize writing the public performance of rhetorical production and the private formation of rhetorical training. Neel advocates exactly this substitution by urging a new sophistry that would make available to all kinds of students an efficacious training in the arts of influence, of constructing arguments, of making truth and recognizing truth as something made. Neel's manageable rhetoric, the rhetoric of deliberation and consultation rather than of contests and verdicts, is removed from the unseemly materiality of work with error, with intractable untruths, and of work with the weak, the playful, the merely literary. And best of all, we are already there: "The direction composition studies has taken over the last twenty years has, in my opinion, been clearly sophistical" (*Plato* 210). Writing has been stabilized as rhetoric, and both terms have been rendered unitary and placed on the narrative path of indefinite amelioration. Writing may need rescue, but rhetoric is doing just fine.

Let us move back to the *Phaedrus* and uncouple, as best we can, the themes of rhetoric and writing. The *Phaedrus* criticizes rhetoric because of its effects on an audience: the rhetorically skilled speaker can mislead listeners about the good and the just, can persuade them against reason. Rhetoric is a danger to the public, to the forums of deliberation and the courts of judgment where it is most efficacious. Writing, however, is a danger to the writer, whose thoughts become abandoned children, shallow and showy growths, sterile seeds fit only for amusement. A person who writes seriously, "patching and piecing, adding some and taking away some," is reduced by that servile labor:

the writer is "a poet [= maker], or speech maker or law maker" rather than a lover of wisdom (328). Rhetoric, then, locates the doubleness of discourse in relation to a public sphere, with its history and contingency; writing locates that doubleness in relation to the subject, including the subject's location in time. The dialogue has shown that writing necessarily doubles the subject; rhetoric suggests a contagion of this doubling, the nightmare of a mobile public opinion, of the inconstant mob. For the sophistic rhetors, control of that mobility was central: it is not surprising that they were distrustful of writing. As Derrida points out, for both Plato and the Sophists "writing is considered suspicious and the alert exercise of memory prescribed" ("Plato's Pharmacy" 108); Plato differs from the Sophists in preferring a living memory to their supplemental mnemonic techniques. We find in Neel a position similar to the Sophists', a similar desire for a rhetoric cleansed of writing; in Derrida we can read a contemporary accounting of the costs of a doubled memory, a doubled rhetoric, and a doubled writing.

We find ourselves, then, with a clear sense of our problem. As soon as we attempt to think through the relation between writing theory and literary theory, we are implicated by the doubleness of writing in a series of divisions, especially divisions of the writing subject. We are faced with a choice: ignoring or erasing this doubleness (Neel's solution) or uncompromisingly following the path of our fragmenting concepts (Derrida's performance). I suggest that this problem can be outflanked, from two directions: first, by working out a model of rhetorical performance from the *Phaedrus* that will contain these doublings; and second, by looking at the work of Bakhtin, which provides a model for nonreductive understanding of the double voice.

Let me begin with the *Phaedrus*, which is rich in models of the writing subject. One of those models is Socrates's doubled performance of the doubled speaker. First, we see the speaker veiled:

> I will veil my face and gallop through the discourse as fast as I can, for if I see you I shall feel ashamed and not know what to say. (274)

In a second instance, Socrates doubles himself by recanting:

> Know then, fair youth, that the former discourse was the word of Phaedrus, the son of Vain Man, who dwells in the city of Myrrhina. And this which I am about to utter is the recantation of Stesichorus the son of Holy Man (Euphemus) who comes from the town of Desire (Himera). (283)

Rhetorical speech can be uttered from behind a veil, demonstrating the rhetorician's shame in the effacement of his or her presence but still permitting the discourse to unfold itself: the doubling of the speaking subject is exploited to heighten and permit rhetorical performances that might otherwise be problematic. This is essentially the situation of Derrida's absent ghostwriter in "Plato's Pharmacy":

> In writing what he does not speak, what he would never say and, in truth, would probably never even think, the author of the written speech is already entrenched in the posture of the sophist: the man of non-presence and of non-truth.   (68)

Or the rhetorician can recant, presenting each performance as an abolition of all prior speeches, as a purgative. Responsibility for the performance is assigned to the audience; to Phaedrus, the substitute for the beloved youth; or to Stesichorus, a reversed Homer who averts permanent blindness by recanting quickly. In this second image of a consciously doubled rhetorical performance, what is exploited is the public stationing of rhetoric, its location in a discursive community, however dispersed and fictional, and the contingency of all propositions uttered in a rhetorical context. More explicitly, in these quotations, we can see Socrates translating the doubleness of writing into a doubled rhetorical performance. There is no attempt to unify the subject, or even to pretend that the performance is coherent, or to suggest that the speaker would not say something else on a different occasion. Rather, the philosopher becomes a rhetor speaking something that comes to him from the neighborhood of desire. This rhetorical position permits a radical freedom of invention: Socrates's recantation turns out to be the supremely ambiguous parable of the chariot of the soul and its divided powers, a speech that records with painful truth, if not with sincerity, the position of the ghostwriter, of the speaker who recognizes that a division of the self is not a fault or a temporary aberration but a necessary consequence of conscious rhetorical performance.

We might consider what such a performance means for the work of the classroom, taking into account Neel's critique of a Platonic theory of writing as so disruptive that students either withdraw or face the collapse of their discourse, and his rejection of the corrosive instability of Derrida's response to Plato. Socrates's performance suggests that these problems are inherent in the rhetorical performance of the philosopher: Socrates, in both cases, speaks fearfully of imagined shame and imagined danger. In both cases, Socrates supports his performance with a fiction, a prop that enacts the contingent and provisional nature of what he has to say. By saying that the speaker is not himself, Socrates contains the necessary doubling of the speaker in writing and establishes a fictional position of stability: Socrates is not the voice that speaks but the consciousness that arranges for the performance.

In the classroom, such a repositioning of the self, such a support for the writing subject, amounts to a permission to lie. Such a permission is one of the most valuable gifts that a teacher can give to students: it allows students to write from the standpoint of fiction rather than from the standpoint of fear. This permission can take many forms: its most benign is simple role playing, the requirement to speak *as if* one were a lab technician, a researcher, a character in a story. Here, the doubling of the writing subject is contained by being dramatized: the teacher, by establishing the important social parameters for the writing subject, supports the students in their orchestration of a rhetorical performance. More complex permissions to lie might include exaggerated, counterfactual, and consciously deceptive assignments, such as those in Robert Scholes and Nancy Comley's *The Practice of Writing*. On the level of classroom tactics, permission to lie implies considerable classroom practice in making things up: Will anyone believe these statistics? What evidence might support this claim? What would be plausible here? Under what circumstances might a reader change his or her mind about this topic? And, of course, such discussions quickly turn to questions of evidence, documentation, and verifiable support, since only writers who can imagine lies are able to consciously and carefully tell the truth.

We can derive, then, a model of rhetorical production from Plato that contains, and makes use of, the doubleness of writing as it emerges in the splitting of the writing subject. We might see this model as broadly responsive to the views Derrida expresses on composition and the politics of composition programs: he recommends transmission and deconstruction of canonical texts; attention, however temporary, to the materials of language production; and an organization of composition programs that is both centered in English departments and dispersed throughout institutions (Olson). Because Neel distrusts such doubling, it is not surprising that he finds Derrida's position both elitist and utopian ("Where Have You").

An examination of the speaking subject in Plato, then, has moved us into political and social concerns: we may contain the movement of writing from the subject to the public position of rhetoric, but we cannot freeze that movement, nor should we want to. At this point, we should call into question the distinction between the writing subject

and the text. Invoking Gracián's *gran ingenio* once again, we move to
the doubleness of Bakhtin's notion of the multivoiced text to help us
understand that the dialogic activity of writing is not a matter of external "historical context"; rather, it is realized in the texture of what has
been written. Here, as in my examination of the *Phaedrus*, I extract a
rhetorical theory from an antirhetorical text: Bakhtin's "Discourse in
the Novel."[2] In this essay, Bakhtin investigates novelistic double-
voicedness, which he defines by contrast to lyric monologism and rhetorical double-voicedness. Rhetoric, then, enters Bakhtin's essay as an
ancillary concept; it is a way of foregrounding a privileged and valued
form of heteroglossia.

Bakhtin distinguishes rhetorical double-voicedness from novelistic
double-voicedness on two grounds: rhetorical double-voicedness is not
conscious of itself, and it is not rooted in history. The first of these
claims requires some investigation, but the second is wrong. Being
"rooted in socio-historical speech diversity" is not a singular quality of
novels (325). Unless we are to reduce historical situation to a mystified
organicism, we must recognize that many prose texts can have this
quality (see Kittay and Godzich). Anyone who has taught a basic writing class has a lively understanding of the ubiquity of sociohistorical
speech diversity.

Bakhtin goes on to say that double-voiced rhetorical genres are "not
fertilized by a deep-rooted connection with the forces of historical
becoming." Finally, and most tellingly, he dismisses the double-voiced
rhetorical text as "merely a game, a tempest in a teapot" (325). Bakhtin
has strikingly reproduced the metaphorics of both the *Phaedrus* and
Derrida's essay on the *pharmakon*. We are to distinguish a vital, genera-
tive, and well-rooted growth from something shallow, showy, and
ephemeral. The good seed is linked to production and living dialogue;
the bad, to play and echo.

We need not agree with Bakhtin's critique of rhetoric to see there the
outlines of an alternative theory of rhetorical production; this theory
is deeply valuable. Rhetoric presents the possibility of a problematic
relation to time, one that foregrounds what is contingent, rather than
historically inevitable, in writing. And from the place of this contingency, rhetorical production refuses to attain seriousness, remains
merely a game. Rhetoric circumscribes gains and losses firmly within
the boundaries of a game and continues to purify the unholy seriousness of war. Within those boundaries, doubleness of voice appears
as something provisional and temporary, rather than as the truth of
the speaker or of the genre. The rhetorical double-voiced text does not
locate itself on the sublime terrain of historical inevitability; it speaks

not for the forces of historical becoming but only for something that has indeed happened to come about, on the quotidian ground of events, of the actual. Bakhtin's essay suggests that writing instruction should not seek to end but, rather, become conscious of the colonization of student writing by multiple discourses—the discourses of the academy, popular culture, and common sense. The multivoiced text permits the writer's location in time to be deployed and activated within the text, to become an element in a persuasive project or in the work of exposition. Historicity is represented in the multivoiced rhetorical text on the level of verb forms, pronoun references, vanishing apostrophes—all the undignified materiality of language. If this materiality is seen as the stuff of writing instruction, rather than as an obstacle to some impossible elimination of the student's double or some impossible performance of a pure and directly representative voice, then writing instruction can orient itself toward an enrichment of the multivoiced text and of the student's control of the text's disparate elements.

For concrete student texts, such instruction might lead to simple exercises. We might ask the author of "Autobiography," for example, to identify the things in the essay that she did not know about when the events were taking place. How does the essay change if the author eliminates this other, more mature voice, or gives it more control, or allows it to speak more directly? While such changes do not necessarily produce better or worse essays, an awareness that students have many available voices and different ways of deploying them is simply another form of the permission to lie that we should give our students. More directly, our understanding of the multivoiced rhetorical text, or of the veiled rhetorical performance, helps us to understand a text like this excerpt from a student essay, written in response to the same assignment that prompted "Autobiography":

> The down side of my life is the same as that which destroys the American dream and way of life. I started to do drugs. I guess it was the influence of the people I hung out with. One day I tried a little pot, and soon I had to have some every day. If one day went by and I did not have it, I would get mad. Then I tried some cocaine. That is when it really started. Shortly I got addicted. Since I did not have a job, I had to steal from people in order to support my addiction. Thanks to the help of some true friends, I was able to find help. It's been three years since I have had any kind of mind-altering substances.
>
> Most of these events have occurred in my neighborhood. Defining my neighborhood is like trying to define Vietnam. There is a

war going on, a constant struggle. It is called the "Drug war". Not one day goes by without someone either dying or getting hurt, for two reasons, the money involved in selling, or the use of drugs. In these neighborhood drugs and drugs dealers rule. They are not scared of anyone, and everyone better be scared of them because they threaten and intimidate everyone. The innocent people affected by this problem are the children. Sometimes getting caught in between shootings or their parents are using money for drugs instead of food and milk. It is not for myself but for them that I now study. So that someday I will be able to help them survive in a war which takes no prisoners.

This remarkable text brings together a rich array of discourses; it also turns, recants, and veils itself in a series of subtle rhetorical moves. The student arrays the expert discourses of therapy ("support my addiction," "mind-altering substances"), history (Vietnam as a war zone), and sociology (effects of the drug war on children); he also deploys the governmental discourse of the "drug war," but with a difference: we are reading not about war on drug dealers but about the state of war that drugs have brought to the writer's neighborhood. These expert and official discourses coexist uneasily with various popular modes of speech: the story of addiction and cure, the initiation through pot and the intervention of "true friends," and the syntax of graffiti ("drugs dealers rule") and of street talk ("they are not scared of anyone, and everyone better be scared of them"). All these discourses perform the act to which the writer commits himself—the "study" that is done in order to help children, study of which the essay is an instance—so that the writer's commitment doubles the text and complicates its location to the future.

The text is also doubled in relation to the speaker. The discontinuity, between the object of the first paragraph's story of addiction and the speaker of the second paragraph's analysis of addiction, is contained, but not resolved, by the speaker's relocating his discursive position into the future and in relation to the children he will, sadly, not teach or save but only "help . . . survive." The text retracts itself and then retracts the retraction, posing an impossibly limited solution to the problem it has described, making clear that its gesture of closure is simply a gesture, a hand pulling the cloak before a face so that discourse can, in some way, continue.

This text, which has by no means been exhausted by my short analysis, represents a doubleness of the speaker and of language that is implicit in writing. This piece of writing does not need to be saved from Plato; rather, we need to save ourselves from the requirement that such writing become single, unitary, "coherent." We all, from time to time, rail against doubleness, and Neel's book is the most eloquent piece of railing we have had for some years. But when we wish to understand doubleness, we need the most sophisticated critical tools of both rhetorical theory and literary theory. Perhaps in performing many such *progymnasmata,* and in listening to the performance of them by literary critics, we may train our ears to hear the doubleness of our discipline, and we may work up the courage to ask one another whether, finally, after all this trouble, we might experience some pleasure for our pains.

Temple University

NOTES

[1] I would like to thank Heather Sutcliffe for bringing the two student texts discussed in this essay to my attention.

[2] For the relation between rhetoric and its critiques and an argument for considering the interdependence of these discourses, see Gaonkar.

PART II

The Language and
Authority of Theory

Theory, Theory Talk, and Composition

Beth Daniell

In the corridors at CCCC there are complaints that the conference is becoming "too much like MLA." Those who use this phrase elaborate, "You know, too theoretical," and are in turn labeled "theoretically naive." This apparent conflict between theory and practice has been taken up by two recent books aimed at defining the disciplinary status of composition, Louise Wetherbee Phelps's *Composition as a Human Science: Contributions to the Self-Understanding of a Discipline* and Stephen North's *The Making of Knowledge in Composition: Portrait of an Emerging Field*. Phelps believes that disciplinary status for composition depends on the development of theory. North warns that animosity between the practitioners on the one hand and the scholars and researchers on the other could so divide the field that composition might lose whatever disciplinary ground it has gained.

In this essay I reflect on these issues, drawing first on Phelps and then, not on North, whose concern is more with research methods than with theory, but on Stanley Fish. I begin with Phelps's ideas about the relation of theory and practice and then borrow Fish's term "theory talk" to explore the issue that seems to be at the center of the current praxis-theory conflict: the language of theory. Finally, I extend Phelps's notion that theory is autobiographical, arguing its role in the construction of identity and exploring the relation between theory and belief.

Theory

As her title indicates, Phelps seeks in *Composition as a Human Science* to establish composition as a recognized discipline. Though the book both begins and ends with explanations of the need for theory, Phelps urges not the priority of theory, as those familiar with her work might expect, but the reciprocity, the dialogue, of theory and practice. Drawing on Hans-Georg Gadamer's notion of phronesis (practical wisdom, knowledge directed toward right conduct), John Dewey's discussion of reflection and experience, and Paulo Freire's concept of praxis as both action and reflection, Phelps calls for a dialectical relation between theory and practice in composition, a relation in which "theory and praxis mutually discipline each other" (238). She envisions the writing classroom as a hermeneutical circle where teachers' theoretical reflections lead to more critically aware practice, which leads to a more critical analysis of theory, which leads to still more critical application of theory to pedagogy, which leads to greater self-reflection from teachers, and so on. Like many others in composition, I too have invested emotionally in this view of our enterprise. But while I believe that writing instruction may benefit from theoretical reflection by engaged individuals, I also think that our current practices result more from the historical intertwining of several levels of politics than from theoretical self-examination.

Indeed, the major flaw of Phelps's book is her failure to discuss the politics of composition and its theories. Phelps herself admits that she has "neglected power and the political dimension of composition and its praxis" (xiii). A chief reason is her own theoretical approach. Phenomenology, Phelps's theory of choice, encourages the sort of cerebral, distanced reflection that appears inherently apolitical. Because this perspective focuses on individual consciousness, that is, on how a thing is constructed in the mind rather than on how the thing is in itself, phenomenology seems to allow its followers to engage in "pure" theory. Theories, however, are never pure. They are always embedded in a situation that is at once historical, economic, social, cultural, and therefore political. And few disciplines are as blatantly political as composition is—departmentally, institutionally, and nationally. Anyone still unconvinced of this proposition needs to read James Berlin's books on the history of writing instruction (e.g., *Rhetoric and Reality*) or almost any account of literacy by James Sledd or Richard Ohmann (e.g., Sledd's "In Defense" and Ohmann's *English in America* or "Use Definite")—or talk to anyone from the University of Texas at Austin.

Theory, defined as a general explanation of related phenomena (that is, occurrences, circumstances, and facts, not the philosophical counterpart of noumena), is supposed to move us beyond politics, beyond questions of power; theory, we have been taught, is the way to attain neutrality. As Fish explains, theory has been an effort

> to *guide* practice from a position above or outside it, . . . an attempt to *reform* practice by neutralizing interest, by substituting for the parochial perspective of some local or partisan point of view the perspective of a general rationality to which the individual subordinates his contextually conditioned opinions and beliefs.   ("Consequences" 437)

In the technical sciences, a theory has been considered better than its predecessor if it explained and predicted more empirical content. The best scientific theories have been thought not only to include all phenomena accounted for by any previous theory but also to explain anomalies that earlier theories failed to account for.

Theorists in the social sciences and the humanities tried to adopt this model, only to find that their theories don't do a very good job of predicting. Phenomena studied by such disciplines—for example, the behavior of alcoholics or Balinese cockfights or sonnets or student essays—have a way of defying prediction. Theories in these fields serve a more interpretive than predictive function. Unlike scientific theories, interpretive theories tend to be incommensurate rather than comprehensive. That is, a given interpretive theory may explain the anomalies that a previous theory failed to account for, but it rarely, if ever, explains all the phenomena accounted for by previous theories. A deconstructive reading of a sonnet, for example, may explain features of the text not accounted for by a New Critical reading, but the New Critical reading offers insights and reveals "facts" that deconstruction cannot. So, it seems, theories in interpretive fields do not explain all the related phenomena. Since interpretive theories are not comprehensive or cumulative, no clear "objective" criteria exist for judging which theory is best; those of us in the human sciences *choose* which phenomena we want to explain. Interestingly, some of the most consciously theoretical researchers in composition regard the theories in our field as scientific rather than interpretive and thereby fail to see that different perspectives sometimes produce irreconcilable "facts." Despite the hopes of some—Fish calls this desire "theory hope" ("Consequences" 439)—we are unlikely ever to construct any one theory that unifies all the knowledge we have created using different theoretical models.

Even in the natural and technical sciences, theory is no longer regarded as an entity existing outside human affairs. In physics it is now accepted that the stance of the observer influences the phenomena observed. In objecting to Thomas Kuhn's account of scientific theories on the ground that it claims that science ultimately rests on the irrational, Imre Lakatos explains that all scientific research programs are built on an irrefutable "hard core" of assumptions and beliefs at which the *modus tollens* (if *a*, then *b*; if not *b*, then not *a*) may not be directed (133). The "negative heuristic"—the methodological rules that "tell us what paths of research to avoid"—protects this hard core by directing research away from it (132). While a theory may do many things, one of its chief functions is to order and explain phenomena so that the basic beliefs and assumptions on which the theory rests remain unquestioned.

These two terms *beliefs* and *assumptions* do not necessarily connote measurability, rationality, logic, or neutrality—that is, values typically associated with theory. On the contrary, assumptions and beliefs are often, at the same time, socially constructed, inherited, unconscious, value-laden, inarguable, and fiercely argued. The negative heuristic of literary studies, for example, protects assumptions about the priority of the text, the commitment to finding meaning, and the belief in interpretation, values that, according to Jane Tompkins, render reader-response theories far more similar to formalist approaches than different from them. Perhaps not coincidentally, both Lakatos's discussion of metatheory in science and Tompkins's analysis of reader-response theories make connections between theories—which are supposed to be distanced, rational, logical, and consistent—and assumptions—which are believed to be true or valid but which are not always bound by such standards. In these explanations, theory stands not above belief but in front of it.

In the 1983 *Critical Inquiry* debate about theory, Steven Mailloux explains that theories persuade those involved in a discipline to practice the discipline in this way or that, to hold this view or that of certain problems, and to proscribe certain other practices or views ("Truth" 765). Indeed, Mailloux argues persuasively that theories function primarily as persuasion (766). Since Kuhn, we have seen that theories not only explain phenomena but also redirect fields of study. In composition, our theories have persuaded us to teach writing as self-expression or as problem solving or as exploration of the culture. Our theories have persuaded some of us that examining the revision habits of expert adults helps teachers teach adolescents to write better; competing theories have persuaded others that such a research program ignores the different social and political realities in which expert adult writers function and in which inner-city students, for example, compose essays. Theories appear, then, to be rhetorical. As such, they not only derive from power relations within a field of study but in fact shape these very relations. Theories are thus immersed in politics, serving the interests of a discipline, or of groups within that discipline, while protecting the discipline's most deeply held view of itself, its hard core of assumptions and beliefs.

Once we understand that theory is rhetorical and political, then our project as intellectuals goes beyond merely formulating theories or applying them. As intellectuals—"teachers as transformative intellectuals," in Henry Giroux's terms (*Teacher* 125)—we must examine theory, looking for its terministic screens. We need to ask: How valid and how rigorous is the research that supports this theory? What phenomena does this theory fail to take into account? That is, where does it "leak"? Can we state the limitations of the theory, so that we do not claim more for it than it can do, so that we can caution others that this theory works in this domain but not in that one? What are the assumptions, both stated and unstated, on which that theory rests? But also: What is the hard core of unstated beliefs underlying the theory? Whose interests are being served? Is the theory consistent with what we say we want to do? What are the social and ethical implications of this theory? Does it serve our stated beliefs about knowledge, language learning, and the value of human beings? Or does it challenge them? Are we better off with the theory than we are without it?

If Berlin is correct in asserting that the college writing course "responds quickly to changes in American society as a whole, with literacy (as variously defined by the college curriculum over the years) serving as the intermediary between . . . the writing course and larger social developments" (*Rhetoric* 5), then we in composition should carefully examine the persuasive power, the rhetoric, and the politics of our theories.

We have been taught that theory, neutral and arhetorical, determines knowledge. Yet we discover that theory is determined by and protects beliefs. Borrowing from the philosopher Richard Rorty, Kenneth Bruffee has defined knowledge as "socially justified belief" ("Social Construction" 774). If we accept this definition, theory then functions in the academic community as the vehicle by which belief is justified. Accordingly, theory is rhetorical, because it involves persuasion, and also political, because it involves power. As we know from experience, one of the prerequisites of power is the control of the production and distribution of knowledge. The conclusion is, of course, that knowledge is political. Can it be otherwise, since knowledge is a product of the human mind, itself the product of ideological struggle? It seems then that we can no longer expect to develop a neutral theory that will produce neutrality in its proponents. And no theory can lead us to some unsullied, politically correct epistemology. As both Mailloux and

Patrocinio Schweickart point out, each giving as an illustration the characters of Winston Smith and O'Brien in George Orwell's *1984*, any theoretical or epistemological position can be used either to oppress or to resist oppression. Created in and by political relations, all knowledge, all theories, all epistemologies rest on ground already interested, exist in a rhetorical scene. Both theorists and practitioners, then, need to look critically at theory and its uses. Dismissing theory seems not to be a valid option in our postmodern academic situation. It is no longer possible to return to a world in which reading and writing can be thought to exist unmediated by theory. I want composition not to wander around blindly among the theoretical perspectives of other fields but, rather, to examine theories consciously and self-consciously to see what is useful and beneficial to our project.

Theory Talk

Phelps, North, and others believe that the recognition of composition as an academic field is linked to theoretical coherence. I think that our apparently growing disciplinary status derives less from the efficacy of our theories than from the consequences of what Fish would call our theory talk, that is, our talk about theory. Fish's notion of theory talk includes both metatheoretical discussion and use of a particular theoretical jargon. Applying a theory to a particular text, whether a student essay or a canonical work, in order to explain that text, is theory. Arguing that theory x is more useful than theory y is theory talk; so is using the jargon of, say, transformational grammar to explain particular text features when terms from traditional grammar would also serve. While I am not altogether comfortable with this distinction—it breaks down under analysis—I use it because Fish's notion of theory talk can help us discover what theory means in and for composition.

Fish argues in many, if not most, of his essays over the last decade that theory has no practical consequences. Sometimes Fish defines theory in such a way that it does not exist so that he can then argue that something that does not exist can have no consequences ("Introduction" 14). Sometimes he explains that in literature the task is essentially the same regardless of the literary theory espoused: you apply certain theoretical concepts to a literary text to generate a reading, and no matter what kind of theoretical disputation you engage in—no matter what kind of theory talk you do—the reading you present is the one you believe ("Demonstration" 370). Thus, Fish concludes, theories don't alter practice and only rarely change beliefs: "It is belief and not theory that underwrites action" ("Consequences" 445). Though he concedes that people are "on occasion moved to reconsider their assumptions and beliefs and then to change them" and that as a result "there may be a corresponding change in practice," he argues that such changes are seldom brought about by theory: "The impulse to reexamine the principles underlying one's practice can be provoked, moreover, by something that is not even within the field of practice: by turning forty, or by a dramatic alteration in one's economic situation, by a marriage, or by a divorce" ("Consequences" 448). When I was in graduate school, a fellow student used to argue that collaborative learning reflected social-constructionist views of language and learning and that, therefore, those of us who subscribed to that theoretical position should change our pedagogical practice. I began to believe her. But I adopted Bruffee's *A Short Course in Writing* and its collaborative learning techniques only after I saw that, like me, Bruffee emphasized the structure of the essay. It was not the theory that persuaded me to change my practice but the appeal to my experience in teaching writing.

While Fish argues that theory has no practical consequence, he admits that theory talk can have "consequences of a nontheoretical (and *therefore* real) kind" ("Introduction" 14). Because, as Fish explains, theory talk is practice—in literary studies, theory (or, metatheory) has become a form of practice, a subdiscipline like bibliography or Old English—it is "therefore consequential to the extent that it is influential or respected or widespread" ("Introduction" 14). In other words, as "a vocabulary that already commands attention and can therefore be invoked in the confidence that it will be an ornament to one's position," theory talk is talk that has acquired within a discipline "cachet and prestige" ("Introduction" 23, 14). One kind of theory talk in composition studies comes from classical rhetoric—such terms as *kairos, stasis, ethos*, for example.

Engaging in theory talk brings status, then, not merely in literary studies but also in the academic community generally and therefore in composition. Because talk about theory has "cachet and prestige," theory talk helps articles get published in journals and helps panels find places on conference programs. It gets grants, curricular changes, graduate courses. In the wider academic community, we may not understand each other's theories, but we recognize each other's theory talk, and we require it from each other, as I learned when a dean who was a geographer insisted on "more theory" in a grant proposal I had submitted. In composition, it is the theory talk, rarely the theories themselves, that gets us jobs, grants, and promotions. Our English department colleagues seldom care if we follow Peter Elbow, Linda Flower, or Kenneth Bruffee in our composition classes, but they do expect us to use theoretical language appropriately. As we have learned to do so, rewards have ensued. Theory talk helps us attain academic respectability, without which we lack both the practical means and the privilege to act on the insights of our research and experience—for example, to introduce new courses, to change the writing program, to write textbooks that deviate from the traditional.

So I find myself saying, perhaps cynically, that what has helped composition most is not the composition theories but the theory talk, the language that helps us sound like other university scholars. After all, no matter what theory we take into the classroom or into our own research, no matter whether we espouse expressivist, cognitivist, or social theories, we still ask our students to write papers (albeit different kinds of papers), and we still read those papers and then certify to our institutions that these students have, or have not, met the requirements of the course in these varying degrees of quality.

The problem in extending Fish's distinction between theory and theory talk to composition is that Fish is talking, for the most part, about applying theories to literary texts, while in composition we apply theories not just to student texts but also to students. Unlike some other reader-response critics—David Bleich and Louise Rosenblatt, for instance, who argue that teaching literature means helping students make meaning of texts—Fish often seems to speak of literature and theory only in the abstract, even as he discusses composition and undergraduate literature classes (see, e.g., "Anti-foundationalism" and "Is There a Text" but cf. "How to Recognize a Poem"). Phelps, for all her theory and talk of theory, remembers that composition is concerned with more than abstractions; she reminds us that teaching writing means teaching human beings to use literacy to negotiate the world: "Teaching teaches writing to developing persons within concrete life situations" (70). In composition, when we talk about theories, we are talking not merely about paper but about people as well. What defines composition studies, I would argue, is the belief that our central task is to help human beings use language—the one phenomenon that more than any other defines our identity—to create meaning.

Perhaps what the practitioners fear is theory that doesn't in some way talk about pedagogy or students. Maybe the abstraction of literary theory is indeed something to be afraid of, since it has effectively killed off intention, feeling, readers, and authors, leaving only texts of indeterminate meaning, only signifiers in endless play. This much sterility is difficult for a rhetorician—a composition teacher—to accept. Yet we must ask ourselves at the same time whether we want to limit our work in language, rhetoric, and writing to only that which has direct classroom use.

What, then, has made the difference in our professional, institutional, and classroom practices? Perhaps it is not our particular theories but our shared belief that teaching composition is an intellectual activity concerned with the relationships between human beings and the texts they create. And we can thank theory talk for helping us create a community in which we can figure out what we, individually and collectively, believe about our work. Without this community, there is no meaning for any of it—theory, theory talk, or writing itself.

The Language of Theory

In spite of the benefits of theory talk, some practitioners see its "cachet and prestige" not as unifying but as divisive. Typically, the tension between practitioners and theorists (categories far too broad and too simple to be useful—after all, where do I fit?) manifests itself in commentary on the language of theoretical discourse, with the practitioners complaining that theory is impenetrable or stylistically obnoxious. This is an old argument, I know, one that the theorists are tired of hearing but one to which some of them should listen. It is true that some writers of theory seem uninterested in making their work accessible to anyone other than a small group of persons like themselves. In a critique of theory in literary studies, Barbara Christian writes that current theoretical language "mystifies rather than clarifies our condition, making it possible for a few people who know that particular language to control the critical scene" (71). Because of our historical situation as outsiders in the English department, composition people are sensitive to language that is exclusive rather than inclusive.

Another complaint against the language of theory, this time coming from the theorists, is that it can actually trivialize theory, making theory less significant, less useful, than it should be. This kind of theory talk rarely struggles to apply established concepts to new problems or new insights to old problems. Sounding important and erudite, this theoretical discourse accepts theory uncritically, without explaining or analyzing it. Such theory talk is not the "speculative instrument" that I. A. Richards had in mind (*Instruments* 115–16) and that Ann Berthoff keeps reminding us of (e.g., "Instruments" 118), nor is it the tool box that Michel Foucault and Gilles Deleuze recommend as a way to look from specific practices outward (208).

But of course not all theorizing is trivial, and not all difficult language is unnecessarily dense. Warning her audience that *Composition as a Human Science* is not an easy book to read, Phelps explains that in the historical, cultural, interpretive disciplines, writers of theory are currently trying to find language to represent contemporary epistemology. This effort can lead to "hybrid, tortured, mixed, and often unsuccessful discourse forms" (vii). "Writing theory is damnably hard," she tells us (xi). In a review of Phelp's book, I have explained the difficulty of her style by arguing that we have come to expect theoretical discourse to be a series of linear and static statements, whereas her concepts are circular and dynamic. In another review, John Schilb points out that "the attempt to express fresh insights often has to push against the confines of what Richard Lanham famously labeled the C-B-S style (Clarity-Brevity-Sincerity)" (165–66), but he then goes on to ask whether theory has to be so difficult that it loses an audience that might otherwise profit from it. Deconstructing the language of deconstruction, Christian argues that its Latinate, Catholic vocabulary belies its proclamations of disrupting the exclusivity of the tradition. Similarly, perhaps we should ask whether theory written in dense, impersonal sentences of unnecessarily complicated syntax, loaded down with nominalizations and prepositional phrases, is appropriate for a discipline that claims commitment to extending access to literacy, education, and ideas.

But of course it's more complicated than this. Like the experience of literature, theory is a transaction requiring both committed writers and committed readers. Sometimes people who write theory are more concerned with working it out for themselves than with communicating it to other people. In such cases, readers are, in a sense, eavesdroppers who have to work hard to construct meaning for themselves. Peter Elbow tells a story about how Noam Chomsky believed that no one would ever read his dissertation, that all he was trying to do was figure the problem out for himself ("Closing My Eyes" 60). Some readers of theory, reluctant to carry out the work that their end of the transaction requires, do appear to value the C-B-S style over ideas.

Sometimes people resist theory because they are resisting ideas that challenge familiar ways of thinking. Some people in composition don't like what's being written now because they object to the fact that, as John Trimbur puts it, "the intellectual context of composition studies has changed over the past five or ten years as teachers, theorists, researchers, and program administrators have found useful some of the ideas and insights contained in contemporary critical theory, whether feminist, poststructuralist, neopragmatist, or neomarxist" ("Trimbur Responds" 700). These theoretical perspectives call into question values that many have taken for granted, promulgated, and built careers on. Some of the criticism directed at current theoretical language is, in actuality, resistance to canon widening; theory has brought Jacques Derrida, Michel Foucault, Hélène Cixous, and Julia Kristeva alongside the familiar Plato, Aristotle, Hugh Blair, Richard Weaver, and Mina Shaughnessy.

We—the readers and writers united by this theoretical volume—are of course too sophisticated to believe that there is out there somewhere some transcendental entity called Good Writing against which we can measure the text features of any piece of written discourse. We are well aware that good writing speaks appropriately to the particular rhetorical scene out of which it arises, and so we expect theory to be abstract and sometimes complex. Nonetheless, we can test the language of theoretical discourse by subjecting it to some simple but critical questions, mainly about its rhetoric: Is the author closing her eyes when she speaks, as Elbow suggests is often necessary? Does the author appear to remember that the purpose of rhetoric and composition is to examine how human beings use language to make meaning, first for themselves and then for others? Who is the implied audience? Who is the actual audience? What group or groups is the writer aligning himself or herself with? Who is being excluded? Who is being included? Why? What is the tone? What tradition is the work coming out of? If the language is dense, do we come away with something of value, something that makes us see our work in a new light, from a new perspective? Do we learn something? We can use these questions to locate our position as readers in the rhetorical scene of theory. We can keep in mind that all theory is political, coming as it does out of the power relations within a field, trying to persuade us to practice our profession in this way or that, trying to redefine the problems so that we will see our work in this context or that. We can remember that theory talk is a socially constructed way of defining oneself within a community.

Theory, Theory Talk, and Self

Since we know that human beings use language to show affiliation with particular groups, why should we expect ourselves, or scholars in our field, to be any different? As theoretical language proclaims academic allegiances, it establishes membership in a community. Talking and writing, we gain membership in a particular group and thereby define our professional selves. Phelps, in her preface, says that theory is autobiography (vii). And so, while *Composition as a Human Science* follows composition's development over a decade toward a self-reflective, self-critical stance, this at once highly abstract and highly personal book also traces Phelps's attempts to make sense of her own experiences in composition. From one perspective, of course, all academic work is autobiographical, but for Phelps as well as for many others, there is a "personal need for theory" (ix). Anyone who has felt a similar need will recognize Phelps's attempt to explain a significant portion of her life. She uses theory to try to reconcile her disparate philosophical reading—from Paul Ricoeur to Fritjof Capra's *The Tao of Physics*—with her experience in composition—from Donald Graves to Robert de Beaugrande. This personal need for theory pushes us to pick up the separate pieces, our fragmented experiences, and put them into one basket. In looking at my own search for theory, which means trying to make coherent not just my reading but also my teaching, I have begun to see theory as a way to make sense of our professional lives, which rest finally, as Fish points out, on beliefs and values. Existing, like language, before we do, our beliefs and values begin as public but soon become private—or at least they feel private. Theory is then a way to make sense of how our private lives, our histories, our reading, and our experiences with language, writing, and teaching shape the beliefs and values on which rest our practice and our public identities. For me, theory connects public and private selves.

Mike Rose does this in *Lives on the Boundary*. Written in lyrically accessible prose, Rose's book tries to make sense not just of his own life but also of literacy and educational practices in American society. At the beginning of the book, Rose is obviously autobiographical, but by the end he challenges established theory by setting it beside actual lives. He probes human problems, connecting literacy and cognition with social, economic, and political realities. Grappling with various literary and educational theories, Rose's book disrupts theory so that we may see the underlying beliefs and assumptions about definitions and purposes of literacy and about the nature and value of human beings. Using just enough theory talk to establish his authority to speak, Rose reminds us not to make theory more important than human beings.

What is wonderful about composition studies is that there is room for both Louise Phelps and Mike Rose, for both esoteric public-private

theorizing and the private-public narratives of lived experiences, fo
both metatheoretical speculation and the stories of children who fall
through the gaps of our theories. Such richness is not necessarily
available in other disciplines, where the strength and longevity of one
paradigm often restrict conversation, research, and even thought. I
used to think that a coherent theory would help composition become
a coherent field, orderly and organized. Now I doubt that this sort of
theory is possible or even desirable. I have let go of theory hope.

From time to time, I have touched on the relation of theory and
belief. At the beginning of this essay, I meant for my readers to understand Lakatos's use of the term *belief* as institutional and disciplinary,
but my use of the word, like Fish's use of it, slides into something more
personal. My colleague Dixie Goswami regularly reminds graduate
students wrestling with theory (and any faculty members listening) not
to take the theories too seriously, not to confuse them with Truth.
According to Goswami, theories are intellectual tools, and we use them
for protection. We use them, she says, against the obstacles of teaching
literacy—the curricular pronouncements from on high, the bad textbooks, and the inappropriate selections of textbook committees, uninformed writing program administrators, and budget-cutting deans. We
should use theory, she advises, to do the best we know how to do. And
so we are back to theory—or is it theory talk?—as rhetorical and
political. What I hear when Goswami speaks—and it may not be what
she intends—is that at some level she would agree with Fish: that
theory talk has consequences because it has "cachet and prestige," and
that belief, not theory, finally determines action. Perhaps theory is, at
least in part, what we academics use to justify belief, what we proclaim
when we move from belief to action. But as academics we compartmen-
talize too often, allowing theory to become separate from practice and
from belief. When this rift occurs, we end up with theory and theory
talk like the worst freshman essays—alienated from writer, from
reader, from anything that truly matters.

When I went to the University of Texas to study rhetoric and composition after having taught high school for more years than I admit, I
soon discovered that I would have to learn not just the theories but
also the theory talk. This academic language never seems to come as
"naturally" for me as it seems to for others. I have carefully acquired
theory talk and continue to craft it consciously, and I have found
painful many of my encounters with it: translating a paper into "English" so that I could get an A and, later, trying to balance a grant
proposal on the ledge between theory and honesty. A year or so after
completing a dissertation that I considered theoretical, I complained

ın a faculty reading group about an article in which the textual pyrotechnics outweighed the point; the response was, "Well, obviously, you aren't very theoretical." What my colleague meant, of course, was, "I'm a member of this club, and you aren't." What hurt was that I wanted very much to be part of that club, All the Theoretically Sophisticated People in the English Department.

Since then, I've had other opportunities to observe this attitude. I have learned that this profession, not just the literary side but the composition side as well, has its share of insecure people who can feel smart only when they feel smarter than. Once I realized that, I was free of theory fear. Then it became clear to me that theory is an intellectual, rhetorical, and political means to an end, not the end itself. I could see that good theory and good theory talk push against what is merely trendy as well as against what is established, showing us little glimpses of ourselves and our students, giving us insights about what it means to read and write in this culture. Revealing the margins, the gaps, the seams, and sometimes the abyss, the best theory comes in texts that somehow—how?—convey "constructed knowledge" (Belenky et al. 134), where theory is integrated with research and scholarship, with values and belief. Both theory and theory talk have important places in my life, for they keep me critical, learning, thinking. They help me make sense of composition as daily practice, object of study, and community of scholars.

Clemson University

The Rhetoric of Theory

Joseph Harris

In the late summer of 1966, some fifty American and British teachers attended the three-week Anglo-American Seminar on the Teaching and Learning of English at Dartmouth College. The participants in this now famous Dartmouth Seminar were to begin their work together by addressing the question, What is English? Once having defined their subject, they were then to move on to issues involved in its teaching— issues of tracking, testing, curriculum, and the like. The hope seems to have been to give some clear shape to what many at the time thought an almost formless subject of instruction. This goal was not realized. In the first paper given at the seminar, Albert Kitzhaber invoked the standard triad of language, literature, and composition in order to define the subject matter of English. The problem, as Kitzhaber saw it, lay in bringing these three concerns together. He wanted to form a view of English as "an organized body of knowledge with an integrity of its own." What the field needed, he argued, was a definition that did not "[turn] out to be but the lengthened shadow of a specialist's personal interest" but instead collected the various facets of English into a single coherent subject of study (*English* 12, 16).

Speaking in response to Kitzhaber, James Britton next argued that we cannot define English by defining its subject matter. Rather, we must first ask what the function of English is in the curriculum and in the lives of students. For Britton, the key question was not, What is the subject matter of English? but, rather, What do we want our students to do? Britton believed that any map of the subject was bound to be an interested and partial one, an argument for a particular set of methods, aims, and practices. The questions to be asked of such a map, then, are not, Is it true? Is it objective? but, Why take on this view of English? Whose interests does it serve and how? As Britton himself put it:

> Part of what I have done in reading [Kitzhaber's] paper is to
> pursue the lengthening shadow of his own special interest . . . to

find what his stand himself would be upon the topic he is laying before us. And, I have no apology for the fact that what will come out in the end from what I want to say will be the lengthening shadow of somebody else's special interest. (1–2)

Kitzhaber and Britton were speaking out of two deeply conflicting views of work in English. While Kitzhaber was concerned with defining English as an academic discipline, a body of knowledge, Britton looked at it as a teaching subject, a loosely shared set of classroom practices, concerns, and activities. Britton and the other "growth theorists" at Dartmouth defined English as a space in the curriculum where students can be encouraged to use language in increasingly complex and expressive ways. The important issue for them was not whether Northrop Frye's archetypes accurately describe the range of literature or whether Noam Chomsky's linguistics fully account for the way native speakers form sentences. Instead, they wanted to know how basing a curriculum on the work of Frye and Chomsky—as was then being done in the United States as part of Project English—would affect what students and teachers did in the classroom.

In *How to Do Things with Words*, J. L. Austin distinguishes between a constative view of an utterance as a statement (an attempt to describe things or events) and a performative view of it as an action (an attempt to affect its listeners in some way). The exchange at Dartmouth between Kitzhaber and Britton dramatizes a similar conflict between two views of theory in English studies. We have, on the one hand, Kitzhaber's constative view of English as a body of knowledge to be studied and, on the other hand, Britton's performative sense of it as what English teachers and students do, a set of practices and concerns. And so while Kitzhaber looked to theory for a map of the subject to be studied, for a set of principles that would organize what we need to know about how texts are composed and interpreted, Britton took a more rhetorical or performative view of it as a means to an end, a form of reflection on action whose aim is to change teaching in direct and immediate ways. As James Moffett later argued, "The theory . . . is meant to be utilized, not believed. I am after a strategic gain in concept" (15).

The constative view asks whether a certain theory is true or false. It is concerned with theory as knowledge. The performative view looks instead to the possible effects of holding a theory. It deals with theory as persuasion. We can of course look at any theory, just as we can analyze any utterance, for how it functions both as a constative state-

ment and as a performative act—for what it says and what it does.
can ask, that is, not only what a theory has to say about the nature
composing or interpreting but also what changes it would have us
make in our work as teachers and intellectuals.

Let me move to some examples. For many years, the goal of almost
all literary theory was to come up with a set of principles that would
define the correct ways of interpreting texts. In recent years, though,
as everyone knows, this brand of theory has been subjected to a devastating critique by Stanley Fish and others—the argument being, very
briefly, that we can never hope to establish an objective theory of
interpretation, since what counts as evidence in figuring out what a
text means is always determined in advance by the approach we take
in reading it. Thus we cannot settle a debate over, say, whether a
deconstructionist reading of a poem is superior to a New Critical one
by appealing to the "facts of the text," since those facts would themselves be a result of the way we read the text—which is precisely what
is at stake. Both sides of the argument would, in a sense, be doomed
to success, since each would be able to provide full though conflicting
readings of any text offered to it. The set of "facts" the deconstructionists found in the text would simply differ from those that the New
Critics found. Since the meaning of a text thus varies with the ways
and contexts in which it is read, no general theory of interpretation is
possible.

Because of this difficulty, Fish and many other antifoundationalists
have concluded that there is no longer any point in doing theory. As
Fish puts it, "Theory's day is dying . . . and the only thing left for a
theorist to do is to say so" ("Consequences" 128). And Steven Knapp
and Walter Benn Michaels end their polemic "Against Theory" by stat-
ing, "Our thesis has been that no one can reach a position outside
practice, that theorists should stop trying, and that the theoretical
enterprise should therefore come to an end" (30). But instead of revealing the futility of doing theory, such arguments simply show the gap
between what theory claims to do and what it actually can do. When
Fish argues that his position "has no consequences for the practice of
literary criticism" ("Consequences" 106), he means consequences only
in a constative sense—that in refuting the attempts of other theorists
to establish rules of interpretation, he does not mean to offer a new set
of rules in their place. We cannot learn how to do literary criticism,
that is, by reading what Fish has to say about interpretive communities.
But this limitation has not stopped his words from having a marked
effect, in a performative sense, on the day-to-day work of many critics

...d teachers, who are now less likely to talk about the "text itself" than
to raise questions about why and how texts get read in the ways they
do.

Fish thus offers a striking example not only of what theory cannot
do but also of what it can. Theory cannot provide us with a neutral
foundation of knowledge from which we can then derive correct methods of reading, writing, and teaching. But it can offer a way of arguing
about (and perhaps changing) the things we do and believe as teachers
and intellectuals. Stephen Mailloux makes this point effectively in *Rhetorical Power*, arguing that even if theory can never reach a position
beyond practice, it can still "continue doing what all discursive practices do: attempt to persuade its readers to adopt its point of view, its
way of seeing texts and the world" (159). Or as yet another theorist,
Gerald Graff, comments:

> What we call "theory" is a kind of discourse that results when
> assumptions that were once agreed on in a community become
> controversial. Literature (like sex roles, religion, etc.) ceases to be
> something that you inherit without thinking about and becomes
> a contested concept, an object of struggle.   ("Vital Signs" 23)

Such views of theory do not privilege it as a base or ground of
understanding, as something separate from and prior to practice. Instead, theory is itself seen as a kind of practice, a form of discourse
whose subject is the beliefs that guide our work as teachers and intellectuals—and whose aim is to change those beliefs and practices. Fish
describes how such change might occur:

> Beliefs, if I may use a metaphor, are nested, and on occasion they
> may affect and even alter one another and so alter the entire
> system or network they comprise. . . . What this means is that the
> mind is not a static structure, but an assemblage of related beliefs
> any one of which can exert pressure on any other in a motion that
> can lead to a self-transformation.   ("Change" 429)

Even if we cannot use theory to get outside practice, we can still see it
as an attempt to "exert pressure" on practice, to argue for certain kinds
of work rather than others. The final test of a theory, then, is what we
can do with it, what kinds of talk and writing it makes possible for
ourselves and our students.

Yet this performative view of theory has been undervalued not only
in literary studies but, ironically, in the revived study of rhetoric as

well. Instead, the refrain in composition for years has been that we need to know more. Theory has thus usually been seen constatively as an attempt to ground practice in a disinterested account of the processes of language or learning or composing. Timothy Crusius, for instance, cautions in his 1989 *Discourse: A Critique and Synthesis of Major Theories*: "This book speaks to the theories, rather than the theorists (all of whom have written much, barely mentioned here, both before and after their major theoretical works)" (3). What may seem a small disclaimer has large effects. It allows Crusius to abstract something called "theory" from the conflicting aims and histories of the individuals who write it, to argue that, however different their goals as teachers may have been, as theorists people like James Britton, James Kinneavy, James Moffett, and Frank D'Angelo have all contributed to a common project with its own "underlying, developmental logic"—a project that it is now his turn to continue and refine (3). For Crusius, doing theory thus turns out to be an oddly neutral activity, the constructing of a map of discourse that is not connected to any specific program for teaching or writing.

It seems to me, however, that most theories of composing gain interest only when they are linked to teaching. Britton, for instance, in his theory of the functions of writing, makes a familiar distinction between transactional uses of language to get things done, to carry out the work of the world, and the more playful or poetic uses of words that are typical of both gossip and literature. But Britton also defines a third, expressive function consisting of informal utterances "that stay close to the speaker," that have yet to be molded to the demands of a task or audience (Britton et al. 82). This expressive function, he argues, underlies all our mature uses of language. According to this theory, then, most learning should have its beginnings in some sort of expressive talk and writing—in language that is still sorting out ideas and feelings rather than phrasing them as facts or conclusions.

But when Britton's research showed that almost no expressive talk or writing goes on in the schools, this finding tended to be seen not as an argument against the validity of his categories but as evidence for a new kind of teaching practice (Britton et al. 138–73). Why? One reason is that, in speaking of the value of intimate and expressive uses of words, Britton appealed to some teachers' deepest beliefs about language; these teachers were thus inclined to act on his ideas despite the evidence of his schools survey. Britton did not influence their work because he offered an unbiased view of how children learn to use language; rather, he argued convincingly for the value of a certain kind of learning. His theory described not what was but what ought to be;

was justified through the teaching practice it gave rise to. And so, even though Britton failed to offer the map of language learning that he had promised, he still succeeded in changing the way many teachers work in their classrooms (the goal, I suspect, that he most wanted to achieve anyway).

On the contrary, Linda Flower and John Hayes's cognitive process model of composing offers an instance of a theory that, while perhaps accurate in some ways, has failed to persuade many teachers of its usefulness. Through the use of think-aloud protocols, Flower and Hayes try to describe what experienced writers actually do when they sit down to write. The resulting map of the composing process, they reason, can then be used as the basis for a pedagogy in which we teach our students to imitate the problem-solving strategies of these experts. The description Flower and Hayes give of this process has been sharply criticized by theorists like David Bartholomae and Patricia Bizzell ("Cognition")—who argue that the model fails to show how larger social and discursive forces position writers and shape what they can say. While I agree with these criticisms, they also strike me as somewhat beside the point. For what most troubles me (and, I think, others) about the work of Flower and Hayes is not so much their account of the composing process as their single-minded focus on technique. Their work rests on the notion that our job as teachers is to help students write better—with "better" simply meaning that students are technically more able to meet the demands of one institution or another, more able to produce themes, reports, memos, term papers, and the like. But if we want to provide our students with something other than a set of hints on getting by as writers in a corporate world, then we need a problem-posing pedagogy, not a problem-solving one. What is worrisome about the work of Flower and Hayes, then, is not the accuracy of their composing protocols so much as their technocratic aims as theorists and teachers—aims that, I think, have moved many in the field to argue against the cognitive process model.

A last example: in *Rhetorical Traditions and the Teaching of Writing*, C. H. Knoblauch and Lil Brannon try in a different way to ground practice in theory, to articulate a view of language and composing that "comes before method, and makes it pertinent, directed, and organized" (1). This thing that comes before method they call, at various points, "philosophy," "modern rhetoric," and "modern epistemology," which they then associate with the writings of Immanuel Kant, Ernst Cassirer, Michel Foucault, and Kenneth Burke. They then go on to suggest that the teacher who adopts this perspective

no longer stresses giving people a knowledge they did not p.
viously possess, but instead creates supportive environments r
which a competence they already have can be nurtured to yielc
increasingly mature performance. . . .

Finally, they conclude by saying:

> When teachers acknowledge and value the messiness, flexibility,
> and open-endedness of composing, they tolerate those features in
> their classrooms, encouraging writers to accept the obligation to
> make their own way toward coherence, stimulating and sus-
> taining student efforts but not encumbering them with arbitrary
> external procedures or agendas. (15)

This is a view of the classroom that I find in many ways attractive. It
is not, though, a view that I believe "comes before method" or that can
be derived from a certain "philosophical perspective." An attitude that
values flexibility and messiness seems more likely to be drawn from
experience with a certain kind of teaching than to be formed through
reading Kant and Cassirer. What makes *Rhetorical Traditions* a powerful book for many teachers is the striking image it offers of the sort of
place a writing classroom can be. This view of teaching is probably not
a result of the authors' reading Foucault or Burke (or even Berthoff or
Britton); rather, it was most likely formed out of a set of beliefs and
practices to which Knoblauch and Brannon were already committed—
beliefs and practices that their reading then helped them articulate and
refine. Instead of coming before practice, then, theory comes out of
practice—theory helps us explain what we are already doing.

This does not strike me as a problem. As Richard Ohmann has said,
to strip a theory of the particular aims and concerns that give rise to
it is to "reduce it to a kind of ghostly paradigm of argument" (Response
19), and it seems to me that ideas are usually interesting precisely to
the degree that they are meant to have practical consequences. In 1978,
William Coles, Jr., argued that to teach writing better we need not
simply more knowledge but a stronger sense of purpose, of how to use
the things we already know. This is still true. We need not only a fuller
theory of rhetoric but a better grasp of the rhetoric of theory.

University of Pittsburgh

Science, Theory, and the Politics of Empirical Studies in the English Department

David R. Shumway

> *It is clear, then, that the idea of a fixed method, or of a fixed theory of rationality, rests on too naive a view of man and his social surroundings. To those who look at the rich material provided by history, and who are not intent on impoverishing it in order to please their lower instincts, their craving for intellectual security in the form of clarity, precision, "objectivity," "truth," it will become clear that there is only* one *principle that can be defended under* all *circumstances and in* all *stages of human development. It is the principle:* anything goes.
>
> —Paul Feyerabend, *Against Method*

> *"The question is," said Humpty Dumpty, "which is to be master—that's all."*
>
> —Lewis Carroll

In English departments the conflict between science and the humanities has a long history (Graff, *Professing Literature*). If we broaden our scope just a bit to include literary criticism in general, we find that this conflict was already a dominant theme by the turn of the century. In the early years, the philological project of most researchers in English was regarded by others in and out of the university as an abandonment of humane aesthetics and moral values in the name of science. The New Critics, especially John Crowe Ransom, advanced their approach by claiming to have carved out a separate place, or ontological status, for poetry, saving it from the encroachment of science. Because of this history, it is not surprising that people in English departments should feel threatened by another encroachment of science on their territory: empirical studies in composition and rhetoric. Although the New Criticism no longer dominates, the new literary theory is, if anything, more hostile to science. Such theory has been the basis for some of the published opposition to empirical studies in composition and rhetoric, but I believe that a larger, unpublished opposition is motivated by ancient prejudice instead. I would like to persuade my colleagues in English departments that we should abandon our prejudice against the bogey of empirical research and recognize this work for what it is: a sometimes useful form of argument.

To get at this prejudice, this essay evaluates literary theory's critique of empirical studies. Since empirical studies based in cognitive psychology have been the most visible in the field over the past ten years or so, they have been the focal point of the literary-theoretical critique, and hence cognitive rhetoric serves as my instance of empirical research here.[1] By *literary theory*, I mean poststructuralist theory and critical theory, whose major exponents (e.g., Derrida, Foucault, Althusser, Adorno) are not mainly literary scholars and whose theories are not directed mainly at literary interpretation. Thus *literary theory*, as I am using the term, does not concern literature so much as the conditions of possibility of language and other sign systems, as well as the knowledge or truth that they claim to represent. Such theory often understands these issues in specifically social and political contexts. I have chosen the modifier *literary* to distinguish this theory from others, especially that of cognitive rhetoricians.

Although I focus here on James Berlin's "Rhetoric and Ideology in the Writing Class" and mention several other instances of a literary-theoretical critique of empirical studies (Bizzell, "Cognition"; Knoblauch), the position I am interrogating is far more widespread than the print debate would suggest. The absence of open debate between literary theorists and composition researchers is a sign of the radical disjunction between them. Linda Flower illustrates the problem in a 1989 article, where she quotes an unnamed graduate student to illustrate a position that many practitioners of English share:

> Last year at the summer Rhetoric Seminar at Purdue, I talked to a young woman who was working on a degree in literature at another institution. As we were sitting around one night drinking wine, she told me that she didn't "believe in doing research." I was a little taken aback that an aspiring scholar would reject any method out of hand, almost as an article of faith.
>
> ("Cognition" 295)

The opposite attitude also exists. Some graduate students in rhetoric have told me that they do not believe in literary criticism or in what I have been calling literary theory. Although these views may seem extreme, I think they are more typical than not. And even when teachers and students do not hold these articles of faith, the radical differences between the practice of empirical research in rhetoric and the practice of literary theory make dialogue difficult. In part, the problem is that dialogue between the two groups is within the practice of the theorists but outside the practice of the empirical researchers. On the one hand, recognition of this divergence could be the basis for discussion; on the other hand, dialogue is prohibited by the assumption that empirical research stands in absolute opposition to literary theory.

Theorists who take this epistemological position risk ignoring work that they might otherwise find socially or politically important. Even when literary theorists agree with the politics of books like Shirley Brice Heath's *Ways with Words* or Paul Willis's *Learning to Labour*, they may think that the empirical elements of such studies merely repeat what literary theorists have known all along. For example, Willis's ethnography supports his claim that working-class youth in Britain get working-class jobs because of the counterculture of the schools, which values physical over mental work. Class is reproduced not, or not only, by the official culture of the schools but by the counterculture they foster. But since theory tells us that education is a means of social reproduction, literary theorists may not find Willis's explanation a significant contribution to understanding. Willis's work lies outside the practice of theory, and therefore the sorts of statements he produces seem trivial when understood as theory. To the literary theorist, empirical work usually seems either theoretically incorrect or merely obvious.

Since no literary theorist has produced a sustained study of empirical research in composition and rhetoric, we may assume that theorists' opposition to such research is rooted in their critique of science.[2] The critique of science is not, of course, a single intellectual enterprise. There are many different critiques, perhaps as many as there are theorists. But I suggest that, for purposes of this discussion, they fall into two broad classifications: critiques that attack science as a theory of knowledge and critiques that attack the influence of science on social and political life. The second attack, however, usually assumes the first. The first form of attack is dominated by Martin Heidegger and his intellectual descendants, including Hans-Georg Gadamer and Jacques Derrida, while the second class is most closely identified with the Frankfurt school, especially Theodor Adorno, Max Horkheimer, and Herbert Marcuse. While the first of these attacks may not always appear to have science as its object—and, indeed, may be directed at realms of intellectual life that are not normally regarded as scientific—the second clearly makes science a direct target.

Berlin's discussion of what he calls "cognitive rhetoric" appeals to both these critiques. Berlin does not argue against empirical studies in general, but the empiricism he finds in cognitive rhetoric becomes his focus. Specifically, he complains that "cognitive rhetoric . . . in its refusal of the ideological question leaves itself open to association with the reification of technocratic science characteristic of late capitalism." This judgment seems at first glance to be based on the second critique, and in fact Berlin mentions such critics of instrumentalism as Georg Lukács, Herbert Marcuse, and Jürgen Habermas. In Berlin's view, the entire cognitivist scheme "can be seen as analogous to the instrumental method of the modern corporation" ("Rhetoric" 484, 483). These statements associate and compare cognitive rhetoric with dehumanizing industrial capitalism. According to the Frankfurt school's critique, science is both a product and a producer of this dehumanization. Reason under capitalism becomes perverted into a purely instrumental role. Reading cognitive rhetoric in the light of this critique, Berlin asserts that this rhetoric is a

> rationalization of the writing process . . . designated [as] an extension of the rationalization of economic activity. The pursuit of self-evident and unquestioned goals in the composing process parallels the pursuit of self-evident and unquestioned profit-making goals in the corporate marketplace.   ("Rhetoric" 483)

Like modern science, cognitive rhetoric becomes merely a tool that capitalism uses to exploit people more efficiently.

But Berlin's critique ties cognitive rhetoric's instrumentality to its epistemology. Cognitive rhetoric refuses ideology not only because it is intent on its instrumental agenda but also because it calls itself a science: "There is no question that Flower considers her work to fall within the domain of science. . . . Her statements about the composing process of writing, furthermore, are based on empirical findings, on 'data-based' study" ("Rhetoric" 481). Berlin may have an interest in Flower's assertions because they show the faulty epistemology on which cognitive rhetoric is founded. Like the current-traditional rhetoric that preceded it, cognitive rhetoric is positivist. It fails to recognize that the real is an ideological construct and instead assumes that "the existent, the good, and the possible are inscribed in the very nature of things as *indisputable* scientific facts, rather than being seen as humanly devised social constructions always remaining open to discussion" ("Rhetoric" 484). I have italicized *indisputable* because it reveals Berlin's assumption that cognitive rhetoric entails the verification principle. According to his analysis, cognitivists are intent on establishing truth and certainty, and thus they fail to comprehend the roles of language, culture, and society in determining what is to be called truth or knowledge. Patricia Bizzell similarly objects to what she sees as the "quest for certainty" implicit in the cognitivist or, in her language, "inner-directed," program:

> In seeking one universal model of the composing process, inner-directed theorists seek a new set of principles for our discipline that will raise their arguments . . . "above mere ideology" [Hirsch 4]. They seek a kind of certainty they believe is accessible only to science.   ("Cognition" 235)

Here we see that cognitive rhetoric is subject to the first critique, which attacks the claims of science to be able to produce objective knowledge. Cognitive rhetoric mistakenly believes itself to be "based on empirical findings," to be "data-based," rather than to be, like every other way of thinking, "imbricated with ideology" (Berlin, "Rhetoric" 492).

Finally, in Berlin at least, the two critiques merge: "For cognitive rhetoric, the real is the rational." What can be known objectively and indisputably is itself instrumental. Conversely, the process of obtaining such knowledge ensures its continued, narrow instrumentality. The goal of producing such "scientific" knowledge prohibits the cognitive rhetorician from raising questions of value or of social interests ("Rhetoric" 482, 483).

My analysis so far leads me to infer that for Berlin empirical research is inherently instrumentalist and inherently positivist or empiricist. If it were inherently instrumentalist, then it would always be objectionable because of its slavery to the status quo, to those currently in power, to goals that are taken to be natural or essential rather than cultural or historically contingent. If empirical research were inherently positivist or empiricist, it could be nothing more than a way of illegitimately imposing a theory, ideology, or perspective as if it were none of these but simply truth. My view, however, is that empirical research is not inherently instrumentalist and that it entails no particular epistemology at all.

The second of these points is, perhaps contrary to what one might expect, the easier to demonstrate, so let me begin with it. First, one must admit that certain epistemological assumptions of positivism or empiricism are often expressed in the rhetoric of empirical research and that these assumptions may well serve as the motives for undertaking such research. It is not easy, however, to make assertions about the epistemology that different researchers assume since they rarely address themselves to these kinds of theoretical issues. In fact, the epistemological case for empirical research is rarely if ever articulated.[3] But when one attends to the rhetoric of empirical research, one finds that such work regularly appeals to the belief that something in language or the mind—a theory, a hypothesis—can be tested against something not in language or the mind, for instance, in reality. Thus Flower asserts in her response to Berlin, "I would argue that the 'meaning' of an ideology can only be seen in context and that statements of its meaning must be tested by observation of how people . . . actually use it" ("Comment" 767). This response misses the main point about ideology, which is that people do not use it; it uses them. Ideology is precisely that which the culture makes us accept without reflection. Literary theory claims that one cannot get out of language or other constructions "imbricated in ideology" in order to reach some extralinguistic, nonconstructed thing against which statements, beliefs, or hypotheses might be tested.

Flower's rhetoric in the passage I have just quoted strongly suggests the contrary position. And insofar as her argument relies on this rhetoric, it relies on an implicit empiricist epistemology, that is, on the position that one can appeal to pure sense experience, unencumbered or unsullied by human theories or beliefs, as the source of knowledge and truth. This epistemology ought to be challenged not only because it is logically untenable—the proposition that pure sense experience is the source of all knowledge or truth cannot be supported by pure sense experience—but also because of its role in the politics of knowledge. Empiricism is used to dismiss discourses that do not fall within the narrow limits of science and to persuade policymakers to support only work that meets empiricism's standards. As Paul Feyerabend points out, this practice is pernicious because there are no reliable means to know in advance when a strategy of inquiry will work (*Against Method* 23–28). So it is not just oppressed nonempiricists who suffer from an empiricist hegemony but, at least potentially, human culture in general.

This argument assumes an epistemology that few people actually hold, a naive empiricism—pure sense experience—combined with a positivism that says, with Ludwig Wittgenstein, "Whereof one cannot speak, thereof one must be silent" (189).[4] We literary theorists tend to think that anyone who does empirical work must be victim of a naive certainty in the truth produced by empirical research. Flower dispels this misconception quite effectively by arguing for "observation-based theory building," which assumes a postpositivism that "acknowledges both the relative nature of knowledge and the social and cognitive process of interpretation of educational research" ("Cognition" 302). In other words, Flower specifically rejects the claims of certainty and absolutism that have been attributed to her and other empirical researchers. She also refutes naive empiricism, asserting that "theory making is never disinterested," that " 'data' is itself a selected piece of experience," and that terms such as "evidence," "results," and "validity" refer, not "to ultimates or absolutes, but to *tools* that help build more persuasive arguments" ("Cognition" 299, 300).

Flower convincingly demonstrates that empiricists need not build their work on a positivist or naive empiricist foundation, even though she does not avoid falling back on those foundations at certain points. She poses her task, in the section of her article from which I've drawn most of my quotations, as responding to the graduate student who did not believe in research, a rhetorical situation whose difficulty is worthy of some consideration. She imagines her wider audience, correctly in my view, to be prejudiced against empirical research, and she attempts to defeat this prejudice by explaining the benefits of the research. Unfortunately, because she fails to say why empirical arguments might be useful or persuasive and instead relies on the traditional claim of greater access to the real, we are left wondering why one might resort to such research in the absence of epistemological privilege. I believe that empirical research is sometimes beneficial (although I don't have the space to develop that argument here), but my task is to demonstrate that empirical methods are not inherently pernicious. Let us imagine for the moment that exactly the same sort of research that empirical researchers now perform could be presented without resort to empiricist epistemology. Would poststructuralism be obliged to continue to oppose such research on epistemological grounds?

The answer, it seems to me, is clearly no. Stripped of "objectivist rhetoric" (Knoblauch 131), empirical research becomes understood as a particular form of argumentation. All arguments, and all discourse that attempts to have some claim on our intellect, involve or imply the presentation of something like grounds or evidence or examples. Literary theory itself—the writing of Jacques Lacan, or Roland Barthes, or Jacques Derrida—illustrates this point well enough. While all three of these writers would reject the implication that they are empiricists, they routinely engage in offering specific instances of the more general claims they make. Empirical research is simply an elaborate way of giving instances or evidence in support of a theory. But the evidence produced by such research has a priori no greater claim on our judgment than do any other statements that are part of the theory being supported, because such evidence is produced by the theory in the language of that theory. Cognitive rhetoricians like to talk about their projects as being "theory driven," which means, I take it, that their research is organized around explicit premises and assumptions about the matter they are investigating. But these premises and assumptions entail certain kinds of answers. An experiment or controlled study would be pointless if it did not have at least two possible results, but the more controlled the study, the more it is restricted to a yes or no answer on a single question. The "results" of experiments or tests always fall within a narrow range that the research design allows, and they are meaningful only in terms of the categories the theory propounds.

Flower herself seems at some points to share this conception of empirical work. She describes her goal in conducting observational studies as "theory building" rather than "using data primarily to test or confirm a carefully delimited assertion" ("Cognition" 297). This aim suggests that the relation of theory and evidence is circular, precisely in the way that hermeneuts have understood interpretation to be circular. Instead of testing the theory, the evidence provided by research builds it: "The goal of an observation-based theory would be to create a finely-grained explanatory theory [of the interaction of cognition and context and writing], to construct a more fully specified vision of this process, based on the data of sense experience" ("Cognition" 303). Understood in this way, theory is self-reproducing. The cognitive psychological model that Flower uses to understand the writing process can be modi-fied—constructed—by research, but it cannot be confirmed or discon-firmed. The general theory selects and limits what is observed. Looking at a group of protocols and finding evidence of planning and translating assumes that one expects writers to be planning and translating. Find-ing that evidence may modify, but must support, the general theory. The sort of theory building that Flower's studies of student writers allow can be understood as having the same relation to her theory and to truth as, say, Derrida's deconstruction of a group of texts does to his theory and to truth. In both instances, a theory is shown to "work," and in both, the theory itself may be modified by the results of the activity.

When understood in this way, literary theory can have no objection to empirical research on epistemological grounds. The data derived from such observations are nothing other than statements, language like any other language. Their status as evidence is a function of their relation to other statements in a particular discourse. On this reading, empirical studies turn out to have the same epistemological or theoretical status that other forms of discourse do. The upshot is not that we should avoid empirical studies because the results they produce are somehow illegitimate but that we should do them with the full knowledge that they will not allow us to escape the limitations imposed on us by our theories and by ideology.

At this point, we can assert that empirical research is valuable in just the way that other forms of theory construction are valuable. Literary theory can help us to see that academic disciplines, government agencies, foundations, and others in a position to influence the activities of scholars should not regard empirical research as intrinsically more valuable—that is, as deserving of the habitual valorization it now receives. Science, or the claiming of science, is a form of power (Aronowitz), in part because nonscientists do not understand the skeptical nonabsolutist character of science. This lack of understanding is not entirely an accident; in presenting itself to the public, science still claims to provide the truest knowledge. In the absence of such an assumption, people who want to do empirical research must ensure that the information they seek to produce will be not only "factual" but also meaningful and socially useful and that their methods will yield that kind of information rather than merely "verifiable" information. There is no disinterested place from which to judge these projects, but by getting rid of the empirical red herring, we can now attend to the interests that it has masked. Empirical studies understood in this way can no longer "refuse the ideological question."

The other objection to empirical research—that it is inherently instrumentalist—still remains, but only if this objection is not a function of the now discarded epistemology. In Berlin's argument, the charge of instrumentalism is greatly dependent on the critique of epistemology. Cognitive rhetoric, however, may yet prove to be instrumentalist, even if empirical methods are not. Consider the similarities between cognitive rhetoric and Taylorism. Frederick Taylor's scientific management program is often proposed as an example of the ill effects of instrumentalist thought. Taylor observed workers doing their jobs in order to discover how those jobs might be done most efficiently. Thus the task of shoveling could be broken down into a series of small movements, and shovelers could be taught to shovel in the most productive way. But Taylor's research makes the workers' own bodies betray their interests; workers are thus doubly subjected. Furthermore, management's objectives of efficiency and profits do not take into account the workers' ow. experience of their labor and thus further cause them to be alienated from it. Taylor's method turns workers into machines.

Berlin accuses cognitive rhetoric of serving corporations in more or less the same way that Taylorism served them. Such a research program teaches students to complete their writing tasks efficiently but not to question the tasks assigned to them. Like a computer, the student's mind is understood to be available for any problem that needs solving. But problem solving and instrumentalism are almost synonymous. Since the cognitive model treats the mind as an information-processing machine, instrumentalism seems to be entailed.

The cognitivist would doubtless respond that anticapitalists also need to solve problems in communication. Yet the left-wing literary theorist could counter that nothing in cognitivist-inspired pedagogy leads students to question the problems others ask them to solve. Furthermore, the demand for well-defined, solvable problems pushes students away from writing about other problems that cannot be so conceived. The pedagogical issue here seems to be, What should college writing students learn in what is often their only class outside the business or science department? At one time, composition students were typically asked to think, and then write informal essays, about large, open-ended questions. Ironically, however, this current-traditional practice was criticized from the Left on the grounds that such acontextual assignments imply the possibility of explaining one's opinions to anyone, regardless of his or her interests, a position that ignores real-world conflicts in order to instrumentally serve capitalism (Ohmann, *English* 156).[5] In this pedagogical dilemma we see the conflicting demands of freedom and necessity. Many people in English imagine their subject as a kind of "necessity shelter," a place for questions to be raised but not answered, for problems to be investigated but not solved. This orientation corresponds well to literary theorizing and its goal of challenging ideology. The task of wresting freedom from the realm of necessity cannot go on in discourse alone, but it must go on there if it is to go on anywhere. Yet we cannot deny that this project has instrumental moments. English professionals typically understand empirical work as impinging on the intellectual freedom that they believe the discipline offers them and their students. Thus, understanding empirical research as just another form of discourse should make it less objectionable, but not if it still leads to a pedagogy that narrowly restricts students' intellects. Some empirical methods of educational research, however, are better suited to anti-instrumentalist projects.

,or example, an ethnography can, at least in principle, allow its subjects to assert their values, make their interpretation the dominant one, and in the process disrupt any instrumental agenda.

We in English should resist further instrumentalizing our field, but it is silly to define our field by excluding methods of knowledge production that can potentially tell us what other methods cannot. Epistemologically, Feyerabend's point must be accepted: the best policy for knowledge seeking is "anything goes." But time and resources are in practice distributed on Humpty Dumpty's principle, not Feyerabend's. Each of us must advocate the production of knowledge that best serves our interested ends. Those who share the goals of social justice and equality need to design arguments to serve those ends, and they should use any available methods that do not violate those ends.[6]

Carnegie Mellon University

NOTES

[1] See Hillocks for evidence of the broad range of empirical research in composition and North for his division of such research into four types—experimental, clinical, ethnographic, and formal—with cognitive research falling under the last classification.

[2] This is not to say that theorists would identify empirical writing research as science. Indeed, they might well call it pseudoscience. Nevertheless, they make the same critique of it as they do of "real" science.

[3] See the volumes by Braddock, Lloyd-Jones, and Schuer and by Hillocks, both of which demonstrate the practical contributions of empirical research to knowledge about composition. Neither book, however, presents theoretical arguments in favor of empirical research. Both simply assume it to be superior.

[4] By "positivism" I mean a philosophical position. For some representative statements of this position, see Ayer.

[5] For an argument that the English department has been historically instrumentalist, see Watkins.

[6] I would like to thank David Kaufer and Alan Kennedy for their helpful comments and suggestions on this paper. The usual disclaimers apply.

Teaching Composition and Reading Lacan: An Exploration in Wild Analysis

Robert Brooke, Judith Levin, and Joy Ritchie

This essay emerges from our search, as composition teachers, for a learning theory that can explain and guide our common pedagogical practice. With individual variations, we three share teaching methods derived from the writing workshops described by such teachers as Nancie Atwell, Lucy Calkins, Mary Field Belenky et al., Donald Murray, Peter Elbow, and Elbow and Pat Belanoff. Our classes provide a range of predictable occasions for responding to drafts on topics that students have chosen. The questions we ask about our teaching emerge from our experience of responding in such workshop classes. In thinking about the uses and abuses of workshop classes, we have found it helpful to explore connections between our teaching and Jacques Lacan's ideas of transference and countertransference. Seeing learning as guided by transference—that is, by a person's projecting onto another person the authority of a "subject supposed to know," one who can give answers to fundamental life questions—has helped us understand our own and our students' learning. Similarly, seeing learning as threatened by countertransference—by an authority's naive belief that he or she can decide life questions for another, can accept the role of the subject who is supposed to know, even though the authority is only human—has helped us understand some of the mistakes we continue to make as teachers.

But Lacan's work developed in a particular context, and our work develops in quite other contexts. Lacan attempted to explain the dynamics of training analyses, decade-long relationships between an analyst and a patient who wants to become an analyst. By contrast, we work in semester-long writing classrooms, where relationships are plural (student-to-student as well as student-to-teacher) and where students may not desire to be like us. And our own teaching contexts differ. Consequently, we find ourselves translating and changing Lacan's ideas as we interrogate them, for if they apply at all in our contexts, they must apply differently than they do in his.

Jane Gallop, in her discussion of Luce Irigaray's book *Speculum*, identifies two stances that analysts might hold toward their practice. One stance tries to be loyal to the teaching of Freud and Lacan, practicing analysis in strict accordance with their principles. Gallop calls the other stance "wild analysis" (72)—a stance not so concerned with Freud and Lacan, instead improvising and interpreting each analyst's particular context. Such wild analysis is also the only stance that can extend psychoanalytic ideas outside analysis. We must read Lacan for connections to our own practice, always aware of the possibility that such connections may not firmly exist. We must read Lacan while being attentive to our own mental contexts, attentive to the way signifiers like the word *transference* shift meanings as the signifying chains in which they occur also shift. As writing teachers, we must read Lacan wildly if we are to read him at all.

This essay, consequently, develops as wild analysis, interpreting transference as a learning pattern and countertransference as a teaching problem. Such wild analysis requires us to be explicit about the contexts involved—and about the differences between our contexts. Hence this text: a collage of ideas, interrogations, and personal narratives organized around our shared topics of learning and teaching. To present this text otherwise would be to believe that we can be loyal to Lacan (or that we would want to be), that knowledge can remain static across contexts, that the signified does not slide under the signifier. But such ideas we are wild enough to discount.

Transference as a Learning Process

Transference outside Analysis
by Robert Brooke

When I was just beginning to teach, I turned to my office mate Dexter Westrum (an older man with over ten years of teaching experience) for insights about teaching. I'd come into our office, frustrated with my students or myself, and he'd lean back in his chair, put his feet on the worn oak desk, and look out the window at the bare trees against the winter sky. (It was always winter in Minnesota.) Then he'd say something aphoristic and turn back to his papers. I now recognize, ten years later, that many of my teaching practices developed from understanding of his comments.

"We always design our courses for last year's students," he would say, looking at the trees—and I'd go away thinking that the course I'd been struggling with was appropriate for the students I'd had *last* term. But this was a new term, and these were new people, with slightly or radically different needs.

"Never ask a question you already know the answer to," he'd say, turning up the radio, and I'd walk over to the student union pondering how I was inhibiting my students' writing because I was directing them into subjects where I already knew what I thought.

"As soon as there is a subject supposed to know, there is transference," says Lacan. "This in no way excludes the possibility, where no analyst is in view, that there may be, properly speaking, transference effects that may be structured exactly like the gamut of transference phenomena in analysis" (*Concepts* 230, 125). We may often learn through the process that psychoanalysts call transference, even if we are nowhere near an analyst's office.

As a young teacher, I think I learned this way from Dexter. Our brief encounters matched Lacan's description of transference as a mode of learning. I came to Dexter frustrated and confused by patterns (in myself, in my interactions) that I did not understand. I was looking for a "subject supposed to know" (Lacan's term for a person who holds a position of personal or institutional authority for you, who you believe knows the "truth" and cares for you). He had for me, after all, personal and institutional authority in teaching. He had been my small-group leader in Minnesota's training seminar; he impressed me with his insight into our group's writing; he was known as one of the staff's best teachers. Dexter would listen to my complaints and then utter one of his aphorisms—and I would go away, transforming myself in my thinking about it.

In psychoanalysis as Lacan wrote about it, transference follows exactly this pattern. The patient speaks to the therapist, demanding a solution, an answer, to problems; the therapist does not reply directly to the demand but instead listens and intervenes in the patient's discourse in such a way that the patient becomes involved in thinking through the situation (a thinking through that operates on all levels of the patient's psychic structure); in time, through this internal psychic work, the patient comes to reorder his or her experience and sense of self in ways that are more effective. The dialogue between patient and therapist prompts the patient's internal work. For the process to function effectively, the patient must initially project onto the therapist status of a "subject supposed to know"; then, over time, the patient omes to understand that the therapist is just another human being who cannot possibly know the "truth" of the patient. Learning, in analysis, depends on how the patient experiences the "subject supposed to know." The patient initially needs it to prompt internal reorganization but finally grows beyond it to escape dependency. So the therapist's interventions are critical: the right kind of intervention guides the patient through this process; the wrong kind keeps the patient a willing slave, dependent on the therapist's supposed knowledge.

My relationship with Dexter was such a learning relationship. When I look back on it, I realize that the authority I initially saw in him was a projected authority. I don't have any way of knowing what Dexter actually meant when he spoke. The aphorisms could have been jokes (he had a reputation as a humorist at parties) or perhaps a measured attempt to confuse me, to stop my rush of words long enough to get me out of the office and let him get back to work (I had a reputation for being overly intense). But I didn't take his words this way. I assumed that they had a message for me, a message tailored to my particular needs, and that Dexter had the best interests of me and my students at heart when he spoke. So I'd leave the office deeply engaged in internal dialogue, building insights that led to changes in my teaching practice.

Now, years later, I wonder about Dexter the person beyond the projection. I regret that I did not go to parties with him and see his reputed humor in action. I regret not being able to talk with him now, both of us as reasonably successful teachers. But at that time maybe such a relationship wasn't possible, wasn't what I needed. Maybe then I needed someone on whom I could project the "subject supposed to know."

Perhaps we need a "subject supposed to know" in order to learn at all. For learning to have meaning to us, for it to help us restructure our lives, choose careers, lovers, friends, perhaps we need a range of knowing subjects. When I look at my relationship with Dexter and see this transference process, it isn't hard to find it in other relationships as well:

One of my students this year is journaling about his girlfriend, a young woman he has known for three months. She "knows what's good for me," he writes. She "understands me better than I understand myself." To read his descriptions of his dates with her, though, is to realize that he doesn't know whether she understands him or not. He takes her to his places (football games, the bars he likes); he explains to her his opinions and his visions for his or their future; he introduces her to his friends, and they all go bowling. She listens supportively, and she makes him feel important and liked, but she doesn't describe what's important in her life, nor does she explicitly disagree with him. Neither of them would articulate it this way, but she is a "subject supposed to know" for him: transference writ large in love.

Other students have experienced transference relationships in their reading. In my class last year, at least three students looked to Stephen King as a knowing subject and tried with various degrees of success to structure their own work around the discourse that his novels propose. Here in Nebraska, in a far northwest corner of the Bible belt, some students also structure their lives around the knowing subject they find in the Gospel of John or the Epistles of Paul. And among my colleagues, I repeatedly find scholars in transference with their favorite authors, the people they've devoted their lives to understanding—Dickens, Cather, Austen.

Even this article and my other work on Lacan, I now realize, are examples of such transference. Why, I find myself asking, would a composition teacher read Lacan anyway? Lots of other writers are looking at dialogue and learning. Why not read Lev Vygotsky's *Mind in Society* or Adrienne Rich's "Notes towards a Politics of Location"? Why not Stanley Fish's *Is There a Text in This Class?* or Ann Berthoff's *The Making of Meaning?* Why would I write about Lacan, or investigate my own practice by borrowing concepts from Lacan's field, if I weren't experiencing a transference relationship?

(I never met Lacan. I'm too young and too American. But I note with shock and interest that the one Lacan article I find most important ["The Direction of the Treatment"] was delivered to the Colloque de Royaumont on 13 July 1958, the day I was born. How's *that* for transference?)

Transference, Feminism, and Falling in Love
by Judith Levin

I see transference as a natural and powerful process that can help students locate their learning in themselves. This process can be especially important for women, whose belief in their own ways of knowing is often undermined in traditional education. At the same time, I am concerned about the potential danger that transference carries for women, the danger of seeing another person as a "subject supposed to know." Unless the knowing subject deflects it, the student's belief in that person's powers can reproduce the one-way, hierarchical relationship that often characterizes women's experience in a male-dominated public world.

My concerns come out of personal experience with a feminist teacher, Barbara DiBernard, who taught a women's literature class that I took as a graduate student three years ago (see her "Feminist Teaching"). I think now that our relationship represents a feminist form of transference. My relationship with Barbara has always differed from the pure Lacanian model, and yet I have no doubt that I've projected onto her the ability to know what I'm about, whether that's all right, and where I should go with my knowing. She has responded with thoughtful observation and empathy and has opened up ways of reading women's literature that stimulate my thinking and writing. This experience reminds me of the image, suggested by my friends Diane Wood and Diane Gillespie, of the feminist therapist or teacher as medicine woman—one who tries not to intrude, observes carefully, and knows where to collect the medicine. The medicine woman may be a feminist image of Lacan's analyst, a female "subject supposed to know."

In the weekly journals that I wrote for Barbara's class I see how a feminist form of transference developed. In these journals I explored my reactions to the learning I was doing in her class and decided that I wanted to leave my full-time job and return to school, changing careers at the age of forty-four. Barbara never advised it; rather, she was an interested and attentive listener as I came to this conclusion on my own in the journals. I felt that I was writing both to myself and to her, and, in a Lacanian sense, our language, the dialogue between us, stimulated an inner dialogue that reorganized my view of myself. Her hearing brought out my telling. I saw her as someone who believed in my powers and wanted to go with me in following out my thoughts and feelings and in finding my own agenda. I think that the writing I did under these conditions is still some of my most thoughtful work.

From the beginning of our dialogue, Barbara emphasized a connected, two-way relationship that I do not see in Robert's interaction with Dexter, and this difference, I believe, has much to do with my story being about women rather than men. In her responses to my journals, Barbara expressed in a feminist way the sense that we were inquirers together. In particular, she did not concentrate only on my learning but shared her own search. Clearly there was no perfect mutuality, since I poured out many pages each week and she wrote at most one page in response, but I felt that we were making meaning with each other. In her comments Barbara mixed thoughts about literature with thoughts about her life. She also showed where we were similar, said several times how I affirmed her, called herself my friend, described our writing as helpful dialogue, said she learned from me. This conversation established our relationship as one of mutual respect. We connected as people with complex lives, providing a context for all the writing, talking, and listening of our ongoing dialogue.

How does this context affect the experience of transference over time? I think that Barbara will always be a medicine woman for me in some sense. At the same time, she consistently responds to me as a colleague and friend, and I believe that the ways I do my work and live my life contribute to her energy for her own work and life. This kind of context allows transference to develop into a relationship in which each of us remains visible. I can see Barbara realistically and differentiate myself over time, so I need not go elsewhere to gain personal authority as a knower. Instead of experiencing transference as a dependency to be outgrown and shed, I can continue to write, talk, learn, and change in an increasingly rich context of connection. I see in our mutual exchange a feminist form of transference relations that may be especially empowering for women.

Of course, teachers can't be this engaged with all their students; I am describing graduate school, where transference issues may be especially strong, interests may converge, and relationships may last for years. Graduate students often develop complex feelings of attachment to faculty members—I've even thought of it as a kind of falling in love. Lacan's idea of transference alerts me to the intensity of these student feelings and suggests their relation to learning.

Lacan describes the real purpose of analysis, and therefore of learning, as the articulation of desire. That is, because I am split from my unconscious, I don't really understand what I want, and I am looking for someone who knows how to help me find it, someone who can unlock the doors to my other self. If I can find someone I trust and believe in, who cares about me, to share this confusing and perhaps frightening search, I am more likely to enter into it wholeheartedly. Now, I wonder if desire for my own completion translates into a kind of desire, that we have not well named, for a person I trust to know and accept and believe in me.

This is tricky stuff. It sounds too close to erotic desire, which is frightening in a school setting—in fact, taboo. And there are real dangers of such feelings generating countertransference that can be harmful for students; we all know of cases where attraction becomes mutual and is acted on erotically. But in transference the explosive possibilities of love do not negate other possibilities.

Looking at the experiences of my fellow graduate students with their teachers, I wonder whether the ones who feel most empowered are the ones who feel a little in love with their mentors. And isn't this really the experience we have, in romance, of falling in love with ourselves? Perhaps it is at the same time a way of getting outside ourselves and deeply involved with ideas. Perhaps it sparks our energies for years of apprenticeship, when an admired person's faith that we have the "stuff" keeps us looking for it. In graduate school, where professional and often adult identities are at issue, it is striking how much students wrestle with their relationships to faculty members. Is there a time, then, when we as students find the reflection of ourselves in the eyes of a respected other to be central for empowering our learning? What are the other stages in this process? And how much does it involve the teacher also needing or wanting the student—not in some out-of-control countertransference but in the sense that the student has something to offer the teacher, so that they both experience genuine and pleasurable exchange?

Transference and Learning in Groups
by Joy Ritchie

Important learning experiences in life often occur in groups, something Lacan's theory of transference, arising from the private patient-analyst relationship, does not recognize. I believe, however, that transference relationships also account for learning in settings like writing work-shops, consciousness-raising groups, and support groups. The ways of using language publicly in such groups make possible a dialogue that can lead to a decentering process essential for internal reorganization. In addition, these groups have in common a restructuring of the tradi-tional relationships of teacher and student, patient and analyst in which transference has commonly occurred. The relationships be-tween members of such groups allow the role of patient or analyst, teacher or student, to become blurred. Each group member functions as both a knowing authority and a divided self seeking answers, and as a consequence such groups often become safe and stimulating set-tings for working through one's desires.

In a recent writing workshop class, for example, a student, Manjit, wrote consistently in her journals about the anger and frustration she felt as an Asian woman student living in the United States. She turned her journal writing into a series of essays that gave voice to the divisions she experienced as a result of her racial, sexual, and academic posi-tions. Eventually she read these essays aloud to her small group and to the class. Her writing and ongoing revisions indicated that the supportive context of the workshop allowed her to engage in an internal dialogue that led her to reconceptualize her experience. In addition, the contradictions Manjit articulated about her identities as an Asian, a woman, and a student served as a catalyst to decenter other women students' understanding of their own roles. Many of the women in the class (twenty-year-olds, midwesterners, members of sororities) were shocked, both by the attitudes about women that Manjit described in her culture and by the racist and sexist parallels that she pointed to in her experience in the United States. Her essays provided an alternative perspective for the other women's analyses of their own lives. One young woman, for example, had written about her experience in the Miss Junior Nebraska Beauty Contest. Her essay acknowledged but dismissed the negative aspects. Manjit's essays, however, gave her a framework from which to reconsider the assumptions underlying beauty pageants, her family's contradictory values in pushing her into them, and her own personal goals. Another student, who said that Manjit's essay on sexual abuse helped her revise her attitudes about date rape, explained, "She helped me see that I really had been blaming the victim."

Manjit's freewriting in her journal began a personal dialogue in which suppressed voices emerged through ongoing self-reflection. At the same time, her private exploration, turned public, allowed other students to recognize, articulate, and reexamine their own questions and desires. The activity of sharing her life story in this context set in motion a learning process (for her, for her colleagues) that became a powerful catalyst for personal and social change. Lacan's theories can help clarify this learning process.

In transference, learning occurs as a result of decentering, which is made possible by language's capacity to touch off feelings we had not intended, to illuminate ideas we didn't know existed, to double back and contradict us, and to intrude on the deceptions we construct for ourselves and on those our culture constructs for us. Underlying the learning in writing workshops is a group transference relationship, one that occurs in the operation of language and the unconscious.

Lacan describes how language works in the social interaction of the analyst-patient relationship: teaching and learning always involve the relationship of the individual to language (*Ecrits* 234). This relationship to language accounts for learning in group contexts like the writing class in which Manjit was a student. In Lacan's theory, psychic structures are organized symbolically, through language that surrounds us. Our sense of self is thus constructed in language, in the array of discourses in which we are immersed. But the meaning of signs is not intrinsic but relational, and thus each signifier gains its meanings from its relations to other signifiers. The learning that occurs through patient-analyst discourse, or through conversation and writing in workshops, occurs because of the new relations made possible as one signifier jostles against others in the chain of signifiers. As one signifier comes in contact with others, it touches off relations of meaning that were not possible before. Lacan writes to his analysts in training that interpretation can produce something new only when "signifier effects the advent of the signified" (*Ecrits* 233). Writing served this interpretive function for Manjit privately, but, made public, it also became a catalyst for learning among other women.

Because each member may assume various complex roles in these groups, the transference that takes place is strikingly different from the hierarchical pattern of transference in the traditional patient-analyst relationship. In group contexts, the "subject supposed to know" is no longer the individual analyst; instead, various individuals actively share the role and shift it among themselves. A person who is a knowing authority in one instance may become a "patient" in another, as roles are changed or reversed.

This collective role of knowing authority extends Lacan's insistence that the knowing subject's own desire is always fully implicated in the interpretation of another's questions. In groups, the role of knowing subject does not merely shift from one member to another. Rather, each member of the group is simultaneously involved in a double role—as a patient who needs to articulate and pursue a desire and as an analyst who possesses knowledge and authority. I see this doubleness most strikingly in our department's composition colloquium, a writing group of graduate students and faculty members.

I ask the colloquium to read a draft of an article I have written, because I know that alone I cannot adequately understand what it says and where it is going. I present my writing to the group members with the belief that they possess the knowledge to help me understand and that they care about my well-being (they want me to succeed, get published, gain tenure). I don't believe that one authority will know how to fix my text, but having worked with this group for a few years, I anticipate a variety of responses: from some people I'll get help with the structure of the piece; from others, help on the theoretical aspects of the draft or a readerly response telling me where they had problems with the text. From these responses, I believe that I will be able to move forward. But I also recognize that the readers' own desires are implicated in their reading of my work, and thus their responses may be limited or false. Sometimes, for example, a response may grow out of work that an individual is doing at the time, or from another theoretical perspective, and he or she may attempt to steer my writing in a direction that confirms a favorite point of view. Peter Elbow says it more directly: "The reader is always right and always wrong" (*Power* 100).

I come away from these group discussions with an array of responses, some supporting one another, others contradictory. But I've come to trust the confusion and decentering that result for me. It sends me back to my draft with new insight to reconsider *my* purposes. It sends me back to *myself*, to an internal dialogue with the responses and my own strategies. The resulting essay is never tailored to the prescription of any member of the group, but it is almost always my translation of, or improvisation on, their responses.

The same potential for internal dialogue is present for me and for others when one of my colleagues brings his or her writing to our group. I read the draft with the expectation that it will add to my understanding of my own questions and concerns about writing and teaching. I listen to others' responses to the draft not just in relation to the writer's work but also in relation to my own writing, my teaching, or some other aspect of my life. The social nature of this group "therapy" allows each of us to participate as therapist and patient simultaneously, to use the external dialogues that arise in the group to carry on our own internal dialogues, and inevitably to articulate and pursue our own evolving desires.

Countertransference as a Teaching Problem

(Mis)Managing Countertransference
by Robert Brooke

One day late in this semester, a young man from my writing class came to my office. Officially, he wanted help finishing his final paper, but unofficially he wanted help dealing with his father. He wanted to go back to California, where his mother lived, he said, but his father would pay for tuition only if he continued at Nebraska. "From what you've written in class about your father," he said, "I thought you might know what to do."

I was, of course, flattered. But I was also dismayed. He was asking me for something I couldn't give. I knew next to nothing about his father and their dynamics, and I doubted that my own history would connect in any but opaque ways. So I asked him to explain what he felt his choices were and suggested that he might try keeping a journal about the issue as a way of clarifying his mind.

Countertransference, the counterpart to the patient's projection onto the therapist, is the therapist's own desire for (the adoration of) the patient. Most often, claims Lacan, this desire ends up being for a strange kind of power over the patient: "The inability to sustain a [transference] praxis in an authentic manner results, as is usually the case with mankind, in the exercise of power," he writes. "Certainly the psychoanalyst directs the treatment. [But] the first principle of this treatment is that he must not direct the patient" (*Ecrits* 226–27).

Transference calls out for countertransference—the analysand does desire the "subject supposed to know," and the analyst often desires the power that comes from seeming to fill that projected role. But if learning is to occur, if the analysand's psychic structure is to reorganize, this call must go unanswered. Because the "subject supposed to know" is a fiction, a lie, the only real answer to the call is to say, "Wait a minute. The 'subject supposed to know' is not at home. In fact, it never even lived here. It's only *me* answering, and I'm only human like you." The only moral response to the projection is to show, through time, that it is only "me" speaking, only another "animal of the species" ("Direction" 232).

I am not an analyst but a writing teacher; yet, having read Lacan, I find that his notions challenge me as well. As a teacher, am I in the same position of risk that an analyst is in? Am I at risk to countertransference, to the belief that my conscious strategies of intervention actually teach students when, if Lacan is right, they may be impeding learning instead? Am I at risk of substituting domination and power for learning because I so little understand myself?

I think of the various ways that I could have responded to my student, and I recognize in most of them a risk of countertransference, of assuming that I know more than I do. I might have responded by telling him what to do, under the false assumption that I really know what kind of life male undergraduates seek. Or I might have responded by refusing to tell him what little I do know (in this case, only about journaling as an aid to clarifying his own mind), under the false assumption that only those who hold degrees in counseling are knowledgeable enough to discuss such choices. Both of these potential errors come about when I fail to distinguish what I know from what I do not, when I accept the projected position of knowing subject instead of recognizing that it is a fiction.

Teaching as a Feminist and a Writer
by Judith Levin

In thinking about countertransference in the classroom—the danger of acting out the authority that students project onto teachers—I find help in the structures of feminist groups, because they are designed to re-form traditional authority relations. I belong to three groups that diffuse authority and encourage equality and mutuality, and I draw on them in my composition teaching.

In a feminist writing group, a women's support group, and a feminist teaching and learning group, time to speak is distributed equally (each of us takes a turn), or the format is built around mutual sharing of stories, and we agree on a commitment to listen and learn from one another. Some members may carry extra personal authority, but they do not present themselves that way and certainly do not share only the authoritative side of themselves. They are there with a need to share experience, expression, questions, and dilemmas. They recognize that each person in the group has the capacity to teach by telling her experience and by listening and responding to the others.

In my writing classes I decenter authority in ways similar to the workings of these feminist groups. I do not give up my own authority in this process; rather, I define it in a way that students can identify with and share: I am a writer. I do the same assignments they do, and I share my work so that my process is visible to them. I read aloud the writing I do that is close to their own concerns—figuring out my family, finding my way with the pressures of time. I always write and speak about my real concerns of the moment. Because I have been writing for many years more than they, I have a natural authority with language that relieves me of the need to assert authority in institutional ways. I believe, and they say in their comments, that I have the right to act as a guide because I can do this thing that we are there to learn. At the same time, I am clearly still learning—they know I'm not a "finished" writer. And they know that I write about my life because I take seriously the same issues that concern them and I see these issues as material for thinking and learning, with many implications. They respond with papers that are often thoughtful about concerns that are clearly their own.

In this context of authority coming out of personal experience and ideas shared in writing, I use other structures to diffuse authority among the students. These structures include sitting in a circle, students choosing their own writing topics, each student taking a turn in informal speaking exercises, many student interactions in small groups and pairs, all students regularly reading papers aloud, my responding to their writing in ways that ask rather than tell, and my showing how they can respond this way with each other. These and similar approaches boil down to giving students many chances to look into themselves, compare with others, and receive responses that encourage further expression.

These methods are not only feminist, of course—they are well known in workshop teaching of composition. What I find empowering about them is what they share with feminist teaching: a series of structures that discourage countertransference and send students back to themselves and each other.

I see students in such classes responding with a sense of personal discovery. When I ask my students to describe what they are learning, they say in their own ways that writing, speaking, and listening are all part of the same process of exploring what is on our minds and that this use of language is revealing about the self. In Lacanian terms, the experiences of dialogue with others and dialogue with oneself constantly interact, so that one is always having, sending out, receiving, and processing thoughts about one's reality. This process, enacted in language, increases access to unconscious material, which comes into consciousness and changes it: I know myself in a new way.

Of course, this teaching style has its dilemmas, and they are not minor. How do we grade personal writing? What do we do with the pressure from students and the institution to teach academic writing? How do we respond to resistance from students who feel that they aren't really learning unless the teacher tells them what to do? What if their verbs are in the wrong tense? The list goes on, and there is a large literature in composition theory and teaching practice that deals with these issues. I don't want to suggest that all is rosy and there are no problems, but I want to call attention to the ways that Lacan, feminism, and workshop teaching all offer something powerful in their recognition of a natural learning process that they are able to support. In the classes I teach, I am still a "subject supposed to know" in the sense that I am an exploring writer with knowledge of a path the students may want to take, and I am actively interested in their progress on it. But they go on from my class recognizing that I am not a source of their power. They locate this power in the freedom and invitation to say what they want to safely and to share it with accepting and responsive others. The structures that make this happen also help the transference

process work, so that students develop in their learning beyond dependency to mutuality and personal authority.

Resisting Countertransference and Teaching as a Woman
by Joy Ritchie

Reading Lacan helps me understand the power relationships that exist
between me and my students. Despite all the changes that workshop
teachers are making, we are still the authority in the classroom. Furthermore, the academy itself takes on a symbolic transferential authority for many students, and I am part of that structure. But I am also a
woman, and my position and Robert's are complicated in different
ways.

Because I am a woman, it ought to be easy to position myself as
teacher-learner in the class. I am accustomed to working in the background, to accepting a role as gentle nurturer. But these very aspects
of my socialization can also lead me to mismanage my responses to
the trust students have bestowed on me. Though I am not used to
wielding power, I am accustomed to asserting control in subtle ways.
I am good at solving problems, giving advice, and nurturing. But even
this nurturing can be a subtle exercise of power.

It ought to be easy to position myself as teacher-learner in the class,
so that transference can work as a process of learning. But all our
socialization and the medical, military, and banking metaphors that
pervade our professional discussions of teaching lead us to believe, like
the analysts Lacan chastised, that we are obligated to teach students,
to "train [their] weak ego" by the strength of our strong egos (*Ecrits* 7,
229). Our metaphors for teaching and the practices that result from
them assume that teachers *do* know what students need, that we can
fix them, cure them.

Other seductions exist for women. Though as a woman I have learned
to remain in the background without asserting myself, I am, at the
same time, accustomed to being the object of others' gaze. It is a
seductive trap to become the object of attention, the object of adoration, the one to whom students go for advice, the one on whom attention is focused as the clever or charismatic performer.

Teaching in a university poses still other problems for female teachers. Though we hold a place of authority, it is, in part, a fictional
position for women. Luce Irigaray learned well, when she was thrown
out of the Ecole Freudienne by her "master" Lacan, that the position
of authority is reserved for men and that the dutiful daughter remains

submissive to the father's law. Because women lack the symbolic status—what Lacan calls the "signification of the phallus"—around which language and thus our individual and social identities are constructed, our authority is suspect in the paternalistic structure. Because we recognize our marginal position in academia, it is tempting for us to take a defensive position and thus attempt to bolster our authority, by demonstrating how much we know, by imposing our position wherever possible, by pushing into the dialogue.

In "Notes toward a Politics of Location," Adrienne Rich describes a way to carry out the displacement of authority that is necessary if we are to manage countertransference while we also acknowledge the complexity of the role of teacher. Rich talks about the importance of locating ourselves, defining our points of view, naming the ground on which we stand. As a teacher, I have a responsibility, then, to make clear my personal and intellectual assumptions and also to let students see the contradictions in my social and political position as a teacher, a scholar, and a woman. I can demonstrate that I speak as a participant within a complicated and sometimes conflicting cultural and political framework rather than as an objective, unified, and monovocal authority figure.

But Rich does not offer guarantees or panaceas. When I sense students' belief and trust in my authority, their affirming messages (often lacking to us as women in professional socialization) become seductive. It is easy to revel in the external accoutrements of authority, as if they take the place of a missing internal sense of authority.

Last spring a woman in my seminar on composition theory came to my office, ostensibly to ask for advice about her graduate program. I was surprised when she began the conversation by saying, "What I really want to know is, can we, I mean women, really do what you're doing? Is it really possible for me to have this life? I mean, can we have it all, as you seem to be having it?" Her question took my breath away. It allowed me to see myself as she saw me and to understand that who I believe I am and what I believe I am doing when I teach can never be entirely what I imagine and may never have the result I intend.

This woman's real question had little to do with our graduate program or my composition seminar. She was responding to me in relation to my symbolic position in the social structure of the university, but she was also responding to me in relation to my symbolic position in the wider social structure, to my position as a woman. Her interpretation of my behavior, what I said in class, my response to her work in class, had little to do with what I intended. It had everything to do with some of the basic questions and desires of her own life and with the projection that she had constructed of me in relation to those needs. That projection is difficult to resist. Had I not been amazed at the enormous implications of her question, for me and for her, I might easily have said, "Yes, let me tell you what to do."

University of Nebraska

PART III

Narrative Theory and Narratives

Is There a Life in This Text? Reimagining Narrative

Judith Summerfield

> *There is no story that is not true.*
>
> —Chinua Achebe

In the afterword to the second edition of *The Rhetoric of Fiction*, Wayne Booth describes what he might have revised had he undertaken sweeping changes of the first edition, published twenty-two years earlier, in 1961. What would he revise, he asks himself, had he the time or the inclination? To begin, he would change his title from *The Rhetoric of Fiction* to *A Rhetoric of Narration*. The new title would constitute a sign of the times, he says, the enlivening preoccupation in the humanities and social sciences with narrative—particularly with how and why we tell (and write) stories and with what stories represent about our ways of knowing. The change would reflect the "true importance of narrative in our lives," Booth says, citing Kenneth Burke, who "has often argued that the telling of stories, the construction of 'symbolic actions' is the defining feature of human beings." Booth assures us that his hypothetical revision would, nevertheless, remain essentially the same as his first edition, because "what we will say about any story, whether we call it fictional, historical, philosophical or didactic, will in some respects resemble what we will say about all stories" (408).

Because narrative is implicated, in one way or another, in much of our work in the teaching of college composition, Booth's comments apply. We can ask ourselves his questions: What have we revised in our thinking and our teaching about narrative in the last twenty years? What do we say about "any" story? And what have we gleaned from the rich harvest of narrative studies that comes to us from various disciplines?

One matter is certain: none of us in discourse studies can escape the impact of the isms on our discipline—structuralism, poststructural-

179

ism, Marxism, and feminism, not to mention deconstruction, semiotics, anthropology, sociolinguistics, psychoanalysis, speech-act theory, reader-response criticism, folklore studies, and narratology—all lifting the enterprise of interpretive analysis into metadiscourse. We cannot read innocently these days, or write, or teach writing or reading without considering, analyzing, defining, scrutinizing what we do as an act of language, particularly when we are in the business of teaching language use. We can no longer depend on the unquestioned, unexamined support of the transcendent absolutes of the "natural," "real," "essential," or "authentic." In fact, as Stanley Fish reminds us in *Doing What Comes Naturally*, it is precisely what we consider natural that should be scrutinized most scrupulously. But trying to recognize, understand, and take a healthy critical look at the assumptions that shape our beliefs about teaching writing and reading is not simply a matter of scratching beneath the surface of practice to uncover theory. The surface-depth metaphor denies the dialectical play of theory and practice; theory is implicated in every move we make. We often fool ourselves, says Fish, into thinking that we can simply "do" theory, when doing theory usually adds up to talking theory or, as he puts it, to "theory-talk" (*Doing* 14).

But current theory talk in these post-Saussurian, post-Freudian, postmodern constructivist moments has, nevertheless, been influential. As the novelist and critic William S. Wilson puts it in an essay entitled "And/Or: One or the Other, or Both": In "everyday life in the postmodern world . . . , most concepts should be pluralized." It is "Not The Truth, but truths. The answer to the great question of agenda, What is to be done? is twofold: pluralize, relativize, and expect answers not to be one answer" (11). These currently fashionable constructs of plurality and relativity are implicated in recent narrative theories: we know that there is no one story of an event, but there are stories; no history, but histories. Stories arise out of specific rhetorical situations, cultural contexts, and historical moments: they are relative to time, place, gender, race, ideology. They represent ways of knowing, ways of constructing our lives and our values. To *narrate*, according to the word's Greek etymology, is to know.

We know that all narratives are narrated; that however they are shaped into chronicle or news story, diary or lab report, autobiography or gossip, they are selected, ordered, and formed, used by the teller to tell a tale at that moment, at that time; and that the "same" tale told tomorrow or the next day will be shaped, in part, by the pressures of that telling at that moment. We know that representation of an event is always belated, always deferred, always after the event; that memory in language unsettles the already told; that each telling tells differently; that there are multiple positionings or versions; that the textual conventions of fiction and nonfiction must be called into question. "Stories . . . they're all composed; they're all fiction. Somebody made them up," says the villager Hugh Nolan in Henry Glassie's remarkable study of the Irish ceili in *Passing the Time in Ballymenone* (37).

From Bible stories to the psychoanalytic couch, from the six o'clock news to the *National Enquirer*, from history to soap opera, we are engaged in narrative acts. Narrative theorists are considering not only how but also why we use narratives in our daily lives. In transforming events into narrative discourse, what are we doing? Are we passing the time or teaching a lesson, entertaining or preaching, remembering or criticizing, making sense of our lives by repeating the past to rehearse the future or trying to settle the unsettled by holding things still? Or is it perhaps the opposite: reopening the past to disrupt, deconstruct, reinterpret, renegotiate, unsettle? Some narratologists make claims for universal stories, for deep structure, for Ur-narratives: Cinderella *is* Cinderella, from China to France. Others resist the notion of universals and deep structure as a Neoplatonic illusion, or idealization, and situate each tale in context, in history. Some of the most compelling work in narrative these days comes to us from folklore and anthropology (Kirshenblatt-Gimblett; Toelken; Glassie), history (Darnton; H. White; Ricoeur), sociolinguistics (Hymes; Goffman; Labov; Shuman), and even the natural sciences, as scientists look at how scientific discourse is made (Gould; Fleck)—and from literary critics who are reading for "master plots" and narrative metaphors (Jameson; Kermode; Beer; Bowie) to determine the ways in which the tacit knowledge of a culture overdetermines the ways we give and receive stories. These authors all learn, especially, from the inexhaustible flow of stories in daily life, from the ordinary, typically unremarked uses of story. What is remarkable here is that the daily and the literary are often juxtaposed, even intertwined, so that traditional disciplinary and generic boundaries are brought into question: What is the difference between the well-formed story in literature and in life? they are asking. What are the differences and similarities between fiction and nonfiction? And how useful are these distinctions?

So where are we in composition? What are our constructs in our work on narrative? How do we "give" narrative assignments—and what do such assignments represent about our inherent assumptions about representing actual events, our epistemologies? Do we consider narrative problematic? Or do we, rather, take it to be natural for student writers to automatically and unproblematically transform events into narrative discourse?

I wonder if this assumption isn't still generally true: when narrative assignments are given, I suspect that they are presented uncritically and unproblematically. I speak here specifically of what has come to be known as the personal essay, the personal narrative, the autobiographical essay, or the narrative essay. Students at all levels of the curriculum, from elementary to postsecondary school, are asked to write about or represent or "re-create" or even "reproduce" their actual experiences, to write about a so-called significant or memorable or meaningful experience in their own lives, to represent in narrative discourse something that actually happened to them. The "what I did on my summer vacation" assignment is still very much alive, albeit well disguised.

Typically, the personal essay appears at the beginning of a course or even a curriculum: it is assumed that students can write easily, "naturally," without much thought, about what has happened to them. They have the data—the "reality"—at hand. Writing, according to M. H. Abrams's metaphor for classical poetics, is a mirror, a reflection of the real world. The text is, therefore, a reflection of the student's real life, the assumption being that the narrative will virtually write itself. Students are often advised to let the order of things order the discourse or to begin where things "naturally" begin, as if beginnings were not composed. (Textbook talk tells much about the ways we construe narrative: if we ask students to "reproduce" or "re-create" or "represent," it makes a difference.)

Narrative is typically positioned within the traditional four modes of discourse and seen, along with description, as one of the "simple" modes: on the other side of the great divide are exposition and argument, considered more complex, more "cognitively" demanding modes. Narrative is typically the beginning point; argument, the end. This is still the narrative form—the plot—of countless composition courses and textbooks, of writing samples collected at the beginning of semesters, and of proficiency exams. Here is a characteristic assignment for writing a personal essay, used, in this case, for a recent research study of "teachers' comments":

Please write a brief essay on the following topic:

Think of a time when you had to make a decision about something of major importance to you, or the last time you had to choose between some significant alternatives. In your essay, describe the situation and your decision in as much detail as possible. Some things you might want to consider in writing your essay are how you felt about having to make the decision, what factors influenced your decision, and how you felt after you made the decision.

(Anson 341)

The key words, for me, are "major importance," "significant alternatives," "felt about having to make the decision," and "felt after you made the decision." The assumption here is that this is a manageable task, that students will have little difficulty in producing a text; in fact, the researcher labels this "instrument" for collecting data "an easy task" (341). The teachers' comments, as reported in the study, generally attended to the life in the text—not to the text—and to asking students to tell more about the life, encouraging them to be forthcoming about what actually happened, to be concrete, to provide evidence, to say how they felt, and to tell the truth.

Would we? Should we rightly expect students who are writing on-site, to strangers, to write on events of major importance, in the first place, and on their feelings, in the second?

There is no doubt that the life, for all of us, is there for inscribing, for providing material. But what do we do with the material, and how should we frame representations for inscribing or authoring a life? How should we frame such representations in the teaching of composition, and how might we revise our own assumptions and discourse about narrative? These are the questions we need to ask.

Life versus Text

For one, as teachers of composition, we can usefully distinguish the life from the text, the events being represented, the "what happened," from the procedures for representing what happened—the textual options. We ask students, then, for their texts, not their lives. The distinction is crucial: the discourse is not the event. It is not real life. To distinguish event from discourse is to respect the confusions, mutabilities, shifts, and needs of memory, to problematize memory; it is to foreground, in the classroom, questions about how and why we remember, how writing itself transforms memory, and how discourse arises out of the writing or telling situation. Writing about the past represents a play between voices of the past and of the present writing moment, between what Virginia Woolf, in *Moments of Being*, calls the "I-then" and the "I-now" (75). Sherwood Anderson, in a metadiscursive moment in *A Story Teller's Story*, remarks on the difference:

> Could I then have had all the thoughts I am now about to attribute to myself? Probably not. But these notes make no pretense of being a record of fact. . . . [I]t is likely that I have not, and will not, put into them one truth, measuring by the ordinary standards of truth.   (100)

The present writing moment works on and reworks the past: we enable our students to recognize that the event and the discourse are always in dialectical play, involving several voices—in harmony, in discord—and that the writing itself offers opportunity for exploring the differences and similarities between the *then* and the *now*. The rhetorical situation, the pressures of the task, the moment itself, the listener, the context, and the writer's "affective volitional" needs and desires (as Vygotsky puts it, in *Thought and Language*) all influence and shape the writing. As writers, we can then explore the textual conventions, constraints, options, and possibilities of the particular task—transforming an event into an autobiography or an essay that makes a point or states a thesis, if need be, or transforming the event into a sociological case study, or transforming the event into fiction. Genre, too, becomes problematic (what, after all, is an essay? what is fiction? nonfiction?), and with various transformations of the "same" event into different genres, student writers can confront writerly questions: If I want this transformation to "feel real," then what do I have to do? What are the textual and cultural conventions for making a narrative feel real? What choices do I have? Dialogue? The present tense? Paratactic (rather than hypotactic) syntax, to give the sense of hitherto unknown events unfolding before the reader's eyes? Saving the point for last? Using implicit evaluation? If I want to use this material to make a point about a childhood event, then that is how I will use it—but that is not the only way events can be transformed, and however I choose, I am a writer choosing.

The questions raised by this poststructural embrace of pluralism and multiple perspectives might disturb: What is the truth? Writing the personal essay is not now automatic, not taken for granted. Thrown into relief are questions about writing and language, about truth and truths. As Woolf puts it in *Orlando*, "Green in nature is one thing, green in literature another. Nature and letters seem to have a natural antipathy; bring them together and they tear each other to pieces" (3).

In teaching literature, we meet some of the same collisions when students read naively, as if the text were life, as if the characters were real people whose actions could be stopped, modified, reversed: "Oh, stop! Don't do it!" or "Now look what you've done!" They use their powers as readers for soap-opera readings, for divine intervention, treating characters like real people and not textual moves. To read critically, as Roger Shattuck tells us in *The Innocent Eye*, is not to have to forgo the pleasure of this kind of innocence—or hope—but to recognize that other, more educated, less innocent ways of reading are possible—not either/or but both/and or and/or (424).

To ask students to write authentically or truthfully or sincerely about events from their past lives is to deny the truths of language: not only that discourse is not the event but also that discourse transforms events. The event becomes the telling. There is no return to the event, except "virtually." The event is overtaken, mediated by language. And language is always belated, always deferred, always after the event. Freud's contribution to us—Jacques Derrida calls it *différance*—is the inescapable fact of belatedness, that we are always a step removed from this moment, that the telling is further removal, that we know things only belatedly—in rehashing the events of our days, in our dreams, our journals, on the psychoanalytic couch—and that we are continually revising those retellings.

When we look to events that are new, sudden, not yet cooked into language, we see story in flux, story in the making. We watch the language in the news story that is still unfolding: the nouns are fluid; the event is not yet named. It is not yet a war but an operation, an intervention, a deterrent, a defensive act, or an undeclared war. George Orwell, writing in 1937, remarks that "every war when it comes, or before it comes, is represented not as a war but as an act of self-defence against a homicidal maniac" (Editorial). When the "something that happened" stuns, shocks, rocks our senses, as, say, the destruction of the space shuttle *Challenger* did, the problematics of naming are brought into relief: as more and more information was presented, revealed, confessed, the event was transformed from tragedy to accident to human error to politics. We know from our own lives that we often fumble for words when still-raw experiences have not yet been cooked into stories: we rely on the already givens of euphemisms for what we do not want to or cannot yet say: death, disease, illness. We may have difficulty in transforming the event when we are victimized, overtaken, rendered powerless. With an accident or emergency surgery, where we are taken to the hospital in the middle of the night, months later we may find ourselves still playing with words, reduced to the passive voice: we were "taken ill," "operated on," or "stricken."

The language may not yet fit comfortably. The story has not yet solidi-
fied. The telling itself will be fundamental for finding the language that
suits, comforts, makes sense of what may still feel like surprise, shock,
or trauma. We fumble with the verbs, with the active or the passive: "I
went to the hospital"; "I was taken to the hospital." We keep telling,
repeating the story, showing our scars. These liminal states, where the
events are not yet easy in language, give us a good opportunity to see
how we transform and inscribe events, to see, as well, how time and
memory further transform; when the event is cooked over a few years,
we may find ourselves telling a comic version of being cargoed by
ambulance to the hospital one dark and stormy night. Not so, yet. And
then other voices and memory and time work on the event, so that
often we do not know what is ours and what is someone else's, particularly when we recall moments of crisis or childhood events. What is
"actual" memory, what is hearsay, what is family story?

> I look around at the walls, the window: it's the same, it hasn't
> changed, but the shapes are inaccurate as though everything has
> warped slightly. I have to be more careful about my memories. I
> have to be sure they're my own and not the memories of other
> people telling me what I felt, how I acted, what I said: if the events
> are wrong the feelings I remember about them will be wrong too.
> I'll start inventing them and there will be no way of correcting it,
> the ones who could help are gone. I run quickly over my version
> of it, my life, checking it like an alibi. . . .   (Atwood 82)

In this passage from Margaret Atwood's novel *Surfacing*, the protagonist returns to the cabin where she had spent her summers as a child
and considers now the slippage of memory, checking versions of the
past against the present moment, particularly now that the other witnesses, her parents, have died. How can she be sure (how can we?)
that the memories are her own?

All these questions—of memory, of the present reworking the past,
of representing time and distance, of witnesses and versions, of the
kinds of transformation (Atwood's text sounds autobiographical, but
it is called fiction)—enter the writing classroom as opportunities, considerations, invitations for writing, and for writing about writing. We
realize, too, that we can learn from writers of all genres—of nonfiction,
fiction, and poetry (Atwood the essayist, novelist, and poet), often dealing with the "same" material—and that we can play one off against the
other, to try their different waters.

Narrator versus Narratee

The transformation of events into narrative discourse assumes a listener or a reader or both; in fact, story grammarians (Prince; Genette, *Narrative Discourse*) typically distinguish four figures in narrative: the writer, the narrator, the reader, and the narratee, the term ascribed to an addressee (a "you," singular or plural) designated as such within the text ("Reader, I married him").[1] The term *narrator*, typically associated with works of fiction, can be used to represent the writing voice or persona or role of any story, fiction or nonfiction, prose or poetry. In literary studies, we accept the persona as a convention: Mark Twain is not Huck Finn; Ben Franklin is not Polly Baker; Marguerite Yourcenar is not the Roman emperor Hadrian. The problem with personal, autobiographical, or narrative discourse in composition, in large part, is that the "I" is, paradoxically, not problematized. Who is this "I" of student writing, and what are its potentialities? Not the least, it is an actual student writing for an actual instructor within an institution, where the instructor is paid to give the student a grade. The student cannot escape these constraints, nor can the instructor. Yet composition talk often asks students not only to write of significant, meaningful events in their personal lives but also to tell the truth, to be sincere and authentic, to write about their feelings or intentions. Smuggled into such demands for the truth is the essentialism of the real, authentic, stable self; ignored are questions about who we can be as writers and the opening up of writerly possibilities that arise out of considering multiple perspectives and voices, multiple versions and truths. We can offer students the enabling notion that, even in their autobiographical writings, the narrator is a stance, a perspective, an angle, in this version, this representation, and not the student confessing his or her authentic feelings or truths. The narrator becomes a role, a position, an angle of vision.

Students know full well about role: in childhood play, they try on voices, adopting others' incumbent rhetorics and affects. They know how to sound like the distraught parent, the loving grandmother, the frantic teenage sibling, the irate car driver. We know, too, that we play various roles as adults and that the voices we use do not necessarily remain constant as we move between our public and private worlds. Problematizing narrative, and particularly the narrator's role, enables students to try on different writing voices as rhetorical choices, with the realization that to transform any event into discourse is to frame it and that frames, as Erving Goffman puts it, call for analysis of the rhetorical and social situations. (For more on role and frames, see Summerfield; Summerfield and Summerfield, *Texts and Contexts*, "States of Mind," and *Frames of Mind*.)

I wonder if we need to know, or should even inquire, whether there is a life in the text, whether students are telling "the truth." Is it any of our business? If we do inquire, aren't we ourselves conflating life and text? Shouldn't our business be language, an exploration with our students about the writerly choices of, say, narrating—about the choices of noun or pronoun, the implications of such choices, and the possible effects on the reader; about the position the narrator takes toward the subject, where the "I" stands in relation to the event, as a participant or spectator, how much the "I" knows at the beginning of the text, how much the "I" knows at the end; about ways the narrator can effect changes of circumstance and consciousness within the text; or about ways the narrator might evaluate the events represented?

The Outer and the Inner Landscapes of Narrative

Evaluation is a key word here. E. M. Forster, in his durable collection of essays on fiction, *Aspects of the Novel*, talks of time and values in daily life:

> So daily life, whatever it may be really, is practically composed of two lives—the life in time and the life by values—and our conduct reveals a double allegiance. "I only saw her for five minutes, but it was worth it." There you have both allegiances in a single sentence.   (28–29)

Forster's terms *time* and *value* are the building blocks of William Labov's well-known work on the transformation of events into narrative discourse. Although Labov's primary purpose was to demonstrate the artistic merit and complexity of oral stories, specifically those of black street kids, his work is relevant to the personal narratives that we ask for in our composition classes. Labov distinguishes between the narrative, which must include at least two temporally related narrative clauses, and what he calls evaluation: "the means used by the narrator to indicate the point of the narrative, its raison d'etre, why it was told, and what the narrator is getting at" (366).

Evaluative devices value the narrative explicitly ("but it was worth it") or implicitly, through selection and ordering of detail; through grammar, particularly modals and adverbs; through emphases, pauses, repetitions, patterns, metaphors, rhythms, subtle shadings of detail; through putting the evaluation into another character's mouth ("he said that it was worth it"). All these devices our students can explore as rhetorical choices, potentialities, opportunities. The mere fact of telling or writing "this story," they realize, constitutes an evaluative act: we say that "this" story is worth telling, because we need to pass the time or fill up space or confront a break in the ordinary flow of daily life, because we want to settle our unease or discomfort with the new or unknown, or because we want the opposite—to unsettle, stir things up a bit, renegotiate meanings. What we get in the telling, we hope, will be any number of responses from our listeners: arousal, confirmation, support, agreement, disagreement, sympathy. We engage our cohorts in an exchange of values, and through them, we accommodate, assimilate that which unsettles and unnerves. Such an exchange is precisely what occurs in Jamaica Kincaid's remarkable novel *Annie John*, when the narrator, eleven-year-old Annie John, has just viewed a dead person for the first time, and she needs to tell her friends at school:

> At school, I told all my friends about the death. I would take them aside individually, so I could repeat the details over and over. They would listen to me with their mouths open. In turn, they would tell me of someone they had known or heard of who had died. I would listen with my mouth open. One person had known very well a neighbor who had gone swimming after eating a big lunch at a picnic and drowned. Someone had a cousin who in the middle of something one day just fell down dead. Someone knew a boy who had died after eating some poisonous berries. "Fancy that," we said to each other. (6–7)

We see here enactment not only of the need to tell but of the need to retell, much in the same way, I am sure, that young children need to be read the same story over and over again—particularly those tales that delight or terrify. How do we read Annie John's needs in this text? "Fancy that" is an explicit evaluative statement, but what is the unsaid, the illocutionary? We might well imagine Annie John's British-influenced elders on the island of Antigua exclaiming to each other, "Fancy that!" The speakers would, most likely, be the women the child hears talking with her mother—conferring with one another on daily events, gossiping. It is an adult phrase, equivalent, perhaps, in other more familiar contexts to "Would you believe it?" or "That's amazing!" or "Imagine that!" It is susceptible to a great variety of intonations—

skeptical, dismissive, delighted, and so on—which we can hear if we try the words aloud, if we perform the text.

The explicit evaluation, then—what the narrator claims that the story says or adds up to, the point of the story—can turn on any number of positionings, from the ostensibly serious to the ironic, from hyperbole to understatement. It is the locus for listeners to locate themselves on a wide spectrum of appropriate responses, from total acceptance to total rejection. Such explorations of language are available to us in any ordinary speech act: it is not a far distance from observing the workings of ordinary language to those of the literary text. Students themselves can become ethnographers of language, reading and interpreting the language they and their peers use to tell stories and comparing their findings with what they see in print. As teachers, we have much to glean from such speech-act theorists as Mary Louise Pratt in *Toward a Speech Act Theory of Literary Discourse*.

Exploring evaluative devices becomes much of the business of composition, as students consider how they want to affect their readers—whether they want to hit them over the head with a conventional thesis statement (an explicit evaluation) or to mystify, unsettle, and intrigue readers through implicit evaluative devices. Students must consider the problematics of the tellable; why we tell or write some narratives in the first place, which ones keep nagging at us and repeating themselves, often unbidden. Here, we might appeal to Kierkegaard on repetition and to Freud on the repetition compulsion.

Subjunctivization

In problematizing narrative, when we foreground questions about memory and language, about the potentialities of our transformations and the rhetoric of narration, we call into play what Jerome Bruner calls the "narrative imagination." Bruner is best known as a founder of cognitive psychology, a cohort of Piaget, and a scientist keenly committed to learning and teaching. A recent convert to narrative studies, he is currently collecting the autobiographies of four members of one family, to study multiple versions of the same story. His book *Acts of Meaning* challenges the directions of the so-called cognitive revolution, in which he was a leading participant. In *Actual Minds, Possible Worlds* he sets forth an agenda for the study of narrative. Bruner distinguishes two modes of thought, the "logico-scientific" and the narrative. The logico-scientific orders experience by constructing "general causes," "verifiable reference," and "test[s] for empirical truth," all leading to "good theory, tight analysis, logical proof, sound argument, and empirical discovery guided by reasoned hypotheses." The second mode of thought, which Bruner claims that we know less about, is the narrative, which leads to "good stories, gripping drama, believable (though, not necessarily 'true') historical accounts" (11). The logico-scientific rests on theoretical arguments being "conclusive or inconclusive"; the narrative rests on possibilities, uncertainties, contradictions, and gaps, and it is characterized by a superabundance of modals—what Bruner, building on the work of Labov and Todorov, calls "subjunctivization," a rhetoric not of certainty but of the possible.

Narrative constructs two landscapes simultaneously. One is "the landscape of action: agent, intention, or goal, situation, instrument, something corresponding to a 'story grammar.'" The other, an inner landscape, is that of consciousness: "what those involved in the action know, think, or feel, or do not know, think, or feel." The two landscapes, says Bruner, are "essential and distinct: it is the difference between Oedipus sharing Jocasta's bed before and after he learns from the messenger that she is his mother" (*Actual Minds* 11; see also Pavel). The outer landscape, we might say, neatly corresponds to Forster's notion of time, while the inner landscape corresponds to his notion of value.

There is much to consider if we try on Bruner's construct. If the logico-scientific takes us to the well-formed argument and the narrative takes us to the well-formed story, then where, in the teaching of composition, does narrative belong? To situate personal or autobiographical writings within the logico-scientific is to take on a rhetoric of the verifiable, the conclusive, the certain. We know these conventions well in composition: thesis, assertion, support, evidence, coherence, unity. Bruner would probably argue, however, that, such pigeonholing of narrative limits its potentialities, denies its possibilities, ignores the subjunctive, the speculative, the possible. I would argue that the conflation of memory and certainty that we often ask for in personal, autobiographical, or narrative writing is problematic. If the logico-scientific trades in certainties, the observable and verifiable, and if narrative trades in multiple perspectives and gaps, uncertainties and contradictions, then aren't we conflating two competing rhetorics: one deriving from science, logic, mathematics and the other from the literary, the humanities, the human sciences? These distinctions are worth exploring and debating.

To foreground our own uses of language in teaching language, we must weigh every word we use, every assignment we make, and consider the possibilities and impossibilities of what we ask students to do. In a recent graduate-level course on rhetoric and composition, I gave graduate teaching assistants the assignment of writing about a decision of "major importance." I asked them not to write the assignment but to "read" it, to imagine themselves at the beginning of a semester, writing for an instructor they did not yet know; I asked them, then, to subjunctivize the situation, to jot down what might be going through their minds if they were students about to do the task. They were surprised: they all remembered having written such "innocent" assignments as students, and they had frequently given such assignments in their own classes. In our discussion, many of them reported that the prompt did evoke memories of significant events in their own lives but that as each memory surfaced, they immediately vetoed it, precisely because they didn't want to reveal anything of importance to an inquiring stranger. Nor did they want to funnel their memories into the confined space of what they saw as the conventions of the brief essay. They spent much of the time trying to find a safe subject, one that did not reveal their feelings. The task, which called for "psychologizing" about feelings, was, in the end, not manageable, not automatic.

Bruner's construct, the narrative imagination, invites us to reconsider our notions of narrative in the teaching of composition, to explore it as an act of mind. Such imaginings invite us to consider the potentialities of subjunctivization; to consider the "as if" or the "if I were"; to stand in another's story, to entertain multiple, even opposing, voices in our own stories, a Bakhtinian *heteroglossia*; to consider, as it were, possible worlds. And we are asked to consider the binary of narrative and argument itself, its usefulness, its logic, and to set it against other models, as we find, for example, in Dick Leith and George Myerson's *The Power of Address*, which suggests that all narratives constitute parts of an ongoing argument, that the timeworn distinction between narrative and argument, whereby argument is valorized or privileged at the expense of narrative, demonstrates a failure to recognize the pervasiveness of fiction as argument, that all great fictions (*War and Peace*; *Middlemarch*; *To the Lighthouse*) can be read as great arguments. It may be time for new constructs altogether. We can problematize these issues and use them to initiate a debate both for ourselves and for our students about the relations and the interactions between narrative and argumentative modes. In the writing and reading of narratives across disciplines and across cultures, we can foreground these and other problematics of narrative, considering questions about memory, time and value, event and discourse, and metadiscourse. We can foreground, particularly in our multicultural classes, alternative ways of telling stories that, in turn, challenge our notions of narrative and make us realize how reliance on narrative conventions is formed out of particular oral and textual conventions. If stories are fictions, if they are all made up, then who does such making up, and how do the stories we tell or write fit or not fit within the history of such conventions in the culture? And is one version of, or perspective on, a story better than another? What do we mean by *better*? What is history? Where are the gaps and uncertainties in this story, in this history? Where are the opposing voices? the oppositions? the resistance or tension or other points of view? the other arguments? the other truths? If such postmodern inclinations and explorations lead us to uncertainties, to few or possibly even no conclusions, to more questions, then how do we work within such constraints or freedoms? Will we find such constraints or freedoms constricting or freeing? Will we find that if we tolerate or embrace uncertainties or contraries, as Blake would put it, that we can live with the inconclusive?

Do we have any choice? Anna Chiarelli, a senior in my nonfiction writing workshop, responded to my comments about an autobiographical text she had written:

> It disturbed me when you referred to me several times in the third person [the narrator]. This is *my* story not that of some character I made up. It's a slice of my past as I see it now. I chose the areas of focus that I felt would convey an accurate impression of what my childhood was like. It's not *a* story, it's *the* story, in the most condensed form possible. *A* story sounds to me like a made-up fairy tale or the telling of a single incident. "The parents" are *my* parents, not some fictional entities I made up.

We talked about her response. I wondered if she was saying, in effect, "Just let me be; let me get on with this kind of assignment as I've always done it." Or was she saying that my use of such language (character, narrator, versions, multiple perspectives) challenges long-held beliefs and values about writing, beliefs that she isn't ready to tackle or doesn't want to tackle? Shouldn't writing, she wondered, be coherent, noncontradictory, and conclusive? At the moment, she is absorbed by some of these questions, which she says she now finds "interesting." We'll see.

Queens College, City University of New York

NOTE

[1] In narrative studies, we find rather heated debates on what to call the life and the text. If we are so inclined, we can problematize each move we make, scrutinizing each word: event, experience, story, plot, discourse, narrative, narrative time, actual time, and so on. For a useful and comprehensive introduction to narrative and literary studies, see Martin, and Mitchell, *Narrative*.

Essays and Experience, Time and Rhetoric

Douglas Hesse

I pass the time when it is bad and disagreeable; when it is fine I have no wish to pass it. I savour it and keep it back.
— Michel de Montaigne, "On Experience"

So it is meaningless to ask: Which is real, "real" or "imaginary" time? It is simply a matter of which is the more useful description.
— Stephen Hawking, *A Brief History of Time*

In *Time and Narrative* Paul Ricoeur contends that the relation between narrative and the temporal nature of human experience is "a transcultural form of necessity" (1: 52). He argues, in one of his characteristic and frustrating circularities, that we experience time only as it is articulated through narrative and that, furthermore, narrative is fully meaningful to the degree that we apprehend its temporality. Yet this is not to say that storytelling is inevitable. In fact, Ricoeur fears its demise:

> Perhaps, indeed, we are the witnesses—and the artisans of a certain death, that of the art of telling stories, from which proceeds the art of narrating in all its forms. . . . Nothing, therefore, excludes the possibility that the metamorphosis of the plot will encounter somewhere a boundary beyond which we can no longer recognize the formal principle of temporal configuration that makes a story a whole and complete story. And yet . . . and yet. Perhaps, in spite of everything, it is necessary to have confidence in the call for concordance that today still structures the expectations of readers and to believe that new narrative forms, which we do not yet know how to name, are already being born.
>
> (2: 28)

My central argument here is that essays, although hardly "new," offer one of the narrative forms that Ricoeur imagines. If Ricoeur is right in his postmodern fears and my argument is reasonable, a desire for concordance drives much of the current interest in the genre. This desire surfaces in such disparate places as Annie Dillard's (obviously self-interested) speculation that "the narrative essay may become the genre of choice for writers devoted to serious literature" (Introduction xvi) and the announcement in the program of the 1990 Conference on College Composition and Communication of a "series of sessions dedicated to reclaiming *the literary status of the essay*" (10).

There is a tremendous paradox in an assertion that, as other genres increasingly deny what Jean-François Lyotard calls the "solace of good forms" (*Postmodern Condition* 81), readers and writers might take consolation in the essay. After all, Samuel Johnson's characterization of the essay as a "loose sally of the mind" has long typed the genre. As Carl Klaus has illustrated, essayists throughout time have celebrated their freedom from convention and order, and promises of openness and democratic tolerance have lured teachers and scholars to argue that students should be encouraged to write essays. But the essay is less formless than it is resistant to traditional analytic methods. It can be understood as a peculiar relation among time, narrative, and experience. To grasp that relation is to resolve the paradox of the essay as concordant discordance and to understand the genre's current appeal.

Formlessness

Discussions of essay form have traditionally relied on analogies either to genres already possessing status in the English curriculum or to formal rhetoric. Robert Scholes and Carl Klaus's *Elements of the Essay* uses the tactic most directly, sorting the genre into the essay as poem, as story, as drama, and as argument—or the essay as essay. The basic division in this taxonomy—between three aesthetic-literary forms and one practical-rhetorical—has been implicit in essay criticism since at least 1915, when Hugh Walker distinguished between "the essay par excellence" and "all the rest" (3), and well before that, in Thomas De Quincey's "Letters to a Young Man" (53–61).

A recent instance of this tradition appears in W. Ross Winterowd's *The Rhetoric of the "Other" Literature*. Winterowd contrasts two sorts of texts. First are those that rely on discursive symbolism and semantic knowledge. These texts are efferential, in Louise Rosenblatt's terms, read to be consumed, their points to be abstracted from the hierarchical structures in which they are embedded in order to be "used" in new contexts. In contrast are texts that rely on presentational symbolism and episodic knowledge. These texts are aesthetic, in Rosenblatt's terms, read to be experienced, lyric, more "valuable" during the act of reading than after (*Reader*). Winterowd argues that essays may be of either type, with the degree to which they are presentational determining the degree to which they are deemed literary. Here, however, a problem encroaches. What is the source of the presentational? For Winterowd it is the text, even though only to the extent that the reader grants it:

> (1) Presentational works are often densely textured and hence reified. (2) The author frequently uses fictional devices such as invented dialogue. The author and the reader enter a special interpretive contract sanctioning the devices named above and others. . . .   (*Rhetoric* 16)

But where is that contract negotiated? Either the text is framed as presentational—perhaps by a book-jacket blurb that announces the contents as "literary nonfiction," perhaps by its presence in an English department course—or the text cues the reader to take it as presentational. In the latter case, readers make generic judgments, determining that when they encounter certain techniques, tropes, or types of narrator, then they are contending with a presentational text.

Deciding the presentational-discursive issue is important in Winterowd's rhetoric because it indicates the method of analysis to be used. Winterowd, like most recent critics, is interested in the "neglected" literary dimension. As a result of this focus, the ontogeny of essay criticism and theory now appears to be recapitulating the phylogeny of twentieth-century literary theory in general. Viewing essays as aesthetic objects has foregrounded the devices of aestheticism, and our vocabulary, as George Dillon notes, has been largely New Critical. But arguing that "what we can do to a poem or short story we can do to a presentational essay" does not grasp the "uniqueness" of the genre. I value the presentational-discursive dichotomy as a strategy for classroom discussions. I would value more having the relation between the two more shrewdly articulated.

The need to do so can be further seen in a book widely embraced in composition studies, Jerome Bruner's *Actual Minds, Possible Worlds*. Bruner's most often quoted proposal is that there are two basic modes of thought, one paradigmatic, the other narrative. These modes differ because "arguments convince one of their truth, stories of their life-likeness. The one verifies by eventual appeal to procedures for establishing formal and empirical proof. The other establishes not truth but verisimilitude" (11). Even if we leave aside the problematic conception of "lifelikeness," Bruner's invitation to slice the narrative so neatly from the paradigmatic fails in the analysis of works that are neither purely stories in the traditional sense nor arguments in the sense of thesis and support. The essay is left outside the taxonomy.

In contrast to this formalistic tradition, hermeneutic theories of the essay have scoffed at analysis. "Essay form is essay form," they claim. If the shape of the essay is the shape of anything, it is that of "thought" or "life." The essay, then, is mimetic of the author's mind and experience. As long as "mimetic of experience" indicates "experience as it has been socially constituted and mediated" rather than "as it really is," these pronouncements are reasonable. Where they fall short is in analytic power, for claims of form are at best profoundly tautologous, as in Georg Lukács's avowal that "in the works of the essayists form *becomes* destiny, it is the destiny-creating principle" (7) or in William Carlos Williams's musing that "the essay is the most human literary form in that it is always pure. . . . Whatever passes through it, it is never that thing" (321). We can escape this tautology by exploring the relation between experience as narrated in the essay and things said about, or as a result of, or in juxtaposition to, that experience.

Storied Propositions

In a previous discussion of this relation, I distinguished between *stories as essays* and *essays with stories*. Stories as essays consist entirely of first person narratives of experience, works like George Orwell's "A Hanging." In essays with stories, narrators recount incidents, but these stories are set pieces in a larger text that contains other elements, such as reflection, commentary, information, assertion, and so on, works like Virginia Woolf's "Thoughts on Peace in an Air Raid" or Lewis Thomas's "My Magical Metronome." And yet, the borders between "narrative" and "not narrative" in such works are hazy. Demonstrating this haziness would entail a more elaborate excursion than I wish to take up here, but the difficulty can be seen when we try to determine what counts as an "event" or "action" or "experience." For example, explaining experience as "lived events" that occur before being textualized, a distinction Jeannette Harris offers in characterizing some writing as "experience-based" and some as "information-based," only puts the problem off a step (145). Any text could be said to be a text of experience—of the author's experience with language, at the very least. Limiting experience to events ordered by a specific slice of time occurring before the writing of the essay may get us further. And the difference between story and not story may be cued by the tendency of narrators in essays to represent themselves as agents of, or participants in, the experiences they narrate. But the hallmark of the genre itself, not just its narrative elements, is the ever-present agency of the narrator.

As a result of this stickiness, I propose conceiving of the essay as story, its propositions as events, its traditionally narrative elements not as proving the essay's points but as giving those points a place in the story, in time. Such works are persuasive, finally, because stories are persuasive, offering readers the consolation of form. The truth of Orwell's assertion in "Shooting an Elephant"—"When the white man turns tyrant it is his own freedom that he destroys" (8)—depends not on his having marshaled sufficient evidence but on his having presented the events as causing the thought. The thought becomes a consequence, an entailment, of the events, and the proposition itself holds a place in narrative time.

Of course, propositions cannot avoid being in time. Passing through a text, the reader encounters one sentence after another and in doing so temporalizes both. And, of course, even an "isolated" proposition exists historically. I mean this observation in a fairly mundane way. If out of the blue I decide to look up a word in the dictionary, the act of reading the dictionary definition becomes an event in my own life.

If all language is language in time, it appears trivial to assert that essays are essays to the extent that they give propositions a place in time. Other texts contain self-reflection and abstractive commentary. But essays are essays because they present the timeliness of propositions more explicitly than do other texts. When Lyotard, in *The Postmodern Condition*, declares that "the essay (Montaigne) is postmodern, while the fragment (*The Athaeneum*) is modern" (81), he recognizes that essays offer truth not as timeless, logical, and stable but as always situational, constructed in experience, their tar paper and Sheetrock showing.

The timeliness of essays is figured by their narrators, who model a way of reading by presenting themselves as readers of their own experience. We can understand how they do so by recognizing two layers of experience in the essay. First (or at least having the rhetorical effect of being prior) are the experiences, the encounters with a scene, a thought, or a text that figure the essay's temporal dimension—Virginia

Woolf watching a moth die, for example. These are the propositions of existence: this happened; this is. Experience at this level is narrative in the conventional textbook sense: a story of something that happened. To help address a complication later, I'll call this Experience 1. As the essayist writes about or with or against or because of the occasioning experience, he or she produces a second layer in the essay, the experience of writing about Experience 1. I'll call this level Experience 2. Why call this level experience at all? Because the essayist represents it *as* experience, as if certain ideas or events cause others to come into existence. In the essay as story, Experience 2 subsumes Experience 1.

Readings

To illustrate these abstractions, we can start with an "easy" example, an essay that is classically narrative. Kathleen Stocking's "Graduation Day at Lake Leelanau St. Mary's" appears in her *Letter from the Leelanau*, a collection of "essays of people and place" (iii), the place a peninsula jutting into Lake Michigan west and north of Traverse City. The frame of "Graduation Day" is a May afternoon and evening, commencement for thirteen seniors at a venerable Catholic school. The essay begins in Stocking's childhood, "one spring evening," as she and her father fish from a bridge in Lake Leelanau, a village "at the narrows of the twenty-mile-long lake by the same name" (30). The scene is brief, a single paragraph, yet her physical position "at the narrows" figures her temporal position between the village's past and its present. Consider the movement in the following section:

> There was also in this village, on the shores of the lake, an ancient Catholic school. I remember the old cobblestone buildings, the broad lawns and the lake, the long shadows of late spring at eight o'clock and people strolling in the golden light.
>
> There are ways in which certain scenes, those observed from a train or car window, or certain magazine illustrations, those mindlessly gazed at while sitting in a doctor's office, impress themselves on one's mind so that they become images in the memory bank indistinguishable from the memories in one's own life, as if one had lived those moments, or is remembering them for some purpose as yet not encountered. And that's the way it was with that cobblestone church on the banks of the lake, as if the image was being saved for later use.

> Now I live in the village of Lake Leelanau, for reasons no more complex than those of people the world over who live twenty miles from where they grew up.   (30–31)

The first sentence of the second paragraph above is virtually a non sequitur except that, of course, we recognize the strategy as a leap characteristic of essays. Cohesion analysis easily establishes collocative ties between "scenes" and the static images of the preceding sentence, between "impress themselves on one's mind" and "I remember." And yet this sentence is more abstract than are others in this short passage. It makes a universal claim rather than a claim grounded in the time and place of the surrounding sentences. But the next sentence ("And that's the way it was . . .") embeds this "universal" assertion in the narrative, as if Stocking winks at her readers for assuming that she would aspire to something so grand. She uses the generalized memory of "this is how things always were in Lake Leelanau," which is Experience 1 material, to occasion the broader assertion, resulting in Experience 2 narrative.

The opening section continues with background, brings us to the present, and concludes with an explanation of why Stocking attends the graduation. She finds herself "walking between cobblestone buildings . . . almost as if time had collapsed around three decades," suddenly feeling that she "was living in the moment of the image or the memory" (31). The story is sparse and scenic. Writing about the rehearsal on the last day of school, a walk she takes between school's end and the ceremony, and the ceremony itself, she presents a succession of small details: a trout jumping in the lake, titles of tracts from the church narthex, the entire class roll, snatches of conversation overheard in classrooms. The stance is "objective," the technique one Chris Anderson has labeled "radical particularity" (*Style* 133–34). Several times Stocking departs from reporting what happened that day.

For example, when Mrs. Petroskey's fifth- and sixth-grade class is released for recess, Stocking presents information about Mrs. Petroskey, who we learn had herself gone to St. Mary's before moving for a time to Boston. Old yearbooks picture her at the prom. Mrs. Petroskey observes, "It's very odd to come back. . . . It's like going back in time to the early 1930s—without the Depression. I see myself walking up the stairs on the same floors" (35). Then the children return from recess, and we're back in the time of the story. A conventional view might be that this "digression" is a step out of time, mere exposition to action. But each step out of time retrieves material into the narrative present of the essay. Mrs. Petroskey links past and present both in the account of the school and, formally, in the essay itself.

The last half of the essay is more densely marked by these departures than the first is and the distance between past and present collapses. Walking through Lake Leelanau, Stocking perceives that "[i]n the dead air that exists between the afternoon of graduation and the onslaught of the tourist season, in the temporary vacuum, the illusion that the past is present is almost palpable"(35). Then the sun disappears, a cold "wind blows low upon the ground," and everything becomes "temporal . . . suddenly wispy, make-believe." In that moment, Stocking grasps that "[i]n order for this village community to come alive and really live again in the old way, new people coming in will have to be able to identify with it, with its values, and have practical reasons for being a part of it; nostalgia alone won't do it, and the chill [she feels] is partly that realization" (36). She represents the realization as coming in the moment of sudden darkness, as if it were brought on by the events around her. It is as though the physical changes cause the idea by putting Stocking not between past and present, where she's been throughout the piece, but between past and future. The cost of our accepting this proposition is slight, and it depends on our accepting the proposition as reasonably entailed by the events to this point in the essay. Curiously, in a short story we'd likely perceive the relation between the chill wind and the premonition of the future as hokey; by convention we're compelled to grant it in the essay. We accept the proposition because it has a place in Stocking's experience, not because it is empirically verifiable.

Stocking reads the day she narrates against the past and the future, both the town's and her own. The experience is meaningful because it can be extended through time, and Stocking's doing so models how we might read her experience against our own, not for extractable information, but for the associations it triggers. Now, all texts signal ways that they might be read. But essays (and certain intrusive first person fictions) provide an agent of reading in the text, an I who reads and who relates the traces of that reading. In essays like "Graduation Day," this I collapses Experience 2 into Experience 1. Readings of the experience are presented as occurring within the same time frame (in this case, the same day) as the experience. (For other examples, consider Gretel Ehrlich's "Looking for a Lost Dog" or E. B. White's "The Age of Dust.")

Dillard's "Singing with the Fundamentalists" offers a different model of reading by locating propositions "outside" the time of reported experience. The essay's first few pages describe its occasion. Dillard has spent several mornings singing with a student group in a campus courtyard. Then she moves the essay to another level: "I have taught some Fundamentalist students here and know a bit of what they think" (13). This section of the essay is not narrative in the sense of reporting events as preceding one another in chronological order. While the discussion in the section is thematically linked to the singing experiences (both are "about" fundamentalists), it does not comment directly on them. Dillard presents herself as writing about the experience at a distance, eschewing tags like "this is what I thought about the morning ritual." Instead, speaking generally of fundamentalists that she knows, she observes, "[They] read the Bible. I think they all 'believe in' organic evolution. The main thing about them is this: There isn't any 'them' " (13). And then, moving even farther "away" from the occasion, she comments on how the media have depicted fundamentalism and then returns to narrate other singing sessions.

If we find these observations compelling, it is substantially because Dillard has placed them within a form, a story, that we accept as "natural." Narrative is self-occasioning—or at least we treat it as such; the mere fact that something is a story compels us to read it, the form serving as its own justification. (We may stop, of course, if it's badly told.) The middle section of Dillard's essay, the apparent step out of narrative time, from Experience 1 to Experience 2, functions as an event in the essay as story. It invites us to view the group differently after Dillard's general pronouncements than we did before. Before the break, we may take the singers as odd and out of touch, but after it we're asked to regard them more seriously. While Stocking collapses Experience 1 and Experience 2, Dillard juxtaposes "lived events" and "ideas." As a result, the relation between events and ideas is reflexive, each adding to the other. In other words, while Stocking explicitly configures events and thoughts about those events by locating abstractive commentary within Experience 1, there is no explicit "about" in Dillard's piece. Rather, readers perform the configurative act, having learned to do so by their familiarity with the genre. The way students read such texts is a good indication of their previous experience with essays. Students in my advanced writing classes, for example, respond either with total dismay or with delight to David Quammen's "Strawberries under Ice," a piece that cuts a fairly complex personal narrative against technical information about glaciers. Those who like it tend to see the relation between the two as metaphoric and to see a progression in the technical material. Those who don't tend to see the piece as chaotic bits of information.

A more complicated essay as story, combining both Dillard's and

Stocking's strategies, is Langdon Winner's "The Whale and the Reactor." Winner begins with a day's visit to the Diablo Canyon nuclear power plant, which is located in a section of California coast that was inaccessible to him as a boy in the 1950s. Approaching the plant, he crests a hill and the reactor appears, its tandem domes looking slightly "like breasts protruding from some oversized goddess who had been carefully buried in the sand" (165). Winner continues:

> At precisely that moment another sight caught my eye. On a line with the reactor and Diablo Rock but much farther out to sea, a California grey whale suddenly swam to the surface, shot a tall stream of vapor from its blow hole into the air, and then disappeared beneath the waves. An overpowering silence descended over me.
>
> In "The Virgin and the Dynamo" Henry Adams tells of an epiphany he experienced during his visit to the Great Exposition in Paris in 1900. . . .   (165–66)

Like Stocking in the opening of "Graduation Day," Winner steps out of time, filling the silence with Henry Adams. Simultaneously, he puts Adams's text (the summary continues a medium-length paragraph) into time when he returns to the opening scene: "My own epiphany when confronted with the nuclear dynamo did not suggest anything as grand as a law of historical development. But that moment at Diablo Canyon crystallized a lifetime of experience" (166). Adams's text is thus gathered into Experience 2.

Winner then launches into several pages of memory, analysis, example, and assertion. In pieces of shuffled chronology, he tells of his childhood in San Luis Obispo. While an undergraduate at Berkeley and a participant in the free speech movement, he works summers at the Pentagon as a systems analyst intern. His parents buy their first television set in 1953. He sees the bones of his feet through a shoe store fluoroscope. He watches a late-1950s television commercial for a dairy conglomerate that bought out local dairy concerns, thus ending glass bottles on doorsteps. About two-thirds of the way through, Winner offers perhaps the best candidate for his thesis: "If there is a distinctive path that modern technological change has followed, it is that *technology goes where it has never been*" (174). As evidence, he briefly characterizes the urbanization of the countryside and then moves, climactically, to the deepest time of the essay.

In the eighteenth century, missionaries under Junípero Serra discovered that they could end the local Indians' burning of mission buildings by replacing thatch roofs with tile. This tactic signals "the beginning of the end of native American resistance in California. . . . At present, the Vatican is studying Father Serra's qualifications to see if he will become the first North American priest to achieve sainthood" (175). Then Winner inserts a break and returns, for three final pages, to Diablo Canyon. But before I discuss the end, let me characterize some aspects of the long middle section of Winner's essay.

First, it *is* a middle section. The Diablo Canyon incident is best seen not merely as a frame tacked on to "catch the reader's attention," in best composition textbook advice. It does so, of course, but more profoundly it gives the middle text a physical and temporal position in the middle; thus the incident stands in the same relation to Winner's essay as Dillard's observations in "Singing" do to her essay. Winner, too, presents a mode of reading that is additive and reflexive. Experience and assertion gather significance as they stimulate other experiences and ideas around them. Consider this brief passage:

> It was this tendency of our California community to accept radical transformations of its way of life, to accept sweeping changes generated from far-away sources with little discussion, deliberation, or thought to the consequences that I now see as something truly astonishing. We were technological somnambulists wandering through an extended dream.
>
> Much of this sleepwalking was, in retrospect, a product of pure innocence and ignorance. For instance, when I was a boy, my parents and I used to engage in a wonderful ritual of buying shoes. One of the things I liked best about it was that as you were being fitted, you walked over to a little machine, stepped onto a platform, and stared into an eyepiece that enabled you to take a long look right through the Buster Brown shoes and into your feet.   (169)

Now, the shoe incident might be seen as evidence—even sufficient evidence—of the ignorant somnambulism posited in the previous two sentences. Certainly, though, the truth of that assertion could be challenged, perhaps with a call for other examples. Winner, however, points readers away from that kind of insistence. These propositions are embedded in a sequence, the mention of technological ignorance seeming merely to occasion his recalling the Buster Browns of his youth.

Rejecting the propositions as undemonstrated would not only mark a reader as callously unwilling to grant the writer the memory of his past but also resist the successive "this then this" nature of the piece. Early in the essay, Winner confronts us with an explanation of his technique. Characterizing the customary demand that writers give "adequate evidence to back up assertions of fact, and proffer arguments in an unbiased, logical way," he stresses that

> writers owe their readers something more. To be self-reflective, self-critical about the substance and method of one's thinking can help resolve puzzles that readers have about a work and its relationship to their own sense of things. I do not favor personal confessionals for their own sake, but, when all is said and done, books have intensely personal origins. Communities are shaped by the shared experiences of the people in them. To talk about these experiences directly may help reveal the ideas and sensibilities we hold in common. (167)

Winner is disingenuous—or more likely just crafty—in avowing that the good of the readers requires writers to share the personal origins of ideas. Essaying in this manner protects as much as it exposes, removing propositions from clear view as propositions. Like Stocking, Winner realizes, "[S]omehow I'd gotten caught in the middle" (168), between past and present.

This being in the middle—between experiences, between layers of the past, between experience time and essay time—appears to be the essayist's characteristic stance. E. B. White, for example, inhabits it always, as do Richard Selzer, Joan Didion, and Loren Eiseley. It is the stance of the narrator, fixed in a present, making of a past a story that is but a future to readers as they read it. Didier Coste characterizes narrative not as inherently temporal writing but as "the discourse that elicits thinking about the passage of time" (9). Essayists create such a discourse by presenting their ideas as experience.

In the final three-page section of "The Whale and the Reactor," Winner returns to that sunny day at Diablo Canyon and, in that context, discusses technical demerits, protests, the licensing of the reactor. The last paragraph jumps to a time "two years after [his] epiphany" and to a speech that Winner gave in San Luis Obispo. The final section rounds everything off; the last paragraph offers a triple closure: of the section, the essay, the book. The preceding parts of the essay are put into a more distant past, transformed by the history of the essay that has brought us to this conclusion.

Essays and Mimesis

In the 1960s and 1970s narratologists aspired to provide a systematic and exhaustive accounting of what stories are and how they work; this narratological tradition mirrors the work of classical rhetoricians who attempted to catalog tropes and strategies of persuasion. An instrumental assumption was that narrative is inherently mimetic, that it naturally mirrors reality. Positing mimesis in such a way provided a fulcrum of analysis, since narratives could then be discussed in terms of their deviation from "the norm." Seymour Chatman's description of the long-standing distinction between "story," or *fabula*, and "discourse," or *sujet*, caps this tradition. Stories tell the events as they really could have happened in "normal" chronological time, whereas discourse reports the events as the writer or filmmaker ordered them for presentation. By the later 1970s the idea of narrative as mimetic of the "natural world" was replaced by the fulcrum of narrative as symptomatic of cultural practices. The cultural critique, given early formulation by Fredric Jameson in *The Political Unconscious*, rejects the idea that narrative is natural and accepts narrative as a master trope that, drawing power from the assumed naturalness of storytelling, indicates what is possible and good. Instead of being unproblematically mimetic, narrative is "an inherently distortive form" (Brodsky 9).

Ricoeur's phenomenology mediates the natural-cultural dichotomy of narrative theory. It contests readings of Aristotle's *Poetics* that shallowly interpret mimesis as the imitation of the world, the tracing of form that exists in nature. In fact, Ricoeur frets that modern novelists, believing that since the world is fragmented and chaotic so should be fiction, have merely returned "mimesis to its weakest function—that of replicating what is real by copying it" (2: 14). He argues, rather, for an understanding of mimesis in terms of *muthos*, which he defines as "emplotment," "the organization of the events," and "activity," the "operation of organizing the events into a system, not the system itself" (1: 34, 48). The test of mimesis, then, is whether a plot exists. And the test of a plot? The "combination of the incidents" (Aristotle, *Poetica* 1450a), the creation of a beginning, middle, and end. Note that Aristotle does not mention bringing incidents into some "shape" or "chronology" provided by nature. The apparently shallow formula of beginning, middle, and end is shrewder, since it describes the function of plot in its own terms. This conception of emplotment is significant because it broadens the concepts of event and narrative. Instead of events consisting of "physical occurrences as they may happen in the world," they might be seen as movement from a past to a future. Narrative is better understood as the creation of plot. Plot, further, is the configuration through time of disparate events. (Keep in mind the broader definition of *events*.)

Ricoeur's view of emplotment aligns closely with Walter Fisher's narrative paradigm, which asserts that there are two modes of human communication—the rational, largely needed by experts "to conduct or account for their special fields of argument," and the narrational, which the public needs to "conduct or account for good moral argument about major decisions of the day" (McGee and Nelson 139). Unlike Bruner, Fisher sees narrative as necessarily rhetorical and probabilistic. It draws power not from mapping reality correctly but from matching an audience's beliefs about what reality is and how it is constituted. Wlad Godzich summarizes the process of identification through narrative, a process "in which the narratee finds himself or herself interpellated by the narrative program of the work he or she is receiving and thus reconstituted into the subject of this narrative program" (xiii). The persuasive appeals of narrative are partially ethical, dependent on the audience's sense of a reliable teller, but they are more significantly formal, since "reality" is presented in a form deemed to be real.

To see essays as stories requires our perceiving them as emplotted. We have long internalized the conventions for recognizing and following the plots of "typical" stories: realistic novels, television sitcoms. To read essays as stories, though, we must attend to the guidance provided by essay narrators themselves. The essay as story persuades through two dimensions. One is the configurative. Readers perceive experience as having caused ideas or the narratives of other experiences and these, in turn, still others, until a sense of closure allows readers to grasp all as part of a larger whole. The second is the extensive. The essay pushes experience beyond the mere succession of fragmenting nows. As the writer transforms Experience 1 into Experience 2, he or she creates the possibility of Experience 3, readers making the essay part of their experience, invited and taught to do so by the figure of the essay narrator. Proponents of transactionalist theories of reading may reasonably protest that configuration and extension are "located" in the reader, not in the essay. But the essay, through its narrator, tells readers how to read experience in a way that even, say, Joseph Conrad's Marlow does not.

The Rhetoric of Concordance

In the summer of 1990 my family took a vacation to the north of Michigan's lower peninsula. Scott and Mary Beth, friends from graduate school, were living in a cabin on a hill overlooking cherry orchards and Good Harbor Bay. We joined them. One afternoon, after scrambling over the Sleeping Bear Dunes, we visited land they owned. Distant vistas, especially of water, are prized here, and atop a ridge on this acreage were concrete footings from an old observation tower. Built near the turn of the century, it was billed as the Top of the World. For a few pennies, visitors used to climb above the pines. There they could make Glen Lake and Lake Michigan, blue slivers from the ground, take on depth as well as breadth. We hiked around what used to be the base of the Top of the World and then back to our cars, to buy ice cream at a small country store.

The store, a 1950s version of a 7-11 or Quick Trip, one-eighth the size, carried milk and bread and Chapstick and fishing bobbers and yesterday's Detroit papers. We learned that the young woman running it, the owner's daughter, was a student at Hope College, where Scott had taught two years earlier. On the glass case above the butter brickle and fudge swirl are a half dozen copies of *Letters from the Leelanau*. I'm drawn to the book by the oil painting of the Manitou Islands on the cover. The top copy is signed by Kathleen Stocking, "June 1990," and I buy it. There are no other books in the store.

In September, as I wrote this chapter, the reason that I turned to "Graduation Day" is complicated beyond my desire to challenge the already-forming essay canon. For in writing about Stocking's book, I vicariously drew that summer, those friends, that country store into my broader experience. And just now, in telling the story of my "finding" the essay, I place my experience into yours. At the 1990 MLA convention in Chicago, John Schilb asked me to send him a copy of "Graduation Day." The book is not yet in University of Maryland bookstores. A month later, Schilb reports having read a review of *Letters from the Leelanau* in the *New York Times Book Review*.

The essay is the latest high ground for teachers and scholars troubled by continual assaults on the individual author and the very desirability, in political terms, of order. Some claim that writing essays gives students a kind of authority that is lacking in an academy dominated by "the hegemony of exposition" (DiPardo 86). The benefits of this authority are simultaneously motivational (students who think that their writing matters will take the role more seriously), political (the essay offers a means of resisting academic totalizing), epistemic, and cognitive-developmental. Others counter that the personal essay, in fact, does not empower students because the genre is not valued in the ways that more "practical" discourse is. Beyond this view is a more serious challenge: social constructionism's contestation of the autonomous self. Even the staunchest apologist for this "democratic genre" must realize that it is a genre and it has a history; students asserting selves within it do so in ways that they do not themselves wholly invent.

Carl Klaus suggests that the essay "seeks to convey the sense of a human presence" (173). Of course, the reader's desire for such a presence in these trans-Derridean days can be read symptomatically as the ideology of stability and natural order. Ricoeur's work itself, and the Heideggerian tradition from which it stems, has been critiqued in these terms. It's beyond my scope here to defend Ricoeur—beyond my interests finally, too, since I share much of the skepticism. But the discussion of narrative emplotment in *Time and Narrative* conveys to me a sense (perhaps a better word is *symptom*) of why the essay has gained recently in popularity. Essays invite us to believe that individual consciousness can order the experiences of life and ideas, can make some progressive textual whole of elements that have no intrinsic relation to one another—my summer vacation, for example, and Paul Ricoeur. We find that belief somehow comforting.

This is the narrative rhetoric of the essay. Its ideology can and ought to be thoroughly blasted by cultural criticism. And yet, the essay directly confronts a paradox of postmodern theory, one that Vincent Pecora formulates succinctly:

> [N]o matter how theoretically necessary the dismantling of the individual subject might be, theory embarks on such a course at its peril, for the hypostatized center of domination that the abstract individual represents is also in many cases the last form of resistance to domination available. (16)

A strange political expediency may compel us, then, to preserve the enabling fiction of the autonomous essayist rendering personal truths. While the genre may seem nearly reactionary, its writers and critics woefully naive in their celebration of "the individual," it depends on something shrewder. By foregrounding themselves as agents of order, essayists display knowledge as entailed by experience; when readers extend "truths" beyond the text, they reveal their own desire for order. A version of things is always a version of things to someone. As a consequence, we should view personal or familiar or exploratory essays not as presented artifacts but as emplotted experiences, persuading by storying propositions into their readers' experiences, giving them time.

Illinois State University

Street Fights over the Impossibility of Theory: A Report of a Seminar

Lester Faigley

> *You wrapped your head in theory like yards of gauze.*
> —Marge Piercy, "Song of the Fucked Duck"

1

E387L: The Politics of Writing

Instructor: Lester Faigley
Fall Semester 1990

In *The World, the Text, and the Critic*, Edward Said describes an exchange between Noam Chomsky and Michel Foucault on Dutch television in the early 1970s:

> Both men agreed on the necessity of opposing repression [but] for Chomsky the sociopolitical battle had to be waged with two tasks in mind: one, "to imagine a future society that conforms to the exigencies of human nature as best as we understand them; the other to analyze the nature of power and oppression in our present societies."
>
> Foucault assented to the second without in any way accepting the first [since for Foucault] "justice in itself is an idea which in effect has been invented and put to work in different societies as an instrument of a certain political and economic power or as a weapon against that power." [246]

Foucault's position in this debate aligns him with theory referred to as "postmodern," which abandons the possibility of transcendent, universal truths and instead places truth within local discourses.

For Foucault and Jean-François Lyotard, totalizing truth entails closure, and the striving for the certainty of reason brings about authoritarianism; witness the Jacobins and Lenin. By overturning the logocentric philosophical tradition and the rational, centered subject of liberal humanism, Foucault and Lyotard privilege giving voice to difference even when those differences are uncomfortable for us to accommodate.

Opposed to postmodern theory is a tradition following from Marxism called "critical theory," whose most active proponent today is Jürgen Habermas. Habermas sees postmodern theory as an abandonment of the Enlightenment and a return of irrationalism. Habermas would preserve the project of the Enlightenment by shifting rationality from the centered subject to the pragmatics of language use.

This course will engage these two positions in a dialogue by introducing a third position, nonessentialist feminism, which draws from both bodies of theory. These theoretical discussions will then be directed toward specific issues of writing and writing pedagogy, such as how textual selves are constructed in the play of discourses, how intentionality is presented in writing textbooks, and how electronically mediated communication has led to multiple subjectivities.

Students can expect to write one-page reaction papers to readings, a short analysis, and an article-length paper for the course (15–20 pp.).

Texts:
> Michel Foucault, *Discipline and Punish*
> Jean-François Lyotard, *The Postmodern Condition*
> Linda J. Nicholson, ed. *Feminism/Postmodernism*
> Mark Poster, *Critical Theory and Poststructuralism*
> Chris Weedon, *Feminist Practice and Poststructuralist Theory*
>
> James A. Berlin, "Rhetoric and Ideology"
> Patricia Bizzell, "Beyond Anti-foundationalism"
> Linda Brodkey, "On the Subjects of Class and Gender"
> Hélène Cixous and Catherine Clément, "A Woman Mistress"
> Marilyn M. Cooper, "Unhappy Consciousness in First-Year English"
> Rosalind Coward, "Feel Good, Look Great," "Pouts and Scowls," "The Royals"
> James Donald and Stuart Hall, Introduction
> Lester Faigley, "Judging Writing, Judging Selves"
> Michel Foucault, "The Subject and Power"
> Ann George, "Analysis of *The St. Martin's Guide to Writing*"

Julia Kristeva, "Woman's Time"
Suzanne Moore, "Identity Shifts"
John Schilb, "Composition and Poststructuralism"
John Trimbur, "Cultural Studies and Teaching Writing"
Victor J. Vitanza, "Three Countertheses"

2

I wondered who would take this course. Six people signed up.[1] Three were from the English department; one each came from speech, journalism, and American civilization. Three were women; three men. Three were foreign students: two from Britain and one from Germany.

"Why did you take this seminar?" I asked on the first day.

One of the students, Bill Shanahan, answered, "What you're trying to do is impossible. I want to see how you're going to attempt to pull it off."

3

Shanahan's response was surprising only because it came before the course had even started and because of his certainty that we could not do what my course description suggested we could—that we as a group could bring debates within and among poststructuralism, postmodern theory, critical theory in the tradition of the Frankfurt school, and feminist theory to bear on practical issues in the teaching of writing. On the first day, I took Shanahan's reduction of my course to a theater of the absurd for his amusement to be something like Stanley Fish's dismissal of the practicality of theory (though I soon came to realize that I had underestimated Shanahan). In "Anti-foundationalism, Theory Hope, and the Teaching of Composition," Fish admits that there is an affinity between antifoundationalism and a process-oriented approach to composition, but he questions whether being more aware that meaning is situated somehow leads to more effective teaching. He contends that our being "able to announce that we are situated does not make us more situated, and even when we could not announce it, being situated was our situation" (348).

I began from the opposite assumption: that realizing we are situated very much changes our situation. Efforts to apply the theory that Fish calls antifoundationalist and others call postmodern drift toward the impossible not because theory is irrelevant but because theory is too relevant to practical issues of pedagogy. Instead of being too abstract to be useful, which is a commonly held perception of theory, postmodern theory is often too specific and too particular to be easily applied in a classroom. In a conversation with Gilles Deleuze reprinted in *Language, Counter-memory, Practice,* Michel Foucault reiterates that "theory does not express, translate, or serve to apply practice, it is practice" (208). This apparent paradox becomes evident when we examine how many abstractions are necessary to justify current practices in the teaching of writing—abstractions such as *clarity, intended readers,* and *authentic voices* that become slippery for those who depend on them most for classroom authority. One of the insights teachers of writing gain from postmodern theory is an understanding of how these abstractions turn out to be not things but systems of mobile relationships, and one of the benefits of teaching theory in a class that invites the active participation of all students is that these mobile relationships are constantly demonstrated, as I would again come to appreciate in this particular seminar.

Much theoretical work in composition studies during the 1980s critiqued the central abstraction in current-traditional rhetoric and in many process-oriented approaches to teaching writing—the image of the writer as a discrete, coherent, stable self capable of rationally directing and rationally evaluating its own activities.[2] Postmodern theory not only would redefine that self as a historically contingent subjectivity on axes of social class, gender, age, race, sexual orientation, and ethnicity but also would emphasize the multiplicity of the subject populated with contradictory desires and emotions. Furthermore, the multiple, contradictory subject is only the beginning of the critique; the world at large is no more coherent or stable than the subject, nor is there any transcendental reason or discourse to appeal to beyond contingent existence. Without abstractions of self-presence, universal reason, and belief in the social benefits of scientific knowledge, institutional practices such as those in the teaching of college writing begin to look more and more like a succession of forms of domination, the conclusion Foucault unrelentingly points toward in *Discipline and Punish.* Foucault's vision of dispersed power at times appears to deny the possibility of opposition, like the workings of a huge, automated machine that has been assembled part by part without a conception of its function and without any operators in control of its mechanisms.

But I'm an optimist (chalk it up to desire), and I still cling to thin reeds of belief that knowledge can transform our situations, even if it is the knowledge of rhetoric and not of science. One of those reeds is at the end of a passage in *The History of Sexuality,* where Foucault makes an eloquent argument that the sources of power do not descend from authority above but bubble up from practices below. He advises those who would analyze power to look not for the headquarters but for the local workings that often form comprehensive systems without prior design. This conception of power as omnipresent—as netlike and circulating—seems to give the subject no opportunity to get outside of power.[3] Some take such passages as evidence that Foucault sees subjects as the passive vehicles of power. But Foucault ends this section by maintaining, "Where there is power, there is resistance" (95). He continues:

> Just as the network of power relations ends by forming a dense web that passes through apparatuses and institutions, without being exactly localized in them, so too the swarm of points of resistance traverses social stratifications and individual unities. And it is doubtless the strategic codification of these points of resistance that makes a revolution possible, somewhat similar to the way in which the state relies on the institutional integration of power relationships.   (96)

Admittedly, such passages on resistance are infrequent in Foucault's work. He does not work out the relation of disciplinary power to overt kinds of repression, such as physical violence, nor does he supply a theory of domination from which political movements could be based—lacunae that lie outside his project but for which he has been much criticized by theorists on the political Left.

Foucault, like Jacques Derrida, has been often accused by critics on the Right of promoting irrationality through his critique of Enlightenment reason. Foucault's response to these charges is similar to Derrida's: "If it is extremely dangerous to say that Reason is the enemy that should be eliminated, it is just as dangerous to say that any critical questioning of this rationality risks sending us into irrationality" ("Space" 249).[4] Foucault even wishes to maintain the spirit of Enlightenment inquiry. What he wants to change is the Enlightenment's goal of finding formal structures of universal value. In "What Is Enlightenment?" he theorizes that the negative critique of universal values can be turned into a positive one: by questioning what is held up as necessary and universal, it is possible to discover what is arbitrary and subject to change.

4

Students in the seminar began by reading Chris Weedon's *Feminist Practice and Poststructuralist Theory*, an activist book that takes Foucault's positive critique as its charge. Weedon recognizes that poststructuralist theory and the theories that led to poststructuralism are almost without exception unsympathetic to feminism, but she distinguishes between the usefulness of theory and the political attitudes of its authors. For Weedon political inaction is a far greater evil to be avoided than contradiction or naïveté. The last sentences of the book give a good sense of its spirit:

> We need not take established meanings, values and power relations for granted. It is possible to demonstrate where they come from, whose interests they support, how they maintain sovereignty and where they are susceptible to specific pressures for change. It is a framework that can be applied to all forms of social and political practice. It is my hope in attempting to make this framework accessible that others will take it up and use it in the fight for change. (174–75)

To make this appropriation of poststructuralist theory, however, Weedon must reject other lines of feminist theory as essentialist, including the major French feminists Hélène Cixous, Julia Kristeva, and Luce Irigaray (a problem that bothered me more than it did anyone else in this seminar). Along with Weedon's book, students read essays by Rosalind Coward on ideologies of female beauty and on the British royal family as soap opera, Ann George's analysis of *The St. Martin's Guide to Writing*, selections from Cixous and Clément and from Kristeva ("Woman's Time") that were placed in dialogue with Weedon's dismissal of their writing, and two essays on poststructuralism and composition, one by John Schilb ("Composition") and one by me. We did not proceed far without running into difficulties.

5

Students took turns writing one-page reactions to what we read. In one of the first reactions, Brenda Sluder discussed the contradiction of merging poststructuralism too easily with a political agenda:

One issue in Weedon's work I find bothersome: her political agenda could be implemented as well by other theories, some of which are overtly essentialist. Why does she choose the theory with the most sophistication, the one requiring the most strenuous exercise of mental acrobatics, the smoothest logic?

Students pointed out other passages where Weedon declares her situatedness and then goes on with politics as usual, and certainly there are numerous places where Weedon glides quickly over some of the most difficult issues in poststructuralist theory, as in the following passage:

> Although the subject in poststructuralism is socially constructed in discursive practices, she none the less exists as a thinking, feeling subject and social agent, capable of resistance and innovations produced out of the clash between contradictory subject positions and practices. She is also a subject able to reflect upon the discursive relations which constitute her and the society in which she lives, and able to choose from the options available.
>
> (125)

Some students in the seminar found highly problematic Weedon's assertion that the subject "none the less exists as a thinking, feeling subject and social agent" who can "choose from the options available." Weedon's insistence that poststructuralism become useful in service of social justice leads her at times to forget the situatedness of the subject and to revert to a conception of the subject that looks very similar to the one she attacks.

Others in the seminar probed Weedon's criticism of poststructuralism; like many other critics, Weedon notes that Foucault's work lacks a theory of what forms power takes in a particular society. Alison Regan wrote:

> Yesterday, while I was thinking about feminism, poststructuralism, language, and subjectivity, I happened to open a box of Tampax. It was no ordinary box of tampons; it contained a coupon advertising a film called *Who Am I Now?*
>
> "WHO IS TEACHING YOUR DAUGHTER THE FACTS OF LIFE?" ask the promoters of this special video offer. (The real question here, of course, is Who is constructing your daughter's subjectivity? Other children in the school yard? The Greenham Commons women?)
>
> The cover of the video shows a representation of a woman in motion—a woman with pink skin and bright aqua hair wearing

a blue leotard. She is subjectivity in progress; she is the universal pubescent female.

She is like the gymnast doing her floor exercises, moving forward through life, leaping high and landing on her feet. I want to be like her. I want to send in the $7.95 and find out who I am, now.

The makers of Tampax tampons may well have read the poststructuralists. If so then they, like Weedon, have taken what they liked and left the rest. They understand that the individual is a site of discursive struggle, and they believe they can influence the outcome of the struggle. They believe in consciousness raising and (both personal and parental) agency. They don't waste much time thinking about the continuous redefinition of the individual's sense of herself; they are more interested in fixing an individual's consciousness as a Tampax buyer.

Regan astutely perceived that others outside the academy also consider the individual a site of discursive struggle, but their political ends differ from Weedon's. This perception challenges those who would see the world and social practice only as textual constructs and would reduce all conflicts to matters of language. While the poststructuralists make compelling arguments for the mediating role of language, a political theory should give some account of how particular discourses are used within a social formation and of the relation of those discourses to material relations and dominant ideologies. But almost all poststructuralist theory moves in the opposite direction, beginning at the margins instead of at the center, focusing on heterogeneity, examining the "micro" level, and denying broad categories of social analysis. The seminar discussions rephrased this dilemma again and again through the semester.

6

From Weedon the seminar plunged directly into Foucault, reading *Discipline and Punish* along with a late essay, "The Subject and Power," that characterizes his project.[5] While we were discussing how the efforts of prison reformers led to more thorough and ongoing means of controlling prisoners through surveillance, the October 1990 issue of *College English* arrived with a remarkable essay by Patricia Bizzell. In "Beyond Anti-foundationalism to Rhetorical Authority," Bizzell articulates the impasse the seminar had reached. She writes, "There has recently been much talk of a rhetorical turn in English studies, and it arises from the new anti-foundationalism of our philosophical orientation" (664). As a consequence, she sees work in literature and in composition being drawn into a larger discussion of rhetoric. The problem with this trend is that English studies is still preoccupied with "exposing truth claims as historically, ideologically, rhetorically constructed" (665), and it has not taken the next step to find what useable truths do exist. Bizzell argues that, to take the next step, we as teachers "will have to be more forthright about the ideologies we support as well as those we attack. . . . Perhaps a way to begin the rhetorical process would be to aver provocatively that we intend to make our students better people, that we believe education should develop civic virtue" (671).

Bizzell does not discuss, however, what can happen when an English department "avers provocatively" toward allowing students to write about major social issues. The University of Texas English department took the step Bizzell describes. During summer 1990 the director of lower-division English, Linda Brodkey, and a committee of faculty members and graduate students wrote a syllabus for a new first-year writing course, Writing about Difference, that would engage students in important public debates on racial, sexual, and ethnic diversity. The text materials for the new course were to come principally from United States Supreme Court cases and cases from federal courts, including majority and dissenting opinions that would provide a spectrum of political positions. The approach to argumentation taught in the course was to be based on Stephen Toulmin's *The Uses of Argument*. But even before the syllabus was finished, it came under such heavy attack that its implementation was "postponed" for a year, apparently from pressure on the administration, and later canceled. By the second week of the fall semester, full-page ads were running in the student newspaper and other campus periodicals, arguing that " 'multicultural education' should not take place at the expense of studies that transcend cultural differences: the truths of mathematics, the sciences, history, and so on, are not different for people of different races, sexes, or cultures" (*Daily Texan* 13 Sept. 1990: 11). In September, George F. Will also condemned the course in his nationally syndicated weekly column, and shortly the course was drawn into the growing national debate over the teaching of multiculturalism.

In the wake of the controversy, I realized that my course description for the Politics of Writing seminar, which I had conceived as a good wrestle with theory, displayed the characteristics of the alien "other" that so disturbed the opponents of the first-year course, beginning with the association of writing and politics in the title. But the problem the students in the seminar and I were having was that we were not doing a very good job of constructing an other, and wherever the manual was for political correctness, we certainly had not found it. Indeed, it seemed to us that the Right was faring much better with their appropriation of the Left's concepts of ideology and hegemony than the Left was in trying to determine what those concepts signify. Meanwhile, our seminar was given another lesson in the social construction of gender and race when three hundred fraternity members staged a counterdemonstration at an antirape rally, yelling football cheers to disrupt the speeches and shouting "Nigger! Nigger! Nigger!" when the student body president, a black woman, went to the microphone.

7

Even though questions of the politics of writing were being put to us almost daily in columns and in letters to the editor in the *Daily Texan*, some of the students were still struggling with how to incorporate politics into postmodern theory. Richard Watkinson wrote:

> I want to accept the idea that we can have a political agenda, but the "state of the art" at the moment seems to deny this possibility at every turn. For instance, when Bizzell says, "We will have to be more forthright about the ideologies we support as well as those we attack" (671), I am in complete agreement, but her next step seems more problematic: "We will have to articulate a positive program legitimated by an authority that is nevertheless non-foundational" (671). This is the crux of the biscuit! What kind of legitimating authority is nonfoundational? I confess (and Foucault here shudders!) that I cannot think of one. However, as the world apparently prepares for war in the Middle East, with barely a serious dissenting voice to be heard, hardly anybody asking if there is another way, I remain convinced that the greatest catastrophe would be to stop looking for an alternative. There *has* to be a better way!

Chris Schmidt wrote about a similar problem he had when, in agreeing with the thrust of James Berlin's "Rhetoric and Ideology in the Writing Class," he found a large gap in Berlin's justification:

Social-epistemic rhetoric, Berlin's answer to [expressive and cognitive rhetorics] does not see language as a mirror of "reality" or the "true self" but as the place in which reality, self, and community are constructed in dialectical interaction. Here, however, Berlin has to change his terms in order to make this model coherent: ideology all of a sudden no longer serves the capitalist power but is an open system of interpretations that negotiates the material, the social, and the subjective. In addition, a mysterious agent appears that "must" "constantly challenge," "constantly revise" the interpretations "in the interest of the greater participation of all, for the greater good of all" (490). I have absolutely no quarrel with this goal, but the foundations Berlin laid out for it seem to be shaky. Who does the challenging, in whose interest, and who is to define the greater good that is supposed to result from this? It seems to me that Berlin, although denying absolutes, comes very close to creating new ones, such as democracy, greater good, greater participation, and challenging the status quo.

Others, however, took heed of Bizzell's admonition that at some point you have to stop worrying about getting it right and act, revising or discarding later if necessary. The bashing of the proposed first-year writing course was convincing everyone except Shanahan that there are political questions in the teaching of writing and in the essays we were reading from composition scholars. Regan noted the connections in her response to Brodkey's "On the Subjects of Class and Gender in 'The Literacy Letters' ":

After reading this essay I am even less surprised that Brodkey's proposed course was canned this summer. Her insight that "law does not protect these students . . . from the ideology that classroom language transcends class, race, and gender" (139) amounts to an indictment of the system on which this and every other educational institution stands. Now more than ever, we need the Writing about Difference course. Without it we are left with a pessimistic vision of education that suggests to me that I might as well give up teaching. I don't expect the new curriculum to answer all of my concerns, but it may offer a chance to participate in the "cooperative articulation on the part of students and teachers who actively seek to construct and understand the differences as well as similarities between their respective subject positions" (140), which Brodkey suggests as a possibility at the end of her essay.

8

Our ongoing seminar debate was rephrased once again in response to the exchange between Jean-François Lyotard, who advances postmodernism, and Jürgen Habermas, who defends modernism. In *The Postmodern Condition*, Lyotard defines as "modern" those discourses that look to a grand narrative, such as the progress of scientific reason, for their legitimacy. Lyotard charges that these grand narratives of legitimation are no longer capable of legitimating even themselves and that, moreover, we have lost our nostalgia for these narratives. By grand narratives, Lyotard refers to the overarching narratives of history, such as those of Enlightenment humanism and Marxism, that are characterized by a belief in reason and science and a faith in progress toward human emancipation. Lyotard argues that these narratives are not only outmoded but also sinister, because over the past two centuries they have been used to justify wars, nuclear arsenals, concentration camps, gulags, social engineering, assembly lines, and other forms of centralized social control.

Opposed to Lyotard in this debate is Habermas, the inheritor of the Frankfurt school tradition of critical theory, who maintains that the horrors of the twentieth century are the end products not of Enlightenment reason but of the failure to fulfill the goals of the Enlightenment. Modernity, therefore, is an unfinished project. Habermas attacks postmodern theorists for giving up on the possibility of rational democracy and of justifying the resurgence of political conservatism (*Philosophical Discourse*). In turn Lyotard attacks Habermas's argument for the goal of rational consensus, accusing Habermas of attempting to stifle what is most liberating in postmodern culture—the splintering of culture into a multiplicity of differences. Consensus for Lyotard is precisely what we should not strive toward because in this aspiration we oppress the other.

Mark Poster, in *Critical Theory and Poststructuralism*, attempts to mediate between these two positions, and he does not go far toward a synthesis. But Poster is suggestive in explaining how Foucault's analyses of the practices of power might be affected by the advent of electronic media and information technologies (see also Poster's *Mode of Information*). When Foucault writes of the technologies of power operating today, he describes the collusion of power and knowledge that became institutionalized in the eighteenth and nineteenth centuries. Lyotard and other postmodern theorists, however, have offered new theories and analytics of power in response to what they believe to be a dynamic break with intellectual, social, and artistic traditions of modernity. Lyotard even uses metaphors of electronic communications technology in describing the social bond in *The Postmodern Condition*. He locates a "self" at " 'nodal points' of specific communications circuits" and notes that "one is always located at a post through which various kinds of messages pass" (10). When a speaker makes an utterance, Lyotard argues, a "displacement" occurs that necessarily provokes countermoves, and thus for him a theory of communications is a theory of agonistics or "language games." Lyotard's claims are acted out in forums for electronic written discussions both in networked classrooms and in the national discussion groups on the Internet. In the seminar, we looked at a few transcripts of network discussion groups. At times the conversations facilitated by this technology seemingly produced the regime of phrases, theorized by Lyotard in *The Differend*, that creates a space in which mute voices can speak and opportunities for resistance to the majority's dominant discourses can occur. The hostility that often surfaces in electronic discussions would seem to confirm Lyotard's assertion that agonistics is the inevitable condition of contemporary life and that the best we can do is to allow everyone to speak. At other times, however, discussions moved toward consensus and, contrary to Lyotard's claim that consensus is always repressive, demonstrated why consensus is sometimes politically desirable, as Habermas asserts.

9

When I wrote the course description for The Politics of Writing in spring 1990 and ordered the books, I had a specific narrative in mind—not one that would necessarily lead everyone to the same point but one that I hoped would, through the introduction of postmodern feminism, give some perspective on the debate between postmodern theory and critical theory. Linda Nicholson has assembled the splendid anthology *Feminism/Postmodernism*, which reprints several important feminist responses to the postmodern critique of modernism and Enlightenment reason. In a hostile review of *Feminism/Postmodernism*, Suzanne Moore asks why is it that feminists are always looking elsewhere for partners: "Instead of the arranged marriage between feminism and marxism, this time around the new suitor is postmodernism." She then chides the authors, "The idea that it could ever be the other way around—that feminism itself could be seductive—is not considered." Perhaps Nicholson's book is precisely the one to dispute

Moore's claim because the essays set out an array of well-conceived positions on issues critical to rhetoric. I especially like the first essay in the volume, "Social Criticism without Philosophy," by Nancy Fraser and Linda Nicholson, which asks in its conclusion how a postmodern incredulity of essences and metanarratives can be combined with feminism. Fraser and Nicholson argue that "postmodern critique need forswear neither large historical narratives nor analyses of societal macrostructures" (34). They claim that the endeavor to write new narratives should remain explicitly historical and comparativist, using multiple categories and recognizing that no single solution can be adequate for all.

But for some members of the seminar, the essays in *Feminism/Postmodernism* restated the same problems with the same positions in different terms. Susan Brown wrote that Fraser and Nicholson

> reject essentialism (a large part of the chapter seemed to be spent in a thorough and justified criticism of feminist essentialism), but their version of postmodernist feminism seemed to me to be equally problematic. In essence they would produce the same kinds of theory but would simply add a little footnote saying, "Oh, by the way, this is gender-, class-, ethnicity-, and sexuality-specific and so don't generalize from it."
>
> They wax very lyrical about what it could do and what it will look like ("a tapestry composed of threads of many different hues" [35]) and argue that it will be useful for feminist practice. It seems to me that what they take of postmodernism and attach to feminist theory and practice looks pretty similar to Weedon's marriage of poststructuralism and feminist theory, with perhaps a little more emphasis on practice.
>
> My problem is that I don't see how you can put this into political practice. It may be a sacrilege to say so, but how can you develop practical theory without prioritizing something? Fraser and Nicholson don't seem to have the answer.

10

We were running out of readings and were no closer to resolving anything. We finished the course with one of Victor Vitanza's recent essays, "Three Countertheses; or, A Critical In(ter)vention into Composition Theories and Pedagogies," which Vitanza had sent me in manuscript.

At the very least, I thought, Vitanza could defend the flank so vulnerable to the critique from postmodern theory. Vitanza's essay, one of his most challenging, announces itself as "perverse comedy," not "a mere attack on the status quo but a meditative questioning of it." Vitanza claims to search for a discourse that composition has heretofore disallowed. He organizes the essay around three counterresponses to what he calls the *"will* of the field" to "systematize . . . language," "to be its author(ity)," and "to teach it to students" (139, 140). In response to the will to systematize language, to direct language into channels like a hydraulic engineer, Vitanza counters with Gilles Deleuze and Félix Guattari's "nomad thought" and "rhizomes," a discourse of middles without beginnings or ends (148). For the pragmatics of the rhetorical triangle where the writer takes the position of speaker-authority, Vitanza substitutes Lyotard's notion of the writer as listener. Finally, Vitanza urges a moratorium on attempts to turn theory into praxis or pedagogy. If writing is taught, Vitanza argues, it should be taught as a "nondiscipline" with "postpedagogy" or "paralogic pedagogy" (165). By the conclusion of the essay (or its beginning), Vitanza places everyone else in composition studies whom he cites—for example, James Berlin, Patricia Bizzell, Linda Flower, John Trimbur—in the same leaky boat of modernism, claiming that none of them are adequately suspicious of grand narratives. (In fact, he even describes Berlin's "social-epistemic" group as the one to be most strongly resisted because it is steadily growing [143].)

But Shanahan demonstrated that one exposed flank is just as vulnerable as another by jumping over to the other side, assuming the persona of Habermas in his reaction paper on Vitanza.

> Dear Victor:
>   I recently read a copy of your "Three Countertheses; or, A Critical In(ter)vention into Composition Theories and Pedagogies" and, quite frankly, was surprised. For someone as obviously well-read as yourself, the failure to anticipate my response is glaring. You cite my *Philosophical Discourse of Modernity* yet fail to come to grips with the somewhat predictable answer contained therein: performative contradiction.
>   You explicitly reject " 'rational' thinking and acting, especially about language" (142). You, along with my long-standing sparring partner, Lyotard, endorse paralogy, "an attempt . . . to make the weaker argument the stronger," and favor "a radical heterogeneity of discourses" (147). Your desire to expose the "bad faith" of a "preassigned *telos*" is particularly well-stated. Failure to do so

inevitably ends in the writer's making nothing, since the writer has "already been made" (149, 150). Your displeasure with universals and traditional argument cannot be understated.

Nonetheless, a more cogent, sustained argument I have yet to see. Despite your obvious, contrived graphic alternations, this text would fit perfectly as lecture thirteen in my *Discourse* (stylistically, that is). Your argument is laid out from the outset as an exercise in rational discourse: the title itself provides the predetermined, structural map for your discourse. The body of the paper is carefully divided among the three countertheses. Each counterthesis is then subdivided into a major argument and a section specifically relevant to composition, arguing from the general to the specific as any good Aristotelian might. My God, you have three main points, the cardinal rule of basic rhetoric. The structure is not the natural outgrowth of some rhizomatic wanderings; rather, it operates from a touchstone approach: "And yet, the countertheses are conceptually located according to Gorgias's trilemma of negative propositions . . ." (144). You constantly call on the authority of various "post-" theorists through the use of evidence and properly (formulaically, even) cited endnotes.

Where are the rhizomes? Where is the perverse comedy? Where, for that matter, is the invention part of "critical in(ter)vention"? In order to "make" your argument, in order to communicate with others, in order to language through your attack on rationality, you required rationality, language, argument. You performed the response to your paper. Rather than your paper deconstructing around this performative contradiction as Lyotard's did in *The Postmodern Condition*, yours provides reasons why rationality, instead of being destructive, is constructive and integral to communication. When I read your work, I leave the experience not puzzled about the peculiarities of discourse but convinced of the need for rational discourse.

Try again, Victor.

Jürgen

11

On the last day of the seminar, students wrote their ending for the course.

CONCLUSION 1
Our Last Ritualized Social Maneuver of the Semester

The work of our class this semester has proved profitable for me in that I have faced and grappled with the shadow of poststructuralism. Trained in old-fashioned New Criticism (a pastime I enjoyed) as an undergraduate, I was thoroughly discomfited by UT graduate study and deconstruction in 1984, so much so that I abandoned academia as fruitless, as if meaning were indeed impossible; that is, I accepted deconstruction absolutely.

However, three years in a retail business provided the fortitude (née boredom) I needed to try again. By now, the shock has worn off deconstruction, and the disappointing predictability—predictable in much the same way New Criticism was—of the practice is evident, although deconstructionists seem to enjoy their work much as New Critics did. Things seem to change yet stay remarkably the same.

Having faced poststructuralism and seen that it need not destroy me, I have been swept into the intricacies of Foucault. Since his work is dense and miles away from my experience in academia—I have also worked on the editing of medieval texts—I have quite a task before me of grasping his work and learning to apply it to my own work.

Foucault's ideas seem applicable to our class: in our academic "social maneuver" of class, we clear a space and create ourselves as subjects acting, in this case, harmoniously within a complex grid of power and knowledge.

Brenda Sluder

CONCLUSION 2
The Politics of Writing—Final Position(?) Paper

The question mark in my heading is meant not as a poststructural reminder that it is impossible to have a position but as a question I ask myself: Do I have a position, a theoretically based, practically defensible opinion on issues like politics, writing, poststructuralism, and feminism? One of the virtues of this class has certainly been that I now see these issues as related, but at the same time this makes it more difficult for me to hold a position on them, because I feel that I would have to come up with a version of the grand unification theory.

To be honest, I didn't really think much about the teaching of composition and the politics involved in it before I started this class. It all seemed to be a matter of teaching the mechanics. I am now aware that the roles of teacher and student are not simply givens but that they become defined in the interactions in the classroom. I hope I'll take this into consideration once I start teaching. At the same time, in the segment on teaching composition a problem turned up that accompanied us through the semester: the difficulty of applying pure theory to a practical setting. The classroom situation and the pressure to give grades and enforce standards of writing do not go away simply by my discovery that these situations and standards are arbitrary. This is where this course has helped me most: It acknowledged that it is necessary and possible to suspend (if only temporarily) the indeterminacy, subjectivity, and breakdown of binary oppositions of postmodern theory in order to talk about specific issues. Thus, if in a specific situation it is helpful to frame an argument about domination and subjugation in terms of male and female, it is appropriate to do so while one at the same time can maintain that these categories are nothing more than arbitrarily manufactured cultural constructs.

The format of the class was especially suited for the process of making up my mind about complicated issues. Even though the discussions sometimes did not seem to arrive at any conclusion, I think that this circularity is just an illustration of the difficulty of coming to terms with the political applicability of contemporary theory. In a lucky coincidence, we've had representatives of both directions in this class, and their debates not only helped to liven things up but also to define the terms of my thinking about the issues.

So, have I found the grand unification theory? Of course not, but I've seen that it's OK not to have found it and to keep looking.

Chris Schmidt

CONCLUSION 3

The reason I chose to take this course was that I was attracted to the word *politics* in the title. Politics has always been of fundamental interest to me, along with reading and writing. This was the course for me! At the end of the semester, I can honestly say that it was totally different from my expectations of what it was going to be about.

It is quite difficult now to remember just what my original expectations were, but I am sure that I never expected to have to question my political ideas as much as I have. I find it interesting that, although I had spent three years as a politics undergraduate and political activist, it was not until I came here and took this course that I really examined, and was forced to articulate, my beliefs.

I do feel that I missed a lot of the higher points of debate within the course, owing to my complete ignorance of any of the theories that were being discussed (and my fairly dim comprehension even now). For me this course has been partly an introduction to the ideas of poststructuralism and postmodernism. At times this has meant that I have been struggling to keep up with the debate, an interesting example of how the academy restricts access through its discourse.

The single most important thing about this course for me is that it forced me to think, and to think hard. In fact, it is the only course out of the four I have taken this semester that has required me to think at all. The rest have simply demanded that I cravenly learn (parrot-fashion) the given "truths," never, *never* question them, and generally get bored stiff. I have enjoyed this course and only hope that I can find more like it to take for the next two semesters.

Susan Brown

CONCLUSION 4

i feel happier now that i've come to terms with the fact that "I" don't exist—although it was disconcerting to discover that the rational self i'd been talking about for so long was a myth. It has made it difficult to answer the questions of curious Americans who ask, "So what made you choose Austin?" Replying that the concept of making a reasoned decision is just another manifestation of the ISA doesn't usually result in an understanding smile!

But, joking a/part (which i hope it always is!) this was the most interesting course of the three i took this semester—despite also being the most theoretically challenging. The political ideals which i brought from the UK have been shaken but not completely destroyed (i hope).

For me the central issue of the course, and which i tried to deal with in my paper, was the possibility (or lack of same) of combining what Bizzell calls "anti-foundationalism" with a political agenda which allows for some fundamental truths. It seems to me that this union is very difficult to achieve. Politics and political action assume, even depend, upon the possibility, the necessity in fact, that "things" can be changed for the better. To imagine a different society is to presume you can identify the ills of the present one. To do that depends on having at least one TRUTH that is incontrovertible. However, the more i got into the idea of deconstruction, the more difficult it became to think of anything that wasn't vulnerable to that process.

But then right when I (notice the I reasserted itself) was working on my paper, I went to see *Berkeley in the Sixties*. What struck me was the ferocity with which the state defended its interests—using the army and the police to crush opposition. I am not proposing a return to the sixties à la John Trimbur, but it seems that dissenting voices have been hamstrung by their own desire to avoid foundationalism. The powers that control society (whoever and wherever they may be) have had no such crisis of confidence. Discarding our own foundationalism does not mean it ceases to exist!

To give up imagining change will not allow me to sleep any easier at night—and I think others feel the same. So as Bob Dylan might say, we "keep on keeping on."

Richard Watkinson

CONCLUSION 5

when we began the class, i suggested that the marriage between a modernist politic and a postmodernist critique of meaning, truth, and the like was impossible; those who remembered my pronouncement and have listened to me during the course of the class (the former more likely than the latter) may have questioned my sincerity in approaching *even* the possibility of such a wedding, i myself wondered about my willingness to open myself to the "light" of such a path, but . . .

i suddenly understand what you have been saying and writing all semester: there is such a thing as "good," and the only way to "know" it is not to proceed from a standpoint of absolute certainty but to proceed from a conviction deep inside of us, a conviction that confirms the true worth of *all* humans and with that recognition, goes forth and embraces, enacts that vision

no, bill, we cannot be sure, but we don't have to reject the vision without the certainty, the critique of Truth does not cripple the politic, it empowers it, the only way to proceed is from the body, from the heart, reject rationalism, but don't reject action

so, my course is clear, i must proceed to the barricades, i must act as i have been written, a democrat in search of egalitarianism, equality, human worth

i enlist tomorrow and am on my way to saudi next week

bill shanahan

CONCLUSION 6

This is my last try, and I want this one to be Honest, Authentic, Sincere, and Truthful

we've done time in the carnival . . . I am here to witness . . . the dissolution.

along with the excitement, though, is a concomitant layer of apprehension—after all, what did [this] subject really do to deserve dissolution?

Have we done our work?

Have we changed our minds? Stood our ground?

Let's see. We (of course, when I say "we" I really mean "me." The plural serves as a comforting refuge, doesn't it?) *started out skeptical about the usefulness of postmodernism as a theory which can help the cause(s). . . . It seems we are still skeptical. It this progress? We still favor informed judgment over uninformed. . . . As long as we're on our way to being "colonizers who resist" (activist professors in the university) we may as well know what we're working with/against.*

questions of who holds the power in the modes of information, the relationship of this new power to the one in modes of production or the relationship of Foucault's analysis of surveillance and [our] own remain unanswered.

We've written pages; have we written papers?

Often we have reached consensus: It is strange to accuse men of phallocentrism and then urge women to write only through, about, and because of their sexual desires and awareness of their bodies. *(Are my lips touching as I write?)*

My daughter (a sort of inner child, as i have no biological child) is rarely happier than when negotiating a careful path between the teleological manifestations of the ontological metanarratives of a postmodern hyperspace. *Yet, when she went to the Grand Canyon last year she eschewed the movie for the real thing. There's hope for her yet.*

Alison Regan

12

Regan's concluding remark is an allusion to a talk she heard me give at the Computers and Writing Conference in May 1990. In it, I discussed Jean Baudrillard's vision of hyperreal America, where nothing is "real" that cannot be experienced electronically, as one way of accounting for students' enthusiasm for electronic written discussions on computer networks. I speculated that Baudrillard's vision is confirmed by tourists who drive to the South Rim of the Grand Canyon to see an IMAX movie of the Grand Canyon on a seven-story screen, much as Walker Percy had observed the relation between mass-produced images and the experience of the Grand Canyon in a famous essay written years earlier.

I had wanted to end this essay with the students' conclusions, which had been the ending to the class. In fact, I did end with the statements from the six students in the course when I sent the first version of the essay to the editors of this volume. The major change the editors asked for was to have "Faigley" conclude the essay. I resisted this idea because I didn't make a concluding statement on the last day of class. There was no way I could have fit, like bricks into a conceptual framework, all that we read during the course and all the responses to those materials. To me, the students' disparate conclusions reflected the fluidness of postmodern theory and demonstrated Lyotard's claim that "invention is always born of dissension."[6] "Postmodern knowledge," Lyotard contends, "is not simply a tool of the authorities; it refines our sensitivity to differences and reinforces our ability to tolerate the incommensurable. Its principle is not the expert's homology, but the inventor's paralogy" (*Postmodern Condition* xxv). To write a conclusion for a course in postmodern theory would necessarily produce what Lyotard calls *paralogy*—a discourse that sets up premises and then draws incorrect conclusions.

The editors are justified, however, in asking Faigley to take his turn in writing a conclusion belatedly because, in the context of this volume, he is now a student in a seminar being asked to address the question of what theory means to him. Perhaps the question should be put to him in skeptical fashion. Since Faigley, by his own admission (which the accompanying discourse from the students corroborates), was unable to resolve how a politics of writing was to be defined within contemporary theory and, thus, in at least one sense, lacked "mastery" over the materials he selected for the course, then why should he be allowed to publish an account of the course? Or in even more hostile fashion, why should he be allowed to represent this course as being concerned with composition studies, especially since some prominent members of the discipline have declared from time to time that theorists are the "enemy" and that they distract composition specialists from the task at hand—teaching students to write better?

I find Faigley an eclectic and contradictory thinker, but I think he would answer that "mastery" is possible only in an imagined university classroom, where the professor possesses knowledge that represents something "true" and unchanging about our world, where the professor can transmit this knowledge directly to students through language, and where the accumulation of this knowledge is the means of human progress. Such an ideal would be possible only if professor and students lived outside history. In actual classrooms, knowledge is produced at specific times in specific settings, and it is always negotiated and pieced together at these specific locations. The experience of reading theory collaboratively and dialogically does not rise above contingent existence but plunges everyone more deeply into the historical particularities shaping the scene of instruction. Like Regan's inner child, Faigley too prefers the gut of the Grand Canyon to the movie, even if it means waking up buried in blowing sand, hiding uncomfortably under a tiny ledge for protection from the midday sun, getting punctured by the formidable array of plant life, and drinking the muddy water of the Colorado River. Teaching a seminar that is saturated with postmodern theory for him is something like venturing on an intense and rewarding but frequently uncomfortable journey with unexpected surprises. Theory is indeed practice.

University of Texas, Austin

NOTES

[1] Students enrolled in the graduate seminar that inspired this narrative were Susan Brown, Alison Regan, Bill Shanahan, Brenda Sluder, Christian Schmidt, and Richard Watkinson. In ideal circumstances each of them would have written their own retrospective accounts of the course to go along with mine. Unfortunately, such luxuries are rare in graduate school. Each student did read and comment on earlier versions of this account. For me there were also many resonances from a graduate course I taught at Penn State during summer 1990 that used a similar list of readings. Students enrolled in that course were Susan Bernstein, Ben Click, Rosa Eberly, Grace Fala, Paul Ford, Ann George, Linda Hoover, Dan Punday, and Calvin Troup.

[2] This critique was introduced into composition studies with Bizzell's "Cognition, Convention, and Certainty" in 1982. Later examples among the essays we read in the course include those by Berlin ("Rhetoric"), Faigley, Schilb ("Composition"), and Vitanza ("Three Countertheses").

[3] Similar statements can be found in other writings by, and interviews with, Foucault in the 1970s. In one interview, Foucault responds, "It's my hypothesis that the individual is not a pre-given entity which is seized on by the exercise of power. The individual, with his identity and characteristics, is the product of a relation of power exercised over bodies, multiplicities, movements, desires, forces" ("Questions" 73–74).

[4] Said, in a frequently cited article, divides poststructuralism into two streams: a Foucauldian stream that engages in the politics of knowledge and a Derridean stream that would deny politics as a referential illusion (see "Prob-

lem"). Derrida has many times refuted the charges that deconstruction allows for nothing beyond language (for references and discussion, see Norris). In addition, several scholars in composition studies (Crowley, "Derrida"; Knoper; Neel, *Plato*; Schilb, "Deconstructing") speak to how a Politics of Writing course might arise from Derridean theory.

[5] Shanahan wrote a parody of the unforgettable beginning of *Discipline and Punish*. Foucault tells of the execution of Damiens the regicide, whose executioners, lacking the horsepower to draw and quarter him, were forced to hack at his joints so that the horses could pull him apart. Shanahan replaced Damiens with Descartes and put me astride one of the horses.

[6] Vitanza says of composition studies, "It is astonishing to think of all the time we spend writing and talking about inventional categories only to fail to realize that true invention is born of dissension" ("Critical Sub/versions" 49).

Making a Federal Case out of Difference: The Politics of Pedagogy, Publicity, and Postponement

Linda Brodkey

In April 1990, the Lower Division English Policy Committee at the University of Texas, Austin, voted 4 to 2 to revise and standardize the syllabus for English 306, the one-semester, first-year, required writing course for undergraduates.[1] The decision entailed developing a syllabus that focused on argumentation and required students to read and write critically about "difference" in the context of antidiscrimination law and discrimination lawsuits. Throughout the late spring and summer of 1990, six graduate students and five faculty members met weekly as an ad hoc syllabus-writing group,[2] and by 23 July 1990 they had drafted a tentative syllabus and reading packet for the course, which was to be called Writing about Difference. On that day Standish Meacham, the dean of liberal arts, sent the English department a memorandum announcing that he had decided "to postpone the implementation of the new curriculum for English 306 for one year" because "misunderstandings about the course, expressed within the University community" necessitated "additional time for planning and consultation." On 10 August 1990, Scott Henson and Tom Philpott, editors of an alternative undergraduate magazine, *Polemicist*, published an article in an Austin weekly newspaper tracing some of the most visible "misunderstandings about the course, expressed within the University community" to an advertisement in the campus newspaper paid for by the Texas Association of Scholars (TAS), the local affiliate of the National Association of Scholars (NAS):

> The TAS collected 56 faculty signatures—only seven from the English department—on a "Statement of Academic Concern" ob-

jecting to the revised course. It was published as an advertisement in *Texan* [the campus newspaper]. TAS collected funds for the ad and cut the check, yet its name appeared nowhere on the ad.

On 14 September 1990, the English department faculty affirmed its confidence in the Lower Division English Policy Committee in a secret ballot (46 to 11, 3 abstentions), and shortly afterward the Associated Graduate Students of English followed suit in a mail ballot (52 to 2, no abstentions). . . .

This essay is a narrative in three parts: the committee vote can be read as a story about pedagogy; the advertisement "A Statement of Academic Concern," as a story about publicity; the dean's decision, as a story about institutional postponement. The subsequent departmental votes gloss all three stories, for they are at once votes of confidence in the committee and reactions to media representations of English studies by special-interest groups. By rights, the votes would be an epilogue signaling the end of the narrative and a return to the present. The ellipsis is there, however, as a stark reminder that the narratives of pedagogy, publicity, and postponement could not be independently resolved at Texas, having been inextricably linked, on 23 July 1990, when the university intervened in departmental affairs.

The Politics of Pedagogy

For me, at least, the narrative on writing pedagogy begins in my own intellectual history. When I look back on my published work, I see many efforts to introduce the topic of difference into writing theory, research, and practice. Until Writing about Difference, however, I had focused a fair amount of my intellectual energy on the theoretical dimensions of difference, in particular the practice of imputing negative characteristics to members of a group and then using those differences to devalue the group and ignore the aspirations of its members, and I had written about the importance of analyzing and transvaluing difference in research on writing and teaching practices. In any event, difference crops up in the case study that concludes my *Academic Writing as Social Practice*, the correspondence between teachers and students in my "On the Subjects of Class and Gender in 'The Literacy Letters,' " and my uneasiness, in "Transvaluing Difference," about the reported hostility of some NAS members to work on difference (see Berger; Mooney; Weiner). All the while, however, I treated my work on difference as a prologue to pedagogy, as providing a warrant for teaching college composition. I argued in "Transvaluing Difference," for example, that my own understanding of "the long academic tradition of questioning received wisdom" obligated me to "instruct and support [students] in a critique of received wisdom, which in their case, as in mine, means a sustained interrogation of the doxa out of which claims about reality arise and to which their claims and mine contribute" (597, 600). With the syllabus for Writing about Difference, I hoped to engage students and their teachers in one version of such interrogations.

If, as poststructural language theories suggest, writers articulate relations between a possible self and a possible reality (which includes possible others) in their prose, rather than one real self and one real reality, then it seems to me that writing pedagogy needs a rhetoric to address these issues. Such a rhetoric could do a good deal worse than to begin by assuming that writing in general and arguments in particular are contingent on what Donna Haraway calls partial vision, by which she means, among other things, that knowledge is always situated, since we literally and figuratively can see or account for only what can be seen from a particular vantage point or worldview. Haraway's argument lays new ground for scientific objectivity, wherein "positioning is, therefore, the key practice in grounding knowledge organized around the imagery of vision," wherein "positioning implies responsibility for our enabling practices," and wherein "partiality and not universality is the condition of being heard to make rational knowledge claims" (587, 589). A rhetoric contingent on the multiple selves and the multiple discourses that bear on any human situation would encourage writers to position themselves at the scene of their analysis rather than entice them to obscure their interest in the vain hope of lending third person claims the sort of pseudotranscendent authority that Haraway calls "god tricks" (584), that Michelle Fine and I call "leaving your body to science" (87), and that students call being objective.

The syllabus for Writing about Difference deliberately sets out to articulate in pedagogy what James Kinneavy introduces as exploratory discourse in *A Theory of Discourse* (73–210), what Stephen Toulmin means by everyday reasoning in *The Uses of Argument* (94–107), and what Chaim Perelman and L. Olbrechts-Tyteca characterize as the ultimate warrant for argument itself in the final paragraph of *The New Rhetoric*:

> Only the existence of an argumentation that is neither compelling nor arbitrary can give meaning to human freedom, a state in which a reasonable choice can be exercised. If freedom was no

more than necessary adherence to a previously given natural order, it would exclude all possiblity of choice; and if the exercise
of freedom were not based on reasons, every choice would be
irrational and would be reduced to an arbitrary decision operating
in an intellectual void. It is because of the possibility of argumentation which provides reasons, but not compelling reasons, that
it is possible to escape the dilemma: adherence to an objectively
and universally valid truth or recourse to suggestion and violence
to secure acceptance for our opinions and decisions. The theory
of argumentation will help to develop what a logic of value judgments has tried in vain to provide, namely the justification of the
possibility of a human community in the sphere of action when
this justification cannot be based on a reality or objective truth.
(514)

These modern rhetoricians offer late-twentieth-century language theorists, even poststructural ones like me, a modest purchase on the place
of reason in the production of arguments. Such views make it possible
to value reason without valorizing it and hence to escape both the
hyperboles of poststructural attacks on reason and the tyrannical reduction of reason to mathematical probability by positivism. They
offer, in other words, a rhetoric candid in its defense of the human
longing for community, however improbable that desire may sometimes seem in the face of the terrifying twentieth-century logistics of
social alienation and scientific annihilation.

Such a rhetoric tries to balance the need for a measure of certainty
against the provisional "truths" and "realities" of poststructural language theories. Writing about Difference, however, amplified the place
of reason in argumentation, for students would have summarized and
analyzed the arguments in court opinions and essays by examining
claims and grounds and then asking whether their use is warranted.
The potential formalism of this approach to writing was modified,
somewhat, by the privileging of critique, loosely derived from Kinneavy's work on exploratory discourse. Kinneavy requires teachers and
students alike to explore the assumptions, or what he calls "dogma,"
on which each of us bases our own beliefs about difference, in this
instance, and to explore the junctures at which our assertions about
social reality may or may not be based on good reasons. I hoped that
this course would convince some students to use writing critically; to
identify, analyze, and produce arguments; and in so doing, to learn
that the purpose of academic argument is not to discredit an adversary
(as it often is in debates) but to arrive at, or construct, informed opin-

ions about the profoundly complex and vexing social issues implied by difference. If asked, students could explain their opinions—however provisionally—by laying out reasons for the positions they had taken.

This approach to argumentation and pedagogy justified to a large extent our decision to ask the nearly three thousand students who take English 306 in any given year to read, think, and write about difference in the context of antidiscrimination law and court rulings on discrimination lawsuits. The syllabus mandated "close" reading of the laws, court opinions, and essays, leaving little room for what students would call personal opinions but what we who designed the course think of as reactions to the topic rather than reflections on the material. Because difference is a sensitive topic, instructors (the syllabus was developed for PhD students) would need to conduct open-ended discussions on a topic about which almost everyone has an opinion but hardly anyone, it sometimes seems, has an informed opinion. While a syllabus cannot actually determine pedagogy, the syllabus for Writing about Difference explicity valued the intellectual work of making and qualifying claims in the light of evidence rather than the positions or opinions asserted.

Pedagogical commitment to the possibilities of argumentation is never so critical as when teachers are introducing students to topics like difference, which is not a commonsense notion like diversity but a counterintuitive one generated by poststructural language theories. The most formidable theoretical claims about the subject rely on difference, traces of which are more or less well articulated in discursive practice (see Brodkey, "On the Subjects"). To the extent that structuralism and poststructuralism are understood as descriptive theories of language, difference is a crucial component of epistemology. Yet it could also play a critical role in what R. Radhakrishnan calls transformative theory, in which the subjects of discourse are also agents of social change. Written for graduate student teachers of varying theoretical interests and sophistication, the syllabus was based on a descriptive rather than a transformative theory of difference. That the syllabus did not articulate transformative possibilities does not mean, however, that some instructors and students would not see and act on them in practice, for pedagogy, after all, is where students and teachers animate a syllabus.

One of the reasons some writing teachers may be reluctant to initiate reforms along the lines laid out here may have less to do with theory than with the recent history of composition pedagogy, the remarkably virulent tradition, augmented by trade books, that segregates form from content in the eyes of students and teachers alike. The syllabus for Writing about Difference challenged such rhetorical formalism. While it used some formal notions (claims, grounds, and warrants), the syllabus eschewed more familiar ones (thesis statments, body paragraphs, and conclusions)—on the grounds that most students believe a thesis statement to be a syntactic formulation of the format of an essay, not the rhetorical assertion of a thesis for whose contents they are also responsible. A rhetoric based on these poststructural lines would indeed need to redefine the rights and responsibilities of students and teachers. Teachers would have the right to interrogate the contents of the assertions students make about social reality, a right they would derive from taking responsibility for teaching students to distinguish between personal opinion (as in "everybody has a right to their own opinion") and an informed opinion (as in "here's what I am taking into account"). Students would then have the right to dissent from the realities posed in their classes, a right they would derive from taking responsibility for learning to distinguish between asserting a claim and laying out an argument in support of it. Undergraduates are not likely to be taught argumentation by anyone but us, though much of what they are expected to read and write in their humanities courses requires them to understand that the drama is in the arguments, not in the claims academics make: hence the high value placed on grounds and warrants in Writing about Difference.

Argument as inquiry rather than advocacy makes it possible for teachers to institutionalize difference, or other politically sensitive issues, as a topic, since this view of argumentation values, and so sets out to teach students to value, informed opinions over personal opinions or even received opinions. Students are held accountable only for the arguments they lay out in support of their positions. To me, asking students to undertake such extensive inquiries would be unethical when teachers believe that the material allows for one, and only one, reasonable conclusion. Such a feckless pedagogy devalues argument and topic alike and renders writing, not to mention language itself, pointless.

My interest in articulating difference in a theory of rhetorical practice coincides nicely with similar work in legal studies (see Austin; Bell; Cover; Crenshaw; Harris; Matsuda; Minow). In fact, my desire to make a federal case out of difference—to use antidiscrimination law and federal court opinions as the primary readings in the course—probably arose from my understanding of the ways in which difference problematizes the application of general legal principles to specific cases. In *Making All the Difference*, a portion of which provided the founding essay for the course, Martha Minow writes:

The assumption that differences lie within people obscures the fact that they represent comparisons drawn between people, comparisons that use some traits as the norm and confirm some people's perceptions as truth while devaluing or disregarding the perspectives of others.   (75)

At issue in Minow and Haraway alike, then, is the misrepresentation of what can be seen from a particular vantage point as all that is worth knowing. Neither law nor science, it seems, can hope to achieve an objectivity that transcends the literal and figurative limits of human vision. The most either can hope for, and it is a good deal, is an epistemology that takes partiality into account and seeks in turn to articulate candid and arguable assertions about reality that encourage reasoned discussion and recognize reasoned dissent, goals in line with those of Perelman and Olbrechts-Tyteca's *The New Rhetoric*.

A rhetoric that takes partiality into account would not, of course, be taught as a subset of selected and transcendent principles of logic—as I was taught it and as most trade books still recommend it be taught. Instead it would be taught as a set of contingent principles for examining issues in situ, for asking what could be learned in a course like Writing about Difference by looking more closely and critically at received opinion, congressional opinion, judicial opinion, and academic opinion on the kinds of employment and educational practices described in discrimination suits. Such a rhetoric maps the intersection of critical theory and critical practice by insisting that each legal opinion be examined as a rhetorical case.

I learned quite a bit from developing the syllabus with what came to be known as the ad hoc syllabus-writing group. While the syllabus was far from perfect, those of us who worked on it—writing, reviewing, evaluating, and rewriting the writing assignments; selecting court opinions and essays; and devising ways to make student writing the focus of the course—found even the draft completed a month before the course was to have begun a fair representation of our work. The syllabus asked students to write ten short, informal assignments (called scripts) in preparation for either class discussions or formal essays; drafts for three of the six full-length essays; four peer critiques; and one portion of a group presentation, in which the members would teach the court opinion assigned to their writing group to the rest of the class. I see these not as so many five-finger exercises in writing processes but as crucial experiences in the kinds of social practices attending a sustained exploration of argumentation and difference, practices that might well make otherwise inscrutable processes like planning, drafting, revising, collaborating, and responding worth it to students and their teachers.

I say "worth it to students" not only because the writing and reading assignments made civil law and civil rights the object of civil scrutiny in the course but also because the policy committee, in response to declining student evaluations of the course over the past few years, decided to institutionalize a common topic across the more than fifty sections of English 306 offered every semester. Since student evaluations of literature survey courses taught by graduate students did not also decline over the same period, there was reason to assume that graduate students know how to teach literature but not writing. That they understood the common syllabus as an effort to help them to teach writing may be reflected in their 52-to-2 vote of confidence in the Lower Division English Policy Committee.

The Politics of Publicity

Publicity generated by opponents of Writing about Difference defines the phrase "Don't make a federal case out of it" with a vengeance. Since my mother used to stop conversations cold with the phrase if she decided that one of her children was going on too long about some real or imagined injustice, I presumed it meant that people who make mountains out of molehills will be ignored by the powers that be. Until the publicity about the course, I never gave a thought to another warning implied by the injunction, namely, the danger of changing venues. Scholarship more often than not challenges common wisdom, and it can provoke violent opposition from individuals or groups whose beliefs are challenged. Media presentations of scholarly disagreements invariably focus on concerns that are entirely different from scholarly ones (see Myers). Faculty members who publicize their intellectual disagreements in the popular press not only valorize received opinion, as translated by journalists, over scholarly opinion but also shift the terms of argumentation from reason to ethos.

Serious intellectual disagreements among the faculty members in the English department at Texas were repressed, not resolved, by the relentless negative publicity about the course. Publicity rewrote intellectual controversy as political agonism, wherein substantive disagreements about writing pedagogy were transmogrified into scandals and cover-ups, conspiracy stories that among journalists only Molly Ivins found unbelievable. "Such a tempest in a teapot," she wrote. "What a squall, what an uproar, what a mighty brouhaha. Such grandiose posturings and pronouncements—and all over a plan to change a University of Texas English course." For example, the policy committee had initially agreed to include Paula Rothenberg's reader *Racism and Sexism* in the course but later decided against it because the book did not support the writing of arguments. Yet many journalists not only kept discussing the book but also simply took the position that if the committee voted to adopt the reader, the book reflected our politics. And since they focused on the Rothenberg text and ignored the course's writing assignments, when we eventually dropped the book, no amount of explanation could convince those on the scent of a "good" story that our reasons were pedagogical, once opponents had publicly declared the book radical and our motives political.

I have seen objections to the *idea* of difference but have yet to see one reference, let alone objection, to the *theory* of difference in the press, not to mention the approach to argumentation or any of the writing assignments in the syllabus. This oversight is true of critics not only in literary studies but also in composition. For example, in writing about the course, both Maxine Hairston and John Ruszkiewicz give the impression of being far more concerned with what they took to be a political agenda than with the theoretical issues that shaped the course (see, e.g., Ruszkiewicz; Hairston, "Diversity" and "Required Writing").

Above all else, Writing about Difference provided academic opponents an occasion to publicize long-standing grievances against a perceived hegemony of theory in composition and literary studies alike. Hairston writes: " 'You see what happens when we allow writing programs to be run by English departments?' I'm convinced that the push to change freshman composition into a political platform for the teacher has come about primarily because the course is housed in English departments." The problem, as she sees it, is that critical theories "have trickled down to the lower floors of English departments where freshman English dwells." She summarily dismisses critical theories: "All these claims strike me as silly, simplistic, and quite undemonstrable" ("Diversity" 183, 184).

Some academic opponents took their case to the press, according to one published account, after failing to convince the committee, other faculty members, and graduate students in the department that their objections to the changes were justified. Peter Collier, in a feature article praising the English professor Alan Gribben for his widely publicized campaign against the course and the department, characterizes him as a "resourceful opponent" whose

> strategy was to enlarge the constituency of the controversy from the confines of the department, where the radicals were bound to win. So he began a publicity campaign, writing about E306 in the powerful campus newspaper and then bombarding all the major newspapers in Texas with information about the course. (The *Houston Chronicle* eventually called it "Elitist cant masquerading as tolerance.") He appeared on radio talk shows and television newsmaker programs. When someone from a blue-ribbon alumni group composed of individuals giving at least $1000 a year to the University wrote him for information about the conflict, Gribben sent back an information packet with a cover letter saying that he believed the study of English at Austin was now dominated by a "highly politicized faction of radical literary theorists" and recommended that the department be put into administrative "receivership" while its intellectual priorities were sorted out.
>
> (9–10)

It is true that Gribben launched a publicity campaign along these lines, one similar to a plan he had laid out in the NAS journal *Academic Questions* some months earlier (see "English Departments") and not unlike campaigns suggested earlier and since by other articles in the journal (see Short; Preston and Enck). But it is also true that the course is of surprisingly little importance, of only passing interest, it seems to me, in Gribben's letter to Anne Blakeney, a member of the blue-ribbon alumni group referred to in Collier's article.

The full letter to Blakeney, obtained by Henson and Philpott through the Texas Open Records Act, was published in the campus newspaper. The letter mentions English 306 but never discusses the syllabus. Instead, like Hairston, Gribben uses the course as an occasion for airing grievances against theory and theorists in the department and then argues for a radical restructuring of the department. "During my 16 years in this English department," Gribben writes, "I have witnessed its gradual domination by a highly politicized faction of radical literary theorists." "You will hear *highly* derogatory things said about me," he goes on to say. "But you may be assured that I am a dedicated teacher, a producing scholar with a national reputation and a principled person oriented toward stability in his family's life and activities. Can the same be said of my many detractors?" In argument by ethos, speakers or writers deliberately create a constituency by representing their interests and those of, say, voters or jurors as identical. Argument by ethos is rarely subtle. After this introductory material about himself, Gribben recommends not only that the English department be put into " 'receivership' while its intellectual priorities [are] sorted out," as Collier states, but also that a chair (not from the English department) appointed by the provost oversee dividing the faculty "into a Department of Critical Theory and Cultural Studies and a Department of English Literature and Language," since this "division of radical literary theorists from the remaining traditional scholars would give the latter the freedom to offer a true literature and writing program" (Gribben, Letter). Gribben's letter uses the course to justify what I take to be the impropriety of publicizing these or any other suggestions about departmental governance to someone outside the faculty without having brought a proposal to the department or even an open letter to the faculty. Yet it was an effective strategy, since many opponents of theory were quick to lionize Gribben, as Lynne V. Cheney did in a talk to the National Press Club.

Publicity about Writing about Difference seemed to create a political reality all its own. "A Statement of Academic Concern," the advertisement opposing the course that was signed by fifty-six faculty members (there are more than 2,200 at the university), was published in the campus paper the *Daily Texan* five days before the postponement. Only the ad accompanied the brief letter (also obtained by Henson and Philpott through the Texas Open Records Act) that the president of the university, William Cunningham, faxed to the chair of the regents on 19 July: "Enclosed is an advertisement which was published in the July 18 edition of the *Daily Texan*. I will call you after you have had an opportunity to review it" (Letter to Beecherl). It is impossible to know exactly what happened subsequently. The president may have spoken personally to the regents and may have shared or discussed other documents related to the course, such as the university's own press release, sent out on 30 May, which described the course as shifting its emphasis to argumentation and civil rights court opinions (see Tindol). But the Open Records documents indicate that he sent only the advertisement. Looking back on everything that transpired during this period, I am inclined to believe that the president acted primarily on the negative publicity.

The advertisement "A Statement of Academic Concern" is yet another example of argument by ethos; its rhetoric of ethos is established in the opening sentence: "We regret the action of the English Department of the University of Texas at Austin that transformed English 306 'Rhetoric and Composition' into a course on 'Difference—Racism and Sex-ism' " (2). In my reading, this document advertises not so much regret as a loss of confidence in both colleagues and the institutional pro-cesses by which decisions are made at a university, and hence I see its sponsors as sacrificing a tradition and practice of departmental autonomy and democratic decision making to an immediate political objective—a desire to reverse a decision made by colleagues with whom they disagree.

The appearance of "A Statement of Academic Concern" was the only occasion before the postponement on which campus opponents pub-licly raised what might be called field-based concerns. For the most part, critics of the course seemed unaware that those who teach and study writing refer to and share a literature on theory, research, and practice similar to that in other fields. In unabashedly reducing writing and the teaching of writing to rules—of grammar, punctuation, and spelling—these critics suggest that the entire field of composition is contained in the handbooks and style manuals published by trade presses for undergraduates. One English professor who took exception to the committee's decision, for example, went so far as to write and circulate his own grammar-based syllabus, which was based on a trade book sold to basic writing students at community colleges. A remark attributed to Gribben in the *Chronicle of Higher Education* probably summarizes the attitude of many academics toward composition as a field:

> Where we used to have chapters devoted to grammar, we now have chapters devoted to oppression. If you really care about women and minorities making it in society, it doesn't make sense to divert their attention to oppression when they should be learn-ing basic writing skills. (qtd. in Mangan)

That many opponents believe writing to be grammar and punctuation, and first-year composition courses to be teaching "basic writing skills," means that things have not changed much—at least not at Texas—in the more than twenty years since Kinneavy first declared composition to be "the stepchild of the English department" (1). As the publicity about the course forcibly reminded me, people who believe that compo-sition teachers should be policing language find it virtually impossible to imagine what we actually *do* when we are not correcting students' errors.

While the opponents of the course, left to their own devices, may have reverted to grammar or punctuation when publicizing their opposition, in the faculty advertisement they spoke in the more familiar idiom of composition, at least at the outset. The opening statement takes the egregious license of changing the title of the course from Writing about Difference to "Difference—Racism and Sexism." This is one of those moments when one can actually see the kinds of "slip-pages" from which political realities are constructed. "Difference—Racism and Sexism" declares racism and sexism to be the real topics, while lending additional credence to the claim that the course is not a writing course:

> Specifically, we are concerned that the new curriculum for Fresh-man English distorts the fundamental purpose of a composition class—to enhance a student's ability to write—by subordinating instruction in writing to the discussion of social issues and, poten-tially, to the advancement of specific political positions.
>
> ("Statement")

The claim imagines and then represents the putative goals of the re-vised course—"the discussion of social issues" and "the advancement of specific political positions"—as inverting the natural order of things. The phrase "to enhance a student's ability to write" is sufficiently vague to mean anything a reader wished it to mean. But the "that" in the adverbial clause "that the new curriculum for Freshman English dis-torts the fundamental purpose of a composition class" implies a causal relationship, which if stated explicitly would read "*because* the new curriculum for Freshman English distorts the fundamental purpose of a composition class. . . ." In asserting that the revised course distorts the purpose of a composition course, the ad not only claims that there is only one legitimate purpose but also implies that anyone who dis-agrees is not teaching writing. That's a serious charge to make, all the more so since it depends on the unexamined assumption that writing instruction takes place only in composition classrooms and only in those classes if content is "subordinated" to form.

Formal conveniences like form and content rarely hold in practice, for writing is a matter of coordinating the what and the how, and pedagogy is therefore an effort to support writers as they go about constructing worlds from words. One cannot but wonder if the signers would level similar charges against writing-intensive courses in the disciplines, that is, if professors who teach writing in psychology or sociology or classics or philosophy or political science classes are also guilty of distorting the very purposes of their courses. I think not. And I think not, because what seems to be at issue in the advertisement is not the teaching of writing or the preparation of graduate-student instructors or even the inclusion of content but the imagined consequences of including a specific content, difference, as well as the materials the signatories imagined students would be asked to read and the positions they imagined students would be forced to take. That writing is an ostensible concern seems even more evident in the remaining three assertions, in none of which is composition pedagogy itself at issue. Instead, there is concern that graduate students in English do not know enough about law, sociology, and so on to teach the course; that students would not have materials on logic and argumentation, which they need not for rhetorical invention but for determining "by what standards their papers are being judged or to what extent an instuctor's political opinions might be influencing the evaluation of written work"; and finally that the course itself might be "biased" by a "single hegemonic view."

In the advertisement, the concerned "we" were fifty-six faculty members, seventeen of whom, according to the *NAS Newsletter,* were also members of the TAS ("NAS Impact"). The NAS report does not mention, as do Henson and Philpott in their report, however, that "the majority of the faculty we talked to who signed the ad weren't associated with the TAS and non-members weren't told that TAS had coordinated the effort" ("Chronicle" 4). If true, the lapse seems serious to me. The ethos in the advertisement was echoed in the letters and editorials that academic opponents published in the summer of 1990.

To my knowledge, public advocacy is not the stated agenda of the NAS or its journal, *Academic Questions,* which does, however, publish articles that recommend publicity along with this disclaimer: "The opinions expressed in *Academic Questions* are not necessarily those of the Association." In 1988, for instance, the journal published an essay by Thomas Short (now the executive editor of the journal), who, after laying out arguments against cultural diversity and interdisciplinarity, both of which he represents as political undertakings in intellectual trappings, concludes on this ominous note:

> Our concerns will need to be presented to alumni, parents, and the general public as well as to our colleagues in faculty meetings and to student bodies. For within our institutions we are now outgunned. It is not that we do not have the better arguments on our side, but only that too few of our colleagues are willing to make them, perhaps because the rest are unwilling to listen. Students' minds have been deadened by miseducation, many faculty have already learned the easy pleasures of politicization, and adminis-

trators are now dependent on winning the foundation support that is available only for curricular innovations (often involving, as an added incentive, the expansion of administrative offices to manage extra-departmental programs). The public needs to be made to understand that politicization is occurring, that it is dangerous to democracy, and that it helps to account for the rising costs and declining quality of American education at all levels. In our society money talks no louder anywhere than on college campuses, and it is about time for those who are paying the bills to take an interest in what their money is buying. We who are trying to stop the politicization of higher education can use their support.   (27)

I quote Short's concluding paragraph in full because I see it as the most cynical political spin on statements professing "academic concern" published to date. Short says he will continue to present his concerns on campus, but in my view, by taking his concerns off campus, he is exhorting like-minded readers to abandon academic debate and turn dissenting colleagues over to the public (who he seems certain will identify only with professors who oppose cultural diversity and inter-disciplinarity) because he and others like him feel they cannot win at the local level. In Short's imagined universe, those who count—every-one who pays taxes, that is—will be compelled by his argument that " 'cultural diversity' is a sham that fronts for a politically motivated attack on liberal democracy" and will join with him "to expose the fraudulence of most 'interdisciplinary' studies" (26), whereas in his actual experience some students, colleagues, and administrators at his university are neither compelled nor persuaded by his argument.

   That the negative publicity increased rather than decreased after the syllabus was postponed may explain how a college composition course in Texas could have become a national fetish for what ails America; newspaper and magazine accounts made the "politically correct" course seem for a brief moment to be as powerful a token of reactionary anxiety about the nation as, say, welfare mothers, single parents, gays and lesbians, feminists, and communists (see Adler; Bernstein; Will). In his article praising Gribben, Collier says of the course or, perhaps, of the controversy: "It became a metaphor—for those disturbed by new developments, an indication of the politicization of the campus; for those who approved a blow in the fight for 'diversity' " (10). I would call it a fetish rather than a metaphor, since media versions of Writing about Difference tended to extend the metaphor solely as I once argued that definitions of literacy too often do, as tropes that "stipulate the political as well as cultural terms on which the 'literate' wish to live with the 'illiterate' " ("Tropics" 47). The media fetishizing of Writing about Difference defines the political terms on which its opponents plan to live with its proponents, and the political spin academic and media opponents put on the course suggests that the magnitude and imminence of the threat presumably justifies verbal transgressions as various as dropping *writing* from the course title and imputing insidious motives to those who inaugurated and supported the changes.

The wildly imaginary course referred to by George F. Will in his column nearly two months after the university postponed Writing about Difference is presumably justified by his conclusion: "The troubles at Texas are, as yet, mild. But the trajectory is visible: down. So is the destination: political indoctrination supplanting education." In Will's world, the actual title of the course, which he glibly misquotes but makes no attempt whatsoever to describe, is never used: "But the pressure is on for political content, thinly disguised under some antiseptic course title such as 'Writing about Difference—Race and Gender.' " He goes on to describe *not* the course at Texas but another, at the University of Michigan, that illustrates his point more conveniently. Curiously, a few months earlier, the NAS journal *Academic Questions* published a similar account of the Michigan course (see Versluis).

Gribben, the man credited by the NAS and Collier (see "NAS Impact" and "Incorrect English") with engineering the successful publicity campaign, voiced no complaints against the course in the spring 1990 department meeting, where faculty members and graduate students had the opportunity to ask questions, express reservations, and make suggestions, some of which were taken into account when we wrote the syllabus. Nor did Gribben ever speak or write to me about his concerns. I first heard about them when I read an article in the *New York Times* of 24 June 1990, reporting that Gribben, in a letter to the editor of the local newspaper, had called the course "the most massive attempt at thought control ever attempted on the campus" ("Civil Rights").

My loathing of the negative publicity about the course we developed should not be construed as an aversion to academic popularization. The times emphatically call for academics to explain, to interested members of the public, what they do and how they do it and even why they do it one way rather than another, seemingly more commonsensical way. Surely one reason that it was ridiculously easy to set aside the policy committee's work is that many of the people who heard or read about Writing about Difference believe writing to be a matter of knowing and applying spelling, grammar, and punctuation rules. Those of us who teach and study writing are accustomed to having our jobs explained to us by those who do not, often in terms that set our teeth on edge (see Watt). I find that I am not nearly as steeled, however, against public accusations from others in composition that my views on writing pedagogy are antipathetic to the field. This is the reason, I suppose, that even though the media focused on Gribben's objections, I was more concerned by allegations colleagues in composition at Texas made against the course.

John Ruszkiewicz was a member of the policy committee who voted against the changes. In his editorial in the *Daily Texan* and in the advertisement "A Statement of Academic Concern" the threat of subordination loomed large. Ruszkiewicz claims that "the original point of the class—instruction in writing—is being *subordinated* to a more compelling goal, in this instance, versing students in the provisions of Title VII of the 1964 Civil Rights Act" (emphasis mine). The faculty members in the advertisement express concern that the course "distorts the fundamental purpose of a composition class—to enhance a student's ability to write—by *subordinating* instruction in writing to the discussion of social issues and, potentially, to the advancement of specific political positions" (emphasis mine). Both pieces remind me of the NAS advertisement, which says that the organization "is in favor of ethnic studies, the study of non-Western cultures, and the special problems of women and minorities in our society, but it opposes *subordinating* entire humanities and social sciences curricula to such studies and it views with alarm their growing politicization" (emphasis mine). The postponement of Writing about Difference suggests that at the University of Texas composition pedagogy was in far greater danger of being subordinated to the interests of the NAS than it ever was of being displaced by the theory and research on writing that supports the syllabus developed for Writing about Difference.

What is radical in the syllabus for Writing about Difference is not the topic but the view that rhetorical principles are historically and culturally contingent; hence our insistence that students cannot be taught to write independent of the content and context of writing. This principle, and the scholarship on which it rests, challenges the various instrumental approaches to instruction that have dominated writing pedagogy in this country from the outset. Reasonable arguments can of course be made for both contingent and transcendent approaches to writing instruction. But the publicizing of one view as writing instruction and the other as political indoctrination dismisses the syllabus, the authority of committee votes, the right of departments to determine the contents of their courses, and the value of scholarly books and journals as the preferred and, I would argue, proper site of academic argumentation and dissent. Because intellectual and professional disagreements are commonplace in the academy, many of us belong to professional organizations, attend and speak at conferences, and read and write for publication. Disagreements about writing pedagogy inside the field differ markedly, however, from those that arise between composition and other fields and between the field and received opinion.

My concern that only one of the faculty advertisement's four claims even broaches writing in field-based items is heightened by public reactions to negative publicity about the course. For instance, we were forbidden by the college catalog description of English 306 to use literature in the course, but because some ill-informed journalists either said or implied that we had replaced canonical literature with, in most instances, the Rothenberg reader, many who called or wrote demanded that we teach what they called the "classics." Others insisted that students who take composition classes need to learn how to think, spell, and punctuate correctly. That some people believe writing instruction to be a matter of remediation, despite the work of many who have labored for years to correct this view of composition at their home institutions, suggests to me that publicity of the sort generated at Texas is likely to make it harder than ever for departments to implement process approaches, launch writing-in-the-discipline initiatives, and fund writing centers for reasons other than remediation, and even remediation will be an increasingly difficult case to make in the coming years. Such programs cost money, and obtaining money in turn requires widespread administrative as well as collegial support for writing instruction. Such support is tenuous in the best of times, and these are not the best of times. So I doubt that most departments can afford the high cost of adjudicating their professional and intellectual disagreements in the popular press, and I suspect that it would not take many such battles to convince quite a few institutions that writing simply isn't worth it.

The Politics of Postponement

Apparently ignoring reasoned letters, statements, and articles that professionals in English studies wrote in support of the syllabus and the faculty, the University of Texas, Austin, effectively legitimated the strategy of negative publicity by postponing Writing about Difference. The NAS may credit its members and their allies for waging a successful publicity campaign (see "NAS Impact"), but the NAS did not postpone the course. The university did. Specifically, Standish Meacham, then dean of liberal arts, postponed Writing about Difference, even though he had publicly supported it and funded its development. While the dean took official responsibility for postponing the course, he made it clear in his memorandum of 23 July 1990 to the department that he did not act alone: "I have asked Professor Kruppa [the department chair], and he has agreed, to postpone the implementation of the new curriculum for English 306 for one year. We have arrived at this decision after consultation with a number of faculty members and administrators." A good many faculty members in the English department at Texas believe, along with Kurt Heinzelman and Ramon Saldívar, who made their position known in the student paper, that "something induced them [the president and provost] to short-circuit not only E306 but also their normal process of scholarly inquiry and skeptical analysis of data." But even though Heinzelman and Saldívar called on the provost to "explain clearly his reasons for interrupting normal curricular procedures and publicly affirm his faith in faculty governance and in the value of innovative, challenging courses like the new E306," the provost kept his own counsel.

In standing mute throughout the long months of negative publicity, the central administration only confirmed my early impression that Writing about Difference would be permanently postponed. To the best of my knowledge, the media cited no one in central administration except the dean of liberal arts on the postponement or the syllabus. To my certain knowledge, no one in central administration except the dean of liberal arts ever broached, much less discussed, the postponement with me. Little wonder, then, that when the members of the Lower Division English Policy Committee finally resigned in February 1991, they cited the president of the university's refusal to meet with them as their first reason (Brodkey et al.). In the dean's memorandum, the only official explanation of the postponement, the dean says that he made the decision because of the "need to address concerns and misunderstandings about the course, expressed within the University community, and because . . . additional time for planning and consultation will ensure the best course possible." The memo may leave the impression that these unspecified concerns and misunderstandings could be alleviated through planning and consultation. But since the dean's decision about English 306 did not follow the usual protocol regarding course offerings, there were no specified formal procedures for appealing or reversing the decision, nor did the administration offer any. In the absence of institutional remedy, the fact of postponement eventually negated the departmental votes of support for the committee.

The eleventh-hour postponement sent not only the syllabus but also the Lower Division English Program into academic limbo. No one in the administration seems to have given a thought to the more than 1,500 students registered to take English 306. We were left with no course and less than a month to throw a new one together. We had to rush-order a textbook, develop instructions for its use, redesign all the teaching workshops we had prepared for Writing about Difference, and meet with demoralized faculty members and graduate students. An already overworked support staff was besieged by phone calls from parents, students, faculty members, assorted members of the fourth estate, and cranks. In my view, institutional postponement of the course that we had spent several months planning egregiously jeopardized the right of teachers to teach and students to learn, since the writing classes we were forced to offer that semester were necessarily hastily planned, though many graduate students worked overtime to compensate for the extraordinary time constraints. Meanwhile, the negative publicity continued unabated and unanswered by the administration.

In September 1990, Henson and Philpott, editors of the *Polemicist*, concluded that William Cunningham, president of the University of Texas, Austin (he subsequently became chancellor of the entire system), had decided "to cancel the class sometime between 9 and 11 July—more than a week before either Brodkey or English department chair Kruppa had heard of the postponement of the course" ("Chronicle" 7). Their evidence comes in the form of a letter protesting the course (secured by Henson and Philpott under the Texas Open Records Act) written by Banett Valenta and received in the president's office on 9 July. "At the bottom of the letter, presumably in Cunningham's handwriting," wrote Henson and Philpott, "the following was scrawled: 'Send her a thank you note. Tell her that the English department has decided [illegible] rethink their decision and that the course will not be modified this fall'" ("Chronicle" 7). According to the copy of his letter of 11 July to Valenta, secured under the Texas Open Records Act, the president did indeed reply along these lines: "After careful consideration, the Department has decided that the course will not be modified this fall" (Letter to Valenta). Asked about the letter by the student Scott Henson at the university council meeting held on 17 September 1990, Cunningham stated that he had made a mistake:

> I tried to reconstruct [what I did on that one] as best that I could. (If you will remember, that was the time in which the textbook was being taken out of it; the initial thrust of the discussion of English 306 really was not on the content as much as it was on the book, *Racism and Sexism*.) The best thing I can do in reconstructing it is to say that the English Department was not going to modify the course using (and the letter did not say that, and it is my mistake; I made a mistake) *Racism and Sexism*.
> ("Minutes" 18720/13207)

Taken at face value, the president's explanation is an example of how effective the spin of negative publicity was.

In the same meeting, the president agreed to take questions from Susan Hays, an undergraduate, who let it be known in her summary comment that she thought he had hedged her questions about alumni interference with curriculum and political influence by the regents in academic matters. Cunningham reminded her that not he but the dean of liberal arts had made "the decision to *cancel* the course" (emphasis added). "Just for the record," Hays is quoted as saying, "I do not think most of the students here are buying that. I do not think we are buying what your reaction was to the letter, and I find a big problem that there is such a lack of confidence in the University president" ("Minutes" 18722/13209). It is disturbing everyone, including the president, who spoke about English 306 at the council meeting in mid-September was referring to the postponement as a cancellation.

While a lot was said and written in September and October 1990, by me and by other faculty members and students who supported or opposed the syllabus, the institutional silence that accompanied our words seemed to render all public efforts moot. The silence was broken a few months later when, in a published speech delivered to a group of donors on 22 February 1991, the president, without mentioning English 306 explicitly, nevertheless made a coded reference to the debate surrounding it:

> "Multiculturalism" is, as you know, a much-discussed topic on virtually every campus in the nation. You may have read something about the debate at the University. Unfortunately, "multiculturalism" has become a code word for some people, a signal of

efforts—real or imagined—to use the curriculum to promote "politically correct" ideologies or viewpoints. We must not, and we will not, permit such a development at the University.

("UT Excellence" 8)[3]

In this oblique reference to Writing about Difference, the president seems to have accepted that the course was designed "to promote 'politically correct' ideologies or viewpoints." Things changed irremediably for me when I realized that the president who was unwilling even to speak with the faculty committee that voted to revise the course was apparently ready to make in public coded allusions to our work, in disparaging and, to me, alarming language.

Though it could be coincidental, since a national debate about political correctness was simultaneously taking place, media hostility toward the course and the faculty members involved seemed to rise dramatically at about the time that the president began borrowing liberally from the lexicon coined and popularized by media opponents of multiculturalism. At the very least, his language reflects knowledge of the spate of feature articles that followed in the wake of Richard Bernstein's October 1990 warning to readers of the *New York Times* announcing "the rising hegemony of the politically correct." I cannot help but wonder whether a different response from the president would have influenced the general reception in the press.

In the verdict from *Newsweek* handed down in December 1990, Jerry Adler, in his eagerness to capitalize on the political correctness spin, got his facts wrong. According to *Newsweek*, the course we designed was being taught—not true—from Paula Rothenberg's *Racism and Sexism*—also not true (52). While various other inaccuracies and guilty verdicts have been published since, I believe it may still be true in this country that you can't be tried twice for the same crime (though that may not apply to trial by press). It is worth repeating here for the record, however, that no journalist from a magazine or newspaper that published articles fetishizing Writing about Difference as a politically correct course interviewed me or even asked to see the course materials (see Brodkey and Fowler). Students flunk courses for making the kinds of research "errors" that these journalists are seemingly paid to make. But as one journalist who later admitted "off the record" that he should have checked his facts put it, "Come on, it was only a hook. I needed a hook, and Texas was perfect." No doubt. Fabricated versions of the course were considerably more newsworthy than the syllabus was.

The final verdict was handed down by the *Houston Chronicle* on 6 February 1991, shortly after the Lower Division English Policy Committee finally resigned en bloc. The harsh sentence is worth reading in full:

> A University of Texas freshman English course, restructured with strong overtones of a new McCarthyism of the academic left, has died aborning. To which we add our heartfelt "good riddance."
>
> There is, indeed, a line to be drawn between instruction and indoctrination. A cabal of UT professors crossed it in their attempt to refocus a freshman survey English course onto a highly ideologized social agenda called "politically correct" thinking.
>
> They were called on it. Good for UT-Austin.
>
> "PC" thinking is shorthand for a laundry list of newspeak ideas on subjects ranging from sexism and racism to society's attitudes about physical appearance and handicaps. It tolerates no deviation from strictly prescribed thought formulations. It has been variously described as a new McCarthyism of the left, a new fascism of the left; its adherents damned as latter-day versions of the Hitler Youth or Mao Tse-tung's Red Guards.
>
> PC thinking deserves every bit of that criticism. It is elitist cant masquerading as tolerance; it is, in short, an idea inimical to the concept of a university.
>
> PC thinking has no place in Austin—or anywhere else for that matter. It is certainly no substitute for a survey of literary works widely regarded as forming the foundation of Western thought, which is what that UT freshman English course has long been and should remain.   ("Good Riddance")

Although one might expect the president of a university to respond to negative comments of this sort about the institution he or she leads, as far as I can determine the president of the University of Texas did not take public exception to this verdict on the course and the faculty members who had designed and developed it. He stood mute, as he had during all the other trials conducted in the press. Into this silence, the *Houston Chronicle* and other newspapers and magazines were free to read whatever they pleased.

The administration denied the department the only effective rebuttal it could have made—the course itself. Since there was no course and since neither the president nor the critics seemed interested in the syllabus, anyone could indict Writing about Difference on any grounds he or she wished. And the grounds were invariably political, since the course fetishized in media accounts seemed to be a political Rorschach for its critics. The course was used to excoriate the professoriat for its sins of omission—not teaching a literary canon, spelling, or grammar. It was also used to rehearse sins of commission—teaching noncanonical writings, indoctrinating students, insisting on political correctness, teaching oppression studies. And when people in composition added their voices to these complaints, they lent credence to those whose opposition to the course might have also included writing processes, collaborative learning, and peer response—had they ever gotten past the topic and the reader and looked at the syllabus itself.

The politics of postponement amounted to cancellation. In the absence of any institutional procedures for reversing the postponement, negative publicity generated by opponents seems to have taken precedence over the committee's votes and the departmental votes supporting the committee's right to make and implement policy for lower-division courses. In the *Texas Academe* newsletter, another colleague in the department, Alan Friedman, concluded that as a result of "the postponement (or cancellation as it increasingly seems to be)," there is a "growing sense of frustration and despondency on the part of the departmental faculty that it no longer 'has primary responsibility for such fundamental areas as curriculum, subject matter and methods of instruction'" (3). I believe that, in allowing the fourth estate to govern, and discipline, the English department faculty, without once interrupting these ill-informed scoldings with so much as a statement about the principle of academic freedom, the institution needlessly demoralized a department, some of whose faculty members had for the first time in many years publicly expressed a desire to teach writing. Moreover, the administrative intervention at Texas is cause for further concern. Faced with the threat of negative publicity from individuals or special-interest groups, other institutions may also prefer to limit faculty responsibility for composition programs to the management of the graduate students and part-time teachers who staff the courses rather than to confront the obvious fact that conscientious faculty members simply will not accept responsibility for courses and those who teach them without the institutional authority to implement policy.

A number of the opponents of Writing about Difference drained of all intellectual content what properly would have been a field-based disagreement about writing pedagogy by publicizing their complaints outside the department and outside the university. In raising the alarm, they unleashed a fair amount of free-floating public anxiety about higher education, which in turn was leveled at colleagues with whom they disagreed. In writing this narrative about events at Texas, I have raised no issue more important than the possibility that on any given campus someone or some special-interest group is apt to see not only courses like Writing about Difference but also any number of curricular reforms as threatening to topple the very foundations of Western civilization, which some NAS members seem to have decided that they and only they represent in their individual and collective persons. It would seem that only such a conviction could even begin to justify the extreme measures taken by some faculty opponents on the University of Texas campus, for when they make a federal case out of difference, I hear the House Un-American Activities Committee in their allegations, echoes of a clear and present danger to the nation that reverberate in the *Houston Chronicle* editorial.

If every syllabus or course or policy that the NAS, or any other special-interest group, may deem heretical is put on public trial, and every institution waits to hear the verdict of whatever negative publicity some of its faculty members are willing to generate, many of us can expect to spend the next few years defending ourselves against such allegations to little effect, since course plans do not readily translate into the sound bites and spins of public advocacy. To my mind, the university needlessly ceded the course and the academic freedom of those who worked on it and voted for it to the special interests evoked in "A Statement of Academic Concern," a very small group whose reservations about Writing about Difference were, however, leveled in terms that alarmed people inside and outside the university. I would not want my own son to take the course they described, and I have no trouble understanding the concerns of people who wrote or called about it. Yet the university seemed to have listened *only* to their alarm and to have ignored articles and letters of support for the syllabus and the faculty. And in so doing, the university validated the strategy of negative publicity and invalidated research, along with the decision made by the policy committee, the syllabus drafted by the ad hoc syllabus-writing group, and the votes taken by faculty members and graduate students in the department.

"Does anybody understand," asks Molly Ivins, "what causes so many academics to have this curious penchant for dramatizing the trivial? Not that the fact we live in a multiracial society is trivial, but must the slightest attempt to deal with that on campus always look like the third act of an Italian comic opera?" I confess that I do not understand. Yet the debacle at Texas is a timely if melodramatic reminder for all institutions that wish to continue defining themselves as communities: they simply must face the fact that, for many scholars and students, differences are a condition of community. To deny these differences—

in the name of tradition or unity or expediency—in order to preserve not consensus but an illusion of consensus dismisses the intellectual work of scholars and forgoes any hope of building an academic community wherein intellectual dissent is as basic to writing pedagogy as it is to writing theory and research.

University of California, San Diego

NOTES

[1] The faculty and student members of the Lower Division English Policy Committee that I chaired in spring 1990 were James Duban, Elizabeth Fernea, Shelli Fowler, Susan Sage Heinzelman, Sarah Hinman, Sara Kimball, John Ruszkiewicz, and John Slatin. Duban and Ruszkiewicz, who resigned in July, were replaced in fall 1990 by Lester Faigley and Stuart Moulthrop. Maria Villalobos, the administrative assistant for lower-division English, attended these meetings and contributed to the discussions.

[2] The faculty and student members of the volunteer ad hoc syllabus-writing group chaired by Richard Penticoff were Linda Brodkey, Margaret Downs-Gamble, David Ericson, Shelli Fowler, Dana Harrington, Susan Sage Heinzelman, Sara Kimball, Alison Mosshart, Stuart Moulthrop, and John Slatin. Maria Villalobos, the administrative assistant for lower-division English, also attended these meetings and contributed to the discussions of writing and reading assignments.

[3] Interestingly, according to notes taken by an undergraduate reporter, the president made remarkably similar impromptu comments on multiculturalism in a speech delivered to parents in October 1990, providing at least a glimmer of what his position might be.

A Writing Program Administrator's Response

Ben W. McClelland

The matter of English 306 at the University of Texas, Austin, has been a serious concern for writing program administrators across the country. In the light of the case, many of us have reexamined the place of rhetoric in college composition courses, called for a renewed adherence to internal university governance procedures in the face of external pressures to ignore them, and worried about the professional welfare of our fellow administrator Linda Brodkey. We have addressed these issues in our professional associations as well as on our individual campuses. For example, the Executive Committee of the Council of Writing Program Administrators studied the case and acted formally in December 1991, sending a letter to the University of Texas administration. The letter stated the committee's firm commitment to the right of composition directors to design and implement curricula in consultation with appropriate faculty committees; moreover, it stated the belief that university administrative practice must emphasize faculty governance and due process. Other colleagues, in the Conference on College Composition and Communication, developed courses like English 306 on several campuses and reported the results of those experimental course offerings at their 1992 annual meeting.[1] And finally, Brodkey has been invited to present her views on the matter in many professional venues, including this collection. I have been concerned about the case's implications for progressive curricular reform elsewhere.[2] Thus, I have analyzed "Making a Federal Case out of Difference" to address the question, What can a writing program administrator learn from Brodkey's administrative experience with English 306 at the University of Texas?

At a recent national gathering of writing program administrators, opinion was divided over whether UT's "mighty brouhaha," as Molly Ivins dubbed it, was an isolated incident or whether it could likely occur on any American campus. Some administrators held that it was peculiar to one time and place: Texas, the comp-lit split, the NAS, and political correctness. Period. Those forwarding this view called the national news coverage exploitative media hyping of a one-time tempest in a particular Texas teapot. Those of us at the meeting reflected on the merits of this view. Certainly, unique elements were at work in the University of Texas case. Conflicts over the composition program were not new there, and earlier controversies appeared to leave the campus primed if not programmed for the intramural conflict that spread to a local crisis and then caught on as a national newspaper conflagration. Others at the meeting took an opposite position, however, holding that, except for the national news coverage, the events at Texas represent what can, and frequently does, happen at colleges everywhere. Proponents of this alternative view posited that foes everywhere are continually trying to wrest the local college's curriculum from one another. Thus, writing program administrators should be ever wary, alert to imminent attacks from myriad opponents.

Each view has merit. But sole reliance on either leads to a partial interpretation of the situation. One reading pigeonholes the case as unique to a single time and a singular place. The second renames the Austin campus "the University of Everywhere" and brushes extremism and paranoia across every scene of curricular contestation. Neither the parochial nor the xenophobic view yields much value for administrators interested in inferring some administrative practices from Brodkey's experience, because in viewing one university's experience as a case study for others, neither accounts for the place of history and political context. A more fruitful reading negotiates some elements of both interpretations, providing useful information for reform-minded writing program administrators.

Multiple Political Contexts

I believe that part of the English 306 story could occur in numerous American locales. While Brodkey's story is rooted in the Austin campus and regional politics, it is also located within a web of political interstices that includes national politics, state politics, campus politics, the politics of English composition, and the politics of race and gender in higher education. Seen this way, the development of English 306 evolved out of a confluence of ideologies with which many other writing program administrators work daily. Few, however, experience the storm that Brodkey did at Austin. To infer from this case ideas useful in administrative maneuvering requires us to look more closely at academic history and current political contexts.

Spokespeople from various political orientations attest to the tumultuous political milieu in which we live. Virulent racism and sexism are evident in our institutions, including American higher education. For example, in *Illiberal Education: The Politics of Race and Sex on Campus* the conservative writer Dinesh D'Souza details numerous racist and gender-biased incidents on American campuses. From the perspective of a black, female academician, Patricia Williams analyzes incidents interpenetrated with racism and gender bias in *The Alchemy of Race and Rights: Diary of a Law Professor*. Within the same political world, members of academic professions vie with one another for the authority to conduct curricula. Advocates of culturally diverse, progressive writing curricula are contending with conservative forces that are attempting to reinstate traditional values-transmission pedagogies and back-to-basics instruction with a tilt toward the Right. Books such as Richard Bullock and John Trimbur's *The Politics of Writing Instruction* and Susan Miller's *Textual Carnivals: The Politics of Composition* analyze the complexities of these continuing engagements.

The politics of race and gender contributes powerfully to the context of writing program administration today, whether the issue is multicultural understanding or analysis of street violence between individuals of different groups. The sites of recent public conflicts are located not only in the South but also in Bensonhurst, Philadelphia, Milwaukee, and Los Angeles, among other places. From personal experience, I can attest that racial and political strife exists in university communities, too—for example, at Brown University in Providence and at the University of Mississippi in Oxford.[3] Anyone reading the newspapers in either region could see that both communities manifest some degree of racism, whether it takes the form of verbal abuse or more serious occurrences. While the manifestations differ, many issues for writing program administration are common to universities like Brown and Ole Miss, just as they are for writing program administrators at, say, the University of Wisconsin, Milwaukee, and Morehouse College. In the wake of the Los Angeles riots and the Senate confirmation hearings of Clarence Thomas, writing program administrators across America deem it appropriate to include issues of race and gender in the writing classroom. Arguably, students should write in real rhetorical situations, and conscientious students need to consider their individual and collective responses to race and gender issues, such as local racist and sexist uses of language, local claims of race or gender discrimination, and pertinent university policies. Moreover, they need to consider public policy issues posed by social and political practices in our multiracial country. How a writing program administrator contextualizes such pedagogical matters in a program's curriculum is a central question.

Wherever he or she is located, the writing program administrator navigates a program in a political stream that has strong eddies and hidden undercurrents as well as visible islands and banks. Like Samuel Clemens, the writing program administrator needs to learn the river to avoid shipwreck. Owing to administrators' shrewd piloting, curricular reform succeeds in writing programs on American college campuses despite some conditions similar to those at the University of Texas.

Curricular Reform at Ole Miss

A university administration can significantly influence the curriculum by the way it structures its academic positions and the way it fosters certain academic areas. For example, with funds donated from the Schillig Educational Trust, the chancellor of the University of Mississippi endowed a chair of English composition, giving impetus to writing program development. In 1986, when I was hired into that position, the chancellor charged me to build a comprehensive writing program that would be a resource to the region. Implementing well-funded summer and winter workshops for teaching assistants and a seminar for new teaching assistants, the program sought to send invigorated teachers into the classroom, newly informed with teaching strategies aimed at quickly redefining English composition on the Oxford campus. As the program administrator, I have initiated radical innovation by working according to university policies and through official channels, while also addressing issues raised through invisible networks, such as hidden power alliances among individuals who felt threatened by a new power center and a different academic program. In addition to demonstrating the intellectual force of the new program, I also had to find allies within the established power centers and create new ones to gain institutional approval for the program. Program development in first-year composition made quantum leaps.

To go beyond program development, however, to implement a comprehensive, theory-based writing curriculum took several more semesters of planning—and waiting—for the addition of other composition and rhetoric colleagues, namely, Ellen Gardiner and Sherrie Gradin, who brought more expertise and leadership opportunities. Moreover, the three of us owe thanks to a number of bright and tireless graduate teaching assistants for their transformative work and to our English department colleagues and administrators for their support. Over several years the English composition program has developed a pedagogy based on the social development of knowledge; the course readings present multicultural perspectives, and the assignments ask students to address various challenging questions, including differences in gender, race, and socioeconomics. Developing the current process-writing curriculum, we debated contentious issues with colleagues. Yet, in time, the program was ushered in, along with a costly facility for processing student texts: a writing center equipped with word processors and staffed by writing consultants who offer peer readings of works in progress. The writing center equipment was purchased through competitive internal grants from the Chancellor's Associates' Program and through private funds donated by Ole Miss alumni, friends, and benefactors. Fortunate as it is, this program today faces serious administrative issues, ranging from budget woes to teacher-training demands and the continuous need for vigilant and vigorous leadership. It continues to rely on broad support from the central administration as it faces difficult programmatic decisions each semester. Certainly, the University of Mississippi could not have developed such a large and diverse program without firm support from central administrators and sure direction from the writing program administrative office.

In a move unrelated to the reshaping of the writing program, the university developed another progressive course that is required of all freshmen. In the fall semester of 1992, the university began offering University Studies 101, a lecture course that covers a range of ethical and moral issues, including the concept and history of the University of Mississippi; the values of the university community; race, racism, and the university experience; gender, sexism, and the university experience; and substance use and abuse in campus life. The impetus for the course can be traced circuitously back several years to a fraternity hazing incident in which an Ole Miss pledge and an active fraternity member were dropped off late at night on the campus of nearby, historically black Rust College. The two white students were nude, and racial slurs were painted on their bodies. The incident caused a disturbance but no violence. One of the several rehabilitative measures initiated to deal with the causes of the incident was the chancellor's task force on race relations. The task force recommended, among other things, that a course on cultural diversity be developed. To enact that resolution, two curriculum committees worked for three years to design the course.[4]

During the course-development period, there was significant opposition to the course; for example, some faculty members objected to the course's being required rather than optional. Critics argued that US 101 would be a required course in political correctness, to which the course committee chair, associate professor of philosophy Michael Harrington, responded, "Political correctness is a debate of means to realize values. University Studies 101 is an introduction to the values themselves, not their means" (qtd. in J. Holland). While this course had strong opponents and carried a high profile during its development, the dialogue about it was contained within normal conflictual discourse of the academy. Vigorous, rational opposition continued during the course's first semester. Students and their parents joined the chorus of complainants; still, the din has not reached the occasionally irrational intensity sometimes found in discussion of other values issues, such as religion, state politics, and the place of SEC football in collegiate life.

Since the universities at Austin, Texas, and Oxford, Mississippi, inhabit similar geopolitical waters, why did the development of the two Mississippi programs of progressive curricular reform have relatively clearer sailing than did English 306 at the University of Texas? The development of these two new courses did not constitute remarkable curricular times at Ole Miss. The program developers did not achieve Herculean feats. Yet neither did they eschew the tough decisions to include timely content and local issues of difference. These are the normal, if noteworthy, accomplishments of creative faculty members toiling relentlessly in unglamorous committee work, much as Brodkey did at the University of Texas. No colleague or journalist, however, has written that multiculturalism has stuck a knife into the heart of Dixie. Nobody has declared the mother of all campus wars. Why not, when the same general conditions obtain in Mississippi and Texas?

The answer, I believe, is that the University of Mississippi's academicians work in an atmosphere of tolerance for academic freedom that Brodkey may not have enjoyed at the University of Texas. There are significant historical reasons for this tolerance in Oxford. Early in this century, politicians meddled regularly with university affairs, leaving the university in such a poor academic state that its accreditation was stripped away. University officials worked diligently until accreditation was fully restored, in 1932, and academic freedom was respected thereafter. Three decades later the James Meredith desegregation case again brought disastrous outside intervention. After the cessation of that incident's violence and the departure of occupying federal troops, Mississippians on and off the campus were so eager for reason to prevail that the chancellor was granted the authority to govern the campus according to customary governance procedures.[5] Since then, the university has enjoyed a strong ethos of academic freedom with no intrusion into university affairs by politicians or interest groups. Thus, no disaffected faculty member at Ole Miss today feels authorized to drum up outside pressure from an interest group in the hope that our central administration would quash a program that had been properly approved by the faculty. Ole Miss's central administration feels honorbound to uphold internal governance procedures, even in the face of external opposition such as frequent parental complaints about English 101 and US 101. Program reformers on our campus must endure the scrutiny of colleagues elected or appointed to various academic policy committees. We know that we must learn to navigate the river well. But we know where the river is.

The Storm Next Time?

Writing program administrators who are launching out on their political rivers must learn how to navigate in their unique political contexts. They need to sound the river's depths, sight its banks, and above all, heed local weather forecasts. Some tropical depressions devolve into drizzle; others develop into devastating hurricanes like Hugo and Andrew. While no amount of meteorological data can prevent a tropical storm, certain areas are more storm-prone, and pilots navigating in those areas need to stay informed and know when to secure the vessel against potentially damaging wind and water. If there is one thing that Brodkey perhaps did not do, it was to check the local weather conditions carefully enough. Brodkey writes that she was surprised at the turn of events that spring at the University of Texas. She says that neither of her colleagues who later spoke out against the course had come to her to discuss her curricular plans. Perhaps it would have been prudent for her to have sought them out during the course-development process. One of my administrative mentors regularly took policy proposals to his nemesis well in advance of faculty meetings just to learn how the opposition would react. Since Brodkey saw that she had won the intramural game of college politics, she apparently did not imagine the depth of her colleagues' objections or their resourcefulness in seeking a reversal of fortune. Moreover, she seems not to have known the central administration well enough to see how it might respond to whichever way the wind was blowing. Recent history with an earlier progressive writing program at Texas, however, should have served to warn Brodkey that the university's policy waters were extremely turbulent and that flood watch announcements were continually being broadcast.

Brodkey is certainly right when she says that "some people believe writing instruction to be a matter of remediation." Moreover, I don't quibble with her view about the costs of running our professional lives in the daily press and awaiting public approval or rejection:

> [P]ublicity of the sort generated at Texas is likely to make it harder than ever for departments to implement process approaches, launch writing-in-the-discipline initiatives, and fund writing centers for reasons other than remediation. . . . I doubt that most departments can afford the high cost of adjudicating their professional and intellectual disagreements in the popular press, and I suspect that it would not take many such battles to convince quite a few institutions that writing simply isn't worth it.

I doubt, however, that "quite a few institutions" will emulate the example set by the University of Texas. First, I believe that while writing instruction is generally undervalued, it is highly valued on most state university campuses. And second, while few universities have paid so dearly for academic freedom as Ole Miss has, I believe that most value it highly, because, for one reason, exceptional abuses are well publicized in American higher education.

In reflecting on her experience at Texas, Brodkey envisions an increase in the number of reactionaries who go public in attempts to quash curricular reform. Tolerance for others' views does seem to be at a low ebb in American politics today; however, every administrator's experience, even in conservative localities in America, need not result in a zero-sum game or worse. Few faculty members reach out to private interest groups when they lose academic contests on their home fields. Few campus administrators feel so disposed toward public pressure over collegial governance. But writing program administrators, wherever they are, must learn how to navigate the political waters at their campuses. So, writing program administrators, take heed of other colleagues' experiences! Analyze the wider historical context and current political climate in and about your institution. Before making controversial program proposals, confer with all concerned parties, including potential opponents. Continually interrogate the tactics and strategy of your plan. Nothing short of careful and savvy navigating is required when you are piloting program reforms through academic waters.

University of Mississippi

NOTES

[1] On the panel "E306 in Different Contexts" at the 1992 CCCC meeting, Robert A. Schwegler from the University of Rhode Island, Nancy M. Donovan from Miami University, and Ellen Gardiner from the University of Mississippi reported on courses that were taught effectively with the English 306 syllabus or similar rhetorical and pedagogical principles.

[2] By *progressive*, I mean curricula (1) that integrate discourses of both self and society by, for example, inviting students to write within the context of social or political issues while considering how the self figures in that context and (2) that generally operate as workshop classes proceeding according to active student learning practices. In *The Bedford Bibliography for Teachers of Writing*, Bizzell and Herzberg provide a summary of progressive college curricula in the early twentieth century (3–4). For recent discussions of writing in progressive curricula, read Stotsky's "Conceptualizing Writing" and Fishman and McCarthy's "Is Expressivism Dead?"

[3] I select these sites for examples simply because I know them and because racial incidents have been reported in the news media there. I have lived in Oxford since 1986, and I spent the twelve preceding years in Providence, where I taught at Rhode Island College. I do not intend to denigrate these communities with this observation. I believe that many other university communities exhibit similar interracial characteristics.

[4] With the chancellor's support, a course-development committee was established by the Academic Council, the policy group of deans and central administrators. Made up primarily of administrators, the committee had faculty representation; however, when its course proposal was presented for approval, the Faculty Senate objected to the course proposal's coming from an administrative agency. A second course-development committee of faculty members was then constituted, and its proposal was approved after considerable discussion.

[5] Sansing has written a history of the state's collegiate system in *Making Haste Slowly*. Thirty years after the Meredith desegregation case, the central administration of higher education in Mississippi is again facing the issue of fairness to all citizens, as is evident in the Supreme Court's recent ruling on the Ayers case and the state's attempts to respond to it. Among other things, the ruling calls for equity in funding and admissions standards for all eight of the state's public universities, those that are historically black and those that are historically white institutions.

Response to Brodkey

Topic or Pedagogy?

Mark Andrew Clark

As a reader of Linda Brodkey's "Making a Federal Case out of Difference," I wanted to take away with me a "nugget of pure truth," which, as Virginia Woolf explains in *A Room of One's Own*, a writer or arguer has the duty to offer to a reader (3). I focused on how her essay could inform my pedagogy, provide ways for students to become more responsible readers and writers, and explain how writing teachers can be more equitable, particularly when responding to student writing. I decided that my written response should not develop a traditional argument but, rather, take the form of an exploration, a rhetoric of inquiry, a pedagogical method of writing similar to the method that Brodkey hoped to enact in a course about difference.

I begin with a set of questions: What were the oppositions to E306, Writing about Difference? Did opponents object to the idea of difference? Did they disagree with the theory of knowledge as "partial" that underlay the course? Did they disagree with the distinction between "personal opinion" and "informed opinion"? Did they object to the levels of analyzing arguments suggested by Stephen Toulmin and by Chaim Perelman and L. Olbrechts-Tyteca? Were they arguing that form should take precedence over content? Did they think that a student should not be responsible for the claims he or she makes about the world? Did they believe that students should not be "agents of social change"? Were they rejecting problem posing rather than problem solving? Did they find exploratory writing inappropriate?

These questions are all important, but I don't want to be led too far away from the topic of difference and writing. So I'll ask another question: Why was the topic of difference chosen? Brodkey explains that the "approach to argumentation and pedagogy justified to a large extent [the] decision." Perhaps so, yet I'm not satisfied. I could speculate about why the committee on E306 chose the topic of difference, but my guess would be based on my own assumptions about the intentions for the course, which opponents claimed they knew but clearly didn't. And why was the topic of difference controversial to opponents in the first place? Some opponents argued that discussions of difference would result in political indoctrination. I don't see how that is a foregone conclusion. I had better stop. My speculations about the opponents' conclusions would be based on my own assumptions about their intentions as well.

Perhaps if I think about difference, specifically, I can find some answers. I can't imagine my colleagues objecting to difference as a theoretical construct to explore in published texts and students' writing. Difference is as much a part of reading and writing as comma splices are. The assumptions, biases, and claims that my students make about the world and about others whom they perceive as different from themselves surface in their texts. How could any teacher believe that, when a student writes "I'm sick of gays" or "People on welfare are shiftless and irresponsible," it doesn't have something to do with difference, assumptions, and biases? Am I to believe that we are all part of the same "family" of human beings? Too much happens in my classroom on a day-to-day basis for me to hold that opinion. I teach writing and reading to students who are different from me in race, gender, class, ethnicity, religion, and sexual orientation, and my students often point out our differences. I've witnessed how these differences get played out in their writings and in their interpretations of readings. Their realities of difference constantly surface in their talk, readings of texts, and writings (see M. A. Clark). Isn't it obvious that writers write out of one thing only—their own experience (as James Baldwin might say [192])? And doesn't experience have something to do with the communities of race, class, ethnicity, and gender that students come from? I don't know any teacher who believes that these differences don't matter when students read, analyze, interpret, interrogate, critique, and write texts. I would have to agree with Brodkey that her opponents must not have read or sympathized with contemporary writing theory and research.

Specifically, Brodkey believes that the opposition was chiefly concerned with the writing pedagogy of E306 rather than with the topic. Clearly, the pedagogy developed in E306 rejected traditional rhetorical formalism as laid down in trade books. Yes, it may be the writing pedagogy that opponents rejected, but if writing has something to do with difference itself, then why didn't Brodkey focus on pedagogy instead of topic? I believe that one of Brodkey's pedagogical intentions was to "politicize" reading and writing through the topic of difference. Opponents weren't afraid of making difference explicit, were they? Why would they have been? There is nothing new about focusing on difference when reading and writing texts. Strong allies in both composition and literature have developed deconstructive, feminist, Afrocentric, and Marxist methods for reading and writing texts, methods that put difference at the center of discussion (e.g., Barrett; Belsey; Kaplan).

Maybe Brodkey's opponents were concerned about the implications of institutionalizing this kind of reading. A number of my colleagues believe that highlighting differences causes more problems than it solves—resistances and dissent can often erupt in classrooms. Still, what's wrong with that? Democratic principles are founded on dissent and resistance. After all, smoothing over dissension and resistance has its share of problems, too, since it is a form of silencing. As Michelle Fine explains, "Silencing constitutes the process by which contradictory evidence, ideologies, and experiences find themselves buried, camouflaged, and discredited" (157). Ignoring difference in my pedagogical practices can cause me as many problems as making difference explicit does, and since my students want to ground themselves in their own experiences, which are often based on differences between their communities and mine, I choose to make difference explicit in my pedagogy and in my talk, as they themselves do.

I wonder if opponents would have rejected the course if the pedagogy of difference and not the topic of difference had been written about in the academic and public arenas. A pedagogy of difference was implied in the E306 syllabus. Yet, to imply a pedagogy of difference doesn't seem enough. To me, there's a distinction between pedagogy and topic. Reading for difference and considering difference as a construction in writing are not the same as writing about difference. Pedagogy and topics are not synonymous. I teach several pedagogical methods of reading and writing, one of which focuses on difference. I make students aware of these "politicized" ways of reading and writing and teach them methods to focus on "realities" of difference, both when they read and when they write texts. Yet I cannot expect them to agree that my way is the only way of reading and writing texts, or even the best way, which choosing topics for them strongly suggests. There are hundreds of topics that could be generated from pedagogical principles set down in E306. For instance, if the course were to focus on the law, one topic could be the discourse of law as a constructor and disseminator of knowledge—not only the way law contructs difference in its texts but also the discourse of law itself. To take away a student's power to choose a topic that interests him or her, as well as a teacher's power to generate a topic, can be as oppressive as what Brodkey claims trade book publishers impose on students and teachers. Students do not want to write exclusively what I think they should write; teachers don't like to be told which topics should be the focus of discussion and writing in their classes. Of course, I do have my own biases. I am, for example, suspicious of standardized syllabi, since what usually get standardized are texts and topics and not pedagogy. I cannot fault the E306 committee members, however, since they were asked by their department to formulate a common syllabus for all first-year writing students.

I guess it's possible that some opponents of Writing about Difference believed that the course was about advocacy and not inquiry, about political correctness and not difference, about indoctrination and not exploration, since a pedagogy of difference was not made explicit. Making difference the topic to be explored says implicitly that this topic is the only topic worth exploring. Having a pedagogy about difference says that difference counts when reading and writing all texts. Although difference as a topic arises out of a pedagogy of difference, a pedagogy of difference does not necessarily arise out of the topic of difference. The shift from how to what sends up a red flag, particularly to teachers who come to writing through literature. A focus on pedagogy seems much more critical, democratic, and liberating than a focus on topics, since as a teacher I can test, build on, and critique why I do what I do when different pedagogies are introduced to me; I have little control and power when I'm told which topics to focus on and teach.

The same problem occurs when law cases become reading texts. I can understand Brodkey's rationale for choosing "antidiscrimination law and court rulings on discrimination lawsuits," since these readings illustrate the points and principles of argumentation that her pedagogy develops, and certainly these readings provide a context for the content. I also believe that these readings would make for a fascinating course, one that I myself would elect to take or teach, but I can just as easily develop difference as a theoretical construct and put difference at the center of my pedagogical methods of reading and writing by choosing texts from a number of other discourses—art, education, science, religion, ethics—as well as from law. Difference as a topic is not the same as difference as a pedagogical method of analysis, interpretation, interrogation, and critique. A topic could be interpreted as authoritative and indoctrinating, the pedagogy as inquiry-like, interrogative, and critical. So, I'd have to disagree with Brodkey and say that the topic of difference seems to be the crux of the controversy.

However, my exploration of difference doesn't make me feel any better. I'm still disturbed by conclusions that the opposition drew about E306. Many of those who criticized the course in the press assumed that the topic of difference in the reading of texts would be used in one specific way—indoctrination. They made assumptions about the intentions of the course and of its originators. Brodkey says that "pedagogy, after all, is where students and teachers animate a syllabus." The how of the syllabus is where the why (intentions) surfaces. To assume that the pedagogy developed in Writing about Difference was restrictive, hegemonic, indoctrinating, repressive, and oppressive seems more a personal opinion than an informed judgment. Methods of argumentation, the rhetoric of inquiry, and the exploration of texts around constructions of difference all seem workable and possible, democratic and equitable. Furthermore, a syllabus is only as good as its users. Any syllabus based on any topic can be used for a multitude of intents, malicious or honorable. Teachers may teach law cases and essays about difference, but how they do so with their students will alert students to the whys of the syllabus. Perhaps some opponents thought that even naming the topic of difference meant political indoctrination and correctness. This is also a troubling idea. If these opponents consider the act of naming difference indoctrinating, it says more to me about the opponents in relation to the topic of difference than it does about difference as a topic itself.

I am equally troubled by the assumption that the course would be used in a hegemonic way, namely, political indoctrination. Does choosing the topic of difference presuppose political indoctrination? Again, some opponents assumed that the ulterior motives for the course were to "correct" students' political positions about racism and sexism and hence to indoctrinate them. For teachers on the Right or the Left, this indoctrination may very well happen. But couldn't it happen with any topic that we teach? To assume that students are mindless vessels into which teachers pour opinions that students gladly drink like hemlock seems as ludicrous as Fine's description of public school administrators who say that the word *dropout* actually makes students quit school (159). Why do some continue to posit students as powerless, dim-witted drones who embrace anything and everything we teachers tell them? I'm not arrogant enough to believe I have that kind of power and influence.

Furthermore, the opposition's position implied that those who come up with "objective" topics have no ulterior motives. Highly doubtful. Motives and intentions come through the pedagogy. I hope we know why we teach what we teach. Topics themselves have no ulterior motives; people who put topics to particular uses do.

Some opponents seemed to think that E306 was more of a sociology course than a writing course, perhaps because of Paula Rothenberg's text, which the committee had ultimately decided not to use anyway. This seems an odd claim to make. The Writing about Difference syllabus specified the assignments to be written; the pedagogical methods of reading and writing arguments—from Toulmin and from Perelman and Olbrechts-Tyteca—to be developed; claims and data from law cases, essays about difference, and students' writings to be analyzed, interrogated, and critiqued; and exploratory writing from Kinneavy to be pursued. Opponents might have disagreed with difference as a topic, but I can't see how they might have reached the conclusion that the course was not about writing. At the very least, Writing about Difference was a writing-intensive course that would be supported by writing-across-the-curriculum programs around the country. If the topic had caused the controversy, opponents who tried to substitute other topics as more appropriate would have left themselves equally open to criticism. For instance, Maxine Hairston claims that writing courses "do have important content: learning how to use language to express ideas effectively" ("Required Writing" B1). I'm perplexed. The word *how* in her statement signals to me the means by which something gets conveyed; it is not what gets conveyed. To use language, one must have something to use language for—namely, a content, a subject—unless, of course, the focus is language itself, or literary discourse as James Kinneavy defines it. When people make this kind of comment, I can understand how Brodkey became convinced that critics opposed the writing pedagogy of E306. What troubles me most is that Hairston seems to see writing as a service to the English department that has no content of its own. In fact, Hairston's position about the content of a writing course has been repeatedly critiqued in the journals of the field as equally political in its intentions and purposes.

Where does my exploration leave me now? I'll take a risk and assert my own position as a teacher of writing, reading, and literature. I want students to understand that they construct a reality in their texts; they do not simply mirror a reality that all their readers share. I want students to understand that any view they develop in their writing is a limited, partial one, tied to a context and its connection to classroom and teacher, framed by assumptions they have about the world, and tied to biases and assumptions they have about others who are different from themselves. I want students to take responsibility for the claims they advance in their texts on any topic they discuss. And I want students to recognize that their implicit and explicit representations of others whom they perceive as different from themselves have consequences, particularly for readers who are not of the same race, gender, class, ethnic background, or sexual orientation.

From where I stand, Writing about Difference intended to put into practice a pedagogy of difference. Unfortunately, topics and texts, and not pedagogy, became an issue once again. Reading and writing are political acts—of self, of other, and of institutions. The drama that unfolded about Writing about Difference is a good demonstration of this reality.

Great Lakes Colleges Association, Philadelphia

Response to Brodkey

Narrating Conflict

Patricia Harkin

Linda Brodkey's "Making a Federal Case out of Difference" forms part
of a volume of essays about theory. In such a context, the generic
conventions of the response and the traditions of the academy encourage me, as a respondent, to use theory competitively, to find lacunae
in Brodkey's "narrative in three parts," to make other stories, or somehow to distance myself—and you—from the pain at Texas. But it will
take more than such decontextualized "theoroids" to alleviate the personal and social pain that this story describes. If theory has social
value, it must go beyond metacommentary to explain how people act
in painful circumstances and what their actions might be said to mean.
I shall try to do so by looking at Brodkey's postmodern story in the
context of modern theories of narrative.

Theories of narrative tend to be modernist inventions. They work
best, therefore, to describe and explain modern narratives. Modern
theory, Wallace Martin reminds us in *Recent Theories of Narrative*,
treats narrative in three ways: as a sequence of events, as discourse
proposed by a narrator, and as verbal artifact that is endowed with
meaning by its readers. Postmodern theory, by contrast, specifically
warns against master narratives that presume to make sense of the
world by positing beginnings and endings and by assuming stable
conceptions of author, narrator, or reader. Indeed, postmodern theory
suggests that the particular complexities of commodity capitalism cannot be reduced to, or accounted for as, linear stories. Brodkey and her
students, colleagues, deans, president, and trustees live in a postmodern world. The characters in her story are not stable subjects; rather,
they are positioned by the several institutional agendas that call on
them. This essay shows how the limits of modern narrative theory may
elucidate the specifically postmodern pain occasioned by the contradic-

tory and conflicting agendas at the University of Texas, how theory itself is a part of that pain, and how theory might still help us act, within our situations, to change things. I begin with a modern observation: "Making a Federal Case out of Difference" is a story told by its hero.

This is a *story* told by its hero. By calling her account a "narrative in three parts," Brodkey defamiliarizes the events at the University of Texas. She directs a specifically theoretical attention to questions of how and why these narratives work (or fail to work) to make sense of (or efface) contradictions that have their source in history. One such contradiction emerges between theory and traditional notions about the service function of composition courses. Virtually every historical narrative about composition studies points to an "original" desire to help students improve their socioeconomic positions by regularizing their verbal behavior. One explanation for the emphasis on correctness of grammar and usage in the so-called handbook tradition is the notion that students can and should be "helped," with skills and drills, to overcome "faulty" discursive patterns.

As Michael Halloran points out, however, the idea of the service function creates a paradox for teachers of writing. They are expected to help great numbers of students develop enough mechanical facility to enter another class. But because teachers are members of an educational system charged with evaluating, they must also make it more difficult for these students to achieve this upward mobility. "The rhetoricians," Halloran writes, "prepared students to leap social hurdles, while at the same time elevating those hurdles" (167).

For this modernist notion of service as teaching conventions of correctness, Brodkey has substituted a postmodern—and distinctly theoretical—notion of service. Theory permits us to help people in a different and more challenging way. Theory explains how the socioeconomic positions that our students putatively seek to overcome are produced through difference, a poststructuralist concept not to be confused with diversity.

This theoretical move produces another paradox, however. Theory helps us to see a content for freshman English as instruction in the social workings of language. Theory encourages teachers and students of composition to understand this content as a body of knowledge that might belong to rhetoric rather than as mere practice in patterns of "correct" discursive behavior. Theory also helps us to see that, when nonspecialists conflate the two and reduce the teaching of composition to instruction in the discursive patterns of white male Americans, the composition course can only contribute to the situation it seeks to dispel. A painful contradiction occurs when the culture tells composition teachers to work toward reducing inequities that have their source in ethnicity, gender, and class but nevertheless rejects theory.

That contradiction is manifest in what Brodkey calls the professional debate about content in composition studies. Theory helps us to see that course content is not natural. We make it, using disciplinary procedures. Theory reveals these procedures as contingent. A debate ensues about how to mark off some body of knowledge that might belong to rhetoric. Brodkey's suggestion is that the course should show how the discursive patterns that characterize white male Americans have come to dominate through processes of legal argument. But another contradiction arises as a function of this desire to further our students' understanding of contingent cultural forces. They resist our efforts to help them. Our ethic tells us that resistance is good, but this particular resistance troubles us. What we call our students' "conservatism" is in part a resistance to these efforts to show them that the culture has conspired against them by making "literacy" a constantly rising hurdle. In an important sense, they already see, and they have responded with their own kind of theorizing: boredom, inattention, and a marvelous vengeance captured in Sinead O'Connor's lyric: "I Do Not Want What I Haven't Got." Brodkey makes virtually no mention of this potential or of actual student resistance. Although I find that lacuna somewhat troublesome, it is readily explicable. Brodkey had no chance to experience student resistance because more powerful resistance, inside and outside the university, prevented her from teaching the course at all.

That resistance is the substance of the story about politics and the source of another paradox. Both sides of this controversy warrant their practice in the doctrine of free speech and accuse the other of violating that right. Brodkey seems to see the Texas Association of Scholars and some of her colleagues at Texas as undemocratic; perhaps she even believes that democracy is not a workable conception of government in a commodified, reified, technologized culture.

Theory helps us to see and naturalize this contradiction, too, as a paradox about the narratives that inform our actions. Postmodern theory holds that narratives do not come to comfortable closure; stories do not have morals. Postmodern circumstances are juxtaposed like the cuts on MTV, not like the sequence of events in a thriller. Still, as Fredric Jameson maintains, narrative is "the fundamental *instance* of the human mind" (13). There is no humanity outside the stories we tell ourselves and one another as we try to make sense. As contradictions beset us, we try to construct ourselves as subjects, and specifically as members of groups, by the narratives to which we give allegiance. These narratives are fundamentally and inevitably political. And in these relations of power, competing stories can be adjudicated on the basis of how well they coincide with other narratives and (hence) account for events. Ideology then becomes a contingently changing set of coincident narratives that resolves or effaces uncomfortable contradictions. Brodkey's naming permits her to grant the impossibility of arriving at unilateral truth but still to seek our approval for her story. She earns that assent, or makes it, through ethos.

This is a story *told* by its hero. Brodkey constitutes the events in her first person narration. Narrators of history must show us how a situation at the beginning of a temporal series leads to a different situation at the end, how earliest happenings take on their meaning because of the later ones—as, for example, when the vote of the Lower Division English Policy Committee became important as a precondition for the TAS ad.

In the choice of plot elements, the construction of events, and what Hayden White has called the modes of employment (*Tropics* 84), Brodkey's story of pedagogy is a tragic romance. It begins with our hero at the top. Her course, her ethic, and her definition of rhetoric's *techne* had carried the day. Her new world seemed anarchic to traditionalists, however, who perceived her as tragically flawed by an intellectual pride that comes from theory. Northrop Frye might see here a displacement of the hero's power of action (33) onto the terrain of theoretical awareness. Brodkey narrates herself as sharing ontology and environment with her opponents and interlocutors but as being intellectually superior to most of them. Theory gives her a different relation to the environment. Like Superman's X-ray vision, her theoretical perspective helps her to see what they don't see, even if, or especially since, what she sees is that she has "position[ed herself] at the scene of [her] analysis" instead of aspiring to a "pseudotranscendent authority."

But the story of pedagogy, publicity, and postponement may also be seen as an irony in which Brodkey's own theoretical and narrational power is no match for the well-financed political weaponry of the Texas Association of Scholars. This powerlessness is a condition of postmodern life and a telling mark of cultural *vraisemblance*. This *vraisemblance* is important, for first person narrations often present interesting and even paradigmatic problems in the theoretical construction of "reliability." One thinks, for example, of *The Great Gatsby* or "Araby." For modern authors like Fitzgerald and Joyce, the unreliable narration of Nick Carraway or the boy in "Araby" was marked against the possibility that a narrator could be reliable. Now, though, like Joyce's boy at the bazaar, we are all driven and derided by the vain narratives we are constantly telling, stories in which we are decidedly unable to hold any ideal aloft like a chalice. Everybody's love song gets mixed up with political ballads.

Brodkey wants us to find her credible, not reliable. Chaim Perelman and L. Olbrechts-Tyteca might say that she seeks an audience capable of hearing her argument. Richard Ohmann might say that she constructs one (*Politics*). Clearly, she establishes the values that her audience has to have by envisioning with them a course in which

> rhetoric would not . . . be taught as a subset of selected and transcendent principles of logic—as [she] was taught it and as most trade books still recommend it be taught. Instead it would be taught as a set of contingent principles for examining issues in situ, for asking what could be learned in a course like Writing about Difference by looking more closely and critically at received opinion, congressional opinion, judicial opinion, and academic opinion on the kinds of employment and educational practices described in discrimination suits.

Brodkey represents herself and constructs her audience as piously concerned about the well-being of the academy. But could she actually believe such a reification—that there could be such a thing as *the* academy and that its well-being could be singular, stable, and describable? Is Brodkey's entire academic career not full of instances of political activity that stems from a "loss of confidence in both colleagues and the institutional processes by which decisions are made," the very bad faith of which she accuses her opponents? Postmodernism's thorniest problems can often be described in high modern platitudes: here is an instance of the pot calling the kettle black.

But to show that Brodkey herself uses the rhetorical strategies for which she excoriates her opponents is to hold her to a kind of modern consistency that postmodern theorists know to be impossible. Moreover, the kinds of arguments that uphold such consistency tend to be associated with particularly aggressive phallocentrism. I see Brodkey's use of these devices as a modified, somewhat reserved instance of the laugh of the medusa. She chooses to violate patriarchal conventions such as maintaining consistency, invoking authoritative metadiscourses, and essentializing value-laden terms like *the academy*. But she reserves the right to invoke and use those conventions when they serve her purpose. This strategic inconsistency is, for me, a salient mark of a politically active, postmodern feminism that is as close as we are likely to come to the heroic.

This is a story told by its *hero*. Brodkey is not a helper or a donor or a sought-for object. She embodies her culture's sense not of identity but of shifting subject positions. Scott Henson and Tom Philpott, the undergraduate editors of *Polemicist*, serve as Brodkey's helpers against the "tricksters" who lacked the courage or the power to kill the new curriculum and so contented themselves with postponement. The real "villain" is, of course, the National Association of Scholars, which is represented as using the doctrine of free speech to deny Brodkey and her students the right to learn how to articulate relations between a possible self and a possible reality.

The postmodern reader appreciates the irony of the situation: logic and rhetoric permit both sides of this controversy to invoke the notion of free speech to warrant their charges. Such a reader can only choose the narrative that makes most sense at the moment, in the circumstances. Brodkey's narrative helps me to cope better with problems that I encounter as a teacher, as an administrator, and as a "member" of a late-capitalist Eurocentric culture. Curiously, Martin provides a possible explanation for my willingness to listen to this story (and others' rejection of it) as he describes the ideas of Viktor Schlovsky. Creating "motivated" defamiliarization, the Russian formalist thought,

> involves the choice of characters. If they stay in one place, variety can be achieved by having them move through different realms and ranks of society. But this creates a new technical problem: How is it possible to make such social movement plausible? The answer is to make use of characters who ordinarily live in more then one social world—servants, for example. (49)

I suggest that a salient postmodern equivalent of the servant is the teacher of English composition at a large state university. Brodkey's story is a picaresque tale about an uppity servant who rises above her station to tell deans, presidents, and "those of us who are paying the bills" what a course in rhetoric needs to do. What Brodkey's syllabus has done most resonantly (for me) is to rewrite the service function of English composition.

Class, then, is the interpretive category that I would choose to account for the Texas story's effect on the academy and the media. Class explains the specific rhetorical tactics by which Brodkey's critics told readers of the *Chronicle of Higher Education*, audiences at the CCCC, and other taxpayers that they objected not so much to the politics of the Brodkey syllabus but to its omission of skills and drills. Brodkey's repudiation of the service function may be the unkindest cut of all, especially to those of her colleagues who have made their careers by dignifying service against what Maxine Hairston, in perhaps her most famous public pronouncement, has called a "mandarin mentality" that prides itself on the uselessness of its sweetness and light ("Breaking" 275). To persons who believe uncritically that their most valuable function is to help students use language correctly, Brodkey's offer to show, instead, how language produces knowledge and power and selves must be understood as a battle cry, a strident *non serviam*. No longer content merely to copyedit the sons and daughters of Texas taxpayers, Brodkey and her helpers took language itself as their province. They dared to come closer to the academic means of production. They trespassed on the academy's orderly arrangement by disciplines and usurped the places that heretofore belonged to philosophy (the queen of the college of arts and sciences) or law (the college whose faculty members make the most money).

This is my reading of Brodkey's narrative. Other readers will find different meanings for this story. Many will refuse to endow this discourse proposed by the narrating hero with the meaning she desires. They will claim that the narrator is unreliable, that some events are left out or that too many are included, or that the motivational or causal sequences can and should be otherwise. They will see this story merely as the imposition of the politically correct.

But those responses, too, are part of postmodern pastiche. The postponement in Brodkey's story may make the tale interminable, but

> picaresque . . . novels are by nature interminable, consisting of one event after another. The technical device most often used to end them is a change of time scale: the last chapter is an epilogue that covers many years, providing an after history for the characters. Epilogues may appear to lack closure in the strict sense: rather than stopping the story and tying up all loose ends, they allow it to drift into the future. But these endings serve another purpose. They graft the novel, which is read apart from life, back onto the real time of history, joining it and the reader to our world.   (Martin 84)

Brodkey wants to be rejoined to the world as the hero of the modern story she has written. She complains that "by rights, the votes [of the English department and of the Lower Division English Policy Committee] would be an epilogue signaling the end of the narrative and a return to the present. . . . [But] the narratives of pedagogy, publicity, and postponement could not be independently resolved at Texas, having been inextricably linked, on 23 July 1990, when the university intervened in departmental affairs." But Brodkey's story, read in the light(s) of postmodern theory, encourages us to see that "rights" did not seem to apply at the University of Texas. And if the "link" among the several disparate opponents to Brodkey's conception of rhetorical responsibility is "inextricable," it is also contingent. Under other circumstances, it may be possible to realize what Brodkey describes in one of the most moving passages in the essay: a view of rhetoric that would

> value reason without valorizing it and hence . . . escape both the hyperboles of poststructural attacks on reason and the tyrannical reduction of reason to mathematical probability by positivism. . . . a rhetoric candid in its defense of the human longing for community, however improbable that desire may sometimes seem in the face of the terrifying twentieth-century logistics of social alienation and scientific annihilation.

If we are to achieve this visionary rhetoric, we shall need heroic narrators of picaresque stories. In Linda Brodkey, we have one.

University of Toledo

PART IV

Symposium: Looking Backward and Forward

On the (Pendulum-)Swinging Eighties

Louise M. Rosenblatt

When asked to give my personal reactions to developments in theory in the past decade, I was struck by the fact that the essay was for a book concerned explicitly with both writing theory and critical theory. In the decades after first expounding my literary theory in 1938, I received dozens of invitations to speak or write, usually about literature, sometimes about composition—but I had to wait forty-five years to be invited to discuss their "connections"!

The eighties decade made up for this and other delays. (In 1980, the widely read anthology *Reader-Response Criticism: From Formalism to Poststructuralism* called me "the first among the present generation of critics in this country" to set forth the reader-response view [Tompkins xxvi].) In 1983, the Modern Language Association published the fourth edition of my *Literature as Exploration*. In that same year, I was asked to present a paper on writing and reading at a session sponsored by the MLA Division on the Teaching of Writing. In 1985, I was invited to give the keynote talk on writing and reading at the CCCC national meeting. (In earlier decades, I had been a member of its Executive Committee.) In 1986, I was asked to give the opening theoretical paper at a conference on reading and writing connections jointly sponsored by the Center for the Study of Reading at the University of Illinois and the Center for the Study of Writing at the University of California, Berkeley. Versions of this paper, entitled "Writing and Reading: The Transactional Theory," were published as technical reports by each of the centers. It was included in the volume of conference papers, *Reading and Writing Connections*, published in 1989. The continuing interest in this subject seemed to me a sign of a changing climate in university departments of English.

To discuss the developments in writing theory and critical theory in the eighties, I find I must sketch the decades-long perspective from which I view them. I began teaching in 1928 (yes!) at Barnard College as assistant in a course on Chaucer given by Charles Sears Baldwin. The Columbia University Professor of Rhetoric, Baldwin had written texts on composition and later wrote three standard volumes on ancient, medieval, and Renaissance rhetoric. Composition was taken very seriously in the department. Everyone, from instructors to full professors, gave a composition course. Nevertheless, as I look back I see that even in that faculty, and throughout my twenty years in university liberal arts departments, the major emphasis was on literature, both for English majors and for their instructors.

The subsequent institutionalized separation between composition and literature in the universities may be to some extent explained by the problems created by the Great Depression and World War II and by the increase in numbers of students. I do not need to describe here the situation that developed, in which composition was taught mainly by untenured teaching assistants, whereas the literature courses were the perquisite mainly of the professors.

Nor do I need to retell the story of how, despite these difficulties, dedicated teachers of composition reacted against traditional formulaic methods and mechanical theories of writing. By the eighties, the importance of writing was becoming widely recognized. Leaders in the field developed various views of the writing process. I was pleased that some of these writing theoreticians cited the parallelism between their theories and my transactional approach to reading.

Note that I have been restricting my comments to the college and university level. The story of composition in the schools is more complex, ranging from widespread neglect of composition to the use of workbooks that fragmented the language into mechanically testable units. Writing, when taught, served primarily the purpose of demonstrating command of conventional forms and "correct" mechanics. Reading was taught as a set of disparate skills to be demonstrated largely through answering multiple-choice questions. Stories, and even poems, were often used for that purpose. Literature at the high school level was taught with the assumption that there is a single "correct" interpretation (often according to Cliff's Notes!). Of course, the separation of the two activities and the prescriptive emphasis owed their authority to the traditional theoretical approaches dominant in the universities.

But throughout the decades, I was aware of another, more congenial, strand of thinking in the schools—teachers and educators who never gave up an emphasis on the writer's or reader's role. Hence my decision, after World War II, to leave my post in a traditional liberal arts faculty, despite its considerable intellectual and financial rewards, and to accept an appointment to a school of education. This school was unusual because it did not limit itself to pedagogy but offered a full undergraduate and graduate program in English, including courses in composition, speech, language, and literature, as well as in "methods." Ultimately, my colleagues and I developed undergraduate, master's, and doctoral programs covering linguistics, semantics, composition, and literature, along with writing theory and literary theory. The programs reflected my theoretical approach more fully than did anything that I had published.

Almost from the very beginning of my work in the field, I have taken an unorthodox stance toward the established theoretical positions. Certain academic strands and experiences—my work in anthropology, research in aesthetics for my doctoral thesis, and my reading of Charles Sanders Peirce, William James, and John Dewey—fostered my tendency to transcend the conventional borders of the discipline of literary study.

Even as an undergraduate, while doing intensive honors work in English, I was also very much involved with discovering anthropology under the tutelage of Franz Boas and Ruth Benedict. My electing to accept a graduate fellowship at the University of Grenoble, rather than a place at Oxford, and my decision to take a doctorate in comparative literature at the University of Paris reflected my desire to combine literary interests with the anthropologist's experience of a different language and culture.

At Grenoble, I attended lecture courses and seminars for French students, took a course in French composition given by a professor from a lycée, and joined French students in a course on translating Dickens from English into French. Having to immerse myself in French in order to write my doctoral dissertation in that language provided a realistic approach to semantics. The book, *L'idée de l'art pour l'art*, dealt with French and English writers whose work I admired but who defended the writer's freedom from social constraints by asserting that they wrote solely "for art's sake." My study revealed that this was mainly a defensive slogan; the literary work could have aesthetic value in itself yet necessarily had social origins, implications, and effects. Tension between these two aspects would be reduced, I suggested, by the education of readers who understood the special nature of the artist's social role.

After completing the doctorate, and while teaching English at Barnard, I took work in ethnology and linguistics in the Columbia graduate department of anthropology. I studied linguistics with Boas, working on Kwakiutl and Maidu, American Indian languages. This course and my experience with French reinforced a sense of the reciprocal relationship between language and culture.

My work in the social sciences and literature led to membership in a commission charged with producing books for adolescent readers on recent developments in the social sciences. After completing my work for the commission, I came to the conclusion that, although books in sociology or psychology were needed, the kind of discussion of human relations that went on in my own literature classes could perform an important social as well as aesthetic function.

It was necessary to present a philosophy of literature and teaching that would explain why and under what circumstances the reading of literary works would have an intrinsic aesthetic value and also make possible the development and assimilation of insights into human relations. My classroom experiences helped me realize that essential to this result was a personal reading of the text rather than the traditional text-oriented promulgation of an interpretation by a teacher. And I had observed the value of interchange among students as a stimulant to the development of personally critical reading, which is essential to citizens of a democracy. Thus the book that I was moved to write, *Literature as Exploration* (1938), although it focused on literature, had behind it a view of language activity that encompassed all linguistic modes in their cultural contexts. *The Reader, the Text, the Poem: The Transactional Theory of the Literary Work* (1978) presented more systematically and more fully the underlying theory of reading and criticism of the earlier book.

In "The Turns of Reader-Response Criticism," Steven Mailloux states that despite "Rosenblatt's prior dismantling of the reader/text distinction," literary theorists devoted the seventies to intense theoretical debate over whether the reader or the text determines interpretation (40). He goes on to explain that the question was kept alive by their continued acceptance of a dualistic epistemology, in contrast to my pragmatist antifoundational epistemology.

The subtitle of my 1978 book explicitly underlined my continued rejection of the traditional epistemology and my differences with the other reader-response critics, a rubric used to cover the spectrum from psychoanalytic to structuralist, poststructuralist, and deconstructionist theorists. All, however, no matter what their assertions, still in practice accorded dominance to either reader or text. In *Knowing and the Known* (1949), John Dewey and Arthur F. Bentley suggested that the term *interaction* had become tied to the Cartesian dualistic paradigm that treats human beings and nature, subject and object, knower and known as separate entities. In the light of post-Einsteinian develop-ments, they proposed the term *transaction* to designate a relationship in which each element, instead of being fixed and predefined, condi-tions and is conditioned by the other. In a transaction, although we can distinguish between perceiver and perception, no sharp separation between them can be made, since the observer is part of the observa-tion. The poem—the term I used to stand for "literary work"—exists, or happens, I maintained, in the transaction between particular readers and the text (the signs on the page). We might refer to reader, text, and poem, but each is an aspect of a relation occurring at a particular time under particular circumstances (Rosenblatt, *Reader* 16–19 and "Viewpoints").

The situation Mailloux describes provides the backdrop for my re-marks. He notes, it is true, that "Rosenblatt's transactional approach finally seems to be getting the attention in literary theory circles that it has long had among compositionists, educational reading theorists, and teachers of teachers" ("Turns" 51). In the eighties, as at any period, one could find in the universities the whole spectrum of theoretical positions, with many still under the sway of some modified version of the formalist approach. But I could feel pleased that some of the theoretical positions I had been expounding for years were now being quite widely espoused in university circles (though not often with Mail-loux's scholarly conscientiousness).

Unfortunately, I found that similar antifoundationalist or relativist premises (often derived from Continental sources) were in various instances leading to conclusions that were quite different from mine. Usually, it seemed to me, dualistic habits of mind persisted: language as a closed *or* an open system, the individual *or* the social, subjective *or* objective, determinate *or* indeterminate meaning. Reactions from one questionable extreme too often led, in a great pendulum swing, to an equally questionable opposite pole. Ideas that I espoused have been carried to what I consider fallacious extremes.

For example, both great pioneers of semiotics, Ferdinand de Saus-sure and Charles Sanders Peirce, saw language as mediating between the individual and the environment. But Saussure's dyadic phrasing of the relation of word and object, "signifier" and "signified," combined with his emphasis on the arbitrariness of the sign, gave rise to a view of language as a self-contained system. For some, this view became the basis for asserting a Nietzschean view of the "prison house of lan-guage," in which the writer is "written" by the language and the reader is circumscribed by an "interpretive community." Both author and reader are seen simply as conduits for arbitrary codes, conventions, and genres. The efforts of "process" writing theorists and reader-response theorists to do justice to the individual or personal were thus frustrated. This pendulum swing, it seems to me, results in a preoccupation with the text that is even more total than in the formalist theory of the autonomous text, though with a "playfulness" that the New Critics would have found irresponsible.

In contrast to Saussure's, Peirce's formulation is triadic: "[T]he sign is related to its object only in consequence of a mental association, and depends upon habit" (3.360). This explicitly human linkage of word, object, and "interpretant" (6.347) had from the beginning strengthened my transactional view of language. While I understood that language is socially generated, I saw that it is always individually internalized in transactions with the environment at particular times under particular circumstances. Each individual, whether speaker, listener, writer, or reader, brings to the transaction a personal linguistic-experiential reservoir, the residue of past transactions in life and language. As William James points out, each is carrying on a process of selective attention, choosing from the elements brought into the stream of consciousness during the transaction (284). "Meaning" emerges from the reverberations of all these elements on one another.

With other reader-response theorists, I rejected the notion that the autonomous text embodies a single determinate meaning. For some, unfortunately, the idea of the potentially pluralistic interpretation of the text induced a pendulum swing to complete relativism. The polysemous character of language led them to see the possibilities of the text as infinite. Moreover, believing that each text carries its own self-contradiction, the deconstructionist ends in a logical impasse.

Again, pragmatism provides a solution for the dualism of absolute truth versus complete relativism. (At one point, I found my views under attack because I believed that some interpretations of a text may be found to be better than other interpretations!) Dewey accepts the antifoundational position that we cannot perceive an unmediated reality. Forgoing the quest for absolutes, in his *Logic* he contributes the idea of "warranted assertibility." What conditions or operations warrant or justify an assertion as true? Agreed-on criteria for what constitute sound methods of inquiry and judgment make possible agreement on "warranted," though tentative, answers. Although Dewey draws mainly on scientific inquiry for his illustrations, the concept of warranted assertibility can be applied to the solution of problems in all areas (*Logic* 9, 345, 4).

Recognizing the differences between scientific inquiry and literary interpretation, we can still adapt the concept of warranted assertibility to literary interpretation. We must indeed forgo the wish for a single "correct" or absolute meaning for each text. *If we agree on criteria for validity of interpretation*, however, we can decide on the most defensible interpretation or interpretations. Of course, there remains the possibility of equally valid alternative interpretations as well as of alternative criteria for validity of interpretation. Such an approach enables us to present a sophisticated understanding of the openness and the constraints of language to our students without abnegating the possibility of responsible reading of texts (Rosenblatt, *Reader*, ch. 7; *Literature* 113–15, 151–53, 281–83).

At the 1978 MLA convention, I presented a paper entitled "The Aesthetic as the Basic Model of the Reading Process." Actually, with my somewhat mischievous title, I was gunning not only for the reader-text dichotomy but also for the false aesthetic-nonaesthetic or art-science dichotomy. The dualistic view of the reader and the text led to the assumption that literariness, or "poeticity," must reside in the words of the text. I argued that the aesthetic is not an inherent attribute of the text. The writer who wishes to write a work of art adopts an aesthetic stance in order to bring forth as many clues as possible for the hypothetical reader. But although a text, say, *Julius Caesar*, may offer great aesthetic potentialities, it can be read either as a work of art or as an example of Elizabethan syntax. And a weather report can be read as a poem. Such differences in purpose would be fulfilled by differences in what I call the writer's or reader's stance toward the contents of consciousness. That stance would guide the choice of what to pay attention to, what to select out and synthesize from the elements stirred up in the stream of consciousness during the transaction with the text. The *efferent* stance (from the Latin *efferre* 'to carry away') is involved primarily with analyzing, abstracting, and accumulating what will be retained after the reading. Examples would include reading to acquire information, directions for action, or solutions to a problem. In the *aesthetic* stance, attention is focused primarily on experiencing what is being evoked or lived through during the reading.

Moreover, I stressed that there was not an opposition, a dichotomy, but a continuum between the two stances. We don't have the cognitive, the referential, the factual, the analytic, the abstract on the one side and the affective, the emotive, the sensuous on the other. Instead, both aspects of meaning—which might be termed the public and the private—are always present in our transactions with the world.

The difference lies in the mix, the proportion of public and private aspects of meaning attended to during a reading. In readings that fall somewhere in the efferent half of the continuum, the elements the reader selects are predominantly more public or cognitive than private. The aesthetic stance, in contrast, accords predominantly more attention to the penumbra of private feelings, attitudes, sensations, and ideas than it does to the public aspects. The concept of the reader's stance in the efferent-aesthetic continuum, as well as the transactional paradigm, differentiates my theory both from the traditional and New Critical approaches and from the other so-called reader-response theories.

We increasingly hear arguments for the reading of a wide range of genres in both writing and criticism courses. All the more reason that, in writing or reading, students need to learn to develop a guiding principle for choice at a point on the continuum appropriate to the situation and their purpose. If *Invisible Man* is to be interpreted as a work of art, it must first be read with attention primarily to what is being lived through. If the purpose is, say, to acquire information or analyze the work's structure, the reader must push personal responses to the periphery of attention and focus mainly on the public, verifiable aspects of what is being evoked during the transaction with the text. For a historical work or a political speech that uses many so-called literary devices, it is especially important for the reader to decide what major stance to adopt.

My reminiscences thus far perhaps explain why I was ready when, in the eighties, I was asked to discuss the relationship between writing theory and critical theory. Pragmatist transactionalism had led me to envision speaking and listening, writing and reading as interrelated aspects of the individual's transactions with the environment. Hence I was in tune with the incipient trend in the eighties toward questioning the writing-reading dichotomy. Reading, it was pointed out, is a "composing" activity, while the very act of writing involves reading. Again, dualism created the danger of a simple annulment of differences. There seemed to be a swing toward seeing reading and writing as mirror images and assuming that there would be automatic transfer of learning from the one to the other in such courses as the traditional formalistic introduction to literature.

In my various talks on the subject, therefore, I pointed out that models of the two linguistic activities overlap yet differ. Both writer and reader are drawing on personal linguistic-experiential reservoirs in a to-and-fro transaction with a text. Both writer and reader develop a framework, principle, or purpose, however nebulous or explicit, that guides selective attention and directs the synthesizing, organizing process of constituting meaning. But these parallelisms occur in very different contexts or situations. We should not forget that the writer encounters a blank page and the reader an already inscribed text. Their composing and reading activities are both complementary and different.

I have been especially interested in differentiating two kinds of "authorial reading" during the writing transaction: the first, expression-oriented, involves reading to test what has been written so far against an evolving inner purpose; the second, reception-oriented, involves reading the text through the eyes of potential readers. When communication is the aim, the first must provide a criterion for the second. This process parallels the reader's experience in reverse, on the one hand testing an evocation for its inner coherence and relevance to the text, as distinct from, on the other hand, seeking both intrinsic and extrinsic means to relate this evocation to the author's intention (Rosenblatt, "Writing" 166–68).

Since it seemed that competence in the one activity would not automatically produce competence in the other, I reflected on the social and educational conditions that would foster constructive cross-fertilization, through the development of generally useful linguistic habits and patterns of thought. The social and classroom environment, what the individual writer or reader brings to the activity, and the sensed purpose of the activity must all be taken into account. Collaborative educational methods, I argued, would include spoken and written interchange among students, the development of metalinguistic insight into their own and others' linguistic processes, and the building of critical criteria.

As the eighties advanced, all the questions raised began to pale in comparison with manifestations of the individual-social dichotomy. Again, premises that I shared—the recognition that each individual absorbs the assumptions and values of the society or culture—became the basis for seeing the individual as completely dominated by the society, the culture, or the community. Thus for some cultural, historical, or Marxist critics, texts became the complicitous indoctrinators of the dominant ideology. At best, it seemed, the reader could be taught to "read against the grain" of the text in order to "tease out" and resist its affirmation of the status quo.

A philosophical and anthropological rationale makes ignoring the individual seem as fallacious as ignoring the social aspect of any event. Each is implicated in the other. But always there is an individual human being choosing, selectively constructing meaning, and consciously or unconsciously transacting with the factors, contextual and human, entering into that particular situation. We can recognize the shaping power of the environment, the society, and the culture. Yet we should understand the possibilities of choice or aspiration within the parameters of our complex culture, with its many subcultures; its ethnic, religious, economic, and social groups; and the diversity of groupings any one individual represents or can join—to say nothing of awareness of alternatives provided by knowledge of other major cultural patterns!

The successive editions of *Literature as Exploration* have maintained my linking of reader-response theory and the need for readers to be critical of the assumptions embodied in the work-as-experienced and also of the culturally acquired assumptions they themselves bring to the transaction. But a critical attitude does not demand a swing to a completely negative or deconstructive approach. In the eighties, I have repeatedly felt the need to insist that to be truly critical is to be *selective*. What, in the views of the world presented to us in life or in literature, should we reject or change? Just as important, what should we accept or reinforce? And, equally important, what positive alternative goals should we construct and work for?

We are frequently being reminded that no teaching is ever completely "innocent." True, but should we accept the swing to the indoctrination of an unqualifiedly negative attitude, which fosters a sense of alienation, of being a powerless victim? And should we permit a simplistic view of "power" to trigger simplistic notions of alternatives and processes of social change? Instead, I argue, let us avowedly inculcate democratic values as the positive criteria for selecting among choices, whether literary or social, whether stemming from the dominant or a minority culture. Preoccupation with one or another of the many ills that call out for correction in our society and our world may lead us to neglect defense of the basic democratic freedoms that make possible any constructive remedies.

Pendulum swings in one direction unfortunately generate equally extreme backward swings. Threatened by the destructiveness of extreme—and, in some academic quarters, fashionable—critical theories, traditionalists have too often rejected the sound premises along with the fallacious extremes. The more moderate positions, with their implications for rational change, tend to be ignored. One reason for this is that the formalists and their postmodern adversaries share the same dualistic ways of thinking. To escape reversion to the academic approaches that set the pendulum swinging, we need to ponder the dangers of false dualisms.

At this time of great upheavals in the world, whole nations are groping their way toward their definitions of freedom, democracy, socialism, capitalism. It is the essence of democracy that our own society, too, should be continuously reviewing and refining its efforts to move more closely to the embodiment of our ideals. Writing and criticism involve us inexorably, I believe, in those broader social and political concerns. Democracy, as Dewey said, "will have its consummation when free social inquiry is indissolubly wedded to the art of full and moving communication" (*Public* 350). Such a vision of our role can free us from the polarities of academic and political debate and inspire a fruitful meeting of minds in the nineties.

New York University (Emerita)

NOTE

This essay first appeared in *College English* under the title "The Transactional Theory: Against Dualisms." Copyright 1993 by the National Council of Teachers of English. Reprinted with permission.

My Life in Theory

Robert Scholes

Having been asked to be "timely" and consider changes in my views over the past decade, I find that to do so I need more time—going back to my beginnings in college. When I was admitted to Yale as an undergraduate, in 1946, prospective freshmen were asked to choose either of two English courses for their first year: English 10, a composition course, or English 15, an introduction to literature that featured Cleanth Brooks and Robert Penn Warren's *Understanding Poetry*, along with Shakespeare and fiction. I chose the writing course without hesitation, since I thought at the time that I was destined to be a "writer." My choice carried no weight, however, and I was put in English 25, a "masterpieces of English" course that was the gateway to the major in English literature. One thing led to another, and with a few deviations I have spent the rest of my life in literature, but always with a rebellious writer inside me, making his presence known on various occasions.

In graduate school at Cornell in the late fifties, my fellow student Larry Dembo made it clear to me that a career in English depended on one's ability to publish literary criticism. This writing dimension of the profession appealed to me, but I quickly discovered that, though I had some gifts as a writer, I just didn't know how to produce the kind of writing that carried critical weight. Knowing what I know now, with the clarification of my thinking provided by Michel Foucault in particular, I can see that my problem was a matter of gaining entry to a discourse that involved a certain cultural stance as well as specific rhetorical procedures. At the time, I sought blindly for models, first trying Edmund Wilson, who was not really academic enough, and then Lionel Trilling, whose lucid eloquence depended on greater learning and harder thinking than I could muster and also on membership in a certain New York City culture that gave his thought the stiffening and confidence that were lacking in my own.

Fortunately, some of my teachers provided models closer to home: M. H. Abrams in particular and W. R. Keast, who, along with his mentor R. S. Crane (Crane was visiting Cornell at that time), gave me some direct and necessary lessons in critical writing. Finally, near the end of my graduate career, I came upon the work of Erich Auerbach and Northrop Frye. Frye was such a powerful model that some of my early writing took the form of a clumsy pastiche of his work, verging on plagiarism in its happier moments. What I was learning from Auerbach at the same time was not a writing style but a way of analyzing prose passages that taught me something about styles in general as well as how to squeeze a short passage of text until it yielded plausible generalizations. The amount of learning it took to write as these critics wrote was not lost on me, and I knew only too well how far I was from that level of scholarly discipline. This realization left me with a severe sense of my limitations, so that I felt quite bashful about writing a critical dissertation and asked my advisers to help me find something humble and useful. The result was that they gave me the recently acquired papers of James Joyce to catalog. This task I did dutifully and with great pleasure, working two levels below ground, five days a week, from nine to five, for a whole year. The result was a dissertation with almost no writing in it at all—and certainly no theory or criticism.

I mention all this ancient history by way of showing that though I had been guided into the paths of literary study, I was thinking about writing all the time. I tried to write every oral report and term paper as if it were for publication, and ultimately a surprising amount of my apprentice work found its way into print. It was my orientation as a writer, I believe, that led me into literary theory. I always took a great interest in how effects were achieved, how texts were constructed, and how invisible generic structures exerted their power. As an undergraduate, I had learned from a great art historian, George Kubler, something about the historical patterns of stylistic change in the visual arts. Auerbach, Abrams, Crane, and Frye directed my attention toward similar processes in verbal texts. The formal qualities of writing itself— all those elements of composition that are summed up in the notion of style—became a continuing source of interest to me.

There are two points about this history that I wish to emphasize. One is that I continued to write fiction and poetry while in graduate school, abandoning those ambitions slowly and with reluctance. Only my resolve to make writing important in my critical work enabled me to reconcile myself to this shift of energies. The other point is that my interest in theory and my interest in writing were aspects of the same concern for language and textual structures. Frye was thus quite important for a young scholar like myself. He was clearly a learned man, a theoretician, a sensitive reader, and yet his own prose was alive with energy, crackling with allusive wit, lucid, sinuous, and elegant. His range of interests extended well beyond belletristic prose. His search for a unified field theory of language, however flawed, however impossible in its goal, was an inspiration to me and many others of my generation.

It was the inspiration of Frye and Auerbach that led Robert Kellogg and me to attempt a combined theory and history of Western narrative in the early sixties, but even this work had a base in the classroom, emerging directly from our experiences in devising a sophomore-level course at the University of Virginia. The book we produced, *The Nature of Narrative*, attracted the attention of a young structuralist theoretician, Tzvetan Todorov, who in the late sixties invited me to a conference on the semiotics of narrative. From there, one thing led to another. The structuralists who interested me at that time, such as Todorov, A. J. Greimas, Gérard Genette, and others, were all interested in grammar, syntax, and rhetoric, both traditional and modern. To understand their work and to contribute to their ongoing discussions meant studying the linguistics of Ferdinand de Saussure and the blend of linguistics, poetics, and rhetoric powerfully deployed by Roman Jakobson. All the materials for a pedagogy that connected literary theory to the practice of writing were there—but, by and large, the Europeans took far less interest in pedagogy than the North Americans did. For me, six years at the University of Iowa had brought pedagogical matters to the foreground of my attention.

In the late sixties—a time that forced many of us to examine the roots of our professional lives—I found that my last line of defense for my life as an English professor was that I taught reading and writing. At that time, I first saw clearly that English teachers from kindergarten to graduate school were engaged in the same process of helping students learn to understand texts more fully and to express themselves more eloquently. I was fortunate, at the University of Iowa, in working with people for whom teaching—and especially the teaching of writing—was a central professional focus. I think of Richard Lloyd-Jones and Carl Klaus (an old friend from graduate school) in particular. At Iowa, in addition to teaching the more usual literature courses, I got to devise my own courses in advanced composition (including one called Histor and Rhetor, in which all the reading came from ancient historians and from Aristotle's rhetoric). I also worked with Lloyd-Jones as he developed a remarkable team-taught course for undergraduates called English Semester, in which literary history was taught with an internal writing component.

In English Semester a group of twenty-five or thirty students registered for four courses and met with a team of three instructors for two hours a day, five days a week. We read English literature from the Renaissance through the nineteenth century, and students performed bits of plays in class and wrote regularly, imitating styles of various works in prose and verse and producing interpretive essays as well. In many ways these courses (which I taught for several years) were the most successful pedagogical effort I have ever undertaken. Participants emerged with a more genuine sense of the literary history of England than most students manage to acquire from any standard set of courses for a major in English. Still, the result left me feeling a bit hollow, especially in the light of what was going on around us in the late sixties. It all seemed too belletristic, too luxurious, too disconnected from other aspects of the lives of the students who had done well and learned much in the course. I could not imagine the job being done better, but I wondered if it were quite the right job to be doing. From this point I date my sense that a major task for critical theory would be to rethink curricular and pedagogical practice.

Moving to Brown in the seventies, I found my first chance for experiment coming as an offer from Andries Van Dam of the computer science faculty, to work with me to devise a humanities course that could engage the capacities of hypertext, a new system he was working on. Thinking the matter over, I came to the conclusion that the most hypertextual items in the English curriculum were poems. Working with two graduate students, Nancy R. Comley and James Catano, I tried to create a syllabus that would use the system's ability to display items from different parts of the database simultaneously. The most important result was that students using the system wrote an average of eighty typed pages (or the equivalent) during the semester—and their writing improved, without any specific attention to their prose by the instructors. The system, which ultimately made all communications available to all participants, encouraged formal and informal exchanges among students as well as between students and instructors. With peer support—and peer pressure—writing about poetry, imitating poetic forms, and thinking about language had generated the kind of results that we long for in composition courses but too infrequently achieve.

Like the English Semester experience at Iowa, the hypertext experience at Brown contributed to my thinking about curricular and pedagogical matters. A challenge from a publisher to put our theories on the practical line led Comley and me to produce *The Practice of Writing*, a composition text using literary materials not as precious objects for exegesis but as samples of effective writing to be imitated, parodied, and responded to in other ways. The theoretical basis for this effort was a Jakobsonian sense that the difference between literary language and ordinary language is one not of absolutes but of emphases. This project also confirmed (and I think I can speak for Comley as well) our sense that the most valuable resources English departments have are texts that embody the expressive possibilities of the English language.

At this point I began to understand that we make a mistake in thinking that we in English departments are properly responsible for all the possible kinds of writing in English. What we can teach about writing involves mainly its literary or rhetorical elements. Members of other faculties send us their students not so that we will teach them to write like social scientists or engineers but precisely so that we will teach them how to achieve the grace, clarity, and energy that we admire in literary texts. I remember discussing these matters with Kurt Vonnegut one evening in New York. He reached into his bookshelves and handed me a textbook, *Engineers as Writers*, which contained an inscription to him by one of the editors, Walter J. Miller. In that volume, which I borrowed, I found, among other things, an interview with Othmar H. Ammann.

Miller and Leo E. Saidla, the other editor, had included in their book Ammann's proposal to build what became, when Ammann built it, the George Washington Bridge over the Hudson River. In the interview, Ammann said two striking things: First, "most engineers think in terms of details. And so most engineering reports are cluttered with meaningless particulars"; second, when asked how he had trained himself to write clear and vivid reports, Ammann replied, "I rely on my studies of logic and literature. Logic taught me how to structure my writing. Literature gives me an understanding of the importance of style" (252). Throughout this exemplary textbook, the editors focus on the literary difficulties faced by each writer in drafting a particular response to a given situation and on the literary methods used to solve those problems. And the texts they offer include translations from ancient engineers as well as the work of contemporaries like Ammann. Even this textbook for engineers, I found, stressed the literary side of writing. But what did the editors—or someone like Ammann—mean by *literary*?

I was still brooding about the various notions of literature active in our culture when I was asked to serve on the MLA's Commission on Writing and Literature. My several years of work on this commission had a radicalizing effect on my thought. The commission was charged with exploring ways of reconciling the split between composition and literature in the profession. What it discovered—or, at any rate, what I discovered while serving on it—was that the culture of English departments is structured by an invidious binary opposition between writing teachers and literary scholars that cannot be improved by tinkering. Because the profession was organized by—indeed, founded on—this distinction, it can only be undone by a deconstructive process striking at its roots. Let me try to be more explicit. What I finally realized was that English departments need composition as the "other" of literature in order to function as they do. The useful, the practical, and even the intelligible are relegated to composition so that literature can stand as the complex embodiment of cultural ideals that are so deeply embedded that they require the deep analyses of a trained scholar. Teachers of literature have become the priests and theologians of English, while teachers of composition are the nuns, barred from the priesthood, doing the shitwork of the discipline. This structure can be undone only by an assault on the notion of literature on which English departments are founded.

What I could do about this discovery, apart from the work of the commission itself, was to use what I had learned from structuralist and poststructuralist theory to perform a deconstructive critique of the curriculum and pedagogy that embody the culture of English. This effort, deployed in *Textual Power* and *Text Book*, and in other ongoing projects, is still my concern. Among other things, I want to make a case for the importance of literariness—and the usefulness of many texts we call literary—precisely by denying the special mystical privileges we have accorded to literature. To accomplish this goal, I am using the resources of critical theory not only to deconstruct our traditional organization but also to reconstruct our efforts as students and teachers of English around the notion of textuality. Under this sign, there is no difference between writing theory and critical theory. In fact, there is precious little difference between theory and teaching at all, since the practice of teaching is based on the teaching of theory, and this theory itself rests on the shared stance of students and teachers as practitioners of writing.

Brown University

Learning to Live with Your Past and Liking It

W. Ross Winterowd

In this brief essay, I am unable to argue for a thesis that, in any case, I take to be self-evident: Romantic theories of language, aesthetics, and rhetoric—originating with the epistemology of the German idealists and transmitted through (and transmuted by) Coleridge, De Quincey, Carlyle, Pater, and others in Great Britain and through Emerson, Thoreau, and others in the United States—constituted the noetic and professional universe of the New Criticism that I entered in the 1950s when I began graduate work. My awareness of the ocean in which I swam was not bonk-sudden, as with Newton and the mythical apple, but excruciatingly slow, as in a surfaceward drifting toward a light that grew progressively brighter and at last radiated blindingly when I emerged into the air: I was able to understand why the "literature of fact" was devalued and made peripheral and why "composition" was ghettoized—why, for most of my career, my interests (and I) have been marginal in the English department and the MLA (if the two are, indeed, separable). I would argue, furthermore, that English department humanities have never recovered from their Romantic "purification."

When I began my formal literary education more than four decades ago I quickly learned that, because of their transcendental value, poems, short stories, novels, and plays were the texts at the heart of the canon and that autobiographies, biographies, histories, and essays were peripheral since they were not "imaginative" literature. Only some years later did I realize that the pruning of the canon resulted from an epistemology expressed most cogently in Coleridge's theory of the imagination (as interpreted and transmitted by such figures as I. A. Richards), with works classed as "imaginative" and "other," the other always at the periphery of courses and curricula, scholarly journals and the MLA. Here is Richards's interpretation of Coleridge:

The Primary Imagination is normal perception that produces the usual world of the senses,

> That inanimate cold world allowed
> To the poor loveless ever-anxious crowd

the world of motor-buses, beef-steaks, and acquaintances, the framework of things and events within which we maintain our everyday existence, the world of the routine satisfaction of our minimum exigencies. The Secondary Imagination, re-forming this world, gives us not only poetry—in the limited sense in which literary critics concern themselves with it—but every aspect of the routine world in which it is invested with other values than these necessary for our bare continuance as living beings. . . .

(*Coleridge* 58)

In other words, the primary imagination is, at best, Matthew Brady or Margaret Bourke-White: a photographer. The secondary imagination is Mary Cassatt or Pablo Picasso: a creative artist. (We can round off Coleridge's faculties of creativity by saying that fancy is Jean Arp: a madcap dadaist.)

René Wellek and Austin Warren further alembicated. For them, the function of literature was to provide a "higher pleasure," characterized by "non-acquisitive contemplation" (30). And Northrop Frye virtually etherealized literature:

> In literature, questions of fact or truth are subordinated to the primary literary aim of producing a structure of words for its own sake, and the sign values of symbols are subordinated to their importance as a structure of interconnected motifs. Wherever we have an autonomous verbal structure of this kind, we have literature. Wherever this autonomous structure is lacking, we have language, words used instrumentally to help human consciousness do or understand something else.   (74)

Immersed in this institutionalized, purified view of literature while I was working on my dissertation, I was trying, in my own terms, to make sense of Plato's *Phaedrus*, Aristotle's *Rhetoric*, Cicero's *De Oratore*, Quintilian's *Institutio*, and *On the Sublime*. Since I had also been a student of Albert R. Kitzhaber, first as an undergraduate at Utah State University and then as a graduate student at the University of Kansas, I became aware that rhetoric was a possible, if not totally respectable, subject of research, as Kitzhaber's now classic dissertation, *Rhetoric in*

American Colleges, 1850–1900, proved. And then I began to read Kenneth Burke, who asked not what literature *is* but what it *does*. As a devout believer in prevenient grace, I realize that I had a primal taint of character that made me susceptible to the corrupting influences of classic rhetoricians, of Kitzhaber, of Burke, and then of Wayne Booth in *The Rhetoric of Fiction*.

For some time, I have been in my anecdotage, so here's a story that characterizes the status of composition, nonfiction prose, and my role in the profession. In a department meeting, my colleagues spent half an hour arguing about who was qualified to teach our sophomore creative writing class. After that weighty matter was settled, we spent roughly thirty seconds deciding on faculty members for our two sections of advanced composition. "We'll give the classes to a TA," said the chair, and then we turned again to Really Important Business. And here's another story. In my twenty-four years at the University of Southern California, a class in nonfiction prose and a graduate seminar with that focus have each been taught one time. In *The Rhetoric of the "Other" Literature*, I have diagnosed this strange situation, which alienates English department "literature" from "factual" texts that are now commonplace (as was the novel in the nineteenth century) and that, in my view, are significant works of art (e.g., Dillard's *Pilgrim at Tinker Creek*; Matthiessen's *The Snow Leopard*; Bryan's *Friendly Fire*).

Since "composition"—under whatever guise, such as Freshman Writing, Freshman English, Writing across the Curriculum, and Business Writing—aims to teach students to write what Nancy Comley and Robert Scholes call "pseudononliterature" (98), it is a less noble and less ennobling enterprise than is "creative writing," which engenders "pseudoliterature." The poem, for example,

> permits its readers at once to cherish its creation as a closed object, one that comes to terms with itself, and to recognize its necessarily incomplete nature in its dependence on us as its readers, on literary history, on the general language system, and on the way of the world.   (Krieger 540)

However, a freshman theme or an advanced composition essay invites us only to mark errors and point out lapses in reasoning, lack of sufficient evidence, incoherence, and the clumsy title.

What Frank Lentricchia says of Murray Krieger holds pretty well, I believe, for literary theory in general:

> The important consideration in the definition of art is not the
> traditional one of art's relationship to other human activities and
> the world of nature, but—a point taken too much for granted by
> too many theorists since Kant—the ways in which art is awe-
> somely independent of nature and other "non-artistic" human
> processes. (216)

Throughout my career, then, English department humanists have
devalued the literature of fact, and they have scorned composition.
"Composition teaching," Richard Lanham remarks, "remains repetitive
and routine. It also takes grotesque amounts of time. If you do it for
long uninterrupted, it threatens to turn your mind to oatmeal" (20).
Unlike literary studies, composition and rhetoric are without theory,
without intellectual content. In composition,

> the emphasis can happily be on *praxis* as opposed to *theoria*.
> Such theory as there is is immediately testable in practice. The
> discipline is required to appropriate only as much theory as it
> needs and as works, while ideas can fairly easily be hooted out of
> court. (J. H. Miller, "Composition" 39)[1]

When I first began to teach composition—as a doctoral student in
British and American literature—the director of freshman writing, the
wife of a senior professor in the English department, was a thoroughly
decent, caring person who did everything possible to help her teaching-
assistant charges be successful in their classes. I remember that we
met at noon on Fridays, for brown-bag lunches and discussion of our
problems: the seemingly impossible task of teaching students to make
verbs agree with subjects, to use proper footnote forms, to write complete sentences, to leave margins adequate for the notations we dutifully would make on the papers. The director always provided cookies
or brownies. The emphasis was definitely "on *praxis* as opposed to
theoria." There were no ideas to be "hooted out of court."

The MLA responded to growing pressures from the ghetto by establishing the Division on the *Teaching* of Writing, giving compositionists
a way to perpetuate their brown-bag sessions while the main body of
serious scholars could go on with their important and intellectually
electric business of theorizing about and interpreting imaginative literature. Interestingly enough, the MLA Division on the Teaching of Literature is sicklier than the Division on the Teaching of Writing, for the
study and interpretation of literature is above the grubby concerns

denoted by that etymologically monstrous word *pedagogy*. (Composition is, of course, all pedagogy.)

The 1990 MLA convention program is the 106th formal statement of the marginalization of composition, rhetoric, and the literature of fact within English department humanities. Of the 699 sessions listed, 64 are indexed under "Literary Criticism and Theory," but none of these seem to concern the "other" literature directly; 11 sessions are indexed under "Nonfictional Prose"; and 6 appear under "Rhetoric and Rhetorical Theory." Seven sessions related to composition appear under "The Teaching of Language and Literature" (e.g., "Feminist Perspectives on Composition"), but none appear under "Composition"—theory, teaching, or other.

My thesis could well be that the MLA tolerates or even encourages fringe activities (the Division on the Teaching of Writing, literacy conferences, and publications such as, for instance, Connolly and Vilardi's *New Methods in College Writing Programs*) merely as a way of co-opting folks like me. If I look at the annual program and complain, the president of the organization can say to me, "But we do meet your interests. Just look at. . . ." And the main body of the organization will tolerate these fringe activities as long as they don't impinge on the real mission of the MLA.

But I've changed my perspective. Certainly the aspects of the MLA that interest me *are* on the fringe and don't interest the great, almost inert body that mills around the Hilton or the Palmer House in December.[2] However, that noddingly somber audience for papers, those thirsty guests at publishers' cocktail parties, the glittering scholars whose period of greatest glory is at the convention[3]—they don't care what goes on at the periphery, which means that outsiders like me can use the organization for our own nefarious purposes. Clearly, the peripheral activities and projects resulted not from an astute political move to neutralize dissidents but from sheer ennui and lack of interest. As long as the unenunciated policy continues to be "live and let live," we "fringies" can use the cachet and resources of the MLA to gain credibility in our own institutions, through membership and activity in the proper club (and such organizations as the Conference on College Composition and Communication are *not* proper), and to sponsor conferences, research, and publications in our fringe areas of interest (for instance, in the vocabulary of our nonstandard dialect, composition, literacy, pedagogy).

Paradoxically, in the long run the fringe may well be more important to the MLA than is the center that glitters so brightly during the holiday season. Like architecture, medicine, and engineering, the study of literature should be an applied field, asking and trying to answer questions about the uses of literature in what Jean-François Lyotard characterizes as the "postmodern condition," about the effects of literature on cognition and conduct, about the most effective methods of teaching literature, about the status and uses of literacy, about teaching reading and writing, about the "common reader" (who is likely to be a reader of nonfiction prose)—just the sort of questions that preoccupy the fringies. Literary study should, then, be depurified. The English department establishment should actually assume responsibility for composition, the field from which it has reaped its yearly crop of fellowships for graduate students. (I would be appalled if one of my fringe colleagues were ignorant of theorists such as Arnold, Bakhtin, Barthes, Bloom, Brooks, Coleridge, Derrida, Eagleton, Fish, Gilbert, Kristeva, Leavis, Lévi-Strauss, Miller, Tate. . . . I *am* appalled that MLA centrists are ignorant of such theorists as Bartholomae, Berlin, Berthoff, Blair, Campbell, Coles, Corbett, D'Angelo, Emig, Flower, Howells, Kitzhaber, Lauer, Miller [Susan], Neel, North, Ohmann, Perelman, Phelps, Toulmin, Whately, Young. . . .)

But I can now have it both ways. I can argue that the central concerns and activities of the MLA are trivial and utterly peripheral to society and its concerns but that through historical circumstance the organization is essential to the fringies, since they are part of the institutionally constituted and departmentalized disciplines (i.e., literature and languages) that the MLA represents and validates. In other words, you can't change history; one way or another, you must learn to live with your past. And I've now found a title for this lament: "Learning to Live with Your Past and Liking It."

University of Southern California

NOTES

[1]As I have written elsewhere, "Invidiously one could say that Miller seems to feel there are two kinds of theory: practical (which works but is, by implication, idea-less) and impractical (which could rescue composition from its vacuity). Miller undoubtedly is arguing that some theory is empirically testable and that some is not, and no one would deny that claim; however, the compositionists with whom I associate are, like our literary colleagues, also concerned with questions of 'ought' or 'should,' with the rational as opposed to the empirical, with dialectic as opposed to measurement, with values as opposed to quantities" ("Purification" 265).

[2] I know. It's a lousy metaphor: an inert body milling around. But, after all, I'm not literary.

[3] As the convention ends, a renewed, buoyant MLA member leaves the Hilton, Americana, or Palmer House to catch a taxi to the airport. The hotel doorman idly inquires, "You one of them English teachers?" And now the dream is over until next December.

"Gender and Reading" Revisited

Elizabeth A. Flynn

Feminism has become *feminisms* in the 1980s and 1990s, an indication of the diversity of feminist positions and the lack of consensus among feminists about fundamental issues. In the 1970s, feminists, perhaps because of their vulnerability, tended to identify themselves as a group with a unified goal and a common enemy, patriarchy. In the 1980s and 1990s, however, feminists have often defined their positions in opposition to those of other feminists. Toril Moi, in the preface to *Sexual/Textual Politics: Feminist Literary Theory,* for instance, defends her frequent disagreements with other feminists, citing the importance of genuine critical debate about the political implications of feminism's methodological and theoretical choices (xiii).

I realized in a personal way that feminists had entered a new mode of discourse when I encountered Nina Baym's critique of my essay "Gender and Reading" in Susan Gabriel and Isaiah Smithson's *Gender in the Classroom.* Arguing that "all interpretations are contingent and none are correct" (75), Baym, in "The Feminist Teacher of Literature," has difficulty with my evaluations of the numerous student response statements included in my essay. She finds in the assessments evidence that my reading is "transcendental," that I impose my own ideological framework on my students, thereby doing them harm.

This is a serious charge. If feminist teachers of a particular persuasion are harming their students, they certainly ought to be stopped. "Gender and Reading," however, says nothing about how I teach or how anyone else should teach. The student response statements I collected came from several sections of first-year English taught by several teachers. I analyzed the statements to investigate the reading process, not the teaching process. Because Baym sees my orientation as pedagogical, she assumes that I want to use the categories I identify to evaluate student writing. In fact, I make no such claim.

"Gender and Reading" takes issue with the radically relativist position Baym espouses, affirming, instead, that some readings are better than others and that misreading is possible. Indeed, Baym's essay is a good example of the gap that inevitably exists between intention and effect. According to Baym, the thesis of the piece is that "men are aggressive, women cooperative" (71), whereas I make it clear that my findings were much more complex. Some men were resistant readers and some women were interactive readers, but most of the students were submissive readers. This essay is a meditation stimulated by Baym's remarks about "Gender and Reading."

"Gender and Reading" was begun in 1980; published in *College English* in 1983; reprinted in *Gender and Reading*, a volume I coedited with Patrocinio Schweickart in 1986; reprinted again in David Richter's *The Critical Tradition* in 1989; and reprinted once more in Melita Schaum and Connie Flanagan's *Gender Images* in 1992. Reflecting on it, then, provides a good focus for this narrative on how my thinking has evolved and how the fields of literary studies, composition studies, and feminist studies have developed over the past decade.

"Gender and Reading" examines response statements of male and female students in the light of a gendered theory of reading. Drawing on Wolfgang Iser's model of the reading process, I argued that effective reading involves interaction between a reader and a text so that the reader achieves a balance between participation in the events of the text and critical detachment. Ineffective reading involves domination of a text by a reader or domination of a reader by a text. I studied the responses twenty-six female and twenty-six male students wrote, under somewhat controlled conditions, about three short stories in a first-year composition course. I selected the students from seven sections of first-year English that two male colleagues and I had taught; students wrote responses before the stories were discussed in class so that their responses would not reflect the influence of the instructor or other classmates. I tentatively concluded that most of the men and the women wrote submissive responses. Some male readers, though, dominated the texts, while no women did, and more women than men were able to achieve a balance between domination and submission.

The essay reflects developments in reader-response theory, feminist literary studies, and composition studies, fields that were not frequently brought together in the early 1980s. Reader-response theory had just become a visible force in literary studies with the publication of books by Norman Holland, Louise Rosenblatt (*Reader*), David Bleich (*Subjective Criticism*), Wolfgang Iser, and others and of anthologies edited by Jane Tompkins and by Susan Suleiman and Inge Crosman. Feminist literary studies was more fully developed, having arisen in the early 1970s. It was just beginning, though, to focus attention specifically on reading, with the publication of work by Judith Fetterley, Annette Kolodny, and others. Composition studies, emerging as a recognizable field in the early 1980s, was very much a hybrid. Dominant influences within composition studies at the time included such fields as rhetoric and cognitive psychology. "Gender and Reading" derived its central research question from feminist literary studies, its theoretical base from reader-response theory, and its method from empirically oriented work in composition studies.

Bleich's "Gender Interests in Reading and Language," which was written after "Gender and Reading" and was no doubt influenced by it to an extent, helps illustrate how feminist literary theory, reader-response theory, and the empiricism of composition studies converge in my essay. Like "Gender and Reading," Bleich's essay attempts to explore gender differences in responses to literary texts. Bleich's theoretical approach is subjectivist rather than interactional, though, and his method is largely interpretive rather than empirical. The major portion of Bleich's essay analyzes the responses of Bleich and three students to literature read in a graduate-level course composed of eight students, but he ignores the responses of the five remaining students. Toward the end of his essay, Bleich reports on a second study in which he seems to have been influenced, to an extent, by empirical methods. He collected 120 retellings of Faulkner's "Barn Burning" and selected one hundred at random, fifty by men, fifty by women. Like an empirical researcher, he informs us of his sampling method and size.

For the most part, though, the essay reflects Bleich's resistance to research that attempts to emulate the methods of the social and quantitative sciences. In "The Identity of Pedagogy and Research in the Study of Response to Literature," published in 1980, Bleich argues that a preferred method is to investigate the reasons and values held by individual readers and groups of readers that motivated the specific shape and character of the knowledge resulting from their reading experiences. The knowledge that results from this procedure is not predictive, he admits. Rather, it aims to create new mental orientations toward acts of reading in individuals and groups (353).

My work has moved closer to the approach Bleich defends. In "Composing as a Woman," for instance, I looked at the narrative essays of only four students, two men and two women. And while I derived the categories I used in the analysis from the work of social scientists such as Carol Gilligan and Nancy Chodorow, I did not attempt to control the study as I did in "Gender and Reading." As I explain in "Composing 'Composing as a Woman,' " the essay is interpretive rather than experimental.

"Gender and Reading" is a product of the early 1980s. Its research question reflects a decidedly American form of feminist literary studies. French feminism, with its poststructuralist orientation, did not have a strong effect on American feminist literary studies until later in the decade. Moreover, "Gender and Reading" bears the mark of the early 1980s in featuring a primarily cognitive rather than social variety of reader-response theory. The method used in "Gender and Reading" also reflects, in its empiricism and objectivism, the development of composition studies at the time.

In short, "Gender and Reading" is innocent of the influence of postmodernism, a movement that has had a significant effect on feminist literary studies, reader-response theory, and composition studies in the past decade. American feminist literary criticism has gained theoretical sophistication as it has attempted to meet the challenge posed by postmodernist thought. Its commonsense beliefs in authors and autonomous texts, which derived from New Critical assumptions, were no longer acceptable grounds for practical criticism. Reader-response theory has shifted its emphasis from individual readers to communities of readers and in so doing has anticipated and contributed to the emergence of a postmodern perspective within literary studies. In composition studies, postmodernism in the form of social construction has taken such a strong hold that experimental research and empirical approaches influenced by research in education and the social sciences often need to be defended.[1]

How might we reread "Gender and Reading" in the light of what postmodernism has taught us about gender, reading, and methods of inquiry? Questions of gender identity are clearly considerably more problematic than they appeared to be in 1980. Postmodern feminists have questioned the idea that men and women constitute distinctly different categories and have warned of the dangers of essentialism—the identification of foundational or essential characteristics on the basis of gender. Postmodern feminists are wary of descriptions of female essences, even if those essences are seen as historical or social rather than biological.[2] They also tend to see male dominance as so pervasive that women can only be defined negatively, as that which is not male.

"Gender and Reading" is not essentialist. Differences between the responses of male and female students were not clear-cut. Most male and female students wrote submissive responses to the short stories, after all. Unquestionably, though, the essay is obviously more a product of cultural feminism than of postmodern feminism. The finding that the female students were more frequently interactive readers than were the men anticipates the work of interpretive psychologists such as Carol Gilligan and Mary Field Belenky et al., who tend to see women's ways of making moral decisions or women's ways of knowing as superior to men's ways. Postmodern feminists would have difficulty generalizing about or seeing "women's ways," if those ways could be positively identified.

Recent reader-response theory also challenges cognitive models of reader-text interaction, suggesting instead that reading takes place within a social context. Stanley Fish and David Bleich are the theorists most strongly committed to this social-constructionist position. Deconstructionists would take the argument several steps farther, questioning the reader's subjectivity, suggesting that reading is a highly problematic activity because a writer's original intention cannot be recovered, and pointing out that linguistic conventions are always already in place and so have a determining force in language activity.

"Gender and Reading" does assume that individual readers are relatively stable subjects, that reading is possible, and that some readings are better than others. In this sense it is prepostmodern. Individual readers by no means project stable identity themes on those texts, though. Their readings vary in accordance with the text they are reading, as do their subjectivities, it would seem. Also, "Gender and Reading" tells a story of misreading rather than of reading. The students' responses to the stories seem so far removed from anything the author might have originally intended that they provide evidence for absent authors and Derridean *différance*.

Finally, what of the essay's empirical method? Of its attempt to create a controlled situation free of the teacher's influence? Recent feminist critiques of science have focused on the androcentrism of claims of objectivity. Such claims are little more than examples of male subjectivity, these theorists would say. Perception is socially constructed, an inevitable result of the situation of the perceiver within a complex social context. Critical theorists and compositionists of a social-constructionist persuasion would no doubt agree. Critiques of objectivity are widespread.

Some feminists, though, have accepted the critique of traditional empirical methods without abandoning the goals of empiricism. In the conclusion to *Feminism and Methodology*, for instance, Sandra Harding discusses feminist empiricism, an approach that aims for objective results, for a kind of feminist science. Feminist empiricists see traditional science as unsatisfactory because, instead of being objective, it is informed by an androcentric bias. They attempt to eliminate this bias, and they think women may be in a good position to do so since women are freer of androcentric ways of seeing. According to Harding, they exhort social scientists to follow the existing research norms more rigorously (184). Harding also points out, though, that feminist empiricism is challenged by postmodernism, which sees feminism as taking an antagonistic position toward any attempt to do science, androcentric or not.

I would like to see feminist empiricists develop their position more forcefully. Surely there are times when we need to attempt to peel away bias and prejudice and uncover the lived experience of women, when we need to attempt to locate "objective" truth, even if we know that objectivity is ultimately impossible to achieve. Feminists need to develop ways of adjudicating among perspectives, of evaluating perceptions, observations, readings.

"Gender and Reading" reflects my own situatedness in feminist literary studies, reader-response theory, and composition studies in the 1980s. As postmodernism might predict, though, the essay has taken on a life of its own, finding its way into collections of essays published later in the decade and into the hands of readers such as Baym who seem to prefer that it reflect their present critical perspectives.[3] I am especially interested in exploring what misreading might mean now that postmodernism has awakened us to the near inevitability of failed communication.

Michigan Technological University

NOTES

[1] Flower's "Cognition, Context, and Theory Building" is a good example of a strongly defensive discussion of the place of social scientific methods in composition research.

[2] Moi makes this point in "Feminist, Female, Feminine."

[3] For appreciative readings of "Gender and Reading," see S. Clark; Gelpi. Caughie laments the essay's "scientifically controlled environment" and its valuation of "critical detachment" (321).

A Letter to the Editors

Sharon Crowley

Dear Johns:

So you want to know what we thought about "literary-critical theory and writing theory around 1980 or so and now"? Come on. In 1980 we didn't think about literary theory; we thought with terms like *structuralism* or *psychoanalytic criticism*. That these isms might have something to say to or about each other was a well-kept institutional secret at that time. Critical theory meant Adorno and Horkheimer, maybe Habermas. And writing theory? You are kidding, aren't you?

This is not to imply that things weren't lively, intellectually, for me during that time, as they probably were for most people in rhetoric and composition. During the sixties, Ed Corbett and other scholars had reminded rhetoricians that their field had a long and mostly glorious history in the West, and I devoted as much of my graduate work as I could to reading Aristotle and Cicero, along with the great traditional histories of classical and modern rhetoric (Kennedy; Murphy; Ong; Howell). But the history of rhetoric was not my only preoccupation during the seventies; I was also interested in current developments in what is now called composition theory.

In the early seventies, Janet Emig and others helped composition teachers to understand that we could teach writing rather than editing. Writing teachers began to theorize about the writing process. And, lo and behold, a new professional category emerged: composition theory. As used in this phrase, however, *theory* meant something like generalizing about what writers do—intellectually, emotionally, ritually, whatever—while they compose. I read stuff on consciousness and creativity, and I read a lot of linguistics too. In those days, some composition teachers thought that psychology and/or linguistics would help us to forge models of the writing process that we could teach to our students, who would then imitate those models to produce writing of their own.

Then, in 1977, one of my colleagues went off to Yale on sabbatical. When he got back to Arizona he was raving about a philosopher named

Jacques Derrida. He insisted that a few of us read Derrida together, and since he was chair of the department, we complied. Northern Arizona's Only Poststructuralist Luncheon Club met every other Friday afternoon, and its members consumed a lot of beer and peanuts while we argued our way through *Of Grammatology*. No doubt I remember the process too simply, but it seems to me now that Derrida just blew my mind.

To understand the effect of deconstruction on my thinking, dear Johns, you have to remember that there wasn't a lot of real intellectual diversity in English departments in those days. Sure, you could argue with your colleagues about the virtues of psychoanalytic as opposed to phenomenological or hermeneutic approaches to texts. But most people used either New Critical or current-traditional approaches, or both, in their teaching. The few rhetoricians who worked in English departments inevitably worked in the shadow of literary studies, and I, at least, tried for a long while to adopt or adapt the institutional example of literary studies to my own thinking about rhetoric and composition.

Literary studies had a well-defined canon, and it employed well-known methodologies for putting some works in and keeping others out. It had a prestigious journal filled with arcana that nobody read. It had a history that had long before been segregated into discrete units around which courses could be organized. Its textbooks featured neat categories like The Age of Enlightenment, or they used thematic divisions that yielded up categories like A Sense of Place. All this machinery gave the impression that the great literary texts were simply there to be studied and admired: they were immaculately conceived, and as a result, they were also universal, timeless, and unalterable.

Rhetoric and composition didn't have any of this stuff. By definition, after all, a rhetorical text is never universal or timeless. Academic rhetoricians were always apologizing for their interest in such ephemera as political speeches. And any composition teacher worth his or her salt knew that student texts, at least, were infinitely alterable. That is to say, our daily practice, as well as our interest in occasional texts, showed us a model of composing that just didn't jibe with the virgin-birth model adumbrated within traditional literary studies.

In other words, I had an intuitive sense that the study of rhetoric ought to be carried on in institutional terms very different from those with which I was familiar. But I was unable to articulate anything more than my frustration with this state of affairs. I carried my differentness around with me into department meetings, curricular debates, budget hearings, tenure decisions. My colleagues were amazingly tolerant. (I was hired to design a series of courses called Writing for the World of

Work. Since technical writing was about the only way English departments defined upper-division writing in those days, my department assumed that because it had advertised for someone interested in rhetoric and composition, it had hired a technical writer. Ha!)

I think that rhetoricians and composition teachers of my generation tried to hide our differentness in our scholarship, though. We tried to identify with idealism, to show that rhetoric really was a philosophy, that composition really did proceed according to a scientifically identifiable process. But no matter how hard we tried, rhetoric and composition—messy, practical, real-world, evanescent endeavors—just wouldn't live up to idealist standards of neatness and control, direction and purpose, unity and coherence, and the Search for Identity and a Sense of Place.

Derrida showed me why we could stop bothering with all this. His insight—that Western thought operates through a set of hierarchical dichotomies—helped me to see that rhetoric, the suppressed half of the dualism of philosophy and rhetoric, is necessary to the maintenance of its more celebrated other. Western culture's continuing forgetfulness of the rhetoricity of all texts was not to be mourned—it was instead something to celebrate. If nothing else, the marginalization of rhetoric afforded its students a unique critical perspective from which to view philosophical thought: of necessity, we spoke its language, but we did not need to buy into its program.

Plato condemned rhetoric because of its indeterminacy, its willingness to tolerate foolishness, to talk to anybody at all, to fool around with tropes and figures rather than search for truth, to celebrate gut feelings over reason. Historians of rhetoric used to apologize for Plato: "He didn't *really* mean it. You just have to read him allegorically, so that true love is really true rhetoric—get it?" Derrida's reading of seminal ancient texts gave me the courage to see and say that Plato condemned rhetoric because he wanted to identify, stabilize, and control meaning in the service of his own ends. That his supposedly universal and transhistorical end served his own time-bound, local, and aristocratic ends (such as censoring the rhetoricians and banishing the poets so that philosophers and kings could own the discursive turf) was merely happy coincidence, if you subscribed to the Platonic myth, that is.

This insight got me to thinking about the supposed discourse theory developed among the sophists who taught in and around Athens at the same time that Socrates was collaring young men off the streets. Since Plato was so hard on them in his dialogues, I began to wonder whether Protagoras, Gorgias, Isocrates, and the rest had understood the deconstructive potential of rhetoric. Standard histories of rhetoric paid only glancing attention to the sophists because their texts had disappeared, for the most part, and because nineteenth-century classicists had invented a reading for their work that condemned it as "mere" sophistry. Despite the textual difficulties associated with studying their work, I discovered that Gorgias doubted the possibility of representation, among other things (nothing exists, and even if it did, it couldn't be talked about). Protagoras was apparently skeptical about the whole project of philosophy and philosophizing, and Isocrates preached attendance on the here and now. (Classical scholars are now coming round to the view that Socrates himself was a sophist. This turn of events is most satisfying, from a rhetorician's perspective. "What goes around comes around," according to Waylon Jennings).

Anyway, I wrote "Of Gorgias and Grammatology," in which I tried to show that the Sophists always already knew what Derrida had recently rediscovered. I am only a little bit embarrassed to report that I really did think that one could responsibly posit similarities between sophistry and deconstruction. You must remember that I was raised in an idealism that posited the transhistorical travel of ideas. Of course, my real agenda must be embarrassingly available to all who have read this far: I wanted desperately to legitimate my interests in rhetoric and its history. To do so I warranted them with the authority of the Sophists and Derrida. The Sophists were ancient enough to serve as distinguished forebears but also just marginal enough to irritate philosophers and other idealists; and Derrida was pretty flashy in those days, although he didn't stay on the margins for long.

Until recently, I could confidently say that Derrida had exerted more influence on my intellectual life than any other writer had. And even though I've moved along, I can't deny that the intellectual tactics of deconstruction have become a big part of my repertoire. It's hard to generalize about effects that are so thoroughly embedded in my working life, but I guess I can say that deconstruction put me in the habit of suspicion. I am especially wary of pronouncements that assert an authoritative origin (as in "Foucault himself says . . .") or a predictably generalized telos (as in "if you teach this way, your students will respond in this way . . ."). Certainly Derrida taught me to be suspicious of any rhetoric that claims to predict the outcome of verbal engagements (as do most modern rhetorics and much contemporary composition theory).

Intellectual dependence on Derrida is not easy to sustain these days, however, when deconstruction in particular and poststructuralism in general are under attack from feminists and Marxists and ethnic critics.

Despite Michael Ryan's heroic (and too little read) effort to read deconstruction as having potential use in radical social programs, you can't deny that deconstructive attitudes problematize or overlook or eliminate human agency. It's still hard for me to think about institutional or cultural change without thinking about people talking and acting. And, as feminists and ethnic critics point out, the modernist "subject" was invented by privileged white males (many of whom were childless bachelors—did you ever notice? Burke did, in *A Grammar of Motives*). People who belong to that same relatively privileged group are now in the business of deconstructing subjectivity, suspiciously enough, just when women and people of color are discovering its uses and its power.

There is also the difficulty that so far, as we all know only too well, Derrida's work has mostly been put to conservative uses in the academy. This situation is complicated, of course, by Derrida's unsatisfactory entries into discussions about sexism and racism. This last consideration raises a couple of interesting questions for a postmodern rhetorician: Should a writer's life (or at least his or her subject position) be taken into account in evaluations of his or her work? And what is the status of an ad hominem or ad feminam attack in postmodern discourse? Foucault fails to theorize his own sexuality; Kristeva looks to America for theoretical salvation; Derrida refuses to become politically involved; de Man—well, we all know that story.

At a recent CCCC meeting, Patricia Bizzell made the claim that a writer's only authority these days derives from his or her ethos: "Believe this because *I* want you to." She is arguing from an antifoundationalist perspective, of course, wherein no transcendental signified can be found to legitimate any argumentative position. But does Bizzell mean, then, that one's life history is on the line whenever she tries to get somebody to believe her about something? In other words, Bizzell's argument legitimates ad hominem and ad feminam attacks; it's not fallacious anymore to hold your life to account when we evaluate your work, Virginia, and you had better straighten up and do right—at least when you write for publication. I think Bizzell is right. (My conviction is strengthened when the editors of an MLA collection ask people to write autobiography for it).

Bizzell's notion of ethos is a bit like Aristotle's, since Aristotle taught that one's ethos amounts to one's reputation in the relevant community. Even though he was writing about a very small and quite homogeneous community (Athenian male citizens), his remarks about ethos, oddly enough, seem relevant within our own postmodern electronic global culture. Certainly, keeping one's work and one's life separate is much harder now than it was when we used to pretend to do it. In an age when the so-called private moral choices made by public figures can disqualify them for office, and when gay activists argue that so-called private discourses like psychotherapy are instruments of oppression, the old liberal distinction between a public and a private ethos no longer holds. The choices that a writer like Derrida faces, then, are these: admit that anything you have to say about women or people of color comes out of a Western male cultural imaginary that has always defined such persons as other or absent; or cease to write about them as though you were an authority on the subject positions they inhabit.

What this predicament implies, of course, is that the modernist dreams of a universal rhetoric (like those of Campbell and of Perelman and Olbrechts-Tyteca) are so much hogwash. Protagoras knew that any rhetoric is partial and exclusionary, and thanks to feminist and ethnic critics, we're learning that lesson all over again. We've also realized that rhetoric can claim to be universal, or impartial, only when it masks the fact of its having silenced whatever voices oppose it. (I think of George Bush, who couldn't seem to understand that some Americans don't share his politics because some Americans are not white and privileged like he is, or of liberal humanist composition theorists who can think that their pedagogy has no politics precisely because it has *their* politics.)

In the light of these recognitions, honest postmodern rhetoricians cannot theorize about much of anything without making endless qualifications about our authority to do so. We must remember that, if cultural or institutional conditions are right, whatever we say or write (and do?) has a potential effect on persons who hear or read it or are affected by it. Of course, we never know what that effect is, or will be, since we've had to jettison our idealized notions of sovereign authorship and reasonable audiences and all the rest of our traditional lore.

But then these problems are now everybody's problems, thanks to poststructuralism. And the problems entailed in unraveling the differences that exist between and among people are better problems than the ones we concerned ourselves with in 1980, when we were trying to make everybody fit into a few ideal categories. They are better problems because they are more challenging and because they immerse us in the times and the people and the culture we live in and with. For example, having jettisoned idealism, we can get rid of the textbook notion of the student as someone whose identity is created solely by the classroom. Instead, we can look at our students as people who bring the discourses of their communities into the classroom with them. Their discourses are not always pleasant to hear and read, riddled as they may be with racism, sexism, elitism. But we acknowledge students' languages as their own these days, more profoundly than we used to. And we don't deny the ugliness and alienation of the world outside the classroom anymore, and we don't kid ourselves that our classrooms are, or can be, warm huggy refuges from that world.

Like the Sophists, perhaps.

Today, I want more and better answers to this question: How does noncoercive change come about? This question presumes, of course, that current cultural conditions need changing. I believe this. I notice that feminist thought has achieved a toehold in the academy. I notice that more and more people of color appear on or in the media. How do such things happen? The ready answer is that the academy and the media are resilient enough to appropriate dissident voices. American capitalism needs workers, and its corporations need to appear to be free of bias, so a few women and fewer people of color get mainstream, high-visibility jobs. But in this process the system-altering critiques mounted by feminists and people of color get diluted: men and women alike can miss the points about the pervasiveness of patriarchy and the imperialism of compulsory heterosexuality; white people don't understand what people of color are talking about when they say that the country and its institutions are riddled with racism, because white people don't have to live with the effects of racism every day of their lives. How do we get past tokenism and into substantial system-wide change? That's what I want to know.

If you are a traditional rhetorician, there are lots of ways to think about how noncoercive change comes about. Depending on your scholarly inclinations, you can appeal to some abstraction like the "universal audience" or "class consciousness" or "ideology" or "fantasy themes." If you're a little bit less traditional, you can read Foucault's studies of the inception of psychiatry or prisons, looking for clues about just how the discourses that enable these institutions were invented. If you want to be a postmodern rhetorician, none of this theory or history helps very much, because you just can't be sure that any feature of any given instance of persuasion will work, in precisely the same way, in a different setting (although Foucault seems to have hoped that his histories would prove helpful to persons who were trying to understand the mechanics of change).

As Gorgias (probably) said, you have to make it up as you go along.

Right now we (or somebody) need to theorize about how we can enact noncoercive change without making damaging exclusions. Rhetoric disappeared as an academic study during the nineteenth century, and that disappearance has allowed its practice to go untheorized, and thus relatively unseen, for far too long. Since literary theorists, feminists, ethnographers, and the rest are not acquainted with rhetoric, they find it difficult to theorize about how noncoercive social change occurs. For example, Rita Felski argues, in *Beyond Feminist Aesthetics*, that women must learn to question "the relative value of one discursive strategy over another in a given context" and that one purpose of feminism is "to examine critically the seemingly natural and self-evident truths of everyday life" (61). While Felski wants feminists to begin these projects, she is not sure where to ground them theoretically, since she finds the discourses of Marxism, poststructuralism, and psychoanalysis to be wanting in this regard.

The projects Felski names are precisely those of rhetorical theory. The second one strikes a particularly resonant chord for rhetoricians, who have made the study of commonplaces—the available means of persuasion in a given situation—a central part of their work. Because rhetoricians know how language has intersected with power in the past and what is going on in public discourse right here and now, they are in an excellent position to help feminists and other postmodern theorists examine the way power relations are constructed in discourse and disseminated within culture. I don't mean to be exclusive or disciplinary: I just mean that we're at your service should you want us.

Well, Johns, writing this letter has raised a lot of old questions about the reliability of narrators and the selectivity of memory. Autobiography is certainly closer to fiction than ever I suspected.

Yours in sophistry,
Sharon

University of Iowa

"Rhetoric Is Politics," Said the Ancient. "How Much So," I Wonder.

Victor Villanueva, Jr.

My life affects my work. It's not as if I hadn't been affected by racism and other systemic forces before I entered academics. It's just that I hadn't recognized those forces before. But now those forces come back to me in pictures.

Bedford-Stuyvesant. The A student, a reader for fun, a spelling bee champ; later, at the neighborhood voc-tech school, a student of drafting, foundry work. White folks have names like Hauser and Steinberg. The Smiths and Joneses were on *Leave It to Beaver*, which I thought depicted another time, as did *The Lone Ranger*. It hadn't occurred to me that there really were Cleavers in other places in my own time. In the end, a high school dropout.

The Army. White folks were officers. Poor whites (not quite "white") and the people of color filled the enlisted ranks. I saw college education as making the difference. It hadn't yet occurred to me that the education line was color-coded. Sitting in a hotel room in Hawaii with my parents, R and R, all of us watching *me* on TV as the newscaster spoke of the day's war events. Today I would think about media manipulation. But then all I saw was myself on TV. In Korea I watched President Pak train guns on his own citizenry and declare that martial law would be lifted when the citizens voted for a change in the constitution that would allow him a third term as president. American soldiers, the protectors of democracy, continued their business as usual. I returned home to find that no one knew. No news on *World News*. I started to think about systemic forces.

The academy. My entry into a community college was made possible by apologies to Vietnam vets: GI Bill, low tuition, no high school requirement, no SATs or ACTs, only GEDs. None of the indignity of special boards for minorities: the economically disadvantaged, marginalized, disenfranchised, developmental, remedial, or basic (though I have since sat on such boards, in which a good deal of time was spent coming up with even more neutral terms). Once in, I enjoyed some success in English courses, enjoyed the glimpses into worlds and minds foreign to me, enjoyed having the authors I read ask questions that were similar to those already forming in my own mind.

Graduate school. Plato tells of the ideal rhetoric: abstract, dialectical, a language that cannot be pinned down. I think of the Bill of Rights: the freedom to pursue happiness, abstract notions, ideals; freedoms I would not wish to do without but that offer few concrete guarantees; no guarantees of food, housing, health. Aristotle, Hermagoras, Cicero tell of the political as the principal business of oratory: discourse for social change. My education starts to take on meaning, something more than fun. Kenneth Burke tells me more on discourse and politics—in our time. Mikhail Bakhtin tells me I cannot deny my past, even if I were to try. Louis Althusser tells me something of the systemic. The Sophists tell me that I can hold contrasting worldviews, that there can be multiple realities, and that they are formulated discursively. Quintilian tells me what I would need were I to teach. Paulo Freire tells me what I would need if I were to acknowledge the political in my teaching.

A professional. A new dimension to racism. I discover more racism in my few years in this profession than I have known in the nearly four decades prior, but not because the people and concepts with which I have come in contact are more racist. Quite the contrary. The great majority, in my experience, see inequity and try to rectify it. But there is a racism inherent in a kind of ignorance that is hard to overcome, a racism that is born of experiential ignorance. The ways in which racism creeps into individual ideologies, into the general hegemony, are only realized when those of us who are normally socially stratified and separated come in contact. People of color, of childhood exclusion from appropriate education, of childhood and adult poverty are decidedly few in this profession. No contact. By the same token, this has been my first prolonged exposure to, contact with, immersion in the white middle class. What I find is that few see beyond surface remedies, perhaps because there are limits to what can be institutionally sanctioned, and that we are subject to what Antonio Gramsci describes as a "directive hegemony" (103–04), which he describes as a hegemony that allows academics to struggle against coercive ideologies as long as basic systems are not too seriously threatened. With a directive hegemony, efforts tend toward reform, reforms that make token changes that can seem substantial. Reform tends to amount to what

Gramsci calls "revolution-restoration" (e.g., 58), changes without change, affirmative action quotas, say, more color in traditionally white positions while the basic inequities remain.

I am, like all of us in the profession who are of color and of poverty, one of the exceptions who demonstrates the rule, one who fell through a fissure in the current hegemony's historic bloc. Yet I am too often the symbol that current systems are working. And they are: systems that allow numbers of the traditionally excluded in, while the proportion of those left out remains relatively unchanged. So I find myself in a strange position: not marginalized yet not of the same class or culture; not of the same history as the majority, a history not of immigrant struggle but of colonialism and the commodified colonialism of slavery. And the strangeness itself—the ways it makes me a commodity, makes me a display of an equal access that is not truly equal—reflect the pervasiveness of difference, of racism. Yet I am a professional, generally accepted and respected as such.

Being a part of and apart from in this way makes for a struggle beyond those typical of the assistant professor. There is always the struggle, the desire within me to silence the differences between those I come in contact with and myself, to give voice to the similarities: language, teaching, a utopian wish and will through teaching and study and writing. Even as I contemplated this essay, I fought the compulsion to bypass autobiography and narrative, to bypass this underscoring of difference, from difference in background to difference in convention.

But I have not always fought the compulsion to silence my differences from those who surrounded me. No minority literature courses. There were none on Puerto Ricans anyway. A master's on Milton. Difference found expression in teaching basic writers and then in directing a basic writing program. But my authority as director could not rely on my having a background similar to that of the students in the basic writing classrooms, as far as I was concerned. Freire provided a political perspective but no specifics on teaching college composition. Authority would have to rest on the literature on basic writers.

Much of the discussion on basic writers hinged on the relation between speaking and writing. Basic writers relied too heavily on the strategies of speech. The precedent in composition studies had been set by Mina Shaughnessy. Another precedent had been set by Andrea Lunsford: that basic writers operate at a lower cognitive level than more traditional college freshman writers do. Thomas Farrell conflates the two notions, generalizing speaking and writing to orality and literacy.

Farrell writes that Arthur Jensen's genetic explanations for black ghetto youths' poor performances in school are untenable. Looking for an environmental explanation, he turns to the work of Milman Parry on oral cultures and the works of Walter Ong and Eric Havelock, who argue that literacy, which came to full fruition in Plato's time, can be credited with the beginnings of abstract thought. Literacy equals abstract thought, orality its lack. Farrell sets about demonstrating that black ghetto children reside in oral cultures. Lunsford and others who hold to the cognitive deficit theory are substantiated.

It's not as if the world of composition embraced Farrell's oral culture hypothesis. It didn't. But most objections concerned the idea that being from an oral culture makes for a cognitive deficit. Most focused on Farrell's ethnocentric notion of literacy. There remained Farrell's monolithic view that African Americans and Africans are of a cultural piece, a view for which he found scholarly authority. One view for an entire race, one culture for an entire continent—without much objection from our profession, which was turning more and more to cultural matters. And there remained the notion of the primacy of speech, that before blacks could write well, they must speak well, "well" meaning in the manner of the literate, the standard dialect. It is a pervasive idea, dialect interference. Yet in my own case, I had never intended to rid myself of the Spanish accent Sister Rhea Marie had told my mother about when I was in kindergarten, never intended to get rid of the Black English of my youth, never intended to get rid of the New York. My dialect altered, it seemed, the more I was exposed to written texts. Writing affected my speaking.

So my entry into the profession, my dissertation, would focus on the speaking-writing relation—without autobiographical references but with the objective cloak of scholarship, the extensive literature on the speaking-writing connection, and the cloak of research, of ethnography. The study involved naturalistic observation of writing groups in a traditional freshman composition course and in a basic writing course. In writing groups, writing, reading, speaking, listening are all at work. What I found, among other things, was that the "better" writers ("better" according to the teachers' grades) knew the sound, the intonation patterns, of written text. The basic writers did not. Spoken dialect was less at issue than was a lack of exposure to written text, to hearing the written read aloud, particularly the kinds of texts the students would be required to write in college.

The research also produced an interesting sidelight. The more successful students of color in each of the classrooms perceived themselves to be of the same class as professionals, believed their parents to have the same occupational prestige as a lawyer or a college professor. But not everyone would be likely to see the parents' occupational prestige as the students did. One student's mother owned a day care center; one's father, a ship's mechanic, was still called "Junior" by his coworkers and bosses after forty years with the same company. But the research was not concerned with psychosocial theories of class, of the complexities that underlie notions of culture. I never played up the class aspect. To have done so, it seemed to me at the time, would have been to enter into a polemic. I intended to be a researcher, not a practitioner of deliberative discourse.

In Kansas City, Farrell's home at the time of "IQ and Standard English," I began another ethnography, a new research project ("Considerations"). The setting: a not-for-profit private school aimed exclusively at low-income adolescents and young adults barred from traditional public schools but wanting back in. All but one of the students were black. So was the teacher: a published poet of overtly political poetry, who not only knew of Freire but had known Freire himself, who had taken part in the Nicaragua and Grenada literacy campaigns. The teacher also knew of Farrell, believed that his students were parts of an oral culture, disbelieved that their orality had cognitive consequences. Here was an opportunity to study and discuss the political while remaining the researcher.

But the research did not answer questions concerning orality and literacy. The teacher's literacy instruction relied too heavily on oral strategies: poetry, song lyrics, raps. Yet other political questions arose. The students, who clearly admired their teacher, who were attentive to his discussions on culture, black history, political systems, nevertheless resisted his calls for a particular political viewpoint: his assertion that the students' educational desires and intellectual abilities made them the potential leaders for substantive changes in the conditions under which blacks live. Why did the students resist? Why did they hold to their already formed predispositions: belief in individual achievement at the cost of the collectivity, or acceptance of black "progress," or simple, undirected defiance? Why the resistance from students who knew very well the more repressive workings of the state and the futility of individual, undirected opposition? I could only figure that they believed education was their way into the middle class; that there, in the middle class, they would no longer have anything to oppose; that they would have transcended the causes of oppression. I had shared those beliefs. I could only wonder at the pervasiveness of our myth systems.

So past research informs the present. Farrell's contention demonstrates the danger of reducing politics in the classroom to history and culture. The research responding to Farrell addressed matters of class as well as of culture. The study in Kansas City made it clear that beyond history and class and culture are race and economics and ideologies to contend with and that these ideologies can be subsumed under something greater—hegemony. My own cultures and ideologies contain the discourses of the urban black of my neighborhood, the Puerto Rican of my family, the working-class white of most of my adulthood, and now something close to the academic middle class, all conflicting, all somehow subsumed under the continuing belief in the possibility for change through education and active—radically active—democracy. Yet the economic middle class still eludes. And I am never not aware that I am not quite the white middle class. I carry what Gramsci describes as a "contradictory consciousness" (e.g., 14). All of us do.

As my research also made clear, the questions that emerged and the speculative answers that resulted were too broad to be adequately addressed in classroom research. Throughout these ethnographic studies my role had been reactive—reactions to an untenable hypothesis and a politically and ideologically (not to mention linguistically) questionable theory. Theory itself now becomes the concern—a rhetorical theory that might account for race as castelike (a concept derived from Ogbu) and for culture and class.

Nagging questions that guide: How do nice people abide by and maintain not nice things, like a system in which certain groups are consistently relegated to the bottom of the structure in disproportionate numbers? How is ideology transmitted rhetorically? How can more oppressive ideologies be countered in the rhetorical enterprise, which includes the teaching of composition?

I begin with neo-Marxian analysis. It attempts to be comprehensive. And it has been a clear influence on recent sociopolitical discussions. More precisely, I begin with Gramsci. Recognizing that we are affected by where we've been, I like that Gramsci himself had a poor childhood; that he entered college through special programs for the poor; that he writes of the peasantry in a way that recalls the American castelike minority; that he was not a philosopher but a linguist, a journalist, a political activist; that, because he wrote as a political prisoner under Mussolini—subject to censorship, without bibliographical resources— his theory is messy, allowing us to read and use Gramsci without having to become apostles of Gramsci.

I like that his theory is not a Marxism as much as it is a Marxian problematic. I like that Gramsci sees individual will and hegemonic power as making for ideological contradictions within us. There are not only the contradictions that arise in our coming from and containing various classes and cultures; there are the contradictions of sometimes having to serve self-interest and thereby knowingly giving in to and maintaining unjust systems. Franchise owners, for example, may know that they exploit their workers and that they themselves are exploited, and they may even know that the world does not have to be this way, but they can rationalize that both they and their workers profit and that those profits are necessary to survival. Because we are often conscious of the inequities by which we nevertheless abide, we in effect consent to the dominant hegemony. We are even partly responsible for the dominant hegemony, since hegemony consists, in part, of the ideologies that the various classes and cultures hold in common, though these varied ideologies tend to be used to the dominant classes' ultimate advantage. Unlike others of the neo-Marxian ilk, Gramsci does not have dominant-class conspirators unilaterally imposing ideas on working-class dupes. We are conscious.

And because we are conscious, carrying a network of ideologies, some of which would necessarily be contradictory, hegemony is not tightly woven. Hegemony can be changed. It can be changed discursively, through what Gramsci calls a war of position. It is not exactly the uniting of workers in Marx's manifesto but a historical situation, a period of critical, general sociohistorical dissatisfaction, in which certain interests can marshal the support of others for the betterment of the whole, the whole generally agreeing that better is crucial.

For a war of positions led by the castelike, by women, by the poor, a cadre of what Gramsci terms "organic" and "new" intellectuals must be created (e.g., 330, 340). Organic intellectuals, essentially, are rhetors who become leaders in their communities: César Chavez, what the teacher in Kansas City hoped his students would become. Or organic intellectuals can be those of us who reside in more traditional intellectual communities who nevertheless speak for and about the communities from which we came and, in so doing, perhaps, affect the views of those from majority communities. Instead of merely giving voice to more of the poor, to more women and castelike minorities, this process holds the promise of the rising of voices—with power and in partnership with those who have greater access to power.

But Gramsci was not a rhetorician. He could not write about how his conceptions of hegemony might complement the work of Kenneth Burke, say, or the work of those who, like Michel Foucault, see power and discourse as inextricably bound. At present the closest we have come to understanding the ideological and the hegemonic in rhetoric, particularly the rhetoric of written discourse and composition instruction, has been through James Berlin's notion of the social epistemic (see "Rhetoric"; *Rhetoric*). We come to know this idea through language, and what we know is constructed through the dialectical interplay of the self, the social group (or discourse community) within which the self functions, and the material conditions under which the self must operate. It is a notion that takes us far in recognizing that we deal less with reality than we do with worldviews, and it takes us far in dissolving the dichotomy between the individual and the collective.

But I do not believe that epistemic rhetoric has been sufficiently problematized. It is still too neat. It provides, for instance, for competing ideologies but does not yet address the competing—the contradictory—ideologies that are contained within the self. It does not yet address how many of us, particularly minorities, form our ideologies from many cultures and discourse communities. The Mexican American is both Mexican and American and yet is neither, not completely, no matter what his or her economic class, no matter the principal discourse community in which he or she functions. Despite an important advance in how we are to regard rhetoric, the epistemic at present still risks the facile categorization of culture and discourse community, which, in turn, risks the continued alienation of those who have been traditionally excluded.

In a 1978 review of trends in recent rhetorical theory Michael Leff cautioned that the epistemic view was too new and too complex to be simply accepted. It warranted cautious, disciplined study and articulation. Yet our caution has not been apparent. There are still the complexities suggested by Gramsci. We assert that writing is a way of knowing; I would like to see the assertion backed by theory, a rhetorical theory of ideology and language that can sustain the notion not only that we come to know through language but also that what we come to know is not all of a piece. The result could have persuasive value, perhaps providing a clearer understanding of how rhetoric is politics, a precedent for action, for more than token changes.

Northern Arizona University

Response to Part IV

Constructing Narratives, Seeking Change

Susan Brown Carlton

As we all learn in the process of constructing that curious document, the vita, which "places" us in our professional universe, the external markers of intellectual thresholds correspond only once in a while to the events that move us to pursue certain inquiries and not others. There is no professional register for documenting the myriad decisions whereby we pose particular questions and leave others unasked, capturing some concerns within a network of scholarship and allowing, even preferring, to leave others free-floating.

Reading the essays in this section, I was struck with the difficulty of the task faced by each author, that of constructing a narrative about how he or she has inquired about, with, and through theory within the forums of literary studies and composition studies. I suspect that each writer could rewrite his or her story with the ordering principles chosen by another, just as the readers of this volume have discovered that their own autobiographies could be reconstructed from any and all of the approaches used in these essays. All told, I can locate five principles of selection for ordering a story of one's encounters with theory: a guiding model of intelligibility, a network of people who exerted a formative influence, a set of texts, repeated interventions in professional controversies, and an accumulation of crises. I should add that these ordering principles run throughout all the essays. They are not mutually exclusive approaches, though clearly some essays are dominated by one or another of the categories, and in some of the essays one or more of these categories may barely surface.

Of course, that I should be drawn to hunt down such ordering principles has everything to do with my own current activities in the profession: a dissertation just completed, in which I analyze disciplinary narratives about poetics and rhetoric, and courses I am preparing to teach on narratives of discovery, cultural definitions of literacy, and rhetorical and literary theory. As this double agenda indicates, I share with these writers their conviction that teaching is a scholarly concern and that scholarship is inevitably pedagogic: the notion that there is any utility in conducting our professional lives otherwise serves certain institutional interests that should be contested. But I differ from these writers in that my postdoctoral professional life is just beginning; I have made my reflections on the intersections of critical theory, rhetorical theory, literature, and composition as a graduate student responding to the work of already established scholars who first mapped the possibility of articulating these fields.

What I find especially compelling about the ordering principles of these retrospective assessments is their relation to the question of what launches an inquiry, an event that Janice Lauer has captured in the term *dissonance*. What moves a felt sense of the problematic into the realm of the discursive possible so that it can be constructed as a topic instead of remaining shrouded in silence? As Jean-François Lyotard makes particularly clear in his formulation of the "differend," such a question is always ultimately a political one and never more obviously so than when we are responding to the conditions of our institutional site.

This collection of essays supports the idea that theory as a mode of conceptualizing the problematic has been a recurring facet of the enterprise to make "what goes without saying because it comes without saying" sayable and hence subject to critique (Bourdieu, *Outline* 167). Making the arena of discursive possibility broader has everything to do with Sharon Crowley's question, What makes noncoercive change possible? It is difficult to formulate responses to this question without recentering inquiry on the individualized consciousness of the humanist subject, and of course for Louise Rosenblatt and for Elizabeth Flynn, such a recentering is precisely what is called for. While I do not share their faith in the efficacy of such a recentering, I was struck by the linkage Rosenblatt makes between critique and discrimination, in the sense of differentiation, and by both Rosenblatt's and Flynn's deft movement among diverse research communities that generally resist paying any attention to one another. Instead of settling in easily within one such community, each subjects her own formulations to the (differentiating and discriminatory) perspectives of alternative traditions. Advocating the appropriateness of charting a middle way, their narratives nonetheless map a series of (intra and cross) disciplinary confrontations that are surely as productive a facet of their work as is the rejection of excess they explicitly forward, and I hope that they address that facet in future essays.

Both Rosenblatt and Flynn argue for continuums and against polarities, a position that contrasts sharply with Crowley's, Winterowd's, and Scholes's deconstructive projects of confronting and displacing binaries, above all the composition-literature opposition, which resists institutional reform. Crowley attends to questions prompted by her cross-contextualizations of the Sophists and Jacques Derrida; Winterowd, to professional collisions between the differing disciplinary ethos of rhetoric and composition studies and literary studies; and Scholes, to encounters with a series of critical movements mediated by mentors, colleagues, and students. For each of these theorists the aesthetic, either as a category of text or as a descriptor of an experiential dimension, has no explanatory power for theorizing writing and reading, yet the aesthetic retains control over the hierarchized taxonomic distinctions that rule English studies. And, for each, insistent reliance on the aesthetic demands both ideological analysis and institutional reform.

The work of all these theorists continues to serve as a resource for theorizing disciplinary relations; their essays in this volume serve as examples for locating the questions and topoi that generate successive phases of such inquiry. These theorists are among those to whom I am indebted, Winterowd and Scholes for work that helped me formulate specific questions about disciplinary discourse and the structure of English studies, Rosenblatt for her role in shifting the focus of English studies to reading as a productive construction, Crowley for her analyses of deconstruction and writing theory, Flynn for furthering feminist theory in composition, and each of the last four, along with many others, for making it easier for women to enter the academy in the nineties and, once present, to be heard.

Victor Villanueva's essay plays a different role in my own work, in that it is helping me formulate new areas for inquiry. I hope that it will be widely read, for Villanueva constructs ethnicity, race, and class as theoretical dimensions of inquiry, an approach too seldom taken in literary and composition theory. James Berlin's social-epistemic rhetoric provides a framework by outlining a rhetoric to address ethnicity, race, gender, and class as issues (see "Rhetoric"). Villanueva, through the operative structure of his narrative as much as through the arguments he forwards, indicates how the contradictions generated by experiences of racism and classism, not as isolated events but as systemic practices and values, have had a formative effect on his scholarship as categories that substantively influence question formulation, critical reading strategies, and rhetorical interventions. In his essay, the subject who inquires constantly scrutinizes the intersections of a life history with the forces of social stratification to complicate, extend, and recontextualize critical discourse. Villaneuva's approach, politicizing the personal and privatizing the public, gives us access to some discursive "instruments for thinking the social world" (Bourdieu, *Distinction* 399).

Those who occupy a dominant position in the social order by virtue of their race, class, gender, and ethnicity repeatedly make a certain assumption, though of course the vast majority of us do not occupy the dominant position in all these categories, a fact that helps to explain the vigilance with which access to instruments for thinking the social world is controlled. I am referring to the assumption that only people of color and women might need to reflect on the isms. This point was brought home to me several years ago at a conference when I overheard a philosophy professor describe how he had redesigned his nineteenth-century philosophy course to deal with issues of gender. When asked how the revised course had gone, its inventor explained that he hadn't offered it after all, replacing it with his standard nineteenth-century philosophy course. And he was quite glad he had done so, for, he commented, there would have been no point in offering the gender-focused syllabus, since no women had signed up for the class.

This professor's view that only women are gendered (and that they are to be included in a gesture of fairness and not because men and women might need to learn about the social construction of gender) is as widespread as the view that ethnicity is a category applicable to everyone except white people, who constitute the blank space around which "minorities" circulate. This fiction acts as a shield from the knowledge of the extent to which whiteness, when combined with the signs of middle-class standing, extends privileges of access and confirmations of one's self-worth. These benefits effect a sense of "entitlement to speak" that is as powerful as is the acquisition of middle-class literacy skills (Bourdieu, *Distinction* 409).

Villanueva's reflections on "racism that is born of experiential ignorance" reminded me of an incident that served to release me, at least momentarily, from such ignorance, although I am sure I have since succumbed many times to the comfort of remaining ignorant of complicity in systemic racism. Once, when I was in high school, the city bus that I and twelve other students took each day was delayed by traffic. Arriving after the beginning of the first class of the day, we went to the attendance office to receive passes to go to class. As we stood side by side behind a long counter waiting for our passes, one of the school clerks smiled at me and said, "That's all right, honey, you go right ahead to class." Although as a high school freshman I had virtually no political consciousness regarding race, it was immediately and embarrassingly obvious that I had received this dispensation because I was the only white student in the group. As I slunk off to class, I reflected on how the clerk had, after all, read the situation correctly. I was the only one whose legal presence in the halls required no certification. It would be automatically extended to me by virtue of my whiteness. I would be spared the delay of questioning and, far more important, my sense of my own right to be where I was would remain intact.

No doubt because this event was a minor one in the history of racism, the other students did not even bother to contest it, but it has stayed with me as a reminder of the "privilege of unnoticed power" granted to the white middle class (Bové 54). At the time, perhaps because I associated the need for "papers" with the operation of a police state, I placed the incident in the context of what I had been taught about the European holocaust. At some historical moments, one's ethnicity either protects one from harm or results in a death sentence, and if one is among the protected, a constant vigilance is required to escape complicity with the executioners. It occurred to me that a history I knew nothing of had led to my moment of embarrassment, a history I would not learn about in school, and the incident sparked my first self-directed research project.

Villanueva's essay gives me a frame for connecting such experiences of social stratification to the recalcitrance of social formations to substantive change, a frame that complicates and enriches Crowley's question about noncoercive change. So much that is coercive escapes that label by remaining undisclosed, outside discourse or at least beyond the reach of discursive instruments for social change. Though I certainly have risked far less self-disclosure than Villanueva has, I too had to fight off a wish to avoid inserting the anecdotal in my response to these essays. My point in including personal events is to concur with Villanueva that they have everything to do with our intellectual histories, if by *intellectual* we mean our attempts to discern significance in the social text.

It is a rhetorical truism that to construct a discourse at all requires an examination of one's position as speaker, however impossible that may seem. In all these essays, that examination is thematized, but the narrative ordering principles I mentioned earlier—models of intelligibility, collegial networks, texts, controversies, and crises—are not equally supple instruments for discussing positionality. Organization according to crisis encounters with one's own position(s) in the social structure gives that theme maximum resonance. By using positionality to explore the ways gender, class, and ethnicity intersect professional life, Villanueva revises the genre of autobiographical reflection, much as Susan Jarratt and Joy Rouse revise rhetorical historiography through feminist theories of positionality (see Jarratt, "Locating Ethics"; Rouse, "Positional Historiography"). I look forward to seeing more writing in which our personal confrontations with social stratification become structuring agents in our public scholarship.

Pacific Lutheran University

Theory, Theories, Politics, and Journeys

Beverly J. Moss

The editors of this book charged me with writing a response to the symposium section that would "indicate how I see myself and my concerns in relation to the issues that the symposium participants have raised." The editors were especially interested, they said, in "underscoring issues of race, gender, and class and of theory and practice." What a task! As a result, I've had to engage in a great deal of self-reflection. As Victor Villanueva aptly phrased it, "My life affects my work." I would add to that statement, "My life also affects how I receive others' work."

Thus, I approached these essays by examining how the concerns raised by many of the scholars in their autobiographies intersect with, coincide with, or parallel some of the concerns I have. I should acknowledge that in my three short years in the profession, I have not often reflected on the relation between critical theory and writing theory. I even wondered why I was asked to do this response. I'm sure it had nothing to do with the race and gender part of the task.

I usually talk theory only when I have to. More to the point, I concern myself with theory only when it's useful for me. This attitude may stem from my membership in communities that have long been victimized and oppressed by Theories. As an African American woman from the South whose parents don't have college degrees, I would believe, if I trusted theory, that I'm genetically inferior to Caucasians, culturally deprived, culturally disadvantaged, educationally disadvantaged, cognitively deficient, and from a primarily oral culture. I would have to accept many other labels attached by theories that were or are meant to explain and exclude people like me. In short, I would be unqualified to write this response. Ideas like these constituted my introduction to Theory. I was well into graduate school before I began to understand the difference between Theory, the universal explanation of all phenomena that answers all questions and ignores context, and theories, explanations that acknowledge the role of context in theory building and the existence of many answers to the question rather than a single answer. The latter, theories, are seen as possible explanations of phenomena rather than as the prophecy that characterizes Theory. As a scholar and teacher, I look to theories to inform my research and teaching and vice versa. Yet questionable theories have had, and sometimes still have, huge followings and a large-scale negative influence on public policies in this country. As one who finds herself repeatedly in the position of rejecting and questioning theories rather than embracing them, I found it all the more interesting to read these intellectual autobiographies and think about my task.

The impressions I offer here mainly concern issues of power and privilege as well as of inclusion and exclusion, issues that underlie many theories. Likewise, these issues are the structuring principles of racism, sexism, classism, and other isms that several of the autobiographical essays address directly or indirectly and that permeate the academy and society in general. I seem to focus on these issues more and more, especially today when white males who feel that their privileged, powerful positions are being threatened cry about reverse discrimination as they dig their heels in deeper and deeper.

Beth Daniell, in her essay in an earlier section of this volume, argues that "theory is rhetorical and political" and, therefore, socially constructed. Daniell's focus on theory, and by implication the academy, as political moved me, initially, to place the autobiographies into two groups: those that in some way recognize and elaborate on the role of politics in their positions (Sharon Crowley, Victor Villanueva, and Ross Winterowd) and those that don't (Louise Rosenblatt and Robert Scholes). Writers in the latter group are not necessarily unaware of the political implications of their positions (one need only read their previous work), but neither do they explicitly indicate any knowledge of how political their beliefs and positions are.

This latter group initially included Elizabeth Flynn along with Rosenblatt and Scholes. However, Flynn doesn't appear to fit in either group. Because she discusses feminist concerns, some would place her with the former group (Crowley, Villanueva, and Winterowd). Yet Flynn's essay doesn't emphasize the political nature of her stances. This dilemma forced me to consider Flynn by herself, and I respond first to her essay.

Flynn chronicles her theoretical shifts through an analysis of one written text, her essay "Gender and Reading." In "Gender and Reading Revisited," Flynn discusses her move toward a social-constructionist reader-response theory and away from the cognitive approach to which she had earlier subscribed. Flynn's essay definitely locates her within a large movement of composition scholars who, in the last ten years, have shifted toward a social-constructionist perspective that emphasizes context and community rather than self and autonomy. Yet Flynn's discussion, like many others in composition, sometimes implies that this focus on social context and community is new. In fact, a major reason this shift has come about is that composition is interdisciplinary. Many composition scholars have begun to look to anthropology and other social sciences for theoretical and methodological frameworks, and these areas long ago recognized the role of social and interpretive contexts.

As Flynn moves from the objective to the subjective, she also calls for an objective, unbiased science as an ultimate goal of feminist empirical research. What concerns me most in that discussion is Flynn's definition of empiricism. Like many scholars who use a positivist model, Flynn sets up a dichotomy between interpretive and empirical research. She narrowly equates empirical research with experimental design and appears to equate *interpretive* with *qualitative*. Many have viewed the empirical-interpretive dichotomy along the quantitative-qualitative split. I take the alternative position that interpretive research—for example, ethnography—is also empirical and that it can be quantitative and qualitative. Another model sees empirical research as that which examines observed phenomena, whether experimental or qualitative. In fact, I see a complementary relation between the interpretive and the experimental rather than Flynn's mutually exclusive one. Finally, empirical research informs theories just as theories inform empirical research.

I consider Flynn's essay alone because it is neither as politically silent as the essays by Rosenblatt and Scholes are nor as politically vocal as the essays by Crowley, Villanueva, and Winterowd are. While neither Rosenblatt's nor Scholes's essay is apolitical, each leaves unasked or unexamined assumptions that are central to their conclusions; hence I label them "silent." Rosenblatt uses pragmatic transactionalism to reach a happy balance between the self and the community. Ultimately, she calls on us to scrutinize our theories and values and to "inculcate democratic values as the positive criteria for selecting among choices, whether literary or social. . . ." Of course, Rosenblatt's position begs the question of whether we can even agree on what is democratic. Who will decide how we define democratic values? Democratic for whom? Whose values? The answers usually involve who has power and who doesn't. We come back to politics, inclusion and exclusion.

Scholes's essay differs from Rosenblatt's because of its explicitly personal tone. Yet, like the previous essay, what seems missing in Scholes's essay is any discussion of the politics of his conclusions. He states that "teachers of literature have become the priests and theologians of English, while teachers of composition are the nuns, barred from the priesthood, doing the shitwork of the discipline." Scholes ends the analogy prematurely. Were he to carry it further, he might point to the political turmoil about the role of women in the Catholic church. The powers that be in the Catholic church see the male-female roles as etched in divine stone, a fixed relation. Is the literature-composition relation also fixed? Although Scholes seems to launch an attack on this position through critical theory (particularly through works such as *Textual Power*), I wonder if his attack will be effective, since he seems to focus on literature (and, in this essay, literary theorists). This view is evident in Scholes' theoretical assumptions and practical applications that teach students to write through imitation of literary styles. Which texts are chosen for them to imitate? Given Scholes's limited definition of *literary*, we would probably engage in a discussion about privileging some types of "literary" texts over other types; in short, we would engage in a canon argument.

The essays that I felt most drawn to were Crowley's, Villanueva's, and Winterowd's, mostly because they elaborate on the politics of their positions. Both Crowley and Villanueva search for theories that don't privilege and that seek to include, rather than exclude, women, minorities, the poor, part-timers, and so on. Both are interested in bringing about change, but Crowley wants to foster noncoercive change on a local level, especially as it relates to part-timers, while Villanueva looks at change on the societal level. This difference in the scope of their concerns may contribute to their differing perspectives on theory.

Crowley's evolution to her current position on theory has led her to a pragmatic approach. That is, Crowley's position—that no one theory can account for all phenomena; that we should take what we can use from different theories for a given problem and discard what is not useful, starting the process over for the next problem—reflects the "theories rather than Theory" position. At the root of Crowley's pragmatic view of theory is the notion that there is no single solution to most of life's complex problems—how we use language, how we decode and encode, how we make meaning in certain contexts, and so on. And if there is no one answer, then no one theory can account for the answers. Crowley does not dismiss theory; she just seems to be realistic about its strengths and weaknesses. Crowley, in her essay, readily admits to jumping on the Theory bandwagon, particularly the Derridean bandwagon, to impress her colleagues in literary theory. Of course, Crowley isn't the only one who has jumped on the Derridean, Foucauldian, or Bakhtinian bandwagon—or the bandwagon of whoever is currently in vogue—to gain respect from and impress colleagues in literary theory. Her admission does suggest, however, that espousing a critical theory is as political a choice as it is a scholarly one. Of course, we readily admit that scholarship and politics go hand in hand.

Villanueva's intellectual autobiography points to the politics of our professional lives (including scholarship) as well as of our personal lives. I was drawn to his essay because Villanueva, more than any other of the symposium participants, focuses on the role of politics in the academy and in the discipline. Villanueva's essay intertwines professional and personal, public and private, and in some ways, reassures me about my own work. I too, seek that same intertwining.

Villanueva's search for an inclusive rhetorical theory leads him to Gramsci's work. His discussion of Gramsci's notion of a "war of positions led by . . . 'organic intellectuals' " reminds me of W. E. B. DuBois's "talented tenth" theory, which held that the brightest and best tenth of African Americans would lead the race to freedom, equality, and prosperity. Both Gramsci and DuBois, roughly contemporaries, promoted positions that they thought would knock down political, economic, and social barriers for marginalized peoples. Of course, DuBois was accused of being a communist (and at the age of ninety-three tendered an official application to the Communist Party) and died in self-exile in Ghana, and Gramsci ended up in jail. There are differences in the two men's approaches, yet the parallels jumped out at me as I read Villanueva's essay. For Villanueva, Gramsci's appeal seems to be his theory that addresses, indeed allows for, contradictory ideologies within the self, an issue that Villanueva argues has basically been ignored in rhetorical theory. Maybe Villanueva's need for a theory that allows for contradictory ideologies parallels Crowley's need (and my own) for theories rather than Theory.

At the root of Villanueva's intellectual autobiography is the statement at the end of his essay that "rhetoric is politics, a precedent for action, for more than token changes." Clearly, this essay is not really about critical theory or writing theory or theory and practice; it is, for me, an essay about what we need to bring about social, political, and economic changes in this society so that those on the margins—in Villanueva's language, "poor people, women, and castelike minorities"—share in the power (if that is desired) and avoid being systematically disempowered and silenced. Again, it comes down to issues of inclusion and exclusion, power and privilege. So far, as Crowley and Villanueva point out, we have only token, surface-level change.

Like Crowley and Villanueva, Winterowd clearly sees exclusion and lack of power as key issues, but his concerns focus on composition as a discipline. Winterowd, more than the other authors, acknowledges the marginal role of composition within English departments and within the Modern Language Association. Yet, unlike Crowley and Villanueva, Winterowd does not seek change in the sense of wanting to move composition from the fringes into the inner circle. While I was, at first, disturbed by this attitude, I've come to make sense of it through my own experience. Initially, I had argued that if composition remains on the fringes, as Winterowd suggests it should, then we will forever be in a position of powerlessness and exclusion. We will always hit a ceiling in our attempts to effect change, to gain power, to have a voice. Occasionally, one or two of us will be let into the circle (tokenism at its best), but the group will remain on the fringes, much like marginalized groups in the academy and in larger society. Composition theorists will still be known only to composition theorists.

Of course, this position assumes that the desired place for composition is in the inner circle with the literary theorists and critics because moving into the center is the best way to effect change. I now have an alternative reading of Winterowd's statement (which may, of course, in no way relate to Winterowd's intentions). From my own experience as an African American woman in the academy, an institution that is historically known for the racist, sexist, and classist attitudes generally perpetuated by the inner circle, I have had no desire to be a part of the inner circle. To seek a place in that circle means to embrace the values and attitudes that it espouses. I am aware that some have taken the position that change can only come from within. Yet the danger of moving within is that many times or most times one ends up playing by the rules of the inner circle, rules that exclude for purely arbitrary reasons. Paulo Freire warns oppressed groups about becoming the oppressors once they have been liberated, and it is very likely that members of marginalized groups may do so when they become members of the inner circle. The outer circle is, in truth, a larger, more inclusive, more broadly based circle than the inner circle is, and eventually those on the fringes will gain a power of their own. Ideally, this power will be unlike that of the inner circle since it will be a shared power to which everyone has access.

So how have these intellectual autobiographies affected me, particularly where theory is concerned? Daniell argues that theory is "a way to make sense of how our private lives, our histories, our reading, and our experiences with language, writing, and teaching shape the beliefs and values on which rest our practice and our public identities." These intellectual autobiographies may be examples that support Daniell's statement. As a reader, I see these essays as part of a useful process that ties the private to the public, that links practical and theoretical through lived experiences. Reading the essays and writing a response forced me to examine the relation between my public and private selves and the way that relation is expressed. I was also forced to reflect on how my experiences (as an African American woman in the academy who is interested in composition studies) have affected my attitude toward the discipline and my own work. Maybe all of us in the profession should have to take stock of where we have come from, where we are, and where we think we are headed—especially before we get there.[1]

Ohio State University

NOTE

[1] I thank Marcia Dickson, Lewis Ulman, and Keith Walters for their comments on various drafts of this response.

Works Cited

Aarsleff, Hans. *From Locke to Saussure: Essays on the Study of Language and Intellectual History.* Minneapolis: U of Minnesota P, 1982.

Abrams, M. H. *The Mirror and the Lamp: Romantic Theory and the Critical Tradition.* New York: Oxford UP, 1953.

Achebe, Chinua. *Things Fall Apart.* New York: Fawcett, 1988.

Adler, Jerry. "Taking Offense." *Newsweek* 24 Dec. 1990: 48–54.

Althusser, Louis. "Ideology and Ideological State Apparatuses: Notes towards an Investigation." *Lenin* 127–86.

———. *Lenin and Philosophy.* Trans. Ben Brewster. London: New Left, 1971.

Anderson, Chris, ed. *Literary Nonfiction: Theory, Criticism, Pedagogy.* Carbondale: Southern Illinois UP, 1989.

———. *Style as Argument.* Carbondale: Southern Illinois UP, 1987.

Anderson, Sherwood. *A Story Teller's Story.* New York: Huebsch, 1924.

Anson, Chris, ed. *Writing and Response: Theory, Practice, and Research.* Urbana: NCTE, 1989.

Applebee, Arthur N. *Tradition and Reform in the Teaching of English: A History.* Urbana: NCTE, 1974.

Aristotle. *The Basic Works of Aristotle.* Ed. Richard McKeon. New York: Random, 1941.

———. *De Poetica.* Trans. Ingram Bywater. Vol. 11 of *Collected Works of Aristotle.* Ed. W. D. Ross. Oxford: Oxford UP, 1924. 11 vols.

———. *Ethica Nicomachea.* Trans. W. D. Ross. *Basic Works* 925–1112.

———. *Rhetorica.* Trans. W. Rhys Roberts. *Basic Works* 1317–1451.

Armstrong, Nancy. *Desire and Domestic Fiction: A Political History of the Novel.* Oxford: Oxford UP, 1986.

Aronowitz, Stanley. *Science as Power: Discourse and Ideology in Modern Society.* Minneapolis: U of Minnesota P, 1988.

Atkins, Douglas, and Michael Johnson, eds. *Writing and Reading Differently: Deconstruction and the Teaching of Composition and Literature.* Lawrence: UP of Kansas, 1985.

Atwell, Nancie. *In the Middle: Writing, Reading, and Learning with Adolescents.* Upper Montclair: Boynton/Cook, 1987.

Atwood, Margaret. *Surfacing.* New York: Ballantine, 1972.

Austin, J. L. *How to Do Things with Words.* Cambridge: Harvard UP, 1962.

Austin, Regina. "Sapphire Bound." *Wisconsin Law Review* (1989): 539–78.

Ayer, A. J., ed. *Logical Positivism*. Glencoe: Free, 1959.

Bakhtin, Mikhail. "Discourse in the Novel." *The Dialogic Imagination*. Ed. Michael Holquist. Trans. Caryl Emerson and Michael Holquist. Austin: U of Texas P, 1981. 259–422.

Baldwin, James. "Autobiographical Notes." *Eight Modern Essayists*. Ed. William Smart. 4th ed. New York: St. Martin's, 1985. 189–93.

Barker, Pat. Rev. of *Triphammer*, by Dan McCall. *New York Times Book Review* 4 Feb. 1990: 14.

Barnet, Sylvan, and Marcia Stubbs. *Practical Guide to Writing*. 6th ed. Glenview: Scott, 1990.

Barrett, Michele. "Ideology and the Cultural Production of Gender." Newton and Rosenfelt 65–84.

Barthes, Roland. "L'effet de réel." *Communications* 11 (1968): 84–89.

———. "The Old Rhetoric: An Aide-Memoire." *The Semiotic Challenge*. Trans. Richard Howard. New York: Hill, 1988. 11–94.

Bartholomae, David. "Inventing the University." *When a Writer Can't Write: Studies in Writer's Block and Other Composing-Process Problems*. Ed. Mike Rose. New York: Guilford, 1985. 134–65.

Bauer, Dale M. "The Other 'F' Word: The Feminist in the Classroom." *College English* 52 (1990): 385–96.

Baym, Nina. "The Feminist Teacher of Literature." *Gender in the Classroom: Power and Pedagogy*. Ed. Susan L. Gabriel and Isaiah Smithson. Urbana: U of Illinois P, 1990. 60–77.

Beer, Gillian. *Darwin's Plots: Evolutionary Narrative in Darwin, George Eliot and Nineteenth-Century Fiction*. London: Routledge, 1983.

Belenky, Mary Field, et al. *Women's Ways of Knowing: The Development of Self, Voice, and Mind*. New York: Basic, 1986.

Bell, Derrick. *And We Are Not Saved: The Elusive Quest for Racial Justice*. New York: Basic, 1987.

Belsey, Catherine. "Constructing the Subject: Deconstructing the Text." Newton and Rosenfelt 45–64.

———. *Critical Practice*. London: Methuen, 1980.

Benedict, Ruth. *Patterns of Culture*. Boston: Houghton, 1934.

Bennett, Tony. *Formalism and Marxism*. London: Methuen, 1979.

———. "Texts in History." *Journal of the Midwest Modern Language Association* 18 (1985): 1–16.

Berger, Joseph. "Conservative Scholars Attack 'Radicalization' of Universities." *New York Times* 15 Nov. 1988: A22.

Berkman, Ronald. *Opening the Gates: The Rise of the Prisoners' Movement*. Lexington: Heath, 1979.

Berlin, James A. "Rhetoric and Ideology in the Writing Class." *College English* 50 (1988): 477–94.

———. *Rhetoric and Reality: Writing Instruction in American Colleges, 1900–1985*. Carbondale: Southern Illinois UP, 1987.

———. *Writing Instruction in Nineteenth-Century American Colleges*. Carbondale: Southern Illinois UP, 1984.

Berlin, James A., and Michael Vivion, eds. *Cultural Studies in the English Classroom*. Portsmouth: Boynton/Cook, 1992.

Bernstein, Richard. "The Rising Hegemony of the Politically Correct." *New York Times* 28 Oct. 1990. sec. 4: 1.

Berthoff, Ann. *The Making of Meaning*. Montclair: Boynton/Cook, 1981.

———. "Speculative Instruments: Language in the Core Curriculum." *Making* 113–26.

Bizzell, Patricia. "Beyond Anti-foundationalism to Rhetorical Authority: Problems Defining 'Cultural Literacy.' " *College English* 52 (1990): 661–75.

———. "Cognition, Convention, and Certainty: What We Need to Know about Writing." *Pre/Text* 3 (1982): 213–43.

Bizzell, Patricia, and Bruce Herzberg. *The Bedford Bibliography for Teachers of Writing*. 3rd ed. New York: Bedford, 1991.

Bleich, David. "Gender Interests in Reading and Language." Flynn and Schweickart 234–67.

———. "The Identity of Pedagogy and Research in the Study of Responses to Literature." *College English* 42 (1980): 350–66.

———. *Subjective Criticism*. Baltimore: Johns Hopkins UP, 1978.

Bogel, Frederic. "Understanding Prose." *Teaching Prose*. Ed. Frederic Bogel and Katherine Gottschalk. New York: Norton, 1984. 155–215.

Booth, Wayne. *The Rhetoric of Fiction*. 2nd ed. Chicago: U of Chicago P, 1983.

Boswell, James. *Boswell's Life of Johnson*. London: Oxford UP, 1965.

Bourdieu, Pierre. *Distinction: A Social Critique of the Judgement of Taste*. Trans. Richard Nice. Cambridge: Harvard UP, 1984.

———. *Outline of a Theory of Practice*. Trans. Richard Nice. Cambridge: Cambridge UP, 1977.

Bové, Paul A. "Discourse." *Critical Terms for Literary Study*. Ed. Frank Lentricchia and Thomas McLaughlin. Chicago: U of Chicago P, 1990. 50–65.

Bowie, Malcolm. *Freud, Proust and Lacan: Theory as Fiction*. Cambridge: Cambridge UP, 1987.

Braddock, Richard, Richard Lloyd-Jones, and Lowell Schuer. *Research in Written Composition*. Urbana: NCTE, 1963.

Britton, James. *Response to Working Party Paper No. 1—What Is English? by Albert Kitzhaber*. Papers Relating to the Anglo-American Seminar on the Teaching of English at Dartmouth College, 1966. ERIC ED 082 201.

Britton, James, et al. *The Development of Writing Abilities (11–18)*. London: Macmillan, 1975.

Brodkey, Linda. *Academic Writing as Social Practice*. Philadelphia: Temple UP, 1987.

———. "English 306: Rhetoric and Composition." Memorandum, 1 May 1990.

———. "On the Subjects of Class and Gender in 'The Literacy Letters.' " *College English* 51 (1989): 125–41.

———. "Transvaluing Difference." *College English* 51 (1989): 597–601.

———. "Tropics of Literacy." *Journal of Education* 168 (1986): 47–54.

Brodkey, Linda, and Michelle Fine. "Presence of Mind in the Absence of Body." *Journal of Education* 170 (1988–89): 84–99.

Brodkey, Linda, and Shelli Fowler. "Political Suspects." *Village Voice* (Summer Education Supplement) 23 Apr. 1991: 3–4.

Brodkey, Linda, Lester Faigley, Susan Sage Heinzelman, Sara Kimball, Stuart Moulthrop, and John Slatin. Letter of Resignation, Lower Division English Policy Committee. 4 Feb. 1991.

Brodsky, Claudia J. *The Imposition of Form.* Princeton: Princeton UP, 1987.

Brooke, Robert. "Lacan, Transference, and Writing Instruction." *College English* 49 (1987): 679–91.

Bruffee, Kenneth. "Collaborative Learning and the 'Conversation of Mankind.'" *College English* 46 (1984): 635–52.

———. *A Short Course in Writing: Practical Rhetoric of Teaching Composition through Collaborative Learning.* 3rd ed. Boston: Little, 1985.

———. "Social Construction, Language, and the Authority of Knowledge: A Bibliographic Essay." *College English* 48 (1986): 773–90.

Bruner, Jerome. *Acts of Meaning.* Cambridge: Harvard UP, 1990.

———. *Actual Minds, Possible Worlds.* Cambridge: Harvard UP, 1986.

Bullock, Richard, and John Trimbur, eds. *The Politics of Writing Instruction: Postsecondary.* Portsmouth: Boynton/Cook, 1990.

Burke, Kenneth. *A Grammar of Motives.* Berkeley: U of California P, 1969.

———. *The Philosophy of Literary Form.* Berkeley: U of California P, 1973.

Cain, William E. *The Crisis in Criticism.* Baltimore: Johns Hopkins UP, 1984.

Calkins, Lucy. *The Art of Teaching Writing.* Portsmouth: Heinemann, 1986.

———. *Lessons from a Child.* Portsmouth: Heinemann, 1983.

Campbell, George. *The Philosophy of Rhetoric.* London: Tegg, 1850.

Carroll, Lewis. *Through the Looking Glass.* New York: Random, 1946.

Caughie, Pamela L. "Women Reading/Reading Women: A Review of Some Recent Books on Gender and Reading." *Papers on Language and Literature* 24 (1988): 317–35.

Chatman, Seymour. *Story and Discourse: Narrative Structure in Fiction and Film.* Ithaca: Cornell UP, 1978.

Cheney, Lynne V. "Political Correctness and Beyond." Address. National Press Club. Washington, 25 Sept. 1991.

Christian, Barbara. "The Race for Theory." *Feminist Studies* 14 (1988): 67–79.

"A Civil Rights Theme for a Writing Course." *New York Times* 24 June 1990: B1.

Cixous, Hélène, and Catherine Clément. "A Woman Mistress." *The Newly Born Woman.* Trans. Betsy Wing. Minneapolis: U of Minnesota P, 1986. 136–46.

Clark, Gregory. *Dialogue, Dialectic, and Conversation.* Carbondale: Southern Illinois UP, 1990.

Clark, Mark Andrew. "The Difficulty in Saying 'I': Identifying, Analyzing, and Critiquing Voices of Self, Difference, and Discourse in College Students' Reading and Writing about Literature." Diss. U of Pennsylvania, 1990.

Clark, Suzanne. Rev. of *Gender and Reading,* ed. Elizabeth A. Flynn and Patrocinio P. Schweickart. *North Dakota Quarterly* (Winter 1987): 246–49.

———. *Sentimental Modernism: Women Writers and the Revolution of the Word.* Bloomington: Indiana UP, 1991.

Clifford, John, and John Schilb. "Composition Theory and Literary Theory." *Perspectives on Research and Scholarship in Composition.* Ed. Ben W. McClelland and Timothy R. Donovan. New York: MLA, 1985. 45–67.

Coles, William E., Jr. "New Presbyters as Old Priests: A Forewarning." *CEA Critic* 41 (1978): 3–10.

Collier, Peter. "Incorrect English: The Case of Allen [sic] Gribben." *Heterodoxy* 1 (1992): 8–10.

Comley, Nancy R., and Robert Scholes. "Literature, Composition, and the Structure of English." Horner, *Composition* 96–109.

Conference on College Composition and Communication. *CCCC Convention Program.* Chicago, 22–24 March 1990. Urbana: NCTE, 1990.

Connolly, Paul, and Teresa Vilardi, eds. *New Methods in College Writing Programs: Theories in Practice.* New York: MLA, 1987.

Connors, Robert J. "The Rhetoric of Mechanical Correctness." Newkirk 27–58.

Connors, Robert J., Lisa J. Ede, and Andrea A. Lunsford, eds. *Essays on Classical Rhetoric and Modern Discourse.* Carbondale: Southern Illinois UP, 1984.

Cooper, Marilyn M. "Unhappy Consciousness in First-Year English: How to Figure Things Out for Yourself." *Writing as Social Action.* Ed. Marilyn M. Cooper and Michael Holzman. Portsmouth: Boynton/Cook, 1989. 28–60.

Corbett, Edward P. J. *Classical Rhetoric for the Modern Student.* New York: Oxford UP, 1965.

Coste, Didier. *Narrative as Communication.* Minneapolis: U of Minnesota P, 1989.

Cover, Robert M. "Violence and the Word." *Yale Law Journal* 95 (1986): 1601–29.

Coward, Rosalind. "Feel Good, Look Great." *Female Desires* 19–25.

———. *Female Desires: How They Are Sought, Bought, and Packaged.* New York: Grove, 1985.

———. "Pouts and Scowls." *Female Desires* 55–60.

———. "The Royals." *Female Desires* 161–71.

Coyle, William. *The Macmillan Guide to Writing Research Papers.* New York: Macmillan, 1990.

Crenshaw, Kimberle. "Demarginalizing the Intersection of Race and Sex: A Black Feminist Critique of Antidiscrimination Doctrine, Feminist Theory, and Antiracist Politics." *University of Chicago Legal Forum* (1989): 139–67.

Crosswhite, James. "Mood in Argumentation: Heidegger and the Exordium." *Philosophy and Rhetoric* 22 (1989): 28–42.

Crowley, Sharon. "Derrida, Deconstruction, and Our Scene of Teaching." *Pre/Text* 8 (1987): 169–83.

———. "The Evolution of Invention in Current-Traditional Rhetoric: 1850–1970." *Rhetoric Review* 3 (1985): 146–64.

———. "Of Gorgias and Grammatology." *College Composition and Communication* 29 (1979): 279–84.

Crusius, Timothy W. *Discourse: A Critique and Synthesis of Major Theories.* New York: MLA, 1989.

Cunningham, William H. Letter to Banett Valenta. 11 July 1990.

———. Letter to Louis A. Beecherl, Jr. 19 July 1990.

———. "UT Excellence Began with Constitution." *On Campus*. 1 Apr. 1991: 2+.

Daniell, Beth. Rev. of *Composition as a Human Science*, by Louise Wetherbee Phelps. *Composition Chronicle* 2 (1989): 11–12.

Darnton, Robert. *The Great Cat Massacre*. New York: Random, 1984.

Davis, Robert Con, ed. *Psychoanalysis and Pedagogy*. Spec. issues of *College English* 49 (1987): 621–91, 749–815.

de Man, Paul. *Allegories of Reading: Figural Language in Rousseau, Nietzsche, Rilke, and Proust*. New Haven: Yale UP, 1979.

De Quincey, Thomas. "Letters to a Young Man Whose Education Has Been Neglected." *The Art of Conversation and Other Papers*. Vol. 13 of *De Quincey's Works*. Edinburgh: Black, 1863, 9–94. 16 vols.

Derrida, Jacques. *Of Grammatology*. Trans. Gayatri Chakravorty Spivak. Baltimore: Johns Hopkins UP, 1976.

———. "Plato's Pharmacy." *Dissemination*. Trans. Barbara Johnson. Chicago: U of Chicago P, 1981. 61–171.

Dewey, John. *Logic: The Theory of Inquiry*. New York: Henry Holt, 1938.

———. *The Public and its Problems*. Vol. 2 of *John Dewey: The Later Works*. Ed. Jo Ann Boydston. Carbondale: Southern Illinois UP, 1984.

Dewey, John, and Arthur F. Bentley. *Knowing and the Known*. Boston: Beacon, 1949.

DiBernard, Barbara. "Feminist Teaching." *Women's Journal-Advocate* 6 (1987): 1–3.

Didion, Joan. *The White Album*. New York: Simon, 1979.

Dillard, Annie. Introduction. *The Best Essays of 1988*. Ed. Dillard. New York: Ticknor, 1988. xiii–xxii.

———. "Singing with the Fundamentalists." *The Graywolf Annual Three: Essays, Memoirs, and Reflections*. Ed. Scott Walker. Saint Paul: Graywolf, 1986. 9–21.

Dillon, George L. "Fiction in Persuasion—Personal Experience as Evidence and as Art." C. Anderson, *Literary Nonfiction* 197–210.

DiPardo, Anne. "Narrative Knowers, Expository Knowledge." *Written Communication* 7 (1990): 59–95.

Donahue, Patricia, and Ellen Quandahl, eds. *Reclaiming Pedagogy: The Rhetoric of the Classroom*. Carbondale: Southern Illinois UP, 1989.

Donald, James, and Stuart Hall. Introduction. *Politics and Ideology*. Ed. Donald and Hall. Philadelphia: Keynes, 1986. ix–xx.

Douglas, Ann. *The Feminization of American Culture*. New York: Avon, 1977.

Douglas, Wallace. "Rhetoric for the Meritocracy." *English in America*. By Richard Ohmann. New York: Oxford UP, 1976. 97–132.

Dowling, William. *Jameson, Althusser, Marx: An Introduction to* The Political Unconscious. Ithaca: Cornell UP, 1984.

Dreyfus, Hubert L., and Paul Rabinow. *Michel Foucault: Beyond Structuralism and Hermeneutics*. 2nd ed. Chicago: U of Chicago P, 1982.

D'Souza, Dinesh. *Illiberal Education: The Politics of Race and Sex on Campus*. New York: Free, 1991.

DuBois, W. E. B. *The Souls of Black Folk*. New York: Signet, 1969.

Durkheim, Emile. *The Elementary Forms of the Religious Life*. 1915. Trans. Joseph Ward Swain. Glencoe: Free, 1947.

Eagleton, Terry. "The Rise of English." *Literary Theory: An Introduction*. Minneapolis: U of Minnesota P, 1983. 17–53.

———. "The Subject of Literature." *Cultural Critique* 21 (1985–86): 95–104.

Eastman, Arthur M., ed. *The Norton Reader*. 7th ed. New York: Norton, 1988.

Ehrlich, Gretel. "Looking for a Lost Dog." *Islands, the Universe, Home*. New York: Viking, 1991. 3–7.

Elbow, Peter. "Closing My Eyes as I Speak: An Argument for Ignoring Audience." *College English* 49 (1987): 50–69.

———. *Writing without Teachers*. New York: Oxford UP, 1973.

———. *Writing with Power*. New York: Oxford UP, 1981.

Elbow, Peter, and Pat Belanoff. *A Community of Writers*. New York: Random, 1989.

Emig, Janet. "Our Missing Theory." *Conversations: Contemporary Critical Theory and the Teaching of Literature*. Ed. Charles Moran and Elizabeth F. Penfield. Urbana: NCTE, 1990. 87–96.

Faigley, Lester. "Judging Writing, Judging Selves." *College Composition and Communication* 40 (1989): 395–412.

Farrell, Thomas J. "IQ and Standard English." *College Composition and Communication* 34 (1983): 470–84.

Felski, Rita. *Beyond Feminist Aesthetics: Feminist Literature and Social Change*. Cambridge: Harvard UP, 1989.

Fetterley, Judith. *The Resisting Reader: A Feminist Approach to American Fiction*. Bloomington: Indiana UP, 1978.

Feyerabend, Paul. *Against Method: Outline of an Anarchistic Theory of Knowledge*. London: Verso, 1978.

———. *Realism, Rationalism, and Scientific Method*. Vol. 1 of *Philosophical Papers*. New York: Cambridge UP, 1985.

Fine, Michelle. "Silencing in Public Schools." *Language Arts* 64 (1987): 157–74.

Fish, Stanley. "Anti-foundationalism, Theory Hope, and the Teaching of Composition." *Doing* 343–55.

———. "Change." *South Atlantic Quarterly* 86 (1987): 423–44.

———. "Consequences." *Critical Inquiry* 11 (1985): 433–58. Rpt. in Mitchell, *Against Theory* 106–31.

———. "Demonstration vs. Persuasion: Two Models of Critical Activity." *Is There a Text* 356–71.

———. *Doing What Comes Naturally: Change, Rhetoric, and the Practice of Theory in Literacy and Legal Studies*. Durham: Duke UP, 1989.

———. "How to Recognize a Poem When You See One." *Is There a Text* 322–37.

———. "Introduction: Going Down the Anti-formalist Road." *Doing* 1–33.

———. *Is There a Text in This Class?* Cambridge: Harvard UP, 1980.

———. "Is There a Text in This Class?" *Is There a Text* 303–21.

Fishman, Stephen, and Lucille Parkinson McCarthy. "Is Expressivism Dead?

Reconsidering Its Romantic Roots and Its Relation to Social Constructionism." *College English* 54 (1992): 647–61.

Fleck, Ludwig. *The Genesis and Development of a Scientific Fact*. Chicago: U of
Chicago P, 1979.

Flower, Linda. "Cognition, Context, and Theory Building." *College Composition
and Communication* 40 (1989): 282–311.

———. "Comment and Response." *College English* 51 (1989): 765–69.

Flower, Linda, and John R. Hayes. "A Cognitive Process Theory of Writing."
College Composition and Communication 32 (1981): 365–87.

Flynn, Elizabeth A. "Composing as a Woman." *College Composition and Communication* 39 (1988): 423–35.

———. "Composing 'Composing as a Woman.' " *College Composition and Communication* 41 (1990): 83–89.

———. "Gender and Reading." *College English* 45 (1983): 236–51.

Flynn, Elizabeth A., and Patrocinio P. Schweickart. *Gender and Reading: Essays
on Readers, Texts, and Contexts*. Baltimore: Johns Hopkins UP, 1986.

Forster, E. M. *Aspects of the Novel*. 1927. New York: Harcourt, 1954.

Foucault, Michel. *The Archaeology of Knowledge and the Discourse on Language*.
Trans. A. M. Sheridan Smith. New York: Pantheon, 1972.

———. *Discipline and Punish: The Birth of the Prison*. Trans. Alan Sheridan.
New York: Random, 1977.

———. *The History of Sexuality: An Introduction*. Trans. Robert Hurley. New
York: Pantheon, 1978. Vol. 1 of *The History of Sexuality*.

———. *Language, Counter-memory, Practice: Selected Essays and Interviews*.
Ed. and trans. Donald F. Bouchard. Ithaca: Cornell UP, 1977.

———. "Questions on Geography." *Power/Knowledge: Selected Interviews and
Other Writings 1972–1977*. Ed. Colin Gordon. New York: Pantheon, 1980.
63–77.

———. "Space, Knowledge, and Power." Trans. Christian Hubert. Rabinow
239–56.

———. "The Subject and Power." Dreyfus and Rabinow 208–26.

———. "What Is Enlightenment?" Trans. Catherine Porter. Rabinow 32–50.

Foucault, Michel, and Gilles Deleuze. "Intellectuals and Power: A Conversation
between Michel Foucault and Gilles Deleuze." Foucault, *Language* 203–17.

Fraser, Nancy, and Linda Nicholson. "Social Criticism without Philosophy."
Nicholson 19–38.

Freire, Paulo. *Pedagogy of the Oppressed*. Trans. Myra Bergman Ramos. New
York: Continuum, 1973.

Friedman, Alan W. "English 306 at the University of Texas at Austin." *Texas
Academe* 1 (1991): 2–4.

Frye, Northrop. *Anatomy of Criticism*. Princeton: Princeton UP, 1971.

Gallop, Jane. *The Daughter's Seduction: Feminism and Psychoanalysis*. Ithaca:
Cornell UP, 1982.

Gaonkar, Dilip. "Rhetoric and Its Double: Reflections on the Rhetorical Turn
in the Human Sciences." *The Rhetorical Turn: Invention and Persuasion in*

the Conduct of Inquiry. Ed. Herb Simons. Chicago: U of Chicago P, 1990. 341–66.

Gelpi, Barbara Charlesworth. Rev. of *Gender and Reading,* ed. Elizabeth A. Flynn and Patrocinio P. Schweikart. *NWSA Journal* 1 (1988): 133–35.

Genette, Gérard. *Figures of Literary Discourse.* Trans. Alan Sheridan. New York: Columbia UP, 1982.

———. *Narrative Discourse: An Essay in Method.* Ithaca: Cornell UP, 1980.

Genung, John F. *The Practical Elements of Rhetoric.* Boston: Ginn, 1894.

George, Ann. "Analysis of *The St. Martin's Guide to Writing,* 2nd ed." Unpublished ms., 1990.

Gilligan, Carol. *In a Different Voice: Psychological Theory and Women's Development.* Cambridge: Harvard UP, 1982.

Giroux, Henry. *Schooling and the Struggle for Public Life.* Minneapolis: U of Minnesota P, 1988.

———. *Teachers as Intellectuals: Toward a Critical Pedagogy of Learning.* Granby: Bergin, 1988.

Glassie, Henry. *Passing the Time in Ballymenone.* Philadelphia: U of Pennsylvania P, 1982.

Godzich, Wlad. Foreword. Coste ix–xvii.

Goffman, Erving. *Frame Analysis: An Essay on the Acquisition of Experience.* New York: Harper, 1974.

"Good Riddance." Editorial. *Houston Chronicle* 6 Feb. 1991: 16A.

Gould, Stephen Jay. "A Triumph of Historical Excavation." *New York Review of Books* 27 Feb. 1986: 9–15.

Gracián, Baltasar. *Agudeza y Arte de Ingenio.* Madrid: Clasicos Castalia, 1969.

Grady, Hugh. "Rhetoric, Wit, and Art in Gracian's *Agudeza.*" *Modern Language Quarterly* 41 (1980): 21–37.

Graff, Gerald. *Beyond the Culture Wars: How Teaching the Conflicts Can Revitalize American Education.* New York: Norton, 1992.

———. *Professing Literature: An Institutional History.* Chicago: U of Chicago P, 1987.

———. "Vital Signs." *Voice Literary Supplement* Oct. 1988: 23–24.

Graff, Gerald, and Reginald Gibbons, eds. *Criticism in the University.* Evanston: Northwestern UP, 1985.

Gramsci, Antonio. *Selections from the Prison Notebooks.* Ed. and trans. Quintin Hoare and Geoffrey Nowell Smith. New York: International, 1971.

Gribben, Alan. "English Departments: Salvaging What Remains." *Academic Questions* 2 (1989): 89–98.

———. Letter to Anne Blakeney. 9 July 1990. Rpt. as "Alumni Relations: Gribben Pushes 'Receivership' for English Department." *Daily Texan* 6 Aug. 1990: 4.

Grumet, Madeleine. *Bitter Milk: Women and Teaching.* Amherst: U of Massachusetts P, 1988.

Habermas, Jürgen. *Philosophical Discourse of Modernity.* Trans. Frederick Lawrence. Boston: MIT P, 1987.

Hairston, Maxine. "Breaking Our Bonds and Reaffirming Our Connections." *College Composition and Communication* 36 (1985): 272–82.

———. "Diversity, Ideology, and Teaching Writing." *College Composition and Communication* 43 (1992): 179–93.

———. "Required Writing Courses Should Not Focus on Politically Charged Social Issues." *Chronicle of Higher Education* 23 Jan. 1991: B1+.

Hall, Stuart. "Signification, Representation, Ideology: Althusser and the Post-structuralist Debates." *Critical Studies in Mass Communication* 2 (1985): 91–114.

Halloran, Michael. "From Rhetoric to Composition: The Teaching of Writing in America to 1900." *A Short History of Writing Instruction from Ancient Greece to Twentieth-Century America*. Ed. James J. Murphy. Davis: Hermagoras, 1990. 151–82.

Haraway, Donna. "Situated Knowledges: The Science Question in Feminism and the Privilege of Partial Perspective." *Feminist Studies* 14 (1988): 575–99.

Harding, Sandra, ed. *Feminism and Methodology: Social Science Issues*. Bloomington: Indiana UP, 1987.

———. *The Science Question in Feminism*. Ithaca: Cornell UP, 1986.

Harkin, Patricia, and John Schilb, eds. *Contending with Words: Composition and Rhetoric in a Postmodern Age*. New York: MLA, 1991.

Harris, Angela. "Race and Essentialism in Feminist Legal Theory." *Stanford Law Review* 42 (1990): 581–616.

Harris, Jeannette. *Expressive Discourse*. Dallas: Southern Methodist UP, 1990.

Hawking, Stephen. *A Brief History of Time: From the Big Bang to Black Holes*. New York: Bantam, 1988.

HD [Hilda Doolittle]. "Oread." *Selected Poems of H.D.* New York: Grove, 1957. 26.

Heath, Shirley Brice. "Toward an Ethnohistory of Writing in American Education." *Writing: The Nature, Development, and Teaching of Written Communication*. Ed. Marcia Farr Whiteman. Hillsdale: Erlbaum, 1981. 25–46.

———. *Ways with Words: Language, Life, and Work in Communities*. Cambridge: Cambridge UP, 1983.

Heinzelman, Kurt, and Ramon Saldívar. "Rhetoric and Composition: Provost Meddles in E 306 Decision." *Daily Texan* 31 July 1990: 4.

Henson, Scott, and Tom Philpott. "E 306: Chronicle of a Smear Campaign; How the New Right Attacks Diversity." *Polemicist* 2 (1990): 4+.

———. "English 306: Reading, Writing, and Politics." *Austin Chronicle* 10 Aug. 1990: 8.

Hesse, Douglas. "Stories in Essays, Essays as Stories." Anderson, *Literary Nonfiction* 176–96.

Hillocks, George. *Research on Written Composition: New Directions for Teaching*. Urbana: NCTE-ERIC, 1986.

Hirsch, E. D., Jr. *The Philosophy of Composition*. Chicago: U of Chicago P, 1977.

Holland, Jesse. "University 101 Begins for Ole Miss Freshmen." *Daily Mississippian* 25 Aug. 1992: 4.

Holland, Norman. *Five Readers Reading*. New Haven: Yale UP, 1975.

Horner, Winifred Bryan, ed. *Composition and Literature: Bridging the Gap*. Chicago: U of Chicago P, 1983.

———. *Historical Rhetoric: An Annotated Bibliography of Selected Sources in English*. Boston: Hall, 1980.

Howell, Wilbur Samuel. *Eighteenth-Century British Logic and Rhetoric*. Princeton: Princeton UP, 1971.

———. *Logic and Rhetoric in England, 1500–1700*. Princeton: Princeton UP, 1956.

Hymes, Dell. *"In Vain I Tried to Tell You": Essays in Native American Ethnopoetics*. Philadelphia: U of Pennsylvania P, 1981.

Irigaray, Luce. *Speculum of the Other Woman*. 1974. Trans. Gillian G. Gill. Ithaca: Cornell UP, 1985.

Iser, Wolfgang. *The Act of Reading: A Theory of Aesthetic Response*. Baltimore: Johns Hopkins UP, 1978.

Ivins, Molly. "For Crying Out Loud, It's Only an English Course." *Dallas Times Herald* 14 Aug. 1990: B25.

Jaggar, Alison M. "Love and Knowledge: Emotion in Feminist Epistemology." Jagger and Bordo 145–71.

Jaggar, Alison M., and Susan R. Bordo, eds. *Gender/Body/Knowledge: Feminist Reconstructions of Being and Knowing*. New Brunswick: Rutgers UP, 1989.

James, William. *The Principles of Psychology*. Vol. 1. New York: Henry Holt, 1890. 2 vols.

Jameson, Fredric. *The Political Unconscious: Narrative as a Socially Symbolic Act*. Ithaca: Cornell UP, 1981.

Jarratt, Susan. "Locating Ethics in Sophistic and Feminist Theories of Rhetoric." Conference of College Composition and Communication. Chicago, 23 Mar. 1990.

———. "The Role of the Sophists in Histories of Consciousness." *Philosophy and Rhetoric* 23 (1990): 85–95.

Johnson, Jean. *The Bedford Guide to the Research Process*. New York: St. Martin's, 1987.

Johnson, Samuel. *A Dictionary of the English Language*. London: Strahan, 1755.

Kaplan, Cora. *Sea Changes: Essays on Culture and Feminism*. London: Verso, 1986.

Kaufer, David S., Cheryl Geisler, and Christine M. Neuwirth. *Arguing from Sources: Exploring Issues through Reading and Writing*. New York: Harcourt, 1989.

Kecht, Maria Regina, ed. *Pedagogy Is Politics*. Urbana: U of Illinois P, 1992.

Kennedy, George. *Classical Rhetoric*. Chapel Hill: U of North Carolina P, 1980.

Kermode, Frank. *The Genesis of Secrecy: On the Interpretation of Narrative*. Cambridge: Harvard UP, 1979.

———. *The Sense of an Ending*. New York: Oxford UP, 1966.

Kincaid, Jamaica. *Annie John*. New York: Plume, 1986.

King, Ynestra. "Healing the Wounds: Feminism, Ecology, and Nature/Culture Dualism." Jaggar and Bordo 115–41.

Kinneavy, James. *A Theory of Discourse: The Aims of Discourse*. New York: Norton, 1971.

Kirshenblatt-Gimblett, Barbara. "Life History as Cultural Construction/Performance." Fife Folklore Conference. Utah State University, Logan, June 1989.

Kittay, Jeffrey, and Wlad Godzich. *The Emergence of Prose*. Minneapolis: U of Minnesota P, 1990.

Kitzhaber, Albert R. *Rhetoric in American Colleges, 1850–1900*. 1953. Dallas: Southern Methodist UP, 1990.

———. *What Is English?* Working Party Paper 1. Papers Relating to the Anglo-American Seminar on the Teaching of English at Dartmouth College, 1966. ERIC ED 082 201.

Klaus, Carl. "Essayists on the Essay." Anderson, *Literary Nonfiction* 155–75.

Knapp, Steven, and Walter Benn Michaels. "Against Theory." Mitchell, *Against Theory* 11–30.

Knoblauch, C. H. "Rhetorical Constructions: Dialogue and Commitment." *College English* 50 (1988): 125–40.

Knoblauch, C. H., and Lil Brannon. *Rhetorical Traditions and the Teaching of Writing*. Upper Montclair: Boynton/Cook, 1984.

Knoper, Randall. "Deconstruction, Process, Writing." Donahue and Quandahl 128–43.

Kolodny, Annette. "A Map for Rereading; or, Gender and the Interpretation of Literary Texts." *New Literary History* 11 (1980): 451–67.

Krieger, Murray. "An Apology for Poetics." *Critical Theory since 1965*. Ed. Hazard Adams and Leroy Searle. Tallahassee: Florida State UP, 1986. 535–42.

Kristeva, Julia. *Desire in Language: A Semiotic Approach to Literature and Art*. Ed. Leon S. Roudiez. Trans. Thomas Gora, Alice Jardine, and Leon S. Roudiez. New York: Columbia UP, 1980.

———. "From One Identity to Another." *Desire* 124–47.

———. "How Does One Speak to Literature?" *Desire* 92–123.

———. "Woman's Time." Trans. Alice Jardine and Harry Blake. *Signs* 7 (1981): 13–35.

Kuhn, Thomas S. *The Structure of Scientific Revolutions*. 2nd ed. Chicago: U of Chicago P, 1970.

Labov, William. *Language in the Inner City*. Philadelphia: U of Pennsylvania P, 1972.

Lacan, Jacques. "The Direction of the Treatment and the Principles of Its Power." *Ecrits* 226–80.

———. *Ecrits: A Selection*. Trans. Alan Sheridan. New York: Norton, 1977.

———. *The Four Fundamental Concepts of Psychoanalysis*. Trans. Alan Sheridan. New York: Norton, 1978.

———. "The Signification of the Phallus." *Ecrits* 281–91.

Lakatos, Imre. "Falsification and the Methodology of Scientific Research Programmes." *Criticism and the Growth of Knowledge*. Ed. Imre Lakatos and Alan Musgrave. Cambridge: Cambridge UP, 1970. 91–191.

Lanham, Richard A. "One, Two, Three." Horner, *Composition* 14–29.

Larson, Richard. Letter to Susan Miller (describing Ford Foundation–sponsored study of practices in composition instruction). 23 July 1987.

Lauer, Janice. "Composition Studies: Dappled Discipline." *Rhetoric Review* 3 (1984): 20–29.

Leff, Michael C. "In Search of Ariadne's Thread: A Review of the Recent Literature on Rhetorical Theory." *Central States Speech Journal* 29 (1978): 73–91.

Leith, Dick, and George Myerson. *The Power of Address: Explorations in Rhetoric*. London: Routledge, 1989.

Lentricchia, Frank. *After the New Criticism*. Chicago: U of Chicago P, 1980.

Literary Theory in the Classroom. Spec. issue of *College Literature* 18 (1991): 1–168.

Locke, John. *An Essay concerning Human Understanding*. Oxford: Clarendon, 1975.

Lukács, Georg. "The Nature and Form of the Essay." *Soul and Form*. Trans. Anna Bostock. Cambridge: MIT P, 1978. 1–18.

Lunsford, Andrea, and Robert Connors. *The St. Martin's Handbook*. New York: St. Martin's, 1989.

Lunsford, Andrea, Helene Moglen, and James Slevin, eds. *The Future of Doctoral Studies in English*. New York: MLA, 1989.

Lyotard, Jean-François. *The Differend: Phrases in Dispute*. Trans. Georges Van Den Abbeele. Minneapolis: U of Minnesota P, 1988.

———. *The Postmodern Condition: A Report on Knowledge*. Trans. Geoff Bennington and Brian Massumi. Minneapolis: U of Minnesota P, 1984.

Macherey, Pierre. *A Theory of Literary Production*. Trans. Geoffrey Wall. Boston: Routledge, 1978.

Macrorie, Ken. *Searching Writing: A Context Book*. Upper Montclair: Boynton/Cook, 1984.

Mailloux, Steven. *Rhetorical Power*. Ithaca: Cornell UP, 1989.

———. "Truth or Consequences: On Being against Theory." *Critical Inquiry* 9 (1983): 760–66.

———. "The Turns of Reader-Response Criticism." *Conversations: Contemporary Critical Theory and the Teaching of Literature*. Ed. Charles Moran and Elizabeth Penfield. Urbana: NCTE, 1990. 38–54.

Mangan, Katherine S. "Battle Rages over Plan to Focus on Race and Gender in U. of Texas Course." *Chronicle of Higher Education* 21 Nov. 1990: A15.

Marius, Richard, and Harvey S. Wiener. *The McGraw-Hill College Handbook*. 3rd ed. New York: McGraw, 1991.

Martin, Wallace. *Recent Theories of Narrative*. Ithaca: Cornell UP, 1986.

Matsuda, Mari J. "Looking to the Bottom: Critical Legal Studies and Reparations." *Harvard Civil Rights–Civil Liberties Law Review* 22 (1987): 323–99.

McCormick, Kathleen. "Always Already Theorists: Literary Theory in the Undergraduate Curriculum." Kecht 111–31.

———. "The Cultural Imperatives Underlying Cognitive Acts." *Readings to Write: Expanding the Context*. Ed. Linda Flower et al. Oxford: Oxford UP, 1990. 194–218.

———. "Reading *Ulysses* within the History of Its Production and Reception."

Approaches to Teaching Joyce's Ulysses. Ed. McCormick and Erwin R. Steinberg. New York: MLA, 1993. 87–96.

McCormick, Kathleen, Gary Waller, and Linda Flower. *Reading Texts: Reading, Responding, Writing*. Lexington: Heath, 1987.

McGee, Michael Calvin, and John S. Nelson. "Narrative Reason in Public Argument." *Journal of Communication* 35.4 (1985): 139–55.

Meacham, Standish. "To: Members of the English Department Faculty." Memorandum, 23 July 1990.

Meese, Elizabeth, ed. Spec. issue of *College English* 52 (1990): 375–456.

Metcalf, Allan A. *Research: To the Point*. New York: Harcourt, 1991.

Miller, J. Hillis. "Composition and Decomposition: Deconstruction and the Teaching of Writing." Horner, *Composition* 38–56.

———. *Fiction and Repetition: Seven English Novels*. Cambridge: Harvard UP, 1982.

Miller, Susan. *Textual Carnivals: The Politics of Composition*. Carbondale: Southern Illinois UP, 1990.

Miller, Walter J., and Leo E. Saidla, eds. *Engineers as Writers*. Salem: Arno, 1953.

Minow, Martha. *Making All the Difference*. Ithaca: Cornell UP, 1990.

"Minutes of the University Council Meeting of September 17, 1990." *Documents and Minutes of the Faculty and Documents and Proceedings of the University Council*. Austin: U of Texas, 1990. 18716–18725/13203–13212.

Mitchell, W. J. T., ed. *Against Theory*. Chicago: U of Chicago P, 1985.

———. *On Narrative*. Spec. issue of *Critical Inquiry* 7 (1980). Chicago: U of Chicago P, 1980.

Moffett, James. *Teaching the Universe of Discourse*. Boston: Houghton, 1968.

Moi, Toril. "Feminist, Female, Feminine." *The Feminist Reader: Essays in Gender and the Politics of Literary Criticism*. Ed. Catherine Belsey and Jane Moore. New York: Blackwell, 1989. 117–32.

———. *Sexual/Textual Politics: Feminist Literary Theory*. New York: Methuen, 1985.

Montaigne, Michel de. "On Experience." *Essays*. Trans. J. M. Cohen. New York: Penguin, 1958. 343–406.

Mooney, Carolyn J. "Conservative Scholars Call for a Movement to 'Reclaim' Academy." *Chronicle of Higher Education* 23 Nov. 1988: 1.

Moore, Sally Falk. "Epilogue: Uncertainties in Situations, Indeterminacies in Culture." *Symbol and Politics in Communal Ideology*. Ed. Sally Falk Moore and Barbara G. Myerhoff. Ithaca: Cornell UP, 1975. 210–39.

Moore, Suzanne. "Identity Shifts." *Marxism Today* May 1990: 41.

Morley, Dave. "Texts, Readers, Subjects." *Culture, Media, Language*. Ed. Stuart Hall. London: Verso, 1980. 163–73.

Mullan, John. *Sentiment and Sociability: The Language of Feeling in the Eighteenth Century*. Oxford: Clarendon–Oxford UP, 1988.

Murphy, James, ed. *The Rhetorical Tradition and Modern Writing*. New York: MLA, 1982.

Murray, Donald. *A Writer Teaches Writing*. 2nd ed. New York: Holt, Rinehart, 1985.

Myers, Greg. "The Social Construction of Popular Science." *Writing Biology: Texts in the Social Construction of Scientific Knowledge*. Madison: U of Wisconsin P, 1990. 141–92.

"NAS Impact, Texas." *National Association of Scholars Newsletter* 3 (1990): 5.

Neel, Jasper. *Plato, Derrida, and Writing*. Carbondale: Southern Illinois UP, 1988.

———. " 'Where Have You Come from, Reb Derissa, and Where Are You Going?': Gary Olson's Interview with Jacques Derrida." *Journal of Advanced Composition* 10 (1990): 387–91.

Nelson, Cary, ed. *Theory in the Classroom*. Urbana: U of Illinois P, 1986.

Newkirk, Thomas, ed. *Only Connect: Uniting Reading and Writing*. Upper Montclair: Boynton/Cook, 1986.

Newton, Judith, and Deborah Rosenfelt, eds. *Feminist Criticism and Social Change: Sex, Class, and Race in Literature*. New York: Methuen, 1985.

Nicholson, Linda J., ed. *Feminism/Postmodernism*. New York: Routledge, 1990.

Norris, Christopher. *Derrida*. Cambridge: Harvard UP, 1987.

North, Stephen M. *The Making of Knowledge in Composition: Portrait of an Emerging Field*. Upper Montclair: Boynton/Cook, 1987.

Oakeshott, Michael. *Rationalism in Politics*. New York: Basic, 1962.

Ogbu, John U. *Minority Education and Caste: The American System in Cross-Cultural Perspective*. New York: Academic, 1978.

Ohmann, Richard. *English in America: A Radical View of the Profession*. New York: Oxford UP, 1976.

———. *Politics of Letters*. Middletown: Wesleyan UP, 1987.

———. "Reading and Writing, Work and Leisure." Newkirk 11–26.

———. Response to "Criticism and Social Diagnosis," by Gerald Graff. *At the Boundaries*. Proc. of the Northeastern University Center for Literary Studies. 1983. Vol. 1. Boston: Northeastern UP, 1984. 16–21.

———. "Use Definite, Specific, Concrete Language." *College English* 41 (1979): 390–97. Rpt. in *The Writing Teacher's Sourcebook*. Ed. Gary Tate and Edward P. J. Corbett. New York: Oxford UP, 1981. 379–89.

Olson, Gary. "Jacques Derrida on Rhetoric and Composition: A Conversation." *Journal of Advanced Composition* 10 (1990): 1–21.

Ong, Walter. *Ramus and the Decay of Dialogue*. Cambridge: Harvard UP, 1958.

Orland, Leonard. *Prisons: Houses of Darkness*. New York: Free, 1975.

Orwell, George. Editorial. *New Statesman and Nation* 28 Aug. 1937: 283.

———. "A Hanging." *Shooting* 13–18.

———. "Shooting an Elephant." *Shooting* 3–12.

———. *Shooting an Elephant and Other Essays*. New York: Harcourt, 1950.

Parker, William Riley. "Where Do English Departments Come From?" *College English* 28 (1967): 339–51.

Pavel, Thomas G. *Fictional Worlds*. Cambridge: Harvard UP, 1986.

Pecora, Vincent P. *Self and Form in Modern Narrative*. Baltimore: Johns Hopkins UP, 1989.

Peirce, Charles Sanders. *Collected Papers*. Ed. Charles Hartshorne and Paul Weiss. 8 vols. Cambridge: Harvard UP, 1931–58.

Percy, Walker. "The Loss of the Creature." *The Message in the Bottle: How Queer*

Man Is, How Queer Language Is, and What One Has to Do with the Other.
New York: Farrar, 1975. 46–63.

Perelman, Chaim, and Lucy Olbrechts-Tyteca. *The New Rhetoric: A Treatise on Argumentation.* Notre Dame: U of Notre Dame P, 1969.

Phelps, Louise Wetherbee. *Composition as a Human Science: Contributions to the Self-Understanding of a Discipline.* New York: Oxford UP, 1988.

Piercy, Marge. "Song of the Fucked Duck." *Circles on the Water: Selected Poems of Marge Piercy.* New York: Knopf, 1982. 86–87.

Plato. *Phaedrus. Works of Plato.* Ed. Irwin Edman. New York: Modern Library, 1928. 263–329.

The Politics of Teaching Literature. Spec. issue of *College Literature* 17 (1990): 1–235.

Poster, Mark. *Critical Theory and Poststructuralism: In Search of a Context.* Ithaca: Cornell UP, 1989.

———. *The Mode of Information: Poststructuralism and Social Context.* Chicago: U of Chicago P, 1990.

Pratt, Mary Louise. "Linguistic Utopias." *The Linguistics of Writing.* Ed. Nigel Fabb et. al. New York: Methuen, 1987. 48–66.

———. *Toward a Speech Act Theory of Literary Discourse.* Bloomington: Indiana UP, 1977.

Preston, James D., and Graves E. Enck. "Retaking Departments." *Academic Questions* (Winter 1992): 70–74.

Preziosi, Donald. *Rethinking Art History: Meditations on a Coy Science.* New Haven: Yale UP, 1989.

Priestly, Philip. *Community of Scapegoats: The Segregation of Sex Offenders and Informers in Prison.* Oxford: Pergamon, 1980.

Prince, Gerald. *A Grammar of Stories.* The Hague: Mouton, 1973.

Quammen, David. "Strawberries under Ice." *The Best American Essays, 1989.* Ed. Geoffrey Wolff. New York: Ticknors, 1989. 212–24.

Rabinow, Paul, ed. *The Foucault Reader.* New York: Pantheon, 1984.

Radhakrishnan, R. "The Changing Subject and the Politics of Theory." *Differences* 2 (1990): 126–52.

Raymond, Charles Harvey. *Essentials of English Composition.* New York: Century, 1923.

Rich, Adrienne. "Notes towards a Politics of Location." *Blood, Bread, and Poetry: Selected Prose, 1979–1985.* New York: Norton, 1986. 210–31.

Richards, I. A. *Coleridge on the Imagination.* 1934. London: Routledge, 1962.

———. *Speculative Instruments.* New York: Harcourt, 1955.

Richter, David. *The Critical Tradition: Classic Texts and Contemporary Trends.* New York: St. Martin's, 1989.

Ricoeur, Paul. *Time and Narrative.* 3 vols. Chicago: U of Chicago P, 1984–86.

Rorty, Richard. *Philosophy and the Mirror of Nature.* Princeton: Princeton UP, 1979.

Rose, Mike. *Lives on the Boundary: The Struggles and Achievements of America's Underprepared.* New York: Free, 1989.

Rosenblatt, Louise M. "The Aesthetic as the Basic Model of the Reading Process." MLA Convention. New York, 29 Dec. 1978.

———. *L'idée de l'art pour l'art dans la littérature anglaise*. Paris: Champion, 1931. New York: AMS, 1976.

———. *Literature as Exploration*. 1938. 4th ed. New York: MLA, 1983.

———. *The Reader, the Text, the Poem: The Transactional Theory of the Literary Work*. Carbondale: Southern Illinois UP, 1978.

———. "Viewpoints. Transaction versus Interaction: A Terminological Rescue Operation." *Research in the Teaching of English* 19 (1985): 96–107.

———. "Writing and Reading." *Reading and Writing Connections*. Ed. Jana M. Mason. Boston: Allyn, 1989. 153–76.

Rothenberg, Paula, ed. *Racism and Sexism: An Integrated Study*. New York: St. Martin's, 1987.

Rouse, Joy. "Positional Historiography and Margaret Fuller's Public Discourse of Mutual Interpretation." *Rhetoric Society Quarterly* 20 (1990): 233–39.

Russell, David R. *Writing in the Academic Disciplines, 1870–1990: A Curricular History*. Carbondale: Southern Illinois UP, 1991.

Ruszkiewicz, John. "Altered E306 Format Compromised by Ideological Freight." *Daily Texan* 24 July 1990: 4.

Ryan, Michael. *Marxism and Deconstruction: A Critical Articulation*. Baltimore: Johns Hopkins UP, 1982.

Sadoff, Dianne F., and William E. Cain, eds. *Teaching Theory to Undergraduates*. New York: MLA, forthcoming.

Said, Edward. "The Problem of Textuality: Two Exemplary Positions." *Critical Inquiry* 4 (1978): 673–714.

———. *The World, the Text, and the Critic*. Cambridge: Harvard UP, 1983.

Sansing, David. *Making Haste Slowly: The Troubled History of Higher Education in Mississippi*. Jackson: UP of Mississippi, 1990.

Saussure, Ferdinand de. *Course in General Linguistics*. Trans. Wade Baskin. New York: McGraw, 1966.

Schaum, Melita, and Connie Flanagan, eds. *Gender Images: Readings for Composition*. Boston: Houghton, 1992.

Schilb, John. Rev. of *Composition as a Human Science*, by Louise Wetherbee Phelps. *Rhetoric Review* 8 (1989): 163–66.

———. "Composition and Poststructuralism: A Tale of Two Conferences." *College Composition and Communication* 40 (1989): 422–43.

———. "Cultural Studies, Postmodernism, and Composition." Harkin and Schilb 173–88.

———. "Deconstructing Didion: Poststructuralist Rhetorical Theory in the Composition Class." Anderson, *Literary Nonfiction* 262–86.

Scholes, Robert. *Text Book: An Introduction to Literary Language*. New York: St. Martin's, 1988.

———. *Textual Power: Literacy Theory and the Teaching of English*. New Haven: Yale UP, 1985.

Scholes, Robert, and Nancy Comley. *The Practice of Writing*. New York: St. Martin's, 1985.

Scholes, Robert, and Robert Kellogg. *The Nature of Narrative*. New York: Oxford UP, 1968.

Scholes, Robert, and Carl Klaus. *Elements of the Essay*. New York: Oxford UP, 1969.

Schweickart, Patrocinio. "Engendering Critical Discourse." *The Current in Criticism: Essays on the Present and Future in Criticism*. Ed. Clayton Koelb and Vergil Lokke. West Lafayette: Purdue UP, 1987. 295–317.

Shattuck, Roger. *The Innocent Eye: On Modern Literature and the Arts*. New York: Washington Square, 1986.

Short, Thomas. " 'Diversity' and 'Breaking the Disciplines': Two New Assaults on the Curriculum." *Academic Questions* 1 (1988): 6–29.

Shuman, Amy. *Storytelling Rights: The Uses of Oral and Written Texts by Urban Adolescents*. Cambridge: Cambridge UP, 1986.

Sinfield, Alan. "Give an Account of Shakespeare and Education, Showing Why You Think They Are Effective and What You Have Appreciated about Them. Support Your Comments with Precise References." *Political Shakespeare*. Ed. Jonathan Dollimore and Alan Sinfield. Manchester: Manchester UP, 1985. 134–57.

Sledd, James. "In Defense of the *Students' Right*." *College English* 45 (1983): 667–75.

Slevin, James F. "Depoliticizing and Politicizing Composition Studies." Bullock and Trimbur 1–21.

———. "The Politics of the Profession." *Introduction to Composition Studies*. Ed. Erika Lindemann and Gary Tate. New York: Oxford UP, 1991. 135–59.

Smith, Louise. Letter. *Chronicle of Higher Education* 19 Apr. 1991: B3.

Spatt, Brenda. *Writing from Sources*. 2nd ed. New York: St. Martin's, 1991.

Spelman, Elizabeth V. *Inessential Woman: Problems of Exclusion in Feminist Thought*. Boston: Beacon, 1988.

Stallybrass, Peter, and Allon White. *The Politics and Poetics of Transgression*. Ithaca: Cornell UP, 1986.

Starr, Jerold. "The Great Textbook War." *Education and the American Dream: Conservatives, Liberals, and Radicals Debate the Future of Education*. Ed. Harvey Holtz et al. Granby: Bergin, 1989. 96–109.

"A Statement of Academic Concern." Advertisement. *Daily Texan* 18 July 1990: 2.

Stocking, Kathleen. "Graduation Day at Lake Leelanau St. Mary's." *Letters from the Leelanau*. Ann Arbor: U of Michigan P, 1990. 30–37.

Stotsky, Sandra. "Conceptualizing Writing as Moral and Civic Thinking." *College English* 54 (1992): 794–808.

Suleiman, Susan, and Inge Crosman, eds. *The Reader in the Text: Essays on Audience and Interpretation*. Princeton: Princeton UP, 1980.

Summerfield, Judith. "Framing Narratives." *Only Connect: Uniting Reading and Writing*. Ed. Thomas Newkirk. Upper Montclair: Boynton/Cook, 1986. 227–40.

Summerfield, Judith, and Geoffrey Summerfield. *Frames of Mind: A Course in Composition*. New York: Random, 1986.

———. "States of Mind, Acts of Mind, Forms of Discourse: Towards a Provisional Pragmatic Framework." *The Territory of Language*. Ed. Donald McQuade. Carbondale: Southern Ilinois UP, 1986. 238–50.

———. *Texts and Contexts: A Contribution to the Theory and Practice of Composition*. New York: Random, 1986.

Taylor, Frederick. *The Principles of Scientific Management*. New York: Harper, 1911.

Thomas, Lewis. "My Magical Metronome." *Late Night Thoughts on Listening to Mahler's Ninth Symphony*. New York: Bantam, 1984. 45–48.

Tindol, Robert. "English Department to Change Content of Rhetoric and Composition Course." University of Texas News and Information Service. 30 May 1990.

Todorov, Tzvetan. *The Poetics of Prose*. Ithaca: Cornell UP, 1977.

Toelken, Barre. "Life and Death in the Navajo Coyote Tales." *Recovering the Word: Essays on Native American Literature*. Ed. Brian Swann and Arnold Krupat. Berkeley: U of California P, 1987. 388–402.

Tompkins, Jane P. "The Reader in History: The Changing Shape of Literary Response." *Reader-Response Criticism* 201–32.

———, ed. *Reader-Response Criticism: From Formalism to Post-structuralism*. Baltimore: Johns Hopkins UP, 1980.

Toulmin, Stephen. *Cosmopolis: The Hidden Agenda of Modernity*. New York: Free, 1990.

———. *Human Understanding*. Princeton: Princeton UP, 1975.

———. *The Uses of Argument*. New York: Cambridge UP, 1958.

Trimbur, John. "Cultural Studies and Teaching Writing." *Focuses* 1.2 (1988): 5–18.

———. "John Trimbur Responds." *College English* 52 (1990): 696–700.

Turner, Victor. *Dramas, Fields, and Metaphors: Symbolic Action in Human Society*. Ithaca: Cornell UP, 1974.

Veit, Richard, Christopher Gould, and John Clifford. *Writing, Reading, and Research*. 2nd ed. New York: Macmillan, 1990.

Versluis, Arthur. "Some New Tricks of Rhetoric." *Academic Questions* (1990): 41–47.

Villanueva, Victor, Jr. "Considerations for American Freireistas." *Politics of Writing Instruction: Postsecondary*. Ed. Richard Bullock and John Trimbur. Portsmouth: Boynton/Cook, 1990. 247–62.

———. "Intonation, Mazes, and Other Oral Influences in the Revision Decisions of Basic and Traditional Writers in First-Year Composition Classrooms." Diss. U of Washington, 1986.

Vitanza, Victor J. "Critical Sub/versions of the History of Philosophical Rhetoric." *Rhetoric Review* 6 (1987): 41–66.

———. "Three Countertheses; or, A Critical In(ter)vention into Composition Theories and Pedagogies." Harkin and Schilb 139–72.

Vygotsky, Lev. *Mind in Society*. Cambridge: Harvard UP, 1978.

———. *Thought and Language*. Cambridge: MIT P, 1962.

Walker, Hugh. *The English Essay and Essayists*. New York: Dent, 1915.

Walker, Melissa. *Writing Research Papers*. 2nd ed. New York: Norton, 1987.

Waller, Gary, Kathleen McCormick, and Lois Fowler. *The Lexington Introduction to Literature*. Lexington: Heath, 1986.

Watkins, Evan. *Work Time: English Departments and the Circulation of Cultural Value*. Stanford: Stanford UP, 1989.

Watkins, Floyd C., and William B. Dillingham. *Practical English Handbook*. 8th ed. Boston: Houghton, 1989.

Watt, Ian. "On Not Attempting to Be a Piano." *Profession 78*. New York: MLA, 1978. 13–15.

Weber, Max. *The Protestant Ethic and the Spirit of Capitalism*. Trans. Talcott Parsons. New York: Scribner's, 1958.

———. *The Theory of Social and Economic Organization*. Trans. A. M. Henderson and Talcott Parsons. New York: Free, 1964.

Weedon, Chris. *Feminist Practice and Poststructuralist Theory*. New York: Blackwell, 1987.

Weidenborner, Stephen, and Domenick Caruso. *Writing Research Papers: A Guide to the Process*. 3rd ed. New York: St. Martin's, 1990.

Weiner, Jon. "A Tale of Two Enclaves: Campus Voices Right and Left." *Nation* 12 Dec. 1988: 644–46.

Wellek, René, and Austin Warren. *Theory of Literature*. 1942. Rev. ed. New York: Harcourt, 1956.

White, E. B. "The Age of Dust." *The Second Tree From the Corner*. New York: Harper, 1985. 115–16.

———. "Democracy." *New Yorker* 3 July 1943: 13. Rpt. in *Wild Flag* 31; Eastman 833–34.

———. "On a Florida Key." *One Man's Meat*. New York: Harper, 1942. 267–74.

———. *The Wild Flag*. Boston: Houghton, 1946.

White, Hayden. *The Content of the Form: Narrative Discourse and Historical Representation*. Baltimore: Johns Hopkins UP, 1987.

———. *Tropics of Discourse*. Baltimore: Johns Hopkins UP, 1985.

Whorf, B. L. *Language, Thought, and Reality: Selected Writings of Benjamin Lee Whorf*. Cambridge: MIT P, 1956.

Will, George F. "Radical English." *Washington Post* 16 Sept. 1990: B7.

Williams, Patricia. *The Alchemy of Race and Rights: Diary of a Law Professor*. Cambridge: Harvard UP, 1991.

Williams, William Carlos. "An Essay on Virginia." *Imaginations*. New York: New Directions, 1970. 321–24.

Willis, Paul. *Learning to Labour*. London: Saxon, 1977.

Wilson, William S. "And/Or: One or the Other, or Both." *Sequence (con) Sequence*. Ed. Julia Ballerini. New York: Aperture, 1989. 11–16.

Winkler, Anthony, and Jo Ray McCuen. *Writing the Research Paper: A Handbook*. 3rd ed. New York: Harcourt, 1989.

Winner, Langdon. "The Whale and the Reactor." *The Whale and the Reactor: A Search for Limits in an Age of High Technology*. Chicago: U of Chicago P, 1986. 164–78.

Winterowd, W. Ross. "The Purification of Literature and Rhetoric." *College English* 49 (1987): 257–73.

———. *The Rhetoric of the "Other" Literature*. Carbondale: Southern Illinois UP, 1990.

Wittgenstein, Ludwig. *Tractatus Logico-Philosophicus*. London: Routledge, 1922.

Woolf, Virginia. *Moments of Being*. New York: Harcourt, 1976.

———. *Orlando*. New York: Penguin, 1946.

———. *A Room of One's Own*. New York: Harcourt, 1957.

———. "Thoughts on Peace in an Air Raid." *The Death of the Moth and Other Essays*. New York: Harcourt, 1942. 243–48.

Yolton, John W. "Mirrors and Veils, Thoughts and Things: The Epistemological Problematic." *Reading Rorty: Critical Responses to* Philosophy and the Mirror of Nature *(and Beyond)*. Ed. Alan R. Malachowski. London: Blackwell, 1990. 58–73.

Index